St. Philip's College

The Peoples and Cultures of Texas

Sponsored by Texas A&M University–San Antonio

St. Philip's College

A Point of Pride on San Antonio's Eastside

MARIE PANNELL THURSTON

Texas A&M University Press

College Station

First edition
Designed and typeset by Graphic Composition, Inc., Bogart, Georgia
Manufactured in the United States of America

This paper meets the requirements of ANSI/NISO Z39.48–1992 (Permanence of Paper).
Binding materials have been chosen for durability.
♾ ♻

Cataloging-in-Publication Data available from the Library of Congress
ISBN-13: 978-1-60344-975-5 (cloth : alk. paper)
ISBN-10: 1-60344-975-2 (cloth : alk. paper)
ISBN-13: 978-1-62349-001-0 (e-book)
ISBN-10: 1-62349-001-4 (e-book)

Contents

Series Editor's Foreword

Dr. Maria Hernandez Ferrier

President of Texas A&M University–San Antonio

Texas A&M University–San Antonio is honored that the inaugural book in our new series shines the light on our nation's one and only community college designated as both a Historically Black College and a Hispanic-Serving Institution. That school is, of course, St. Philip's College, and San Antonio is incredibly blessed to have it as part of the esteemed Alamo Colleges educational system.

A&M–San Antonio has very close ties to all of the community colleges in San Antonio, but St. Philip's stands out for the passion and promise with which it serves its students. From their roots as a training institution for recently emancipated slaves, they have found the right blend of academics and professional development that goes beyond serving the Eastside of San Antonio.

This history is more than the story of how St. Philip's came to be—it is the story of how education can shape a neighborhood and affect an entire city. Which is why *St. Philip's College: A Point of Pride on San Antonio's Eastside* is so appropriate to be the very first title in a series of publications called Peoples and Cultures of Texas, sponsored by Texas A&M University–San Antonio. The line will include titles that explore the history of San Antonio, the state, and the region, the importance of education, and other topics that are timeless and relevant to us all.

I am indebted to Dr. Marie Thurston for bringing to life the story of this historic college, and to Dr. Adena Loston for her outstanding leadership and her generosity in allowing Texas A&M University–San Antonio to be a part of this project. Thank you to the Texas A&M University Press for producing this beautiful publication in time for the 115th anniversary of St. Philip's College.

As a new institution (established in 2009) in a historically underserved area of San Antonio, we at Texas A&M–San Antonio often remember a quote from St. Francis of Assisi, who said "start by doing what is necessary, then what is possible, and suddenly you are doing the impossible." The 115 years of St. Philip's history stand as a model for student success through compassion, service, and commitment to excellence. This book speaks to the genesis of St. Philip's and of Texas A&M–San Antonio, and how, together, we look forward to the future of education in San Antonio and across South Texas. I am proud to be a part of this celebration of St. Philip's College.

Foreword

Dr. Adena Williams Loston

President, St. Philip's College

This oral history of St. Philip's College represents a labor of love, dedication, commitment, and a true desire to acknowledge the journey of this learning institution on the Eastside of San Antonio. Through the more than 100 years of educating all who came, St. Philip's College has stood as a beacon for hope, progress, change, transition, promise, and goal accomplishment. Dr. Marie Thurston has led this history-chronicling project from its inception. The selection of Dr. Thurston represents the most appropriate choice of individuals. She has steadfastly given of herself to ensure that St. Philip's College has its own history, as seen through the eyes of its many passengers along for the journey. Dr. Thurston was exactly the correct choice for this assignment recognizing her academic prowess and most importantly, her abiding faith. She is a woman of deep religious convictions, which have guided her life's journey. Her attributes of faith and religious convictions principally align her with the founding roots of St. Philip's College, St. Philip's Episcopal Church, Bishop James Steptoe Johnston, and the Episcopal Diocese of West Texas.

Dr. Thurston has diligently sought to engage active and past contributors to the history of St. Philip's College by conducting thousands of hours of interviews and conversations. Although she was originally engaged by Dr. Angie Runnels, it was an easy decision to continue her efforts once we met and I understood and felt her passion for this assignment. St. Philip's College upon my arrival was celebrating its 109th anniversary. Dr. Thurston, quite thorough, laid out a plan to strategically capture as many facts as possible, and this publication is scheduled to coincide with the 115th anniversary of the founding of St. Philip's College and to serve as the first edition in a series of publications contributing to the history of the region through Texas A&M University–San Antonio. Thanks to Dr. Maria Hernandez Ferrier, founding president of Texas A&M University–San Antonio, for making this possible.

Since 1898, from our original home in La Villita to our current location, St. Philip's College is truly an institution that has been embraced by its community. Our existence evolved from a desire to ensure that young black girls coming out of slavery attained both marketable skills as seamstresses and leadership skills, to the present day, as we remain committed to our mission as an open-door institution that provides educational opportunity for the academically talented and the academically challenged. Our graduates and attendees have attained phenomenal accomplishments throughout San Antonio, the state of Texas, the United States, and internationally. As we journey toward our next century of service to the community, service to our business and education partners, and service to mankind, we will maintain our original ethos of preparing all who come through our doors with marketable skills and leadership skills.

Many thanks to Dr. Marie Thurston, and I am grateful for my leadership assignment in this journey.

Preface

I wrote this book with one thought in mind: to preserve the history of St. Philip's College. Dr. Angie Runnels, former president of this college, had the foresight to ensure that this rich history be recorded, and she set in motion the mechanism to accomplish that. This book grew out of her vision to publish the history of St. Philip's College, for she said, "This story must be told because no other school has a history like this." It was my good fortune that Dr. Runnels selected me to record the account of St. Philip's history and accomplishments. Rather than use the term, "write the history," I use "record this account," for in truth, those who grew up with the school and others who kept St. Philip's on its course were the ones who wrote this history.

Much like the lives of many African Americans and others who are the oppressed, recognition for St. Philip's did not come easy. St. Philip's came on the scene in America when, so as not to honor the race, even the terms used for identification, *colored* and *negro*, were written using lowercase characters. Recognizing that it may be offensive to some reading this book but wishing to retain the authenticity of the documents used as reference, the lowercase spelling and use of the words "negro," "colored," and "black" appear as in the original.

Henry Hampton, in his oral history of the civil rights movement,[1] wrote of the dilemma he faced in the 1970s and the 1980s regarding the convention of the period, which was (and is) to lowercase the term "black" when referring to African Americans as a racial group. Much like Hampton and his dilemma with the issue of whether to use the upper- or lowercase when using the term "Black" to describe the race, in this book we are faced with the same issue.

We are now in the twenty-first century and America has not settled the issue of recognizing and dignifying the race with uppercase spelling of the term "black" when used to identify African Americans as a specific racial group. Though it is not our choice, but because we are following the *Chicago Manual of Style*, in this history, we have followed the prevailing convention, which is to capitalize names of ethnic and national groups (such as African Americans) and lowercase designations of racial groups based on color, such as black or white.

Appiah and Gates, writing in the twentieth century in the United States, noted that, as contemporary African Americans became increasingly aware of the centrality of a positive racial identity, along with this awareness came an accompanying rise in black consciousness and how African Americans as a people viewed themselves.[2] Suddenly, there was such pride in being black in America that even the terms used to describe and define the race changed. Negro became Afro-American, and, in the 1960s, when Stokely Carmichael[3] burst on the scene, the phrase "Black is Beautiful" became a household phrase, prominent in spoken English among those once known as "colored" or "negroes" and even among other Americans who supported equality.

A few years later, words used to identify the race changed again and rather than Afro-American, African American came into vogue. Still later, in the 1990s, the words used to identify the race were again modified and African American became Black and/or African American, used interchangeably.

How the Project Began

In 2002, President Runnels conceived the idea of an oral history project, the outcome of which would produce a book to tell the St. Philip's story and tell how the college began. Her idea of the project was to have persons from the community, alumni, faculty, staff, administration, and students give an oral account of their affiliation with the school. She assembled a committee whose objective was to offer advice and produce a list of names of persons to interview. The committee was composed of Angie Runnels, president of the college; Levi Jackson, then chair of the counseling department; Mark Barnes, college archivist; Terry Guajardo, St. Philip's test administrator; Joyce Williams, assistant to Mark Barnes; and Marie Thurston, author and project coordinator. The committee met several times over a few months to work on the project. Patricia Williams from the archives department, though not a member of the original committee, gave invaluable assistance and advice in locating material for the history.

The Oral History Committee compiled a list of names of persons to interview and a large part of this history is told from the point of view of those persons. Nearly everyone contacted to be interviewed was delighted to be asked. In fact, several persons not on the original list called and asked to be included. Only two that were asked to be interviewed declined and of the two that declined, one was ill and indicated that she had difficulty speaking and the other said that she could not find her materials and, therefore, did not wish to be included.

The committee suggested that we speak with persons from the following categories:

- Individuals with a faculty or staff connection to the school
- Administrators of the college and from the Alamo Community College District
- Former and current students
- Employees of the school, past and present
- Interested observers from the community

Over the course of the project, 126 interviews were conducted and recorded. Many other informal discussions were held that were not taped. The oldest person interviewed for the project was ninety-six years old at the time of the interview. She gave a delightful and most interesting two-hour interview; however, she was not well, her voice was soft, and the noise from a window air conditioner by her bed made the sound on the tape inaudible, drowning out much of what she said. We simply could not ask her to repeat the interview.

Two of the interviews were conducted over two sessions each. Both interviewees had other engagements scheduled that conflicted with our schedules, but they insisted, "We have more to tell you." They invited us to return and we happily did so. In several instances, when face-to-face interviews were not possible, we used material gathered in our research from secondary sources: families of interviewees, when we could locate them, old school catalogs, school newspapers, and yearbooks. Many persons important to the St. Philip's story were deceased, such as Artemisia Bowden, Clarence Norris Sr., James Steptoe Johnston, Bishop Capers, some faculty, and many of the students.

Again, we contacted secondary sources: families, friends, acquaintances, libraries, newspapers, and the Internet—wherever we could find information written about them. Although we tried to keep the use of secondary sources to a minimum, in these cases, we found secondary sources to be most helpful.

During the interviews, the participants shared their recollections of events in St. Philip's development through stories we taped and later transcribed. Their accounts of what, when, and how incidents occurred varied in length from one to three hours and comprise the foundation of this book. Because of space limitations and the number and length of the interviews, no interview was used in its entirety. We were also told many stories that had no bearing on the history of the school, and while those stories were interesting and we enjoyed listening to them immensely, they were saved for another day. To preserve the integrity, style, and perspective of the interviewees, we limited the editing to a minimum.

Gwendolyn Etter-Lewis wrote that the most important variable in producing an oral narrative is the relationship between the persons interviewed and the interviewer.[4] At times during an interview, we were asked, "Have you spoken with so and so?" If we answered, "No, not yet," they continued with, "Well, you need to talk with them!" This was followed by telephone numbers written on scraps of paper and, in some instances, on-the-spot calls made to provide an introduction to someone they felt was critical enough to the history that we should speak with them immediately. This book, then, became the recollections and experiences of persons who grew up with St. Philip's and others who played a vital part in its history and its survival.

Some of their stories tell of the efforts the community put forth to protect its "Jewel of the Eastside," one of the many names given to St. Philip's. Other stories chronicled the sacrifices made by the administrators, faculty, and staff who guided the college to become "A Point of

Pride" in the community. Recording each of their stories allowed us to be proud partners in preserving the history of the school. For purposes of context, we include a minimal amount of history that relates to what was going on in San Antonio and in the United States at the time. However, it is the interviewees and their stories that give the most credibility to this history. St. Philip's College should be celebrated for its great work and those words cannot be expressed loudly and often enough. However, this is first of all a story about people, what they said, what they did, and how they did what they did to preserve Miss Bowden's School. This is a story that must be told.

St. Philip's College

Introduction

St. Philip's College stands as a beacon, a point of pride on San Antonio's Eastside. For 115 years St. Philip's has offered education and technical training to the community that surrounds it, and that means it has offered light and hope. Within the community, it has been a rallying point for support of the way forward.

There were happy and fulfilling moments in the school's history, such as when Bishop James Steptoe Johnston answered in the affirmative the request from the Negro parents for a school in San Antonio for their children that would provide them an opportunity to receive an education. But when the students excelled, even as their teachers made do with few resources, all too often with reduced or little pay and even at times with no pay, those were the shining moments. There were also glorious times, such as when accreditation was received, marking another important milestone accomplished and affirming that the teachers were doing the right things. These events made their sacrifices worthwhile.

At times in the life of St. Philip's, it appeared that the school would not survive, but Artemisia Bowden and others would not have that happen. They were determined that St. Philip's would succeed. There were times when events of tragic proportions occurred, bringing in their wake discouragement to everyone, such as when Bowden's sister Mary died. Mary Bowden came from Georgia to San Antonio to offer her assistance as a teacher and to help Bowden manage the school. Following a brief illness, she passed away. In dealing with the feelings of helplessness brought on by Mary's death, Bowden experienced many moments of despair; but as time passed, these moments healed.

One can only imagine the stark terror and feelings of abandonment that Bowden must have felt when events such as the diocese relieving itself of all obligations for St. Philip's, including management of its finances, occurred. They added to her already overburdened responsibilities by handing everything over to her, including finding funds to cover day-to-day expenses and for anything else that required an outlay of monies. The search was never-ending. These were the times when she, after doing all that she could, leaned on her faith in God, her family, and her friends to see her through. Even then, despite her best efforts, there were times when there was simply no money to pay the teachers or to cover any other expense. Those moments came all too often, but she always found a way.

Having to make do with less than adequate facilities, few supplies, and secondhand materials might at times have been a distraction, but having to make do was never a deterrent. The administrators, faculty, and staff, who always wore multiple hats, were creative and became masters at substitution.

Through it all, the St. Philip's story became a true love story. Witness in this book the fact that for more than fifty years after many of those interviewed attended St. Philip's, whether they graduated or not, their love for the school was still strong. Their memories of the halcyon days they spent at the school were vivid and they spoke, often in glowing terms, of how meaningful that time was to them. Or, just as important, read testimonies from the faculty and those in the community who fiercely defended and supported St. Philip's, Miss Bowden, and its worth to the community, the city, and the nation. Because of their devotion, and that of the community, faculty, staff, and students, St. Philip's came to be known by many as "The School That Love Built." Bowden, who gave her life to St. Philip's, is reputed to have spurned a suitor, indicating that she was wed to her school.

Miss Bowden led the school for over half a century and

became a legend so revered that she came to be known as the Savior of St. Philip's, one of the many names given to her because of her sacrificial giving to the school. She died in 1969, but her spirit lives on, so much so that it would not be surprising, when rounding a corner, to meet her at any moment and to hear one of her admonitions: "Stand up straight, young man, you have so much to live for." Or to be addressed by her oft-quoted favorite saying, "Find something to do and do that something well."

For sixty-eight years, the first three administrators, Artemisia Bowden, Clarence Norris, Sr., and John Murphy, gave leadership to St. Philip's College. When one includes the years that Bowden gave to the school before it became a junior college, this number climbs to a combined total of eighty devoted years. Eventually, those first three leaders passed the torch to their successors, leaving behind a secure foundation. The leaders who followed seized the task they inherited and in many ways exceeded all expectations, superbly carrying on the school's mission to prepare the students for a rapidly changing world. The leaders who came after embraced the school as surely as their predecessors and their labor was filled with as much love and dedication as that of any of the founders. Today's leaders continue to embrace and fulfill the mission and they, too, pass the torch.

While St. Philip's would not be what it is today if it were not for those founders, likewise, St. Philip's probably would not exist, or be the institution it is, were it not for those who grabbed the torch and those today who continue to run with it. One must surely not forget the role of the community in which the school resides, for much like a mother hen protecting her young, with each crisis, the Eastside community continues to rise to the defense of the school.

When St. Philip's became a part of the San Antonio community, segregation was a way of life and a part of the fabric of life in America. Nettie Hinton, who graduated from St. Philip's College in the 1950s, characterized her community as understanding about segregation because such amenities as downtown water fountains were segregated, with "Whites Only" signs. Blacks were required to sit behind a certain line on the city buses and the only seating for blacks in the Majestic Theatre was in the balcony. Since blacks were not allowed to use the public elevator, they could only access the balcony by using the elevator used to transport freight.

Nonetheless, Hinton and others felt that their lives were full and satisfying where they lived, especially since this law-enforced separation was one of those things that came into their lives intermittently. She described growing up black in her community as "not a real world experience," because she lived in a closed community that provided her and the neighbors most of what was needed.[1]

Teachers in the black schools in San Antonio described by Hinton did not have the most up-to-date textbooks, nor were the science laboratories cutting edge. The quality of materials used to teach and the infrastructure of the schools in the district she attended did not match the quality of the white schools. But, the teachers in those substandard schools gave their all to help the students learn and many graduates of those schools went on to accomplish great honors in their field.

It is certain that founder Bishop Johnston would be pleased at the recognition and honors that St. Philip's continues to receive for its leadership role in higher education and for the leadership role it plays as a part of the Alamo Colleges and the national student completion movement, Achieving the Dream: Community Colleges Count. St. Philip's participates in this multiyear initiative, Achieving the Dream (AtD), funded by the Lumina Foundation for Education. "AtD addresses the challenge of providing low income students and students of color with opportunities for academic success and the issue of how to increase the retention rate in low income students of color."

St. Philip's leaders of today have shown that as the challenges faced by schools continue to increase, the school continues to live out its mission to provide its students and its community opportunities to grow and enhance their lives. The leaders have proven that they are equal to the task, despite continually being called upon to provide more with less. At this writing, St. Philip's is being challenged, as never before, to not only trim but cut the budget. With student enrollment at an all-time high, the test is how to provide more services with fewer resources. St. Philip's has always met the challenges it faced in the past, and St. Philip's—led by leaders who understand the problems, are equipped to deal with them, and welcome the challenge—continues to do so today.

1 1898 and Before

The seeds of St. Philip's history were planted many years before the story actually began, for they were sown in the bowels of the ships that took the first Africans against their wills and brought them to the New World to labor without financial compensation. These seeds took root with the indignities, scorn, and hatred that the prisoners suffered as the ships docked in the South, where they were sold as chattel and ended up as slaves. More than a hundred years later, these roots, along with other events that occurred in San Antonio, had a major influence on the history of St. Philip's College.

We begin this history with a look back at some of the events in San Antonio and in the nation that influenced the history of St. Philip's College. Many Africans, brought to America as slaves, suffered extreme hardships and deprivations. Central to the indignities suffered was the denial of their right to practice their native religion. They were, however, allowed to attend the churches of their masters, but even then they were required to sit in special sections set aside for Negro worshippers. In 1786, as the number of Negro worshippers at St. George Methodist Episcopal Church in Philadelphia, Pennsylvania, increased, some of the white congregation became uncomfortable with the arrangement. Absalom Jones, a Negro worshipper who attended St. George's, was "almost dragged from his knees," as he prayed. Richard Allen, a former slave who had purchased his freedom, was with Jones at the time. Tensions arose from this incident, which ignited flames of racial hatred.

The incident began when Negro worshippers were told to vacate the seats around the wall where they usually sat and to move to a gallery that had been set aside for them. Misunderstanding the instructions, the Negro worshippers sat in the wrong section and, in the confusion, were forcibly removed. Bishop Allen explained:

> We had subscribed largely toward furnishing St. George's Church, in building the gallery and laying new floors; and just as the house was made comfortable, we were turned out from enjoying the comforts of worshipping therein.[1]

Because of this indignity, they left that church and founded churches more suited to the needs of their congregations. As Payne explained, they then held their own services, which were more in accord with their style of worship. Their determination to erect a house of worship, where they could worship God as they wished, came as a result of their unhappiness with their treatment; but the discontent among the Negroes did not end in Philadelphia. It continued in churches across the nation, including Texas, and in 1895, more than one hundred years later, the situation repeated itself in a San Antonio congregation of Negro worshippers. Unhappy with the services in the African Methodist Episcopal Church and feeling unwelcome in the white Episcopal Church, they sought a place of their own to worship. Worship in the Episcopal tradition was important to them; but like the Pennsylvania worshippers, they wanted to worship as they pleased, in a church of their choice.

In San Antonio, the discontented congregants took their petition to Rev. Robert Woodward Barnwell Elliott (Rev. R. W. B. Elliot), first Bishop of the Missionary District of Western Texas. The bishop, sympathetic to their request, outlined a plan of consideration for the Church. As far back as 1877, the bishop recognized the problems created by the growing numbers of former slaves and freedmen living among the white population and he often spoke about the problem of racism and the challenges it presented to the Episcopal Church. He also made mention of the important role the slaves played by providing their physical labor.

Rev. Robert Woodward Barnwell (R. W. B.) Elliott, first Bishop of the Missionary District of Western Texas.

While the bishop, as a representative of the Episcopal Church, was known to be supportive, not all the church members shared his compassionate attitude toward the former slaves, now freedmen and freedwomen, who were struggling to survive in an era in which Southern sentiments and prejudices continued to constrain their lives. There were members who believed that attempting to improve the condition of the Negro was a waste of time and money. The bishop, on the other hand, disapproved of this uncharitable attitude, explaining that it was a question of whether the church could survive refusing to do its part to elevate, educate, and develop the Negro. He believed that the average American would think that the church had given up on the Negro race, regarding it as a decaying branch of the human family.

Bishop Elliott considered the role of the church to be reconciliation, and he suggested that it was a waste of time and money for it *not* to try to educate Negroes. Plans for spearheading education for the Negroes in San Antonio might have ended with his untimely death in 1887, were it not for his successor, James Steptoe Johnston.

Bishop James Steptoe Johnston, Founder, St. Philip's School

James Steptoe Johnston, born on June 9, 1843, in Church Hill, Mississippi—a state committed to maintaining separation of the races—succeeded Bishop Elliott. Though reared in the South, Johnston brought to San Antonio a zeal for improving the conditions of the Negro citizens of the community. Much like Elliott, he believed that the only way to make productive and moral citizens was through the education of the whole person, the mind and the soul. And just as his predecessor's feelings for the Negroes' situation did not reflect those of the majority in the South, neither did Johnston's.

As a child, Johnston attended the local Episcopal church, a congregation that served persons of all denominations. This afforded him opportunities to meet and mingle with people from other religious congregations and where he was exposed to a doctrine of inclusion, principles he passionately espoused as an adult. As bishop of West Texas, on more than one occasion, he wrote to the pope encouraging unification. Johnston served as a priest in the Episcopal Church until 1888, though he had never completed college, nor attended seminary. In 1888, he was awarded an honorary doctor of divinity degree by the University of the South and, in June of that same year, became the second bishop of the missionary district of Western Texas. Johnston constantly stressed the themes of education and stewardship and under his leadership, the Western District of Texas applied for, and, in 1904 was granted, acceptance from the General Convention in Boston as a financially independent diocese (a district containing Christian churches under the authority of

Bishop James Steptoe Johnston, Founder, St. Philip's School

one bishop). The clergy in this new diocese unanimously elected Johnston as its bishop.

During Johnston's time as bishop of the Western District, the themes of education and stewardship distinguished themselves in his work. He established two schools in San Antonio: West Texas Military Academy and the Saturday Evening Sewing Class for Negro girls that became St. Philip's College. Additionally, he further expanded the existing St. Mary's Hall, a school for white girls. West Texas Military School later became Texas Military Institute (TMI), a prominent school, initially only for white boys. The first graduating class of West Texas Military School included Douglas MacArthur, the same Douglas MacArthur who, during World War II, became a highly celebrated general and Supreme Allied Commander of the Southwest Pacific Theatre.

In 1895, Johnston admitted to the district, at their request, a congregation of black Episcopal Methodists calling themselves St. Philip's Church. Under Johnston's sponsorship, the members found a place to worship in a room above a hardware store on West Commerce Street. St. Philip's Church was now officially organized for the Negro congregants. This location was not meant to be a permanent home for the church and, before two years had passed, the district purchased a new home for them in the former German Methodist Church on Villita Street. With the move to the new location, St. Philip's Church experienced renewed vitality and growth as the members became well established in their new home. The following year, Johnston started the sewing class for girls and the students from that sewing class, held in St. Philip's Church, were the beginning of St. Philip's College.

From a Place of Worship to a School for Negroes

When James Steptoe Johnston arrived in San Antonio, he found the Negroes in the city largely uneducated and enduring a hard life. Not only were they deliberately and regularly excluded from participation in educational and community activities but their only hope of sharing in events in the city of San Antonio was through the manual labor they provided or by working as servants. For San Antonio's Negroes, discrimination, both socially and in worship, was a way of life, created by segregation of the races.

The aspiring church members of St. Philip's were not discouraged by Bishop Elliott's death, nor were their plans impeded for a place of worship for themselves or their plans of education for their children, for they found a friend in Johnston. According to the history of St. Philip's Church, a large delegation visited Johnston and begged to be taken under his Episcopal care.

Their plea was so insistent and so urgent, that even though funds had not been allocated for such an undertaking, Johnston consented and took up the burden, declaring that God was in the request and they would press onward, walking by faith and not by sight.

Bishop Johnston retired in 1916 because his health failed and he passed away on November 4, 1924 in San Antonio at age seventy-one. He was succeeded by Rev. William T. Capers. Rev. Dr. Milbrew Davis, retired priest of St. Philip's Church, who served as rector of St. Philip's from 1975 until 1996, and his wife, Shirley, were interviewed in their home in San Antonio. They both affirmed that the Episcopate probably supported the idea of a church and a school for the Negroes because "Historically, one of the major thrusts and traditions of the Episcopal Church has always been to emphasize the importance of education and spirituality."[2]

A Ray of Hope

With a place of their own to worship established, the parents in the congregation of St. Philip's Church turned their attention to finding opportunities to improve their children's education. They compared the limited programs available in the Negro school with the programs in the schools available to the white children and decided that they wanted more for their children. When some of the parents from St. Philip's Church learned that Laura Jackson, a Negro seamstress from Galveston, had recently arrived in San Antonio, they enlisted her assistance.

At that time, public education for the children was limited and enlisting Jackson to teach a sewing class for them would be a way to supplement the education their children were receiving. The Texas State Historical Association noted that the popular belief, prior to the Civil War, was that educating African Americans would lead to discontent and rebellion.

As early as 1865, the Freedmen's Bureau supervised and coordinated training for Negro children that ranged from basic reading and writing to vocational skills. According to Clarence Norris, a public elementary program for black students had been in existence since 1868 with a curricula restricted almost entirely to basic grammar and basic arithmetic.[3] There was little in the way of broader course offerings.

The plan of the San Antonio parents to add to the courses their children were receiving fit well with Johnston's vision of supplementary schooling for the children, for he also believed that they needed additional training. Johnston envisioned a day school for the Negro children that would grow into an industrial school for girls and provide them with not only a good grammar school education, but also knowledge of how to perform domestic duties, which would always "procure for them a desirable position."

Working as a domestic was considered a worthwhile and desirable position for the Negro, and one that could be continued into old age. However, parents wanted more for their children than working as a domestic, which was on the lowest rung of the social strata. In the view of Michael Heintze, on Edward Jones's history of Morehouse College, had it not been for the founding of the independent black colleges, most Southern blacks would have remained in the grasp of ignorance and the associated ills of economic dependency.[4]

The supplementary education provided for the Negro

children was not to mirror the classes taught in the schools for white children; the classes in the Negro school were all to be vocationally based. When Jackson agreed to teach the girls, in 1897, the ladies of the church, assisted by Bishop Johnston and Rev. William H. Marshall, pastor of the church, organized a sewing class for the girls.

There were about twelve girls from the Sunday school of St. Philip's Church at the first meeting of the Saturday evening class held in the rectory of St. Philip's Church. From Norris Jr.'s interview with Minnie Meade (Lowerey), we learn the names of some of the attendees: Electra Brown, Ida Nunely, Arthur Sanford, Fannie Hardaway, Willie Wiggens, UrsaYaborough, Ed Brown, Willie Sanford, Roberta Cushiel, Cora Nunely, Stella Jefferson, Maude Hardaway, Flossie Ervin, May Brown, Middie Meade, Willie Nunely, Roberta Williams, Arthur De Vann, Bernie Lewis, Fred and Johnny Meade, and several unidentified others.[5]

St. Philip's archives include a photograph of the last meeting of the St. Philip's Saturday evening sewing class with a photograph of about twenty children, some unidentified. Norris noted that though the class was organized for girls, a number of boys attended the sewing class.

Minnie Meade Lowerey, first graduate of St. Philip's School

Because the Saturday evening sewing class was very successful, excitement grew for a private day school for the children. Bishop Johnston's support for educating Negro children offered their parents great encouragement, especially after he began a search for a full-time instructor. Johnston's stated purpose of the school was to impart threefold training to Negro girls: training of the head, the heart, and the hand. He believed that the girls should be taught domestic skills that were needed to work in the homes of the wealthier white population of the city. Conversely, the vision of his Negro congregants was to prepare their children for professional careers. The Negro parents even dared to dream that perhaps the careers might be outside of San Antonio, and indeed, some were.

Despite the dissimilar visions of the bishop and the parents, both agreed that the children needed more in the way of educational training. Bishop Capers, who followed Bishop Johnston and later became chairman of the Board of Trustees of St. Philip's Junior College, gave an example of just how successful the school was, even in its early days, in reaching its goal to prepare the children for adulthood and responsibility. He spoke of an interesting conversation that he had with a Pullman porter on one of his visits to the North. The porter's son, a graduate of St. Philip's, was attending an Eastern college and preparing to enter the ministry. His son's ambition was to come back to the South and devote his life to the advancement of his people. The porter then went on to tell the bishop of the great appreciation that the Negro people of San Antonio had for St. Philip's Junior College and what it had done for the youth of the city to prepare them for their life's work.

The bishop mentioned a number of young Negro men who had graduated from St. Philip's "and in every instance, they were prosecuting very useful lives, devoted, of course, to their own people."[6] Dillard Robinson was the son of the Negro porter. Upon receiving a Bachelor of Sacred Theology Degree, the Rev. Dillard Robinson returned to San Antonio to lead the congregation of St. Philip's Church. Under his leadership, a period of successful growth and advancement followed. However, after a few years at St. Philip's Church in San Antonio, "he accepted a call to Trinity Cathedral in Newark, New Jersey, which was, according to Bishop McAllister, "one of the top jobs in the Episcopal Church. He was the First African American elected Dean of a Cathedral in the United States," a proud moment for St. Philip's and for an alumnus.

First class at St. Philip's School

Bishop Gerald McAllister offered the information that Dillard Robinson was also the young crucifer of the first service that he held at St. Philip's [Church].[7]

A Dream Come True

In 1895, when a large Negro Methodist delegation in San Antonio came under his jurisdiction, at their request Bishop Johnston organized St. Philip's Church, reported the Centennial History of the Diocese of West Texas.[8] The bishop raised money in the North and erected a "substantial church and rectory" for the congregation.

> Bishop Johnston and the Standing Committee of the Missionary District (Episcopal) of Western Texas purchased property in downtown San Antonio, Texas in the ten three hundred block on Villita Street. This was the first site of St. Philip's School, now known as St. Philip's College.[9]

A report of the Journal of the Council of the Protestant Episcopal Church spoke of their indebtedness to Bishop Johnston for his several years of hard labor in raising the necessary funds to open the school. According to Johnston, many of the funds that maintained the church came from Northern congregations through the Missionary Board, and he felt that was as it should be. He went on to infer that because the North had made the problem by freeing the Negro, they should step in and help solve it, for the white people in the South were not willing to give money to help to solve the situation.

Johnston was referring to the problems that the Episcopal Church had in providing worship opportunities for Negro congregants, but his words can be applied to their efforts to provide schooling for Negro children as well. Many persons in the South approved of slavery and felt that the loss of the free labor from the Negro was economically unfeasible.

The dream of the members of St. Philip's Church for a private school for their children became a reality early in

1898, when Bishop Johnston hired Alice G. Cowan to run the day school. Cowan, a white woman living in Mexico doing missionary work, came well prepared for teaching, having trained at the Philadelphia Training School for Deaconesses. From the Handbook of Texas, a reference was found to a Mrs. Alice G. Cowan, daughter of Mr. and Mrs. James Colahan, married to Rev. Enoch C. Cowan, a veteran and an Episcopalian rector. According to the unidentified *Lakewood Newspaper*, dated August 29, 1930, she spent many years in the South and Southwest where Rev. Mr. Cowan had charges.[10] We cannot, however, prove that this is the same Mrs. Cowan.

St. Philip's school records indicate that on March 1, 1898, shortly after her arrival in Texas, a Mrs. Cowan opened St. Philip's Industrial Day School, aided by Bishop Johnston and a Negro minister, Rev. William H. Marshall from the British West Indies. Rev. Marshall, the first full-time rector of St. Philip's Church, was appointed to his post by Bishop Johnston.

The accommodations in the small schoolroom were humble, but one can imagine the joy that the children felt at having their very own school. On the first day, March 1, 1898, only one girl and one boy attended; nonetheless, school was open and that made it a momentous occasion. Though the school began with just the two students, Norris records that "a week later, one little girl who had been looking wistfully through the fence was induced to come in. Later on, a small boy gave up some of his abundant leisure to the pursuit of knowledge."[11] Slowly, perhaps even one by one, more children came and the school remained open until July 1, 1898, when it closed for the summer. According to reports to the bishop sent by Cowan, the classes were so successful that, when the first school year ended, the class that began with two pupils ended with an enrollment of thirteen pupils.

In 1899, the bishop, aware of the overcrowded conditions, purchased a piece of property adjoining St. Philip's Church, San Antonio. He paid $400 for the property and built a brick schoolhouse that cost $1,800. There were twenty-one children in the school and before too much time had passed, adequate space again became a problem.

The new schoolhouse, with its two well-equipped school rooms, was very pleasant—they had a "furnished kitchen, closet, two halls and a gallery, plenty of black-board room and a place for sewing and utensils for work."[12] Cowan reported that with the additional space, enrollment increased.

Two years later, when the Committee on Education of the Episcopal Diocese visited, they found the St. Philip's

Dillard Robinson, St. Philip's graduate and later Dean of Trinity Cathedral, Newark, New jersey

Industrial School "domiciled in a new brick building, of ample size, neatly finished and up to date in all its appointments, with an industrial department where the girls are taught cooking and plain needlework."[13]

Glowing reports about the school were given at the Twenty-Sixth Annual Convocation held in San Antonio at St. Mark's Church, May 16–20, 1900. The report reinforced the pleasure that the bishop and other officials of the diocese felt with Cowan and it was reported that, under her, the school more than fulfilled their expectations. Not only did the children receive a solid English education, "they were also taught cooking, sewing, house cleaning, and such like domestic duties, which all girls should know."[14] An account from the Education Committee reported that even after one year's use, the building had not a scratch on the walls, nor were there blotches on the floors.

After two years, Cowan handed in her resignation, and it is probable that some of the children listened to the news of her departure with great anxiety, particularly those children who had started school not too many weeks before the school year ended. They had barely had time to grasp the basics they wished so fervently to learn. It was highly unlikely that the boys in attendance completed a full year of schooling under the best of circumstances, for even the youngest child among them was enlisted to plant

First site of St. Philip's School

and hoe the crops as well as perform whatever other jobs needed to be done around the farms or plantations where they lived and worked.

Mrs. Perry G. Walker, from Baltimore, Maryland, was Cowan's replacement. At least two pieces of correspondence noted that Walker was a Negro woman, though in his report to the diocese, the bishop made no mention of Walker's race or her age. There was a terse statement from the bishop that read, "I have secured the services of Mrs. Walker of Baltimore, Md. to take her [Cowan's] place."[15]

The Committee on Education noted in their report to the diocese that Walker had reported an increase in attendance but they, too, made no mention of her race.

Despite lacking adequate materials and equipment and teaching in an overcrowded classroom, Walker continued to maintain the excellent standards set by her predecessor, Cowan. Bishop Johnston, well-pleased with Walker's services, noted in his report to the Twenty-Seventh Annual Convocation of the Church:

> This school continues its successful work under Mrs. P. G. Walker, [Perry] who has kept the school up to the high standard set by Mrs. Cowan. It is small in numbers, but as an object lesson is most valuable, as showing what can be accomplished in moral and intellectual development of this race, if given a fair chance.[16]

The bishop mentioned Walker's "special training for the work required." When one takes into consideration the great difficulty that Negroes had at that time in obtaining education of any sort, it is noteworthy that Walker received credit from the bishop for her special training. Even then, at a time when travel accommodations and communication were difficult to accomplish, St. Philip's was able to attract well-trained people from places as distant from Texas as Baltimore.

In fact, St. Philip's quest to hire the best faculty and staff continues to this day. In 1949, Dolly B. Davis-Hoover, from Washington, DC, the first African American faculty member at Indiana State University, honed her skills in the library at St. Philip's. Davis-Hoover came to St. Philip's from Tuskegee Institute in Alabama, where she worked as a beginning librarian from 1945 to 1949 under Dr. Frederick D. Patterson, founder of the United Negro College Fund. Patterson was president of Tuskegee at the time. Hiring a librarian away from Tuskegee Institute, a widely known and highly esteemed institution, was quite a feat for Artemisia Bowden and St. Philip's. Davis-Hoover worked at St. Philip's in the library's technical services division until 1955, during which time she attained the rank of librarian.

Likewise, Bishop Johnston reported to the Committee on Education that "[t]he reports from the three Church schools in this city are full of encouragement and hope." Of St. Philip's Industrial School, the committee stated: "This school continues its successful work under Mrs. P. G. Walker, who has kept the school up to the high standard set by Mrs. Cowan. The new Principal of this School has presented to the Convocation a creditable report, showing considerable increase in attendance. The course pursued in the instructions seems difficult of improvement."[17] Considering the conditions under which Walker labored, the commendation was an outstanding accolade.

Proving Their Worth

Few would dispute the success of St. Philip's Industrial School. The parents and the bishop were so pleased with the school's accomplishments that, during the summer of 1902, plans were again made to enlarge the building and this time, to add an assistant. The bishop recognized that the work was entirely too much for one teacher and that the enrollment warranted adding an assistant. With seven grades corresponding to the grades in the public schools, St. Philip's Industrial School boasted a school year with, at times, as many as sixty-six pupils; however, the school still had only one teacher.

Despite being overcrowded and conducting school with not enough equipment, at a fair held in San Antonio, St. Philip's Industrial School won first prize in both cooking and sewing. This happened at a time when the chairman of the Committee on Education acknowledged that the work being done in the school was crippled for lack of simple things that the principal requested, such as cooking utensils and a sewing machine. His constant plea was for friends from the North or for some other benefactor outside San Antonio to supply these materials.

In June 1902, St. Philip's Industrial School held its first graduation from the grammar school.[18] Norris reported that three students completed the course work of the grammar school, with one student completing a two-year course in cooking and sewing and two completing the course in cooking only. Minnie Meade, the student who completed cooking and sewing, was described by Walker as a student with the expectation of reflecting great credit upon the school. The three graduates from the seventh grade were Benjamin Lewis, Minnie Meade, and Rosetta Smith.

At the end of 1902, with sixty-six pupils enrolled and still without an assistant, Walker reported teaching seventy-two sewing lessons and seventy-two cooking lessons. Additionally, besides teaching children the basic classes, she helped them to make seventy-five articles. In spite of the enormous workload, Walker reported that she "missed not a day from school." Furthermore, she added, "It mattered not how stormy the day; some were always there to meet me."[19] The workload took its toll, however, and at the close of the 1902 school year, Bishop Johnston reported to the Episcopal Church that Walker had resigned. Despite losing two excellent teachers in just four years, the bishop was not deterred. He had heard of the work of St. Athanasius School and Church in Brunswick, Georgia (the town where Artemisia Bowden was reared) and, very much impressed by their reputation, paid them a visit. He wished to observe the school firsthand and possibly hire one of their graduates to head St. Philip's Industrial School. The Georgia church school highly recommended Bowden, for they knew her well. Following the death of her mother, and at the advice of her priest, she, along with her sister and brothers, attended and graduated from St. Athanasius School. From the reports he received about Artemisia Bowden, he was satisfied that she would be a very good choice. He offered Artemisia Bowden, a graduate of St. Augustine's in Raleigh, North Carolina, the position of head of St. Philip's Industrial School for Girls, to take the place of Mrs. Perry G. Walker, who withdrew from the institution at the close of the spring session, 1902. Bowden was teaching at High Point Normal and Industrial School, High Point, North Carolina, at the time of her hire. Fortunately for many generations to come, she accepted the position.

2 Coming to Texas

> If you will get someone to look up the schedule and write on what train to expect you, I will see that someone meets you. In order for your identification, you will please have a bow of red ribbon, about 1/2 in made on your left shoulder. I shall hope to see you at my residence Wednesday morning the 3d.[1]

A brief letter can deliver a message of great import. Inside this note, written on August 25, 1902, by the second bishop of the Missionary District of West Texas, were traveling instructions for a trip to San Antonio and $32 to defray travel expenses. The instruction to wear a bow of red ribbon was to enable Bishop James Steptoe Johnston, sender of the letter, to recognize the addressee, but embedded in its contents was much, much more.

For the recipient, Artemisia Bowden, the letter became a symbol of the journey that spanned fifty-two years and countless miles, but for the writer, Bishop James Steptoe Johnston, it marked the beginning of an association that lasted until his death. On Wednesday, September 3, 1902, Artemisia Bowden came to Texas to meet Bishop Steptoe Johnston in his home to discuss a position as principal at St. Philip's Day School. The day of the meeting was the first of many such meetings.

The Journey Begins

The train ride from Georgia to Texas was long and tedious, giving Artemisia Bowden plenty of time to ponder what had seemed at the time a good idea. With so much time on her hands, it is easy to envision Bowden thinking that now her decision to go to Texas seemed reckless and ill advised. Accepting a position at St. Philip's School in San Antonio, a place where she knew no one, in a town that she had never before visited, in an area where the Negro population was extremely sparse, probably appeared not only reckless, but very unwise. One can imagine that she may have had anxiety as the reality of the situation set in—she had left a good job in North Carolina to work in Texas for a man she had never met.

The 1900s: Artemisia Bowden

As the journey continued, we can imagine Bowden reflecting upon the lessons her father taught her—don't get discouraged if things don't work out. When you find something to do, do it the best that you can. Her father, a former slave, had always been her rock of support and it is easy to imagine that thinking of him eased her mind.

The arduous road that St. Philip's College traveled for more than a century on its way to greatness mirrored the long and tedious journey that Artemisia Bowden experienced as she made her way to Texas. The bold and daring spirit in the actions of both Bowden and the college seemed always to be moving steadily, relentlessly, ever toward a new destination, but always with the same goal in mind, to make St. Philip's the great institution it was destined to become. The journey was often made with trepidation, but it also appeared that there was no other choice. It was their destiny. As Adena Loston, the current president, says, "It's in our DNA."

Those who labored for St. Philip's knew that to make the school what it would become, they would have to venture into unchartered waters. They knew that it was a gamble, but they also hoped that when they took those calculated risks, they were ensuring that their fledgling efforts would, in all probability, succeed and someday culminate in a great institution. They were brave, courageous, and determined. Their goal was not lofty in the beginning, for their aim in coming to St. Philip's was simply to teach the Negro children how to read and write.

When the bishop hired Bowden, he also employed Myrtle Hill as her assistant. Hill had grown up in St. Philip's congregation and was a recent graduate of the normal department of St. Augustine's. Noting that there were fifty-four children on the roll, the Bishop was certain that adding an assistant for Bowden would contribute to the efficiency of the school and facilitate a division of labor, as well as lessen the responsibilities of the principal.

Walker, who had replaced Cowan, added her own special touches. She had diligently proven that she was up to the task of teaching children who had never before set foot in a school building. When she left the school, Bowden provided the leadership for the school to continue. Scarcely had Bowden arrived before she began to demonstrate her leadership abilities. She began by changing the name from St. Philip's Day School to St. Philip's Industrial School for Girls. The new name was to reflect the new emphasis. This was the first of its many name changes.[2]

The New Hire

Artemisia Bowden, eldest child of Milas and Mary Molette Bowden, was born in Albany, Georgia, on January 1, 1879, just fourteen years after the Emancipation Proclamation. Her parents well understood the value of a good education, for they were former slaves without formal education. Upon the death of their mother, and at the advice of the parish priest, their father sent Bowden and two of her siblings to St. Augustine's School in Raleigh, North Carolina. When they arrived, she was scarcely more than a child herself, but at St. Augustine's, she became a mother figure, not only to her siblings, but also to her peers and fellow students.

As the older sister, when their mother passed away, Artemisia played the role of mother protector to her brothers and sister. In the years to come, just as she nurtured her siblings in their infancy, and just as she was a mother figure at St. Augustine, she assumed the role of guardian for St. Philip's until, like her brothers, sisters, and classmates, the school came of age and was able to stand alone. As for St. Augustine, the school had a profound influence on her life and she found the curriculum to be rigorous and thorough, staffed with dedicated, outstanding teachers and church men.

Among her teachers was Rev. Henry Beard Delany, who was at one time vice principal of St. Augustine. He later became principal of St. Augustine and was one of the first two Negro bishops of the Episcopal Church to serve in the United States.[3] Another of her teachers was Charles Boyer, a graduate of Yale University. William Augustine Perry, whose father was rector of St. Luke's Church in North Carolina, was a classmate. Perry later led St. Augustine to become one of the finest high schools in the South. These teachers had a great influence on Bowden and the effect left her with the zeal to educate her people, and even to "win some to the Church," as Rev. J. Carleton Hayden wrote in *Linkage*.[4] Moreover, it is also likely that she met both white people and persons of color at St. Augustine who were sincerely interested, not only in education, but also in the advancement of the Negro race. It is also possible that, because of the inspiring associations that she made, that she, too, developed a great desire to be associated with the advancement of her race, especially as her own interest in education increased. At the same time, it could be speculated that, partly because of its liberal views toward education for Negroes, her interest in the Episcopal faith intensified. For whatever reason, she became a devout, lifelong Episcopalian who committed herself to this faith, a faith that sustained her throughout her life and, when all else failed, a faith that she called upon continuously.

Her father, a self-made man and a pillar of St. Athanasius' Episcopal Methodist Church, exerted a great influence on Bowden. Katherine Durvan, a former member of her faculty who was also Bowden's friend, writing about Bowden's retirement, said that her father, "an illiterate man, but a real Christian," became one of the pillars of St. Athanasius Church and School community. Bowden was a young girl when the Episcopal church was being built in Brunswick, Georgia, and she observed her father and his insatiable desire to be helpful, and to be a functional part of any worthwhile community movement. Bowden is purported to have heard her father speak of days of labor carrying the hod, in lieu of giving a contribution.[5] Her father claimed to have said that he had neither silver nor gold to give; rather, he told the minister of the Episcopal church, that in place of money, his labor would be his donation. Bowden, from that day forward, wanted to give of herself.

Even as a young girl in Brunswick, Georgia, Bowden's life was dedicated to serving others and it is entirely plausible to believe that, awed by her father's promise, she was determined to do no less. From the time she came to St. Augustine School until she graduated in 1900, Bowden distinguished herself academically, and this caught the attention of her teachers.

After graduating from St. Augustine, Bowden remained in North Carolina, accepting a teaching position at a parochial school, which she held for a year before moving to a normal and industrial school, also in North Carolina. When Bishop Johnston visited St. Athanasius School, seeking a Negro woman to run the day school in San Antonio, he was told about Artemisia Bowden. He had heard excellent reports of the preparation and academic skills of Athanasius's graduates, and because she was highly recommended, he wrote to Bowden and offered her the position.When she received the invitation to come to St. Philip's Industrial School in San Antonio, she no doubt saw this as an opportunity to put her beliefs and her newly learned skills to the test.

Promises Kept

She was highly recommended for her scholarship and for her moral qualities, but engaging Bowden as a school administrator and principal was a speculative move, for she was young and lacked experience in administration. When she received the invitation to come to San Antonio to St. Philip's Industrial School, Bowden may well have seen this as a great opportunity and considered her age, her ethnicity, and her lack of administrative experience to be of little significance. When she stepped off the train, wearing on her left shoulder a half-inch long red ribbon, "made in order to be recognized," her zeal for excellence was her most important feature, as those around her would soon learn.

The enduring lessons that she taught by word and by deed are what made the visit significant—lessons about striving for excellence, lessons demonstrating self-sacrifice and determination, moral lessons that displayed the power of love. Nothing else mattered. The lessons that she brought with her and that she taught to all with whom she came in contact continues to have an influence today and remains the foundation that undergirds St. Philip's College.

At their first meeting, it is probable that the bishop noted that she had followed to the letter the instructions to wear a red ribbon on her left shoulder. Over the years, he grew to become one of her most ardent supporters, as he took note of her attention to detail. He also became a committed advocate. She, on the other hand, was not only the administrator/principal/teacher, but also the school's chief fund-raiser, all areas in which she greatly excelled. The bishop had many reasons to be her admirer, for under her guidance, the school subsequently became a household name, not just in San Antonio, but in some surrounding cities and states as well. Harry F. Green, at that time Dean of Prairie View College, in Prairie View, Texas, wrote the following to Bishop Capers:

"As far as my studies and investigations go, St. Philip's in San Antonio, Texas is the only one of the so-called junior colleges that approximates in its program what a modern junior college is like. This, I confess, wins my admiration and respect . . . I am very much pleased with the opportunity to indorse [*sic*] the program and work of St. Philip's Junior College."[6]

3 Artemisia Bowden and St. Philip's Industrial School

If she came to Texas expecting to find new equipment, new books, and supplies, she was mistaken. What she found was an overcrowded building with not enough of anything except excited children, eager to learn. Bowden was given a much-needed assistant, but necessities, such as books and equipment, were in short supply.

Artemisia Bowden

During her first visit with the bishop, it is likely that Bowden discussed his expectations of her and her duties as principal of St. Philip's School. Despite her assigned task, in addition to those the bishop outlined, she soon found herself in the role of fund-raiser, leader, and even philanthropist. At St. Philip's, as in many schools for African American students, particularly in the South, used books and furniture for Negro children and Negro schools were the norm, a condition that continued well into the twentieth century. In an interview with a former president of St. Philip's, he stated that if there were furniture, books, and supplies that were no longer needed or wanted at San Antonio College (SAC), the other community college in San Antonio at the time, they were sent to St. Philip's. At St. Philip's, these inequities continued well into the 1970s.

The fifth session of St. Philip's School began September 15, 1902. From the first day that she met her eager students, Bowden made it her goal to make St. Phillip's School a household name. She informed the bishop that this would happen, and she enlisted his aid to ensure it. Her first year was scarcely under way before attendance increased, and by the first of October, 1902, enrollment had increased to forty-two children. The two-room facility, built to accommodate fewer than twenty students, was taxed to its maximum, as were Bowden's organizational skills. Bowden reported that during this fifth session, with an enrollment of eighty pupils, there was a general daily average of fifty-five children attending the school. The overcrowded conditions tested not only her resourcefulness and her mettle, but also her organizational skills and her endurance.

Not to be deterred by the poor conditions, with her assistant Myrtle Hill, Bowden set about making St. Philip's School live up to her dream of being a great school. To begin with, in order to reflect the new emphasis, she gave the school a new name; thus it became St. Philip's Industrial and Grammar School. Using the same format as the public schools, mornings began with devotionals conducted by the minister of St. Philip's Church, Rev. William Marshall. Rev. Marshall was the first rector of the church; he was followed by the Rev. Richard Gordon, who replaced Marshall in 1904.

Bowden found, however, that even with her zeal for excellence and her lofty plans for expansion, she had to first focus on some of the same challenges as that of her predecessors. Inadequate space for the number of students in attendance and lack of materials and equipment were at the top of the list.

Despite the conditions, she maintained a positive attitude, seldom complaining about the quantity of work required or the huge responsibility she carried. It was not unusual for her to work late into the night, just to keep the doors to the school open. In a 1904 report to the bishop, she wrote: "I believe that the people are beginning to see that St. Philip's school is the place to send their daughters in order to make all-round women of them."[1] She went on to say, "I feel that my year's work has not been

Artemisia Bowden

in vain, because I can see signs of improvement. Some of the best girls of the city are "St. Philip's girls." Even then, Bowden felt committed not only to the students but also to the community, which was small and according to interviewee Lois White, sparsely settled. White knew the black community well, and later worked at the college as an instructor.

The city of San Antonio at the turn of the century, according to Norris, "had not only become the largest city in Texas, it had also become a thriving metropolis."[2] But while San Antonio's "black population had increased to 14% of the city's total population," the standard of living for blacks, their employment, and their social life had not appreciated proportionately. Black participation in the community was limited to servitude.

One bright spot that never failed to please Bowden was having Hill as her assistant. With an assistant, she had a flexibility that her predecessors did not have. Having Hill on board made her plans for reorganizing the school into primary, grammar, and industrial departments easier to perform.

The new arrangement, placing courses into departments and establishing a schedule for the day school with set rules for attendance, facilitated what Bowden and Hill were able to accomplish. The school day for primary students began at 9:00 a.m., with primary dismissal at 4:00 p.m. Grammar department students were dismissed at 4:30 p.m. A student tardy six times without parental excuse merited indefinite suspension. Though having an assistant was meant to lighten her load, Bowden taxed herself to do more than she expected of her assistant. In addition to her basic administrative workload, Bowden also taught four sewing classes per week and two cooking classes, while Hill taught one cooking lesson per week, along with the basics. During these sessions, the children were given instructions in the how and why of things related to the kitchen, house economy, and how to clean.

Organization of the Three Departments

Primary Department **Miss Hill** **(Grades 1–5)**	**Grammar Department** **Miss Bowden** **(Grades 6–9)**	**Industrial Department** **Miss Bowden/Miss Hill** **(Grades 6–9)**
Kindergarten methods with word and object method, spelling, reading, writing, arithmetic, geography, language lessons.	Reading, writing, arithmetic, English grammar, geography, algebra, geometry, gardening, rhetoric, US and Texas history, English literature, botany, civil government, and general history.	Sewing 1st yr.: Holding the needle, making stitches, making garments. 2nd yr.: Using patterns, button holes, fancy stitches. 3rd yr.: Tailoring, fabric selection. Cooking. 1st yr.: Cleaning the kitchen, sources of foods, learning to build a fire. Hygiene. 2nd yr.: Fancy cooking, marketing, housekeeping. 3rd yr.: Invalid cookery, sick room care, ventilation. Useful information re: the sick.

Source: Norris, "St. Philip's College," 70.

Girls working in the in the school garden

They learned to prepare menus and meals and to do whatever they could to beautify and keep the school in order.

Classes offered in the industrial department were a popular feature of the school and Bowden took note of the children who were very good sewers. Even the littlest ones were inspired by her to be the best, for it was possible that they might continue their education and pursue the trade of dressmaking. Bowden wrote: "Miss Hill has spent much time teaching gardening. The little ones took great pleasure in sowing the seeds and watching their growth and it not only gave them an idea how it should be done, but helped the cooking school."[3] The lessons in gardening were very important to the school, as both Bowden and Hill used the garden not only to teach the children but also as a source of food for both the children and teachers.

While attendance continued to grow, the school was not free. Various fees were charged: tuition was $0.50 for the Primary department students and $0.75 for the Grammar department. Music students paid a $2.00 fee, which was not an inconsequential sum to pay. This paid for one music lesson per week. Students in the Boarding department were required to wear uniforms purchased through the school at an additional expense. Their uniforms were made of navy blue material with mortarboards (commencement-style caps) of the same. The cost of the uniform for small girls was $6, and $10 for the older and larger girls.

Each girl had to provide an umbrella and overshoes, one laundry bag, napkin ring, three towels and table napkins, four sheets, two pillow slips, two pairs of woolen blankets or quilts, two counterpanes for single bed, and one rug. Two sisters could use bedding for double beds and all items were to be marked with the owner's name. Black shoes and hose were to be worn on all occasions. Students wishing not to work had to pay an extra $3 per month or $12, if paid by the year. Considering the costs of the fees, it seems likely that the families whose children attended were persons with some means, particularly since the cost of tuition and other expenses, such as the cost of uniforms, were major factors influencing enrollment. The inability to pay tuition would not be a deterrent, for Bowden always found a way to assist students wishing to enroll and attend St. Philip's.

Sylvester Mitchell, who attended St. Philip's in the 1930s and the 1940s, and whose family lived near the school up to the year 2000, had this to say about Bowden and St. Philip's:

"She was the type, whether [*sic*] you want it, she'd try to make it possible. If you were living in the rural areas and your parents weren't able to send you to school, Miss Bowden would accept contributions of eggs or food or whatever you had to offer to furnish those kids that she kept in the dormitory."[4]

Mitchell went on to say that some of the parents would give Bowden a cow or a hog or keep the school in vegetables. The Hayes boys had sisters who attended St. Philip's, and they were always bringing fresh vegetables to the school. "Some of the rest of 'em, maybe you had what not, they [*sic*] parents would see that she got whatever they had to offer to keep the boys or girls in school."[5]

Pleas for more space, more supplies, and more equipment regularly appeared in Bowden's reports to the bishop. Despite the conditions under which she had to teach, her teaching and leadership were cited as exemplary. Following a visit to St. Philip's Grammar and Industrial School, the members of the Committee on Education offered their support, suggesting to the Convocation of the Missionary Jurisdiction of Western Texas that encouragement be given to the school for its accomplishments. The committee emphasized that the school deserved the help of the church because of the good that it was achieving.

While academic accomplishments were an important component of St. Philip's School, Bowden stated that her highest ambition was to have the school "produce true, God-fearing women, who do speak the truth and whose characters are spotless."[6] She taught them the importance of having a sense of their own dignity and self-worth and how to live by a strong moral code in a segregated society that devalued them.

Only two years later, in 1904, the enrollment of St. Philip's Industrial School had increased to around eighty-five students, with daily attendance averaging fifty-five children. The teachers continued to follow much of the curriculum taught in the public schools. Because the children were so delighted at having an opportunity to attend school, they did whatever they could to take care of their school, including keeping it clean. Meanwhile, in his reports to the Diocese of West Texas, Bishop Johnston continued to express great respect for Bowden and her work.

In one such report, he noted that when an inspector of colored schools visited St. Philip's, he spoke in the highest terms of its management, its excellent corps of teachers, and its immaculate cleanliness. He went on to praise St. Philip's School, indicating that "the school was found to be clean in all respects, . . . all departments of the school reflecting great credit upon both teacher and pupil."[7]

Though the enrollment continued to climb, out of eighty-five students enrolled, only ten were males. Several key factors may have affected male attendance: boys were a ready source of cheap labor and were kept home from attending school to work in the fields whenever needed. Also, many of the classes offered in addition to the basics were considered to be domestic subjects—for example, cooking and sewing, classes thought to be more suitable for females. It may well have been that Bowden felt it her mission to emphasize training for young women, especially since the school began as a sewing class for girls. Further, she believed that the destiny of a people rests in the hands of its women and, as if to prove her opinion true, female attendance continued to increase.

Growth and Expansion

When Bowden and the bishop found that the capacity of the original structure was taxed to the limits of its ability to accommodate attendance, rather than turn away students, the bishop added a second story to the building he had erected adjoining the church.

The bishop praised the liberality of his friends in the North, for by their generosity, they enabled him to provide a commodious hall for school exercises and social gatherings by adding a second story and to complete the school building by summer. He named the new addition Mercer Hall, in honor of his son, a missionary in the Philippines. Bowden, happy to have the new accommodations, would hold commencement in Mercer Hall that year and she voiced the sentiment of all when she thanked the friends who were so generous in helping to meet their great need.

Bishop Johnston, meanwhile, utilized every opportunity to praise the Northern donors for their generosity. The financial assistance they provided to construct the building also provided opportunities for more black students in the South to achieve an education. It is a certainty that without the support of the Northern friends, many black youths in Texas and the South would not have received an education.

The increase in enrollment kept pace with the school's growing reputation for excellence and dictated that consideration be given to boarding out-of-town students. Since attracting out-of-towners who needed a place to live was a key element of the continued growth of the school, the lack of facilities for boarding presented a problem.

Earlier, attempts were made to house a few out-of-town students in private homes, including renting the house next door to boarders, but this was not an entirely satisfactory solution. Bowden constantly appealed to the Education Committee and to the bishop to purchase the piece of property next to the school. Because of its proximity to the school, it was an ideal location in which to build a dormitory for out-of-town girls and this fact was not overlooked in her reports. The Committee on Education, heeding the continued requests, recommended purchasing the small lot bounded on both sides by the property of St. Philip's School. However, a period of time would

St. Philip's first boarding site

pass before the lot was actually purchased and boarding facilities provided.

As if the lack of space, insufficient funds, and too little equipment were not problems enough, at the end of the school year, Hill, Bowden's assistant, left to be married. Meanwhile, as enrollment for the 1906–1907 school year grew to 102 pupils, with monthly enrollment averaging ninety-five pupils and daily attendance averaging seventy or more, Bowden's younger sister, Mary Bowden, was recruited from Georgia as an assistant.

Because the need for additional space and housing for out-of-town students became so acute, St. Philip's was forced to make a hurried attempt to provide boarding facilities for them. In May, Bowden reported to the bishop: "We have attempted for the first time a boarding department. We have had as many as twenty four [boarders] at one time. I long for a time when you will be able to secure the piece of property next to ours and build a dormitory for the girls."[8]

While her immediate concern was for adequate space for her students, her own living conditions and those for her sister were deplorable. They lived in an old building that even the bishop described as "dilapidated and disgraceful looking." He reported to the diocese that "a new building is greatly needed, for this one is 100 years old and neither safe nor sanitary."[9] When the bishop appealed to friends of the school for the new building, as an incentive to give, he reported that the Board of Missions already made a $500 grant from the Men's Thank Offering to purchase the piece of property and only $1,000 more was needed to construct the building. The Educational Committee was so pleased with the work of St. Philip's School that they recommended each parish and mission in the diocese add a gift equivalent to 10 percent of their pledges to the Diocesan Missions for the prior year to relieve the immediate needs of the school. The committee further recommended that funds for a new building be raised at once, because the need was so great and the school so successful in proportion to the monies expended. The finance committee subsequently reported that quite a number complied. Before too much time passed, the bishop reported that since a few friends who had become interested in the school responded by being generous in their gifts, he was able to erect a comfortable residence for the teachers in place of the old, dilapidated shack in which they had uncomplainingly lived for several years.

More importantly, the addition of the new building meant that not only would out-of-town students have decent accommodations, but lack of housing would no longer be a deterrent to the schools' growth. Among the gifts received was a $100 contribution from the Women's Club, an organization of "leading Colored women in the community." The Women's Club received the highest praise from the bishop, who reported to the diocese that their gift was a testimony of their appreciation of the valuable work of the school. Around this time, the school had sixteen regular boarding students and new living quarters that included the addition of a large, roomy laundry with stationary tubs, large boiler, and hot and cold water for the use of the boarding students. The dormitory included a dining room, kitchen, and bedrooms for the two teachers.

At least two of San Antonio's prominent white citizens, George Bedell Moore and Eleanor Brackenridge, were generous contributors to the construction of the first dormitory building. Additionally, Brackenridge provided the funds necessary to furnish the building. The new building added much to the comfort, looks, and general surroundings.

But, as one problem was solved, another seemed always to be waiting to take its place. After a brief illness, Mary Bowden, Miss Bowden's sister and able assistant, passed away. The bishop, announcing her death, noted that Mary Bowden was much beloved by the students and would be difficult to replace.[10] Bowden's distress was clearly painful as she expressed in writing her anguish at the loss of her sister. Heretofore, her communications had been positive and optimistic but at this writing, she justifiably complained. "This has been a very trying year for me: First, the great loss of my sister and second, the many duties along with insufficient funds to meet the current expenses. I do hope that before the Council closes, you will be able to secure at least one or two scholarships. Having no endowment or any other fund to fall back upon keeps one always at one's wits end trying to meet the demands."[11]

Even as she recovered from the loss of her sister and coped with the lack of funds, when the school opened in 1910 for its twelfth annual session, Bowden had added a Normal department and two additional teachers. The 1910–1911 St. Philip's catalog listed Artemisia Bowden as principal and teacher in the Normal School offering sewing, advanced cooking, physical culture, and manual training. Two new staff members for the 1910–1911 school year were S. L. Allen, in the Grammar and Primary departments, who also taught sewing, and Prof. Herbert Reed, assistant teacher, and vocal and instrumental music teacher.

Music played an important part in the school day, dating back to the first year when Cowan mentioned in her reports the children's love for singing. On one of his fund-raising trips to the East, the bishop had returned with the surprise gift of a piano for the school, which greatly enhanced the student's enjoyment of music. Bowden, writing about their surprise and happiness at the gift stated that "by using it daily, the children demonstrated their appreciation." At St. Augustine School, Bowden had played both piano and organ and before Reed came on board at St. Philip's School, she often played the piano for the vesper services. At times, Bowden played the piano purely for the enjoyment of the students.

Earlier, she had made an unsuccessful attempt to offer music lessons to students after school; however, because of her fund-raising duties, little free time remained for lessons. Reed, a skilled musician, was a welcome addition, and having him assume responsibility for music freed Bowden to concentrate on raising funds and managing the school. As encouragement and as an incentive, families with more than one student taking music lessons were offered a discount.

Since there were no reserve funds to keep the school afloat, and no sources of continuous, outside support, a list of fees for support for the school was established that had to be paid in advance. However, even with the added fees collected, there was never enough money to cover day-to-day operational expenses. The school catalog frequently included a plea for scholarships to help defray operational expenses. There was no endowment fund and the school lacked the finances to be self-supporting. There were only two scholarships: the Bedell-Moore Scholarship and the Eleanor Brackenridge Scholarship.

In an effort to increase the number of students, an off-site kindergarten was launched, and while it was not physically located in the building, nonetheless, there was a connection to the school. Additionally, it was financed by one of her most loyal benefactors, Eleanor Brackenridge. Despite the physical separation, there was a clear-cut relationship between the kindergarten and the school. Information about the kindergarten appeared in the school catalog in the 1910–1911 school year, indicating that it was to be "located in a thickly settled district where it will be convenient for all the little ones to attend."[12] The kindergarten would be a continuing source of student referrals.

Georgia Taylor, born in 1914, and one of the first students to attend St. Philip's kindergarten, grew up in a neighborhood about a block from the college. Her brother (Sylvester Mitchell) and sister (Veola Alexander) attended also. Taylor lived in the area all of her life, along with her siblings, and when the school became a junior college during the 1930s, all three attended. Taylor's account of attending St. Philip's kindergarten is in the following section.

Georgia Taylor's Story

Taylor, whose mother would walk the children to St. Philip's to attend kindergarten, said that the first thing she remembers about St. Philip's is her mother telling them, "That's where Miss Bowden lives." Taylor, five or six years old at the time, remembers Bowden coming to her neighborhood and asking Taylor's mother if she and her siblings could attend the kindergarten that Bowden was planning to start. "She signed me up," said Taylor, "and I went for a full year. The next year, I went to Brackenridge. All classes were in this large two-story building and were held on the first floor. Miss Bowden had girls living upstairs," said Taylor, "and we played games, did coloring and that sort of thing. Then we'd go outside and play." Taylor remembers that at least a dozen children were in her class and that her teacher was a Miss Mote. She did not remember much else, but said that she never will forget Miss Mote because she was such a sweet person. "The bad side of that was no one would take us [to school]. After the first week, our mother decided that we should be able to take ourselves. But it didn't work out like that way. People would pick on us. We'd get to one corner and there would be these white kids at this corner. They would run us every morning. They'd go to the next street and they'd head us off. But anyway, somebody stopped those kids from chasing us every morning. We were too afraid to tell our parents, but it didn't stop us from going to school because our parents insisted we go. We enjoyed it after we got there."[13]

4 The Industrial Side of Education at St. Philip's School

Industrial education, along church lines, is the only wise, expedient, and true solution of the race problem in the South.[1]

Facing Reality

When the West Texas District Episcopal Church Committee on Education met in 1900, their position on education for Negroes was unmistakable: if the church was to fund education for the Negroes, there had to be an industrial component. In fact, any school for Negroes wishing to receive funding and obtain support from white benefactors had to offer training in manual and domestic subjects. Thus, for more than forty years (from 1900 to 1941), St. Philip's School included in its name the term "Industrial."

In 1882, John F. Slater, a millionaire, created an educational foundation devoted to promoting industrial education in the South for African Americans and poor whites. J. L. M. Curry, former Confederate and pro-slavery Congressman from Alabama, exercised control over much of the funds provided for schools for Negroes, thus effectively dictating the subjects taught in the schools. Curry was chosen in 1881 as general agent for the Peabody Fund, an organization that established vocational programs throughout the South, and by 1890, he was head of the Slater Fund. In 1914, the Peabody Fund was dissolved, and, according to Heintze, a considerable amount of the assets of the fund went to the John F. Slater Fund.

Though he had previously defended slavery and the right of secession, after becoming an ordained Baptist minister, Curry's zeal for spirituality apparently grew. With his change of heart, it is said that he then worked tirelessly to ensure that African Americans were included in the educational system. The 2nd Morrill Act of 1890, passed by the US government, assisted states in founding land-grant colleges for Negroes, but the assistance was only given to schools with an industrial or agricultural curriculum.

Economics provided another justification for industrial training. With the expansion of the coal, iron, steel, cotton, and textile industries, both Northern and Southern investors needed a large and continuing supply of cheap labor to expand their operations. Blacks needing employment satisfied that requirement. Controlling the economic status of Negroes by limiting their educational and occupational opportunities effectively guaranteed a continuous source of cheap labor.

Williams and Ashley noted that including "Normal and Industrial" in the names of schools for Negroes was only a cover for the times that wealthy white funders visited the schools. The school "fared much better and received more support from philanthropists when they offered normal and industrial education."[2]

From 1906 to 1917, St. Philip's Normal, Grammar, and Industrial School offered classes in sewing, advanced cooking, physical culture, and manual training. Offering courses in cooking and sewing was a near guarantee of support from the white citizens of San Antonio, as well as support from Northerners. It is a certainty that without the funding support from San Antonio's white citizens and the northern whites, St. Philip's School could not have survived.

While Bowden acknowledged the necessity of providing the vocational arm of the school, she also believed it essential to provide a curriculum in which all students could be helped to develop into young men and women of intelligent action. Therefore, in addition to the industrial training offered, Miss Bowden's School, as it was colloquially known, combined liberal arts courses with vocational and preprofessional studies in several fields. Courses were taught that offered dual training: from Latin and rhetoric, bookkeeping and algebra, to quadratics and geometry.

The emphasis on classical training for Negroes virtually ended when the states assumed responsibility for the education of all children. Then, because teacher training and manual and industrial trades continued to be emphasized, a need was created for teachers to teach these industrial subjects in the Negro schools. As there were no other schools in the vicinity open to Negroes that offered training for Negro teachers and were easily accessible, Bowden viewed this training as a new opportunity for St. Philip's to expand.

Significant Changes

In its sixteenth year, St. Philip's School had thirty-five boarders and fifty day pupils. While providing boarding space for the students was an important component of the school, many additional changes were on the horizon. As an example, the number of teachers increased from two to six. In 1906, Bowden added the Normal department with three additional years of work, and by 1915, the school had become a high school. It was clear that there was a need for facilities beyond high school to provide training in higher education, not only in Texas, but also to provide training for persons in New Mexico and Arizona. Since training opportunities for Negroes were lacking in these areas, the prospects were ripe for St. Philip's to expand.

Meanwhile, a change of great significance emerged that involved Bowden's major supporter, co-fundraiser and mentor, Bishop Johnston. The bishop petitioned the diocese for permission to retire, giving as his reasons, "advanced age and muddled finances beyond his ability to solve, mostly connected with schools in the Diocese." [3] Though his request was first made in 1911, and repeated in 1913, it was not until 1914 that the Rev. William Theodotus Capers of Philadelphia was elected coadjutor. In 1916, it became official; Rev. Capers succeeded Bishop Johnston as leader and bishop of the diocese. Though retired, Johnston maintained his interest in the school. On March 24, 1923, Bishop Johnston wrote a last letter to Bowden, expressing his view of the racial issue:

> The colored people have been made a part of our population by a providential dispensation which brought them here in bondage. To their unrequited labors before the emancipation, the prosperity of the Old South was largely due. I myself have been greatly indebted to them; and have tried to make some compensation to them by fitting them for the citizenship which has been thrust upon them. It is highly important that as many of them as possible should be brought under the elevating influences of the Christian religion, which is the best guarantee possible for their highest moral development.[4]

On November 4, 1924, Bishop Johnston passed away. The words in the previous paragraph, written to Bowden a few months before his death, described not only Johnston's feelings, but also his actions toward the Negroes. Bowden lost a friend and major supporter, as did San Antonio's Negroes. Fortunately for the Negro congregants, Johnston's replacement, the Rev. William Theodotus Capers, shared Johnston's views and continued with his support for Bowden's efforts to provide religious and educational opportunities for the Negro population.

Capers was reared in the Episcopal Church, where he had also served as rector. The attitudes of many parishioners in the Episcopal Church toward Negroes and education were considered liberal; thus, it is not surprising that the bishop supported the Negro petitioners' continued request for increased educational opportunities for their children. Despite the fact that he came to the diocese of West Texas without specific training in Negro education or knowledge of the phases of school control, Capers worked for St. Philip's cause for more than twenty-seven years. In 1943, Bowden would mark the occasion and show her appreciation by presenting a loving cup to the bishop and a bouquet of red roses to Mrs. Capers.

A New Role to Play

While St. Philip's School continually received glowing progress reports, the response to the reports did not include the necessary financial support. The limited monies St. Philip's received from a small number of white citizens in San Antonio barely supported the school, for the contributions received were minimal. *Linkage*, a black

Bishop William Theodotus Capers

publication by the Episcopal Church Center in New York, reported that as St. Philip's developed, Bowden, of necessity, spent more and more of her time raising money. From their account, the diocesan convention and the parishes contributed almost nothing, and even when Bishop Johnston recommended that the school be made a diocesan institution, the convention refused to offer larger contributions. Dr. Davis, former rector of St. Philip's Church, affirmed the difficulty Bowden had in keeping the school afloat.

Over and over at the diocese, he viewed documents attesting to the struggle that Miss Bowden had. "She was very forceful and very aggressive about her St. Philip's School, unyielding to the point of giving much of her own and her family's resources to keep it going. Her little girls' choir travelled across the country, trying to raise money to keep the doors open."[5]

As stated by Davis and others, the diocese helped some, but not as much as they could have. They used the argument that the resources of the diocese were slim. Some Episcopal schools in San Antonio for whites may well have closed during that time because of financial reasons. Bowden, however, was so determined to keep St. Philip's afloat that, despite being unable to pay them, she brought in some of her own relatives to assist her. They gave not only their time, but also their personal resources. Davis could confirm this because he knew her brother Henry Bowden, who was also a priest.

The Women's Auxiliary, an organization of black women within St. Philip's Church, regularly contributed financial support. Even with this support, it was often difficult to find sufficient funds to pay the teachers. Constant turnover became the norm.

Esdale Malloy, perhaps Bowden's dearest friend, who began teaching at St. Philips in 1919, described the difficulties of working under such financial constraint.

> The teachers would try to find extra work to supplement their already meager salaries, but there was constant turnover because of the uncertainty of not knowing when they would receive their salaries and because of the extra workload required.[6]

A constant flow of revenue was needed just to maintain the school, and now Bowden found herself in the unenviable position of not only having to raise funds to operate the school, she also had to find the funds to pay her faculty. Adding the burden of having to find funds to pay her faculty made finding the monies needed seem, at times, an unattainable goal. It was frequently necessary for Bowden to use all of her abilities to convince her teachers and staff to continue providing instruction to the children and to keep the school open, particularly since she had no ready or continuing source of monies to pay them, which they knew. But, with families of their own to support, their choices were limited. They had to be paid.

During the Great Depression, when the shortage of money was so acute as to endanger the school's continuance, the bishop suggested that the faculty accept a 10 percent cut in salary. Following is an excerpt from a letter written to Rev. Capers from Dean J. L. Hawkins refusing to accept the cut in pay.

> I am very sorry but it will be impossible for me to accept the terms as stated in your letter. Miss Bowden assured me and Mrs. Nelson of the State Department

Esdale Malloy, teacher at St. Philip's

> that she had the money to pay the teachers for their services. I have already had a cut in my salary and don't think it is fair to be asked to accept another one. I am sure you can appreciate my position. We have done every thing [*sic*] within our power to keep the school going and I think it is only fair and Christ Like that we receive compensation for our services.[7]

Bowden's suggestion was that each teacher accept a cut of one month's salary, exclusive of room and board, rather than the 10 percent of the year's salary suggested by the bishop. The teachers refused that cut also. Not to be deterred, Bowden met with the teachers and afterwards reported to the bishop that she had spoken with the teachers and thoroughly discussed the deficit, which amounted to $1,300, with them. Though they were still not willing to accept a one month's salary cut, there was a difference in their attitude from the previous reaction. Bowden believed that if she were able to secure $900, she could satisfy the teachers and bring the scholastic year to a peaceful close.

And well she might have, for besides being very persuasive, Bowden's fund-raising efforts for St. Philip's were Herculean. Nonetheless, the Episcopal Church did not reward her or St. Philip's school with assistance in the proportion given to the other Episcopal schools in San Antonio. Even in the face of acknowledgments from others that St. Philip's was exemplary, and notwithstanding her hard work to ensure that the school remain first-rate, the diocese continued to offer St. Philip's a pittance in comparison to the financial assistance given to both St. Mary's Hall and Texas Military Institute (TMI).

The bishop gave credit to individual members who donated funds privately, while indicating that the largest contributions were given almost exclusively by friends in the North. In a report to the diocese, the Education Committee expressed great pleasure with the support from the laity given to St. Mary's Hall, while indicating that this support had taxed them to the utmost capacity of accommodation.

Additional Challenges

Turnovers and salary problems were just some of the difficulties Bowden faced. When a teacher left, the already small teaching staff had to cover the classes of the departed teacher, in addition to their own duties. Even in the face of the extra workload, and the possibility of receiving or not receiving a salary in a timely manner, finding new teachers was not a problem; there were always new graduates needing employment. According to Malloy, Bowden had friends among black college presidents and high-level Episcopalian officials, and they provided her with a continuous source of replacements. The new hires were, more often than not, outstanding college graduates, but without teaching experience. In addition, they were usually young. In a personal interview with Clarence Norris Jr. Malloy recalled:

> She [Miss Bowden] would go to meetings. Her friends were highly educated people. She would go to Atlanta University where she knew the President of the school. She would go there and tell the President she was looking for such and such type teacher. He would put her in contact with them.[8]

Because of the dire need for additional finances, Bowden, with the assistance of Bishop Johnston, began earnestly seeking friendly contacts in the North and South from whom she might cultivate a continuing source of financial assistance.

Pressure to Move

Meanwhile, around 1914 to 1915, the first of several attempts was made to move St. Philip's out of the downtown area. The presence of the military, an increase in the number of immigrants from Mexico, and an increase in the white population, all contributed to an enlarged business community surrounding the school. The encroachment of businesses and the inability of the school to expand were reasons given for moving the school to the outskirts of the city. Among the black population, however, it was believed that the move to relocate the school to the Eastside was politically and racially motivated. They felt that white merchants wanted the school out of downtown San Antonio because it was an institution for blacks. Milbrew Davis indicated that he knew of one or possibly two of the white schools that closed because of business expansion.

When the inspector from the US Department of Education recommended that the school be moved to a suburban site, they knew if they hoped to continue to receive support from the citizens of San Antonio, the school would have to relocate. Then, in 1915, with the business community mounting increasing pressure to move the school out of the downtown area, Bowden and the bishop began seeking a site elsewhere.

The times were difficult financially, the city was expanding in that area, and the cost of maintaining the church and school facilities there was more than the diocese felt they could afford, so the LaVillita location was sold. The diocese said that they could no longer afford to maintain it. Of necessity, Bowden and Bishop Johnston identified four acres in a predominantly black community on the east side of town. The site, in an area on the outskirts of the city, at 2120 Dakota Street, encompassed nearly a city block and was located about two miles from the central section of the city. A trolley car line, within a block and a half of the location, made the site particularly desirable. Despite the fact that ownership of the property had been in dispute since 1853, Bowden and the bishop thought the location ideal for the school.

In addition to a two-story brick building on the property, there were two smaller frame buildings whose structures could be improved to provide classrooms and dormitory facilities for the students. But, the most immediate problem to be solved was how to secure the funds needed to purchase the property. Once again, Bowden traveled to the North to see friends whom the bishop had interested in the school. Earlier, when the number of teachers increased from two to six, Bowden assumed the responsibility of raising funds to pay the teachers' salaries. Sometime later, she undertook the task of raising funds to operate the school. Now, in addition to those duties, she assumed the added responsibility of raising funds to purchase land for the new location.

Bowden successfully canvassed her friends in the North for funds, and with the money she received from them, monies from Bishop Capers, donations from her family, and her own personal donations, she accumulated enough money to contract for the property at 2120 Dakota Street.

With the bishop's approval, she entered into an agreement to have improvements made to the property, a move that increased its value 100 percent. Bowden's duties as principal of the school, major fund-raiser, and school administrator increased as well, probably a great deal more than 100 percent. What had begun as a yearning in the hearts of the members of St. Philip's Church for a place of worship for themselves and an opportunity for education and a better life for their children, culminated in St. Philip's Industrial School. Their wishes were granted. They now had a place of worship and a school for their children that, despite an inauspicious beginning and constantly teetering on the brink of closure, had become known in and outside of San Antonio. St. Philip's Industrial School was well on its way to becoming a school to be taken seriously.

5 Four Acres and a New Home

On March 30, 1917, lots 1 through 9 at 2120 Dakota Street on the Eastside of San Antonio were sold to Miss Artemisia Bowden for the sum of $6,076 and the school moved to its new home.

St. Philip's Normal, Grammar, and Industrial School

In 1917, following two downtown locations and four name changes, St. Philip's moved to the city's Eastside, where Bowden and Bishop Johnston had secured acreage. The word "Normal" was added to its title and St. Philip's Grammar and Industrial School became St. Philip's Normal, Grammar, and Industrial School. Three buildings on the property, humble though serviceable, provided space for expansion and growth.

Both bishops, Capers and Johnston, were instrumental in assisting Bowden to purchase the Eastside property. When they first began seeking a location out of downtown, Johnston was still active in the position of bishop but around 1913, he began asking to be relieved of his duties. Capers, appointed in his stead, came to San Antonio in 1914 and, in 1916, succeeded Johnston as bishop of the diocese. Johnston, however, maintained an interest in the school until his death.

The new site comprised just over four acres of uncultivated land on which there was a run-down, two-story brick house, two smaller frame buildings (each in need of repair), no paved streets, and no streetlights or sidewalks.

However, the acreage provided ample land to plant a garden, which provided practical training for the students. They planted the seeds during the spring, gathered their crops during the summer months, and stored them to be consumed during the winter by both teachers and the students.

When two students from the 1940s, Rose McCann Hall and her sister, Serilia McCann Sanford, arrived on the campus at St. Philip's, they described the campus as "just plenty of mud and rocks." Many years later, Eddie Harris, a student from the 1970s, also recalled that Walters Street on the northeast side of the campus was unpaved and remained unpaved for many years. "This location was before any streets were paved. I mean it was all graveled streets. We had only three streets that were paved: New Braunfels Avenue, Houston Street and Commerce Street. Walters was a little narrow, rocky, gravel road." [1]

It mattered not that conveniences were few and luxuries nonexistent, St. Philip's successfully passed through a critical year. The 1918 Annual Report of the Council noted "through her own strenuous efforts and by the generosity of interested church people from the extremes of our nation, West and East, North and South, Miss Bowden, has made possible the enlargement of the building on the new property and the securing of funds in payment upon the purchase of the property itself."[2]

After modest improvements, the two-story brick house became an administration building with classrooms and dormitory accommodations for twenty-five students. One of the two small frame buildings became a cottage for the teachers, and the other a kitchen and dining room for students. The school then became known as St. Philip's Normal and Industrial School, dropping "Grammar" from the title. This was the fifth name change in the school's history, but it was not to be the last.

Both Capers and Bowden hoped that with the move,

Johnston Memorial Building at St. Philip's College, circa 1949

the property on LaVillita Street could be retained for the use of the Negro people of the province. But St. Philip's received so little in the way of financial assistance from the diocese that there were no funds available to maintain the property. Unless a continuing source of funds could be found, the property would have to be sold. After the bishop reported that with only one or two notable exceptions, no parish or mission of the diocese could provide continuous financial support to the school, both Bowden and the bishop realized that immediate steps must be taken.

Just when it appeared that there was little they could do to keep the property, Brackenridge made a proposal to purchase the LaVillita Street property. The proposition from Brackenridge, who so often in the past had been a benefactor to the school, was available only under the condition that the diocesan relationship with the school be relinquished.

Bishop Johnston—who by now had retired from active duty, but had maintained his interest in St. Philip's—was consulted, along with the standing committee, regarding the sale of the property. Having no other choice, the bishops and Bowden made the decision to consider the sale. With St. Philip's mounting indebtedness threatening to overwhelm the school, accepting the offer seemed to be the most expedient thing to do, particularly when the clergy added their recommendation to that of the standing committee. As difficult as the decision was, when both parties, the bishops and the standing committee, recommended the sale, the offer for the LaVillita Street property was accepted.

At the Sixteenth Annual Council, held in 1920, Capers reported that since neither the diocese nor the church-at-large had given the financial support to the school that was needed, Bowden had to take advantage of the financial assistance that Brackenridge offered. He went on to note that while this assistance was only available upon the relinquishing of the school's relationship with the diocese, Bowden continued to remain faithful in her self-sacrificing efforts to maintain the school as a diocesan institution.

Not everyone was happy with the sale, however, for it appeared to some that the diocese support and concern favored the school over the church. Milbrew Davis visited the priest in charge of the church and Leon Wood, father of a student who attended St. Philip's. The Woods family is

Student at work in the St. Philip's gardens

said to have contributed liberally to St. Philip's Church in its early years.

Davis recalled that "[a]fter they sold that property and bought this property right here on Nevada Street, according to Mr. Woods, the diocese was kind enough to allow the members of the church to worship in the basement over on the St. Philip's Campus. The Church felt that they were kind of like a step child to the school."[3] When the school moved from downtown to the Eastside of San Antonio, some members of the church felt that because a place of worship was not made for St. Philip's communicants, the relocation of the school caused a hardship for the church. It seemed to them that the disposition of the property and proceeds were entirely in the interest of the school's growing needs.

It was business as usual at St. Philip's school. Despite being perpetually short of the basic necessities required to run the school, Bowden began another major reorganization. She extended the course work of the normal department to four years beyond the eighth grade, using it to satisfy preparatory or high school graduation requirements. It should be noted that graduation from high school was not as important as graduating from the normal department, because graduation from the normal department meant that one could be hired for a teaching position in the Negro schools.

Not content with achieving normal school status, and always seeking ways to improve St. Philip's, Bowden began seeking the rank of junior college for the school, citing the fact that the nearest public college for blacks was at least 200 miles away. A successful campaign was launched to erect an administration building that would be named for Bishop Johnston. Adding this building would create the extra space needed to meet the minimum space requirements for a junior college. Capers noted, in a report to the Twenty-Third Council of the Diocese of West Texas, that the Negro citizens of San Antonio offered not only their support for the project but also their resources.[4]

Welcome Assistance: Auxiliary Endorsement

When, on December 15, 1924, the Women's Auxiliary of the Province of the Southwest in the Diocese sent a written endorsement praising the school's work, it could not have arrived at a more opportune time. Their public recognition of the work that the school was doing with Negro girls was an encouragement to other donors to support the school's efforts. In addition to the special offerings contributed toward the building fund by churches in the dioceses, the auxiliary pledged their financial support toward expenses. Just as important, the president of the Women's Auxiliary of the Province of the West Texas Diocesan approved funds specifically allotted for the building fund and for expenses for the operation of St. Philip's Junior College.

This endorsement from the Women's Auxiliary, a major boost for the school's fund-raising activities, was extremely important because the areas they served in Arkansas, Kansas, Missouri, New Mexico, and Oklahoma were located outside of Texas and provided access to a great number of persons not heretofore contacted for funds. The $1,500 promised was never received, however, for the meeting in which the funds were to be approved by the body was not held. Nonetheless, their endorsement was proof that in other cities as well as in San Antonio, people were beginning to take notice of St. Philip's and the work it was accomplishing among the Negro population.

Many of the Negro ministers and the leading Christian women of the various Negro congregations of the city saw the work that the school was doing, pledged their support, and canvassed others in the community to do likewise. The Negro citizens, taking note of the religious and educational influence the school was having on the young women of the community, demonstrated their support by raising $3,000 to contribute to the erection of the Administration Building. Alexander Joske, a San Antonio merchant and businessman, gave a nucleus of $6,000 to begin the project.

Becoming a Private Junior College

Even in the midst of the grave financial difficulties the school continually faced, there was a ray of sunshine, such as happened on May 11, 1928. On that day, J. R. Reid, Chairman of the Board of Examiners of the State Department of Education in Austin, Texas, sent a letter to the Rt. Rev. W. T. Capers, Bishop of West Texas, announcing, "It is my duty and pleasure to advise you that the recommendations of this Board to the State Superintendent of Public Instruction have been approved, making St. Philip's College of San Antonio, Texas, a standard junior college for colored, with privileges of certification of their teachers by this department."[5]

With this turn of events, control of St. Philip's was committed to the bishop of the diocese, Bishop Capers, and when the terms were accepted, the college also agreed to a change in name from St. Philip's Normal and Industrial School for Negro Girls to St. Philip's Junior College. "Under Canon 9, Section 1, of the Canons of the Diocese of West Texas, the Control of St. Philip's Normal and Industrial School for Negro Girls is committed to the Bishop of the Diocese. Acting under this Canon, I have changed the character of this school by accepting from the Department of Education of the State of Texas the grade for it of Junior College. By accepting this grade, the name of the school has been changed from its former name to that of St. Philip's Junior College."[6]

The accreditation given to the college was tentative and subject to their rectifying certain conditions, primarily related to finances; nonetheless, the college was now recognized as an accredited junior college of the state of Texas. In all of the reports written to the diocese about the school, including letters from visitors as well as from the Education Committee, not one was found that criticized the quality of instruction. Unexpected visitors were always welcomed and invariably left impressed with the quality and level of care given to the students and to the physical plant, in spite of the lack of funds, overcrowded conditions, and less than adequate facilities.

As an example of innovations introduced by the school, St. Philip's planned an advanced summer school program at the senior level for teachers needing to renew their teaching certificates. These classes were offered despite the fact that funds to pay for additional faculty were not available. Bowden arranged it so that teachers could attend classes through an affiliation with Prairie View State College in Prairie View, Texas, and Wiley College in Marshall, Texas. The need was there, and by the school year 1928–1929, Prairie View began offering classes on St. Philip's campus. The following school year, 1929–1930, Wiley College offered extension classes at St. Philip's also.

A report from Bishop Capers in the Twenty-Seventh Annual Council held in 1930 credited St. Philip's with continuing to enjoy the distinction of having received from the State Department of Education the rank of A-1 Junior College.[7]

Unavoidable Circumstances

Bishop Capers had prophesied that St. Philip's would someday be a great institution of learning, but before his prophecy could be fulfilled, both the college and the country were engulfed in the Great Depression. While this inescapable advent threatened the very existence of St Philip's, the devastating effects were being felt across the entire country. None escaped its consequences. Financial assistance anticipated from friends and the usual supporters failed to materialize, as did contributions from customarily dependable sources. It was simply too difficult to interest businessmen in philanthropic endeavors when their own and other firms across the country were failing.

There were those who did their very best to help by sending solicitation letters and testimonies to the diocese, the Board of Education, the Women's Auxiliary, and to organizations and persons around the city, as well as to persons out of state. The following excerpt from a letter sent to the Twenty-Seventh Annual Council, Diocese of

West Texas, provides insight into the kinds of appeals that were sent:

> Miss Bowden has given her deepest love and her very life's blood to this institution, and while today it is in difficult financial straits, yet I earnestly hope that before the school closes, there will be found some way to meet the situation and thereby continue the life of the college.[8]

Walter W. McAllister Sr., first president of the St. Philip's Trustee Board, recalling Bowden's recurring and seemingly never ending struggle to find enough money to pay her teachers, mentioned in an interview with Clarence W. Norris Jr. that she regularly called on him for donations. He said that he responded with whatever he could afford at the time, perhaps $5 or $10. Then, he recalled, when she had accumulated a fair sum of money, she used it to pay her teachers a portion of what was owed them.[9]

6 Struggling to Survive: The 1930s

We believe that there is a possibility of rendering a very valuable service to this city by offering the facilities and equipment of St. Philip's Junior College to meet the urgent need of our city and surrounding territory for a Junior College for our Negro youth.[1]

Not content with having achieved junior college status, as early as 1930, Bowden and Bishop Capers began meeting with B. W. Harley, the Superintendent of Public Schools with the Board of Education of San Antonio. They requested that supervision of the curriculum be taken over so that St. Philip's Junior College could meet state standards. This request was denied.

Drastic Measures

While Bowden and the bishop were attempting to convince the Board of Education to place St. Philip's under its jurisdiction, in November 1933, a special committee of the Diocesan Executive Board was appointed, with the idea of removing Bowden from her position as president.[2] A further recommendation was that Rev. Patton from the American Church Institute for Negroes make an immediate visit to the college. They wanted him to look at the school and make recommendations for having new management in place by the beginning of the next semester. In an unsigned letter, dated December 13, 1933, to Dr. R. W. Patton, Director of the American Church Institute for Negroes, the writer solicited Dr. Patton's assistance in "clearing the college of prejudices that have been created against it because of Miss Bowden's visionary and unbusinesslike method of managing the college." The writer continued that the paradox was "[t]he identical weaknesses that Miss Bowden has manifested in the management of the college have created it. If it had not been for her enthusiasm and her dreams of a great institution the college would never have been born. But it is her enthusiasm and her dreams that have led her into statements which have created the prejudices that are now threatening the very life of the institution."[3]

Along with the request for a change in management, the special committee requested that during his visit, Dr. Patton investigate and help them find a capable Negro man to manage the college. The diocese and the Board of Trustees were ready to do everything possible to assist the institution, if they were willing to reorganize the management. Dr. Patton did not make the visit to San Antonio to inspect the school as requested, explaining that he could do nothing by coming.

Because the institute and the other schools it supported were so negatively affected by the Depression, sometime after this interchange, the institute withdrew the yearly support it had provided St. Philip's. Reasons cited were: "We [the Institute] are barely swimming with what we have on us, with our noses just a little above the water, in addition to the fact that the conditions surrounding St. Phillips [*sic*] preclude the Institute's assuming responsibility for it."[4]

"One of the chief reasons the Institute could not accept St. Philip's as an institute school," wrote Dr. Patton, was that "St. Phillips [*sic*] has not had, and apparently has no prospect of securing such financial backing as would prevent its relying almost exclusively on the Institute for its support."[5] In an unsigned three page, single-spaced letter, dated July 1, 1931, sent to Porter A. Whaley, Chamber of Commerce, San Antonio, the writer explains why the institute cannot support St. Philip's, specifically because it does not meet institute qualifications, including the fact that San Antonio's Negro population is small, much smaller than many other deserving cities. In the past, the American Church Institute had given limited appropriations amounting to $1,500 yearly to St. Philip's, but it did so reluctantly, "solely out of sympathy for Bishop Capers and to relieve him of the trying situation and to give him time to align at least the other dioceses of Texas in support of the school."[6] One of the conditions of becoming an Institute School (one that received yearly support of up to about one-third of its expenses), was that all of the dioceses of the Episcopal Church within the state in which the school was located had to guarantee their financial support. On April 16, 1931, at 12:46 a.m., Rev. Patton sent a telegram to the college that was received at the corner of Commerce and Presa Streets in San Antonio. It brought distressing news.

> INSTITUTE PASSED RESOLUTION INSTITUTE SHOULD NOT CONTINUE APPROPRIATION ST PHILLIPS [*sic*] THIS ADVICE ESPECIALLY BECAUSE NATIONAL COUNCIL REDUCED APPROPRIATION INSTITUTE TEN THOUSAND ACCOUNTS DIOCESES FAILURE PLEDGE QUOTE . . . BOB W. PATTON.[7]

The impact of the institute withdrawing its financial support was felt throughout the region, for it was more than the loss of financial assistance; it was also a blow to the reputation of the school. While it is impossible to know how many other individuals and organizations withheld their support because of the influence of the institute's stand, it is a certainty that the action had a negative effect. In his December 13, 1933 letter to Dr. Robert Patton, Bishop Capers wrote

> The withdrawal of the appropriation from the American Church Institute for Negroes acted as a double-edged sword, for it cut off a goodly portion of its income with one edge and with the other edge cut away definite confidence in the Institution on the part of the people.[8]

As grim as the situation was, which was perhaps as bleak as it had ever been, there came a ray of hope, just when it was most needed. This time help came in the form of a contribution from the John F. Slater Fund, donating $1,350 toward the salaries of two teachers for the school year 1933–1934. As welcome and as helpful as the gift was, it was not enough to prevent the economic disaster that seemed destined for the school. The financial woes of the college were so acute that foreclosure of the property to satisfy debts was imminent.

A Crisis Averted

Since Bishop Capers and the Standing Committee of the Diocese of West Texas had signed for thirty-five first mortgage bonds in the amount of $25,000, to purchase the eight lots on which the school was situated, he appealed to the diocese, informing them of the consequences of foreclosure and the effect that it would have on its reputation. However, there were no monies to redeem the bonds from the bondholders, leaving the real possibility that St. Philip's could be sold to pay the debts. Even with the improvements made to the property, the fear was that not enough money would be generated from the sale to pay the entire amount of the debt. Not only could the school be sold to satisfy the indebtedness, if the sale of the college failed to generate enough money to satisfy the amount owed, other properties belonging to the church could also be sold to pay the debts.

Realizing the seriousness of the situation, the Council of the Diocese of West Texas immediately took action, authorizing a special committee that they empowered to negotiate an extension and institute other measures as necessary to forestall the crisis. The committee formulated a series of procedures that successfully held off the creditors, the extension was granted, and the crisis was averted, but only for the moment. Bowden reported to the Board of Trustees that "without the sacrifices we made, the work couldn't have gone on."[9]

Community Support

There were Anglo supporters in the community—such as Eleanor Brackenridge and her brother, George Brackenridge, G. Bedell Moore, and Ned McIlhenny—who gave not just their funds, but also their time and expertise. Bishop Johnston and Bishop Capers, allies whose benefaction could always be depended upon, had consistently been staunch supporters of Miss Bowden and St. Philip's. Edward Keator, again accepting a pivotal position in the school's finances, was appointed to a special committee to study the school's financial situation. He, however, went far beyond merely studying the problem: he kept financial records, secured funds, and served as needed in different positions on the Board of Trustees of the college. Additionally, he negotiated with the school district to convince them to place St. Philip's under its jurisdiction.

Frank Huntress, owner of the *San Antonio Express* newspaper, was an advocate from whom Keator and Bowden received encouragement and support. Other champions of the college were Mayor Walter W. McAllister Sr., and his son, Walter Jr., who followed him on the Board of Trustees. The names of some who were advocates for the school have been lost. As the school continued, support from the community began to grow, partly out of their respect for Miss Bowden. The following excerpts are from letters that shed light on the kind of backing St. Philip's received over the years.

> *San Antonio community:* "In view of the fact that the Negro citizens do not have a principal junior college, nor any form of junior college training for our youth other than St. Philip's Junior College, we, some of the representative citizens, do hereby petition the Trustees of said institution to offer to the San Antonio Board of Education the Supervision and direction of the curricula of the school."[10]

> *San Antonio businessman:* "I received recently a letter from you in which you were making an appeal in the cause of the St. Phillips [*sic*] Junior College, and while money has been extremely scarce with me, still I managed to reserve $10.00 from my Christmas funds and sent Mr. Ned McIllheny, treasurer a check."[11]

> *Sympathetic citizen, 1932:* There were others who had only their sympathy to give: "I have helped with this and wish I could help again. We are living on my farm here now, and you know the situation of farmers. Last year broke us all. Later I may be able to subscribe, if so I will."[12]

Porter Whaley, General Manager of the Chamber of Commerce, San Antonio, wrote:

> Over three hundred letters were sent out within two hours after the meeting of the Educational Committee. Under ordinary circumstances, a letter of this kind should have brought in four or five times as much money as in this case. We are enclosing herein checks amounting to $100.00. We exceedingly regret that is all the money that has come in.[13]

Out of Town Appeals from White Citizens

In 1942, the Rev. George A. Wieland, who was at the time Executive Secretary of the Department of Domestic Missions of the Episcopal Church, offered his assistance by appealing to the Women's Auxiliary to provide seventy-five chairs for the school. He made the request when he learned that Miss Bowden had to move the chairs from one classroom to another in order to accommodate the students. It was inconvenient and created great confusion. His request was not granted, not because she did not need the chairs, but because they had already approved a grant for $500 for repairs and this was all they could do.

Support from the Negro Community

In May 1931, a group of San Antonio's leading Negro citizens petitioned the Board of Trustees of St. Philip's Junior College to take under advisement their request for St. Philip's Junior College to become a part of the San Antonio public school system. (See appendix for petition and list of signatures.) They argued that coming under the umbrella of the San Antonio Independent School District (SAISD) would provide relief from the continuing struggle for operating funds.

Though their correspondence to the Board of Education did not reflect this, they feared that the school would close for lack of funds. They were greatly concerned for the future of the Negro youth in San Antonio, for during these Depression years, St. Philip's Junior College provided the only opportunities for training beyond high school in San Antonio and the surrounding area for Negroes. Employment for Negro youth, beyond common labor, was nonexistent. This contingent of the black community voiced their support for St. Philip's through their written petition to the Board of Education and also through their sacrificial financial contributions.

Negro Support outside of San Antonio

Letters of support and endorsement were sent to Bishop Capers from various sources in other communities and other states. Dr. Harry F. Greene, Dean of Prairie View State College in Prairie View, Texas, was a friend and ardent supporter. He emphasized the fact that of the dozens of schools in Texas that called themselves colleges, St. Philip's was the only one with the intention of becoming a first-class junior college, and the only one whose programs appeared to be like a modern junior college.

For a number of years, in support of Miss Bowden, the bishop and the Board of Trustees continued to petition the school district to take St. Philip's under its supervision. For equally as many years, the school district refused. In an effort to convince the SAISD of the efficacy of an association with St. Philip's, Bishop Capers argued that many reciprocal benefits would flow through to the district. This argument failed to convince the school district. Keator, along with Bowden, attempted to negotiate the operation of St. Philip's by the SAISD, using the argument that it was unfair to fund a junior college for white students while ignoring the Negro students. This argument, too, was to no avail.

Meanwhile, the college continued with business as usual. Student clubs were organized: the Bishop Johnston Literary Society, the Girl's Friendly Society of America, the Drama Club, and the Choral Club. *The Tiger* and *The Opportunity*, two student publications, were first published in 1929 as a forum for disseminating news of the school to students, alumni, and interested friends. Bowden continued as a regular contributor of articles to *The Opportunity*, as did other faculty and students.

A Working Board of Trustees

Despite resistance from the Board of Education to placing St. Philip's under its jurisdiction, Bowden and Johnston eventually succeeded and the board reluctantly accepted St. Philip's. A working Board of Trustees was selected from among the elite of San Antonio, all men of great influence in the city. The 1934–1935 board is an example of the caliber of persons invited to serve on the Board of Trustees who accepted and served.

Considering the caliber of the leaders who served on the Board of Trustees and their influence in the San Antonio business community, it is puzzling that twelve years elapsed before the SAISD gave favorable consideration to accepting supervision of St. Philip's Junior College. One of the vital roles that Keator fulfilled as treasurer for St. Philip's was to keep these men and other important persons in the community abreast of the school's progress. He often sent a personal endorsement such as follows, along with the financial statement from the San Antonio National Bank, assuring them of his role and of the necessity of keeping the school in the community: "This institution, in my opinion, deserves the support of the community and I know that it is being operated economically and carefully—every obligation and every payment going through my hands."[14]

Despite its financial woes, even then St. Philip's was known outside of San Antonio and beyond Texas for preparing its students well. The *Afro-American* newspaper, widely circulated among black readership, cited the fact that the school had attracted the attention of many educators interested in the advancement of Negroes. The article went on to note that there were five teachers in the school and these five were accomplishing commendable results shown by the statement that "out of 48 who graduated since 1928, only three are unemployed."[15]

This is significant when one takes into account that when this statement was made, the country was in the midst of a Depression. Nor should it be overlooked that the Trustee Board sent kudos to the school, pointing out the opportunities that the school offered from an economic standpoint and from the moral contribution in the community that the students made wherever they went.

Board of Trustees, 1934–1935

Name	Profession
Ned McIlhenny	Vice President of Frost National Bank
J. E. Mitchell	Prominent insurance man and son-in-law of the late Bishop Johnston, founder of St. Philip's College
H. H. Ochs	President of Wolff & Marx, a leading department store in San Antonio
Dr. F. G. Oppenheimer	One of the wealthiest bankers in the Southwest
Dr. Frederick Terrell	Retired capitalist, honored citizen of San Antonio
Prof. S. J. Sutton	Principal of Douglas High School, only African American member of the board

Oral Histories Beginning with the 1930s

In the following chapter, graduates and faculty from St. Philip's are introduced as they tell their stories. Their association with St. Philip's began around the time of the Depression and continued during the difficult financial time that followed. The interviews begin with students and faculty from the 1930s who were, at the time of the interviews, in their eighties. The voices of those with whom we spoke gave us insight into some of the many roads that led them to St. Philip's, particularly when it was a fledgling junior college. It is of significance that St. Philip's was the first institution of higher education available to black citizens in the city of San Antonio.

7 Oral History Interviews, 1930s

Let us understand that the present college is just the beginning of a great institution of learning which shall take rank with the first colleges of the land. If we keep these convictions in our minds and ever pressing upon our hearts, we will live to see the day when hundreds will graduate annually from St. Philip's and from her walls will go an ever-increasing influence for the betterment of her people.[1]

This chapter presents a look at some of the oldest living students we located, who attended St. Philip's College beginning in the 1930s. They told us of hardships they endured in their efforts to gain an education beyond high school in a city where little was provided for them. In addition, surviving faculty tells what it was like to be employed at the college when St. Philip's was a fledgling institution and struggling financially.

Rev. Claude Black

Claude Black enrolled in St. Philip's Junior College in the 1930s, at age sixteen, immediately after graduating from Douglas High School. He knew Miss Bowden first as teacher, later as landlord, and, shortly after becoming a minister, found himself (as he put it) "in the unlikely role of advisor and confidante." A native of San Antonio, and former two-term city councilman, Black became a much sought-after preacher and counselor. As pastor emeritus of Mt. Zion First Baptist Church, and having spent over fifty years in the ministry, most of it in San Antonio, Black was considered by many to be the dean of San Antonio's black clergy.

Academic Life

When Black went to St. Philip's in 1933, he described the atmosphere as family-like and really good for students who were just entering college. He spoke of being called "mister" for the first time in his life, and at sixteen, to be called mister was a great thing. It was like a transformation. Teachers called him mister and the young girls "miss." He felt like an adult and considered this the signal for entry into the college environment.

"The major building was the administrative building, a mixture of administration and classrooms. In 1933, the city and the nation were in the heart of the Depression, and many of the students could not go outside of the city because their parents didn't have the money. So a great number of the class of 1933 went to St. Philip's. They [their parents] wanted them to go outside the city and they [students] wanted to go too, but they had no money."[2] Black pointed to today's students, who are in a similar situation when they want to go away from home. It's not that they don't like St. Philip's, it's just that they want to get away from home and enjoy new experiences in a different city.

When Black enrolled at St. Philip's, all students took the basic courses: English, history, science, mathematics, and electives, such as music. Florence Dawson was the musician at that time and she also worked with the choir.

St. Philip's Culture, 1930s

Black was given an opportunity to do a lot of things at St. Philip's that he might not have done at another school, such as playing on the basketball team. Tuition was a small sum, probably in the teens, but even at that, their

Rev. Claude Black

parents could not anticipate whether they were going to have it because of bills, lack of work opportunities, and other obligations. "Our father always told me he would come up with it, and he did and I was able to stay there," said Black.

Black described the school library as "[n]ot as big as my library here at the house. I have a personal library that's bigger than it. Compared with today's offerings, the library was small and inadequate, with few books. We didn't have any great library resources to turn to for study. Many of us, I guess, went to the city library but even city libraries are not geared to academic work, really. We have general libraries, but at that time, you'd not find the kind of material that you needed as a student in science, or as a student in history. You might have found more help in history than maybe any other subject. And those were the basic subjects you were taking."[3]

Black graduated from Morehouse College in 1937 and planned to attend medical school. To earn money, he began working with his uncle in his grocery store but he soon became weary with "sitting there day in and day out, waiting for people to come to the grocery." "Sometimes when going to school," said Black, "Opportunity drives us, not purpose." He was out of college for three years in the 1940s and then he began to deal with the purpose of his life. He then went to Andover Newton, finished in 1943, came back to San Antonio and was called to pastor Mt. Zion First Baptist Church, where he spent the next forty-nine years.

While at Mt. Zion, Black organized San Antonio Mothers' Service Organization, a group of women who helped to send many students to St. Philip's. "Now, the interesting thing that they've done, which thrills me, is that they've sent students not at the top of the class but students whose economic condition would not allow them to go to school," said Black. "This service organization looks largely at the income of the family. They've sent students there whose parents aren't able to get them started, not just the students that have high academic records."[4]

Lola Vernice Warner, 1934 Graduate, St. Philip's College

Warner enrolled at St. Philip's in 1932, after graduating from Douglas High School in San Antonio. She grew to know Bowden well, for in addition to her contact at school, she once spent the night at Bowden's home in Atlanta. Born in the small German town of Weimar, Texas, halfway between San Antonio and Houston, Warner moved to San Antonio with her family during the Depression. She graduated from Kenwood in Los Angeles Heights and because she was a good student, was moved into the sixth grade. At that time, three classes were all in one room; high school ended in the tenth grade and students then rode the bus to Douglas, the high school. Warner finished Douglas in 1934 at sixteen and then attended St. Philip's, where she finished at eighteen years.

She was delighted at the opportunity to attend St. Philip's. For one, though it was an Episcopal school, they not only allowed dancing, they sponsored dances at the school. Warner loved dancing but her parents thought she was a little young for that. Good African Methodist Christian people didn't encourage dancing. They waited until they were grown; not while still in school and growing up. "But," said Warner, "St. Philip's was the church that sponsored student dances and oh my goodness, they got ready! I had never known, never been to a school where they prepared for fun and recreation like that, you know. And I was just amazed, they decorated and the band came

Lola Vernice Warner, graduate of St. Philip's College

and I just danced myself down. This was the first time that I had danced that had been approved by Christian people. Everybody danced. Boys just went around and asked everybody to dance and I danced by myself. That was my first love for St. Philip's."[5]

Bishop Capers would come and have mass at the chapel, which the students were required to attend. Warner remembered that there were two girls living in the dormitory and "a very studious, nice, gentlemanly young man, a singer; Frank Stillwell, and he had a sister named Artie. They were seniors and a boy named Brownie lived across the street. There was a small home cafe where a lady sold hamburgers and sandwiches for ten or perhaps fifteen cents, not more than a quarter. The students were permitted to go over there, cross the street and buy a hamburger if they wanted to or a sandwich or whatever little something she had, maybe even teacakes."

Mr. Tarver, who had only one arm, was the chemistry teacher. Because she had not had science classes before, Warner "was afraid to death of all this fire, steam, and water bubbling." She remembered that the chemistry class produced "about the only 'C'" that she had on her grade card that first year and later on, she decided to do something about that. Being unaccustomed to science classes, she "didn't cotton to chemistry too well. I had heard about it, but that's all."

By the second year, Warner had become the student assistant in the chemistry lab; though she was not entirely comfortable, by then she had learned the basics. She was no longer afraid of the chemistry class. She "began to understand what was happening, then it became very interesting" and she "pulled that 'C' out."

San Antonio Classmates

Despite the passage of time, Warner could recall many of her classmates: "Rev. Black, Frank Kelly, Abner Williams, Amy West, LaVeda Walker and that Stillwell girl." Throughout the interview, we were amazed at the facility that Warnerhad for remembering the names of her classmates. She was in her nineties.[6]

Tommy Crayton, Student, 1930s

Crayton came to St. Philip's in the fall of 1939. After graduating from high school, he joined the military because there was no four-year college that he could attend in San Antonio.

Recollections of Campus Life

When Crayton came to St. Philip's, he called the two buildings on the campus the twin towers. The long straight building he described was the art building, and next to it was a two-story building with a dormitory where the girls lived upstairs and boys lived downstairs. Eight male students stayed in a house across the street from St. Philip's. Crayton said, "That was the first year that they had that many in the dormitory. We ate in a cafeteria across the street from where we lived and the cooks were students. One of the guys that was a chef went on to be a Major in the service and later on became a preacher." [7]

Financing an Education

Crayton joined the National Youth Administration (NYA) Program, started by Franklin D. Roosevelt, and was hired in his last year in high school to keep the yard and buildings clean at St. Philip's. His pay covered his tuition.

The Faculty

When Crayton returned after getting out of the military, there was still not a four-year college that he could attend in San Antonio so he went to mechanics school. St. Philip's did not have auto mechanics in the curriculum at the time, so when he attended St. Philip's, he majored in teacher training. Crayton recalled that Katie Greene, Bowden's so-called adopted daughter, taught the physical education classes. "A Mrs. Jackson, from Philadelphia, taught art. A Mrs. McIntyre taught literature and we had a skit like making movies. We had good teachers who went to different schools trying to attract the children to come to St. Philip's.

"Mr. Johnson was the Dean and he was also one of the teachers. A man from Howard University taught Child Psychology, but he left after the first year because they didn't have money to pay him. When Miss Bowden needed money, she'd go downtown to the people that owned the businesses and of course, she got money. She was good at that. We don't know where she got it or who she got it from but that's how she kept the school going."

Georgia Taylor graduation photo, 2002

Georgia Taylor, Student, 1931, 1970s

Taylor, who graduated from Douglas High School in 1931, attended St. Philip's College with a scholarship that paid a portion of her tuition for the first year. She attended night school at St. Philip's for two years and did not graduate, though she made excellent grades in each subject except math, which she failed. Even after seventy years, she could still recall that Charlesetta Snell and Hadley Hawthorne were her math teachers.

At that time, social life was limited to whatever the churches in the community and the school provided. Taylor remembered going to chapel daily, but not on Sundays. She recalled a building on the corner that she described as "kind of a hall where [they] sometimes went for different types of entertainment such as different kinds of programs but not dances. That building was the only one off campus that was available to the school at that time." She recalled Bowden going around the neighborhood, talking to people when she needed something done and the neighbors were happy to be of help because she was trying to do something for the black members of the community. Taylor also remembered that out-of-town students outnumbered the local students. After graduating from St. Philip's, students from San Antonio often went to Prairie View, Sam Houston, and to a school in Austin.

There were no tennis teams, but there was a place to play tennis and sometimes softball on the vacant lot across the street from the school. The students would begin playing tennis early in the morning and later, when the teachers wanted to play, the students wouldn't leave. The faculty would have to play against the students and win to get them off the courts.

This is the same Georgia Taylor who attended St. Philip's first kindergarten class. She also attended St. Philip's College twice, first in 1931 and again in the 1970s. Taylor did not graduate when she attended during the 1930s; she needed to complete one course in algebra to graduate. When she attended St. Philip's in the 1970s, she again enrolled in the algebra course and again did not apply for graduation. She said that she was unsure whether her course would be accepted. During the interview session, as we looked at her grade report, interviewer Mark Barnes noted that she had made a passing grade, took her information to school officials, and informed them of the situation.

In 2002, seventy years later, Mrs. Taylor walked across the stage at Trinity University's Laurie Auditorium with the midwinter graduating class of 2002 and received her associate's degree. Mrs. Taylor, at eighty-eight years, was four times the age of the majority of her fellow graduates.[8]

Henrietta Stevenson, Student, 1930s

Stevenson was a St. Philip's student in the 1930s. After graduating from the University of Michigan, she joined the faculty at St. Philip's. She was one of the few students whose parents could afford to pay her tuition in full. Most of the students worked to pay for their tuition. Stevenson, known very well in San Antonio, came to be considered by many as the Grande Dame of the Eastside. Her husband, Ernest Stevenson, was also a member of the St. Philip's faculty. Mrs. Stevenson, at ninety-four, was one of the oldest living St. Philip's graduates at the time of her death. She passed away in 2009.

Henrietta Stevenson, student

Academic Life

Stevenson was born at home on July 24, 1915 in a house that still stands on the corner of the 600 block of Pine Street and Martin Luther King Boulevard. At the time, the street was named Nebraska. "I knew about Miss Bowden, even as a child," she said. Stevenson's mother, whom she described as a very outgoing person, had a cordial relationship with Bowden, since it was unlikely back then that someone like Miss Bowden would come to town and not be introduced to her mother.

Stevenson finished Douglas High School in 1931 and spent two weeks at Fisk University, but her asthma was so bad that she withdrew and came back to San Antonio. She spent the year at St. Philip's, while living at home. She recalled that Miss Bowden was head of the school at that time and worked very hard, traveling back and forth to various places to raise money.

Financing Their Education

The 1930s were characterized by financial difficulties across the nation and for the students, meeting the cost of tuition was an issue for all but a few. Only a handful of students were able to pay their own tuition and the jobs that St. Philip's provided seemed to be as meaningful to their education as the academic coursework.

"One of the years, when I was a student, the money was not there and I don't know what month it was, I guess it was mentioned at chapel time. I remember young men crying, you know, they had looked forward to getting an education. Now, the crisis was over, we'll say, in about a week or something like that. What happened, the teachers had said that they would not hold classes. So, that's the way the students found out and I guess Miss Bowden pulled a miracle and got some money and paid them. I remember that crisis."[9]

The Faculty

Stevenson remembered many of her instructors at St. Philip's from the early 1930s. There was a Miss Gray from Chicago who taught English and Miss Moses (or Moseley) taught music. Stevenson described a class in religion that she attended because she said "Miss Bowden was such a lady that she did not think that anyone would have wanted to insult her by not going. The racial climate in San Antonio was strict segregation and separate schools and on the trolley or bus, there was something that you could move up and back, so that if more blacks got on, this thing moved forward to separate and if more whites got on, it would be moved back."

Classmates

When Stevenson recalled her classmates, her memory was impressive. She continued to maintain contact, even after seventy years had passed, with two of her classmates, Dorothy Hood Oliver, who moved to Jacksonville, Florida, and Betty Gace, who moved to Tennessee. Roy Willie Burley of San Antonio was a high-school classmate and Alfred Markins was a brother of Vernis, who was married to Coach Hudgins from St. Philip's.

Stevenson described Bowden as always impeccably groomed, with every pleat and tuck in place, blouse freshly starched, shoes with no dust showing. "I'm sure there was some, you know, from walking around, but just impeccably groomed to the last thing, from the top of her head down to her toes. And also, *excellent* quality of whatever it was: If it was a pocket book, fine leather. Most of the colors she wore were muted, black, navy blue, beige or white. I think she had something lavender too, but always dignified colors that would be suitable for her station, which was the head of an educational institution and also as an example of what a lady should be like and have effect."

Another Side of Miss Bowden

"Miss Bowden would get very excited whenever Bishop Capers was coming. We would laugh behind her back about the way she spoke because of her Georgia accent. When she called his name, it seemed to us that she was saying, 'the bee ship is coming, the bee ship is coming.' She wanted everything in the school to be in order, because 'the bee ship is coming.' I don't remember a specific joke or anything but she would say things and there would be a twinkle in her eye, so she was not all stern and bad or anything like that. When we had chapel, there was an old-fashioned organ that she would pump and play. She did not always lead the song; but, when she did, her song was always 'O Zion Haste, Thy Mission High Fulfilling.' That apparently, was her favorite because she was on a mission.[10]

"Her brother, Father Rev. Bowden, an Episcopal minister, said to us that people thought of Miss Bowden as a spinster lady, but she had had offers of marriage that she declined because she felt the calling of her ministry was to do this work. And so, with that from her brother, it let us understand that she understood life and was willing to make the sacrifice."

Stevenson recalled that St. Mark's Episcopal Church gave donations to St. Philip's but she had no idea how much support because "our money now is so different, you know. If they had given $50 back then, it would have been a lot of money. The Bishop would set the standard for the relationship and the attitude of the parishioners."

Bowden's Family

"Miss Bowden's father had three sets of children and Artemisia Bowden was from the older set. I think she may have had four sisters and brothers. There was Frances, who was, I think, with [by] his second wife. And then, Father Bowden and Minnie were the third ones. I'm mentioning that because Frances was married to a man named Bernard Coleman. And, as far as I know, he's still alive. Miss Bowden's sister Minnie was a social worker and she and her husband lived in San Antonio for a year or so. This was in 1940 or '42."[11]

Stevenson's mother escorted Minnie, the last daughter and sister living when Miss Bowden died. "The Episcopal Church took care of Miss Bowden's last years and all of the hospitals looked after the funeral expenses. She is buried in a mausoleum in Corpus Christi." Mrs. Stevenson passed away in San Antonio on October 30, 2009.[12]

Sylvester Mitchell, Student, 1930s

Mitchell, a San Antonio native and brother of Georgia Taylor, attended kindergarten and St. Philip's College in 1935 and 1936. Mitchell says that he attended St. Philip's at a time when they had the "first tailoring course going on over there." Having grown up in the neighborhood around St. Philip's, he remembers when the college was just a one-story building. After receiving an associate's degree from St. Philip's, Mitchell joined the Army. He attended St. Philip's again in the 1950s and remembers Everett Turbon teaching some of his courses. After St. Philip's, Mitchell earned a degree at Texas State University.

"St. Philip's was there when I was a little boy and I'm eighty-five years of age. Some of the students lived upstairs in dormitories and the downstairs was used for classes. Many times when the out-of-town students were homesick, students from San Antonio would invite them to their homes."

Mitchell enrolled in tailoring classes "that were held in the little garage that was converted into a building to be used for classrooms." He used his GI Bill eligibility from his military service to pay his tuition. Robert J. Washington was the instructor and later on, he became Washington's assistant teacher.

"She [Miss Bowden] tried to get things going with this co-education. She didn't have a place for the boys at first, but she had a little white house across the street and she would get the fellas from the country and let 'em stay in this little house, whether the parents had money for their tuition or not."

Mitchell recalled that at that time, much of the property on Walters Street was owned by whites or Mexicans with "just a few colored." When Miss Bowden wanted to buy the property, they considered it because the school was situated in a mixed neighborhood where everyone accepted everyone else.[13]

Audre Hudson Tavares Adams, Faculty

In 1934, Audre Tavares, a beautiful, petite young lady fresh out of college came to San Antonio from Guanajuato, Mexico, to join St. Philip's faculty. At that time, the faculty and staff were mainly local blacks from Texas. With the frequent changes in staffing that occurred, faculty began coming from other locations in the United States. At the time of the interview Tavares, who married Bernard Adams, had retired from teaching and was a lively, very gracious ninety-eight-year-old lady who was eager to share with us her memories of St. Philip's. When we arrived for the interview, Adams met us at the door, prepared with notes in hand. "In case I forget what I wish to tell you about St. Philip's," she said.

Audre Adams, faculty

Adams grew up as a member of the only black family living in Guanajuato, Mexico. She, however, was born in the United States, "because my mother wanted me to be a United States citizen." Her mother came to the United States and stayed just long enough for Tavares to be born and then they returned to Mexico. She had never experienced racial prejudice prior to coming to the United States to attend undergraduate studies.

Adams attended Howard University in Washington, DC, for undergraduate studies and, following graduation, learned of St. Philip's College through an advertisement in an El Paso newspaper for a Spanish teacher. Texas was close to her home, she said. "So I wrote to the school seeking employment, even though that was the first time that I had heard of St. Philip's College."

Coming to San Antonio

Bowden needed someone to teach Spanish and to be her secretary and Tavares, thinking that it was an excellent opportunity, wrote to Bowden, saying, "I do not type and I do not know shorthand, but by September, I will know how to type. I do not promise you shorthand." Bowden replied in a very gracious letter assuring Tavares that she did not have to know shorthand if she could type.

Tavares's sister taught her to type blindfolded, using an old Olivetti typewriter. Then, when Bowden replied affirmatively with an offer of hire, she left Mexico for San Antonio. Upon Tavares's arrival, she called the school. Miss Esdell Malloy answered, informing her that Miss Bowden was out of town but that they were expecting her. She went by taxi to the school. When she accepted the position, she had only seen a picture in the newspaper of a building at St. Philip's.

"When I first saw the picture in the newspaper, I said, 'What wonderful building is that? I wonder if that's the library or the science building?' After I got there, I remember, I wrote to my mother and I said, 'Mother, the picture we saw, that building, that was the entire school!' At that time, the school was on Dakota Street and the campus was two small buildings, one of which housed classrooms in the downstairs area. Miss Bowden's bedroom and office, the registrar's office, and a family dining room were in the back. All faculty and staff meetings were held in the chapel. The tennis courts where faculty and students played were across the street. And that was the school! St. Philip's, at the time spelled with two l's, was known as St. Phillip's.[14]

"Miss Bowden would be gone, sometimes for weeks or maybe over a month, traveling all over the country on behalf of St. Philip's, raising money everywhere." Adams recalled that the faculty was also required to raise money to help to keep the school afloat. She wrote to people that she knew asking them to send money to help the school.

Leaving St. Philip's

After teaching one year at St. Philip's, the high school principal at Douglas, a Mr. Gates, asked Adams if she would be interested in teaching in the public school system. The Spanish teacher had died, creating a vacant position at Douglas. "Well, I don't know if that's the proper thing to do. I haven't signed a contract with Miss Bowden and I've taught there just one year and I don't know what the law is," Adams said. Gates advised her that she could resign and say that she had another position. "So, I wrote Miss Bowden, thanked her for having given me my first year's experience teaching, and told her that I had accepted work in the public schools." Adams, who felt bad about accepting another position, meanwhile received a letter from Bowden who was very kind, very understanding, and who said that she was happy for her. Adams worked in the public schools until retirement and also taught in the evening division under Mr. Watson at St. Philip's.

Adams stayed close to her students even following retirement and some became language teachers because of her influence. Love of languages was the path that led her to San Antonio and she said, "I've tried to direct my students down the same exciting path that I followed. If I had to live my life over, I'd do the same things. Teaching was so satisfying to me."[15] Adams passed away November 2009 at the age of 102.

8 An Awesome Responsibility: The 1940s

In 1941, the diocese adopted a canon absolving themselves of any responsibility for the school, noting that "henceforth, the property, funds, and revenues . . . should be administered separately and distinctly from those of the Diocese."[1]

Assuming Financial Responsibility for St. Philip's College

St. Philip's managed to survive the Depression years, but just barely. By the 1940s, the difficulties that followed those years heralded the beginning of more troubles to come. The college was doing great work—better work, in fact, than ever before—and the diocese recognized this, but they also knew that, considering the economic times, the risk to the diocese in continuing to accept the school's obligations was simply too great.

True to the fears of Bowden and the bishop, within a very short time, financial assistance from the diocese and from the Western District ceased. Support for St. Philip's from the diocese had always been minimal, and when that help was withdrawn, the consequences were dire, for there were no supporters waiting to take their place. With the likelihood of no additional financial assistance from the diocese, there appeared little possibility that St. Philip's would receive future assistance from the Western District. This was, quite possibly, one of the darkest and most worrisome times for Bowden, for she assumed the burden with no immediate, dependable, or continuing source of outside assistance. A testimony to how highly her decision was regarded is summed up in this letter:

> It is because the Board of Trustees of St. Philip's Junior College has faith in you that your promise to raise ten thousand dollars in behalf of the current budget of the school was accepted and has become an accredited source to the school. This seems like a fearful burden to place upon you, but you voluntarily assumed it.[2]

Bowden was experienced in raising money to support St. Philip's and because of that, the bishop and trustees felt justified in allowing her to assume the three-year indebtedness of the school. In his own words, the bishop advised her not to hesitate to use his name in making her appeal if she thought that it would help. Since he held both the office of bishop of the diocese and president of the Board of Trustees, he thought that making the appeal with his blessing might be of some help.

"Miss Bowden brings St. Philips to this new Board with no indebtedness or defects other than this year's salary shortage," wrote the bishop. "The indebtedness accumulated for 1928 to 1931 has been drawn up in legal form as Miss Bowden's personal obligations, with two years for her to take care of same. Attorney Hall has this matter in hand."[3]

Angels of Support: Family and Faculty

Not enough can be said of the efforts Bowden's family put forth to help her keep the school open or for the financial assistance that she received from them. Her family, along with a few other stalwart believers in the school, remained constant, even as support from the community

Edward H. Keator

and the diocese dwindled. An excerpt from a letter from Edward H. Keator sheds light on the kinds of assistance that Bowden received from her family:

> When Bowden's father died, he left $2,000 of New York Life Insurance to her. Out of this [,] $1,000 was used by her for the payment of school obligations, including both teacher's salaries and supplies.[4]

Keator, an oilman and a faithful Episcopalian, became interested in the struggle to keep St. Philip's going and after committing to render his assistance, became a loyal and trustworthy supporter, a position he held to throughout his life. In addition to serving as a member of the trustee board, he offered his assistance in any way that he could to put the school on a sound financial track, including writing letters of appeal for financial aid and interceding with the bank when needed. Additionally, he met with the other trustees and representatives from the Diocese of West Texas to affect a bond settlement and provided bookkeeping and accounting services.

At one time, Keator wrote a letter protesting what he felt was unfair treatment of Miss Bowden. "At no time during my association with the school operations did Miss Bowden receive a full salary any year—in fact, [she received only] a small proportion of it at all times. Such income as she did receive was given in a large amount to clearing up obligations of the school of many years standing which were direct obligations of the Diocese of West Texas."[5] Keator went on to say that in a judgment against the college and Miss Bowden, which was as much an obligation of the diocese as of her own, she paid every cent of the settlement herself. Because he worked very closely with her at all times, he attested to the fact that her salary was budgeted at around $100 per month. She failed to receive her full salary any of the years indicated in the following chart, which outlines the salary owed to her.

In a follow-up letter, Keator noted that, in addition to paying teachers' salaries and bills from her own funds, Bowden placed a mortgage on her property and gave her personal note for $1,100. These funds from her personal resources were used to operate the school at a time when the portions owed to her of her own monthly salary amounted to more than $5,000.

With support no longer available from the diocese, Bowden set about trying to find a replacement donor and to get funds for operating expenses to carry the institution forward through the remainder of the school year. First, she tried establishing a relationship with the San Antonio School Board. Her plan was to have the school board supervise the curriculum of what was now the St. Philip's Junior College and Vocational Institute. Bowden reminded the board that St. Philip's Junior College had never received public monies, but that public funds had been used to operate San Antonio College from its beginning.

Nonetheless, the board was firm in its refusal. Each time the request was made, it was denied. In fact, even the federal funds that came into the city to be used for relief during the Depression were not made available to the black community for postsecondary training. Following are a few of the measures taken to raise funds:

Unpaid Salary, Artemisia Bowden, 1935–1941

Years	Amount
1935–36	$ 485.00
1936–37	$ 640.00
1937–38	$ 530.00
1938–39	$1,125.00
1939–40	$ 685.00
1940–41	$1,120.00
1941–42	$ 810.00
Total	$ 5,395.00

- An alumni association was formed to promote a "continuing tie" between the college and former students.
- Some class offerings were increased while others were decreased.
- Both elementary and junior high school programs were discontinued, as was the requirement to wear a school uniform.
- The mathematics department taught new and advanced courses that included college algebra and plane trigonometry.

Though increasing the curriculum meant additional work, faculty and staff gave their all in the efforts to raise funds and keep the college open. Members of Bowden's family came to offer their assistance at various times. Following is an excerpt of an interview conducted with Bowden's nephew, Richard Perry Mallard Bowden, or R. P. M., as he preferred to be called. His father, Henry Bowden, also an Episcopal priest, came to San Antonio to offer Bowden his assistance in operating the school. As one of the last living relatives in Bowden's family, we are grateful to R. P. M. for sharing these historical facts with us.

R. P. M. Bowden, born on Mittman Street in San Antonio, was baptized at St. Philip's Church, at that time located in a building on the campus. He was named after both paternal grandfathers. "My auntie, Artemisia Bowden, named me after my mother's father, Richard Perry, and my father's father, Mallard Bowden." R. P. M.'s father, Rev. Henry James Charles Bowden, and Artemisia Bowden were half-siblings who shared the same father. Henry James Bowden, the oldest of the latter set of Miss Bowden's siblings, was born in Brunswick, Georgia, and attended St. Augustine College in Raleigh, North Carolina, in 1918; College of City of New York in 1921; and Shaw University. He graduated from Morehouse College in Atlanta in 1925, and attended seminary at Columbia University, graduating in 1929. Henry Bowden "became an Episcopalian Priest and was canonical [recognized, accepted] in the diocese in Atlanta from 1934 until his death in 1995.

"She [Bowden] was considerably older than he was; he was born in 1902 and I guess you know that she came to San Antonio to work in 1902. 'Auntie' and my father were very much alike, as were her other brothers: dedicated and determined to help people and to make sure that people helped themselves."

R. P. M. Bowden

The last known living blood relative of Artemisia Bowden, R. P. M. shared with us the following history:

"Auntie, Miss Bowden, was the oldest of her generation; she had a brother, Edward, who was a physician and surgeon and another brother who was in pharmacy school." According to R. P. M., the brother in pharmacy school met an untimely death, the details of which were not shared. When Bowden's father, who was R. P. M.'s grandfather, remarried (for what R. P. M. thought was the third time), his father was born from that union, as were his aunts, his father's sisters Frances and Minnie.

R. P. M. recalled that when he lived in Bowden's home for several months during the summer of 1941 the house was across the street from where the security office is now. "Not sure," said R. P. M., "but I think she [Bowden] was living on the corner of Dakota at the time. My father left Atlanta in 1932 to assist my aunt with the administration of St. Philip's and also to teach religion and English. My aunt was always going around raising money and traveling and he had a young family to feed. My father said that there was no need for both him and Auntie to starve, so after a short while, he left San Antonio to take a job

R. P. M. Bowden, nephew of Artemisia Bowden

in Wilmington, NC, as rector of St. Mark's Episcopal Church."

Of St. Philip's R. P. M. had this to say: "I may be jumping ahead, but I think before long, it might be a four-year college—it has the potential."[6] Though he was confined to a wheelchair, R. P. M. traveled extensively. He passed away on October 5, 2010, following an extended illness.

Willing Hands: Faculty and Staff Support and Sacrifice

From the very beginning, whether hired as an administrator or faculty, personnel worked double duty. Stonewall (Stoney) Jackson Davis began his teaching career at the college in 1947, working part-time, teaching one day class and one evening class. After two months of employment, he was appointed business manager and full-time registrar. Describing his position, Davis stated:

> The administrators at St. Philip's were expected to perform more than their regular duties as a supervisor or a manager. I, personally, was regularly assigned classes, teaching from one-third to one-half time, from six to nine hours, in addition to my administrative duties. During the fall semester, when I became the full-time business manager, I continued performing dual duties. This was true with other administrative personnel, who were expected to and did perform dual duties, wherever and whenever needed.[7]

Even after being promoted to full-time business manager, Davis continued performing double duty, teaching one to six hours per week for all except the last three years of his career. Despite the long and often arduous hours, the great cooperation and loyalty on the part of the personnel of the college was given without question. In an interview with Norris, Davis described an incident where a delivery of merchandise and supplies arrived as he was teaching a class. Having no other option, he left a student in charge of the class while he accepted the delivery.

To his friends, he was affectionately known as "Stony," but to St. Philip's, Stonewall Jackson Davis was a well-respected, totally committed member of the faculty.

Even Dean Norris, in addition to his duties as dean of the college, performed double duty, serving as registrar from 1955 to 1966.[8] Before Norris became registrar, the business manager (Stoney Davis) carried the extra duty of registrar. When Norris arrived, the president felt it more appropriate to combine dean and registrar rather than business manager and registrar, since combining the positions of dean-registrar was the practice at many small black colleges. Norris indicated in his autobiography that "when I served as dean-register for fourteen years, my teaching assignment was also indicated in St. Philip's catalog and on many occasions I did some teaching along with my administrative assignment."[9]

Stonewall (Stoney) Jackson Davis

Dean Leonidas Watson, though director of the Evening Division of the college, was not exempt from performing double duty. For ten years, he also taught from six to nine hours per semester. Despite being required to perform double duty, many determined, committed administrators and faculty remained in their positions for decades; such was their dedication to St. Philip's. Their faithfulness was rewarded, for change eventually came.

9 The 1940s, Continued

At a conference yesterday with Mr. Leo Brewer, Mr. Henry Stribling, Mr. Douglas King and myself, representing the Diocese and members of the Board of Education, it was agreed that they would take over the operation of St. Philip's Junior College as a branch of San Antonio Junior College, under the direction of Mr. J. O. Loftin. This operation will commence with the opening of the fall term, shortly after September 1st [1942].[1]

The agreement, which had been under discussion since the early 1930s, took place only because of immense pressure from Negro citizens and some leading members of San Antonio's white community, and then only with great reluctance. Under the terms, the San Antonio Independent School Board agreed to supervise St. Philip's Junior College and make it a part of the city's educational system.

A personal letter, followed by a telegram announcing the acceptance, was sent on August 18, 1942 to the chairman of the Trustee Board, Bishop Capers. He was out of the city at the time. The Western Union Telegram signed by E. H. Keator and sent to Bishop Wm. T. Capers in Colorado Springs, Colorado, on August 26, 1942, 1:51 p.m. read:

> Please call Trustee meeting for Friday, Three o'clock for its action. . . . Board accepted our proposition to take St. Philip's. Dilworth preparing transfers today.[2]

Victory and a New Name

With this piece of correspondence announcing the change, the hard fought battle to place St. Philip's under the umbrella of the San Antonio Independent School District (SAISD) came to a close. The move resulted in the college, which was a privately held institution, receiving another name change and the official designation of San Antonio Junior College—St. Philip's Branch.

Under the new organization, J. O. Loftin, president of San Antonio College, also became president of St. Philip's Branch. This move resulted in a demotion, in title only, for Artemisia Bowden: she was now dean of the college instead of president. St. Philip's College was given to the SAISD as a gift from the diocese, valued at approximately $75,000, under the conditions that SAISD would maintain the school as a junior college and vocational school, free of encumbrances.[3]

Loftin, who came to San Antonio to assume the presidency of San Antonio College, explained that the designation naming St. Philip's as a branch of San Antonio College (SAC) was meant to indicate that St. Philip's College and San Antonio Junior College were one and the same institution. "The move," he went on to say, "made them eligible to receive funds made available to Junior Colleges in Texas by the Texas Legislature—$50 per year, per full time student—and based on the legislative history referring to the school as a branch of SAC, the move allowed it to keep its identity while receiving the funds." During the 1945–1946 school years, as in the previous two years, the SAISD administrators anticipated an increase in funds and this made the affiliation even more desirable.[4]

Jerome Weynand (elected president of the Colleges of the District, September 1, 1973) said that SAC did not merge with St. Philip's; they were separate entities all along: "I want people to understand that. Many times it is referred to in the local press as a branch of San Antonio Junior College; it was not, St. Philip's was an entity all by itself." He went on to say that:

J. O. Loftin, President, St. Philip's Branch

Jerome Weynand, President, St. Philip's Branch

> Miss Bowden pushed for getting the same recognition as the San Antonio Independent School District had given to the fledgling San Antonio Junior College, when it broke away after the first year with the University of Texas. According to the newspaper, Bowden sought equal status for the private school, called St. Philip's, to come under the umbrella and be sustained with tax monies by the San Antonio Independent School District. In 1942, after St. Philip's came under the SAISD, she came over often to see Mr. Loftin at his offices on South Alamo Street.[5]

President Weynand reasoned that the two schools, San Antonio Junior College and St. Philip's Branch, were the same. But in reality, St. Philip's was treated differently. Facilities, equipment, staff, even the instructional programs were different. Having met Miss Bowden from the early days when she was president of the college and in his position as a school reporter for the *Express-News*, Weynand had called on her frequently for news stories. On one occasion, she invited him to speak at the college at one of the civic luncheons. Additionally, he covered the school districts board meeting and the board meetings of the San Antonio Union Junior College District that Bowden attended.

While working at the newspaper, Weynand was hired by J. O. Loftin for the position of registrar of SAC. The first faculty meeting that he attended was held in 1954 at St. Philip's. Weynand subsequently earned a master's degree at Trinity University and went on to earn a doctorate at University of Texas, Austin. After earning his doctorate, Weynand returned to SAC to his position as registrar until a slot opened and he was named director of student personnel services. This position evolved into the position of dean of students. In September 1971, he became vice president of the district and president of the district in 1973. Weynand resigned the position of president in 1981, having served the district faithfully for twenty-seven years.[6]

San Antonio Independent School District Affiliation

The most significant change realized from St. Philip's connection with SAISD was obtaining a firm financial base. The change from having to operate with inadequate funds was good but other factors proved to be limiting. Since the

SAISD had only halfheartedly agreed to take St. Philip's College under its administration, there was no substantial commitment on the part of the district to do more than act as overseer. Consequently, while the school operated under the school district's authority, St. Philip's received scant attention from them. Loftin also treated the two schools as though they were the same. But in reality, the differences in the two institutions were plainly evident—a discrepancy that was not uncommon, of course, in the segregated schools of the South.

If San Antonio Junior College offered science courses, St. Philip's was limited to offering introductory science classes. San Antonio Junior College had departments offering engineering, physics, and mathematics, while St. Philip's divisions offered industrial education and home economics, classes not offered at its sister school.

According to Stonewall "Stoney" Davis, classes at St. Philip's tended to be terminal courses or were limited in terms of providing employment opportunities. The clear intent was to ensure that black students were not offered training that prepared them to become business owners or managers. Davis recalled that inequities in terms of physical plant, programming, supervision, and instructional materials continued into the late 1960s. Making a comparison of the two campuses, Davis described visiting the chemistry and physics laboratories at San Antonio College and comparing them to the laboratories at St. Philip's College. "It was like going into the kitchen of a well-kept home and then going out into a baby's play kitchen. It was many, many years before St. Philip's began to get adequate equipment."[7]

Inequities and the lack of real growth notwithstanding, becoming affiliated with the SAISD was the beginning of a new life for St. Philip's College. With the State Department of Education now classifying the school as a junior college of first rank, recognition was given to its graduates by placing them directly into the upper classes of four-year senior colleges. Prairie View State College, Wiley, Tillotson, Spelman, Morehouse, Fisk, Langston, Virginia Union, and Howard University accepted St. Philip's graduates with full credits given for the courses they had completed. Nonetheless, in the three years of affiliation with SAISD (1942–1945), little growth occurred in enrollment. In fact, the number of students dropped to a low of just over 100 in 1942 and hovered around that number for the three years that St. Philip's was under the school district.

While no new buildings were constructed on St. Philip's campus while the school was under SAISD's jurisdiction, neither did a great deal take place in the way of improvement to the existing buildings. However, the physical plant, originally deeded as a gift of $75,000, doubled in paper value to $150,000. A limiting factor was that the school board, charged with all of the schools in the district, supervised many more schools than St. Philip's and San Antonio College and because of this, the board had little time to attend to the junior colleges.

St. Philip's College under the San Antonio Union Junior College District Board of Trustees (SAUJC)

In 1945, the citizens of San Antonio voted to place San Antonio Junior College and St. Philip's College under a newly created district board of trustees. They also voted affirmatively to a $940,000 bond issue, the funds from which would be used for repairs and construction at San Antonio College and at St. Philip's College. On September 1, 1946, St. Philip's College ceased to operate under the auspices of the San Antonio Independent School District. One favorable consequence that emerged from the alliance with the school district was the stability that came from the connection with SAISD and the allure of having a dependable salary. Both proved to be powerful incentives.

There had always been a stalwart member or two who stayed the course, such as Bowden's good friend, Esdale Malloy. However, even she left at one time, only later to return and remain until retirement. Increasingly, more and more of the faculty began to count their tenure in decades.

Despite the inequities between the physical plants at St. Philip's and SAC, St. Philip's educational programs were strong. The school, while under the jurisdiction of the SAISD and physically away from immediate attention, was seemingly not affected by the lack of proximity. In fact, it had little effect on the day-to-day operation of St. Philip's. The faculty taught students at their own level of preparation and challenged the student body with an ever-growing range of courses. Faculty and administrators made up for the inadequate facilities and lack of materials deficiency through nurturing, tutoring, and encouraging the students.

One month before St. Philip's came under the Board of Trustees, Bowden sent a letter to the board with a contract accepting their offer for properties that she owned. These properties could have been sold for more elsewhere, but she wanted to ensure that the property would be used for "her people."

> **COPY OF CONTRACT,**
> **MINUTES OF TUESDAY, AUGUST 6, 1946**
>
> ALSO ITEM 6, PURCHASE OF LAND FOR ST. PHILIP'S COLLEGE. By Mr. Leo Brewer, resolved, that the contract of purchase of eleven lots from Mis[s] A. Bowden by San Antonio Union Junior College District (SAUJC) be and is hereby authorized; and that the President of the Board be authorized to sign said contract for the District; and that the letter from Miss Bowden accompanied by the contracts, as submitted herewith, be a portion of the minutes.[8]

In 1945, when the proposition to place control of the two schools under a Board of Trustees was presented to voters, the measure passed. The proposition created the Junior College District, with a seven-member Board of Trustees. Though Miss Bowden and the bishop had won the battle to come under the umbrella of the SAUJC, it soon became very clear that the concept of separate but equal facilities was equal in name only, particularly in the classes offered at the two institutions.

St. Philip's was greatly affected by the passage of the proposition because it granted the city the authority to raise funds through local taxation. This meant that the district could receive revenue from the state, had authority over tuition and fees charged the students, and had the authority to come up with its own programs. Clarence Norris Sr., at that time associate dean of St. Philip's, and Jerome Weynand, who later became president of both San Antonio College and St. Philip's College, credited J. O. Loftin with being the prime mover of the proposition.

Having received voter approval for the new board, the trustees of SAUJC District held a meeting on November 5, 1945 to elect officers of the newly created SAUJC District Board of Trustees. The trustees elected W. W. McAllister president of the board, even though he was absent from the city at the time. Other officers elected were Jesse N. Fletcher (vice president), Lee A. Christy (secretary), and A. V. Knight (attorney for the district). Loftin was designated president of both colleges. Clarence Norris Jr. interviewed McAllister, and we are indebted to Norris's family for permitting us the use of his notes, from which the following interview originated.

Walter W. McAllister Sr., Chairman, Trustee Board SAUJC

When J. O. Loftin first proposed formation of the junior college, it was rejected and defeated by the people. In 1945, Loftin approached McAllister and suggested that they go to California to a junior college meeting, which McAllister did and was immediately sold on the idea of having a junior college in San Antonio. Prior to the visit to California junior colleges, "I didn't even know what a junior college was," McAllister said to Norris Jr. "When the idea was proposed again, the issue passed."[9]

McAllister did not attend the first meeting of the board and when he came back to San Antonio, he learned that he had been elected president of the trustees. General Eisenhower was president of the United States at the time. McAllister was in Washington serving in Eisenhower's administration where he was appointed chairman of the Home Savings and Loan Bank. To be eligible to serve, he

Walter W. McAllister Sr., Chairman, Trustee Board SAUJC

had to resign from most of his affiliations, except president of the Junior College Board. As president of the Trustee Board, he came back to San Antonio every three to four months to hold a meeting of the board.[10] World War II limited the growth of the college and took its toll on enrollment by drafting many young persons to fight for their country who otherwise might have enrolled in school. As the war claimed some in the way of students, it provided business opportunities for others.

Dr. Ernest Stevenson, who came to the college in September 1941, was chairman of the department of science. He taught physics, biology, and chemistry. When World War II began, he found opportunities in New York City as a chemist in Macy's Bureau Standards. After working six months at Macy's, he left there and began at Bendix Aviation Corporation in New Jersey. In 1971, thirty years later, he returned to St. Philip's.

Dr. Ernest Stevenson, Faculty and Former Chairman, Science Department

Dr. Ernest Stevenson, Faculty and Former Chairman, Science Department

Stevenson was married to Henrietta Roberts, a St. Philip's student in the 1930s who later became a member of the St. Philip's faculty. Dr. Stevenson, now deceased, was interviewed in 1974 by Clarence Norris Jr. We thank the Norris family for allowing us to use a portion of the transcript from his interview.

St. Philip's received a great deal of help from programs funded by the federal government and the state. It was a requirement that the state legislature give their approval before the Union Junior College District could be set up. Under this arrangement, St. Philip's received subsidies from the state that helped to fund programs in the school. Each student enrolled on the twelfth class day was counted in the determination of the state appropriation for each public school district in the state of Texas. The loss of Dr. Stevenson to Macy's and to the Arsenal was unfortunate at the time, but in later years proved to be a stroke of good fortune for the college. The knowledge of metals that Stevenson gained at Macy's and at Bendix provided inestimable preparation for his reemployment in the science department at St. Philip's.

The following insights are from Dr. Stevenson's interview with Clarence Norris Jr.

While at Bendix Aviation Corporation, Stevenson worked in the field of metals in industry, gaining very sizable experiences. He worked with heavier metals at Englehard Minerals Industries in New Jersey, training technicians in the analysis of those materials. This required becoming familiar with new types of instrumentation where parts per million of gold, silver, or platinum in an alloy they determined. When Stevenson returned to St. Philip's, he had gained enough knowledge to write a proposal for Title 6 money and was able to obtain $20,000, which was used to set up a new organic and biochemistry laboratory. Thus, the experience he received during his leave of absence proved to be a boon for St. Philip's.[11]

Stevenson retired from St. Philip's with the rank of full professor, after a distinguished career at the college and influencing the lives of countless students. The Ernest Stevenson Collection, to be housed at St. Philip's, was established on April 1, 2010 by Dr. William C. Davis, with assistance from Dr. Jeanette Passty and Placido Isaac. The collection, which consists of approximately five hundred books and antique chemistry apparatus, was for five years, under the guardianship of Dr. Davis, who became its conservator. This important collection is to be stored and later housed in a special area in the Sutton Learning Center on the campus at St. Philip's College.

Significant Events in the Life of St. Philip's College

During the latter part of the 1940s, the college discontinued the high school department and stopped providing dormitory facilities for the students as well. However, a modern trailer camp, furnished in cooperation with the Federal Public Housing Authority, provided housing for fourteen families and twelve singles. This housing was limited to the sole use of veterans.[12]Many veterans returning from active duty chose to use their veteran's eligibility for study at St. Philip's and their soaring postwar enrollment caused a major shift in the student body and in the sharp growth of St. Philip's as a college.

The total student body in the school year 1945–1946 rose to 230, the highest it had ever been, and the faculty increased from ten to fourteen members. Changing the courses of study for the convenience of the veterans returning from World War II created, in retrospect, a significant event. This move was, perhaps, as bold a move in the life of the college as joining the SAISD had been, for veteran enrollment continued to increase each semester. When, in 1948, the college celebrated its fiftieth anniversary, veterans made up 76 percent of the total enrollment, which was by then at 485. There were 368 veterans and 117 civilians in the student body.

In the pages that follow, we meet students who attended St. Philip's College in the early 1940s. They give their perspective on what it was like to attend the college in its infancy, when it operated as an all-black school.

10 Students, Faculty, and Administrators from the 1940s

St. Philip's enrollment, while growing, was still small. World War II was a threat and integration in the United States had not yet become law. Finding finances in the amount needed was a continuing struggle for the students.

Oral Histories, 1940s

When World War II became a reality, African American soldiers fought alongside others, first in segregated units and later in integrated divisions. Then, in 1948, when President Harry S. Truman signed into law a bill instituting integration in the military, for the first time, African Americans had the force of the law behind them in regard to equality of treatment.

Rose McCann Hall and Serilia McCann Sanford, two sisters from Egypt, Texas, were St. Philip's students in that era. They had each attended a boarding school in Conroe, Texas, prior to becoming students at St. Philip's. Their former boarding school, however, did not have junior college status. There were nine children in their family, and all earned college degrees; one earned a PhD. They laughingly said, "We started going to school and didn't know when to stop." [1]

Serelia McCann Sanford, Student, 1940s

When Serelia Sanford went to St. Philip's, she was a little country girl who had just finished high school. There was no money for college at that time, and she and her parents were wondering what she would do. She had never heard of St. Philip's Junior College until a Miss Johnson said to her, "Say now, I know a lady in San Antonio who needs somebody like you."Sanford had worked for Johnson, who recommended her to Miss Bowden, so she went to St. Philip's, found a job in the school office, and worked and went to school there for two years.

After two years at St. Philip's, Miss Bowden paid for Sanford to go to Spelman College, located in Atlanta, Georgia. She only stayed one year but had it not been for Bowden, who had taken a liking to Sanford, she says that she could not have gone to school. "I'm really thankful to St. Philip's," said Sanford. "I enjoyed going to school there. That was in '42 or '43. I'm almost eighty and Rose is right behind me, so I guess we did the best we could, huh?"[2]

Rose M. Hall, 1940s

Rose says that she went to St. Philip's because her sister, Serelia, went there. When she arrived, there was a small dormitory, not even divided into rooms, where most of the students from out of town lived. Rose and Serelia were among the last girls in the dormitory, for the year after they arrived, the dormitories were discontinued.

Rose knew Miss Bowden very well, for she lived in the dorm upstairs from Bowden and worked in her home, cleaning house for her seven days a week. Rose was in Bowden's home many times when Bowden was away attending a meeting or perhaps across the street at the college. There were thirteen girls living in the house at the time, all from out of town. They had meals on the campus, at the cafeteria.

"We'd get up, rush to the bathroom, clean up, go eat breakfast and then go downstairs to class. After class, I'd go to the office and I'd work until the office closed, then go back upstairs. On Sundays, we'd go to church. There was no running around town. I guess that was the only time we could leave." Because Sanford worked on the books in the office, she had many opportunities for close contact with Bowden and got to know her well.[3]

Hazel Calhoun Hays, Student, 1945

Hazel Hays was a student in the same era as the two McCann sisters. Born in Monroe, Lousiana, she moved with her family at the age of eight months to Kingsville, Texas, where her father worked as a railroad man. Her father was laid off from his job from May to October and since there was a lot of work during fruit and vegetable season, he, being a young man, traveled with his family between Monroe, Louisiana, and Kingsville, Texas.

Hays finished high school in Corpus Christi, Texas, and won a scholarship to Wiley College but because her parents thought that Wiley would be too far away from home, they brought Hays to San Antonio and enrolled her at St. Philip's College.

Hazel Hays's Story

Hays, who had never visited St. Philip's prior to her enrollment, knew of St. Philip's only from the other children from her high school who had attended the school in San Antonio.In fact, that's how she first heard about St. Philip's. In 1945, when her father brought her to the campus to live, on her first visit, they met Miss Bowden. "I lived in the dormitory," she said, and "it was the only permanent-building there."

Hays said that her father was the kind of person who loved talking to people. "He talked to Miss Bowden and she fell in love with my daddy. He told Miss Bowden, 'She's smart, and with nine children at home, she's used to working, so put her to work.' Miss Bowden started asking me to do things. People would give her things, and she would keep them in the basement of that building, anything that they thought the girls could use, they gave her, including a lot of vegetables, apples, candy and things like that. No food was cooked on the weekend and that [food in the basement] was so we could have something to eat on weekends and sometimes to have snacks at night if we wanted them."

Bowden's house was just across the street and Hays would go over there to polish the silver. By this time, Bowden had moved out of the building with the students and Ruth Madison was dean. Bowden, who served wine and other foods at her business and professional women's meetings, would say to Hays, "whatever food is left, the girls may eat," continuing with, "take this to the girls." But what she didn't know is that the girls had already been there to get some; Hays had given them food and wine out the back door. Bowden did not offer wine to the girls nor did she know Hays was dispensing it, but Hays was sure that since Bowden was serving wine at her meetings, she would not miss the wine given to the girls.

Hays graduated from St. Philip's at the top of her class and won another scholarship to Wiley College and this time, she was allowed to accept the scholarship. After finishing Wiley, Hays returned to San Antonio and moved into a small apartment located in the back of Bowden's house, on the corner of Mittman and Hedges. Hays lived in the apartment for perhaps two to three years after finishing Wiley College.[4]

Clara Etta Williams

Williams, a student from the 1940s, grew up in San Antonio, attended St. Philip's in 1946, and graduated as a member of the first Practical Nursing class at St. Philip's. Williams recalled that Bertha Storey was the first nursing instructor and that she taught her class. "In fact," said Williams, "All of my family attended St. Philip's: my mother, my father, my sister, who finished Douglas high school in 1933, and my brother who finished Wheatley high school in 1934. It was a tradition in our family to go to St. Philip's."

Clara Etta Williams's Story

Back then, it was a struggle for parents to send their children to school, especially for advanced education beyond high school. Money was tight and parents could not afford to send their children out of the city. Williams remembered seeing her father wear shoes with holes as large as a half dollar in them.

Williams's mother attended St. Philip's from 1913 to 1915. At that time, according to Williams, the curriculum was limited. "In 1913–1915, all they were taught back then was cooking and sewing and little bit of writing; i.e., the basics. It was not geared to be just college oriented. She [mother] came to San Antonio because her family was here and the family put their pennies together and paid for her, so that she could go to St. Philip's."

Clara Etta Williams, student, first nursing class

After St. Philip's, Williams's mother went to Wiley College, graduating in 1937. Her father went as well. He attended Tillotson (not yet named Huston-Tillotson). Though she finished college, Williams said that her mother was a cook all of her life. She worked at a job where she was making about a dollar or two a week and, for many years, her father worked at Brackenridge Park and Guaranty Shoe Company.

Williams, who finished high school at seventeen years of age in January 1946, had either to go to school or go to work, so she enrolled at St. Philip's, majoring in prenursing. Between 1946 and 1948, because economic conditions were very difficult, her parents could not afford to send her away to school. Williams dreamed of going into military service, but at seventeen years of age, she needed parental permission. Her mother refused to sign the papers giving permission.

Bowden told Williams's mother about the nursing class in the making, indicating that she could attend, learn nursing, and find work in a hospital. Williams was one of the first to register for the class, at the time called Practical Nursing. Eleven students enrolled in the first class and eleven graduated. Describing Miss Bowden as a scouter who was always looking to see if there was someone that she could bring in who was qualified to make St. Philip's a better place, Williams said that on one of her journeys, Bowden found Bertha Storey, the first nursing teacher.

Storey and Bowden arranged to have the students perform their practical nursing duties at Santa Rosa and Baptist Hospitals, a rarity at the time, because in those days, the local hospitals did not hire blacks in those professions. Blacks hired at Santa Rosa and Baptist Hospitals worked as janitors, not as nurse's aides.Williams was one of the first LVN's hired at Santa Rosa and she was hired in her last year, before graduating from the LVN course. She was employed at Santa Rosa for about twenty-five years.

Williams recalls an anecdote, paraphrased here: "You know what they [the nuns] say about you," Miss Storey said to Williams, who laughed and said,"What do you mean?" "They said, you're good, but you're cocky. You're just so sure of yourself," said Storey. And Williams replied, "Well, Miss Storey, you put that in us." Expecting her students to be the very best, their uniforms the most crisp, she wanted to hear them "squish" when they walked the hall, and she expected to see her face in their shoes. "And she did," said Williams.[5]

Madelyn Gardener

Attending St. Philip's was often a family affair. During the interviews, a number of the interviewees spoke of family members who attended with or before them. One such interviewee was Madelyn Gardener, the granddaughter of Mrs. T. L. "Minnie" (Mead) Lowery. Madelyn described her grandmother as "one of the very enthusiastic, first graduates of St. Philip's School." Mrs. Minnie Meade Lowery, Gardener's maternal grandmother, attended when St. Philip's was called St. Philip's Episcopal School. Meade, a very good seamstress during her lifetime, named one of her children after a customer for whom she sewed.

Not only was Gardener's grandmother a student at St. Philip's, her mother, brother, and aunt were students as well. Gardener attended in the mid-1960s and went into nursing under Peggy Peterson Powell, who, by that time, was over the department.When Gardener graduated from the LVN program in 1976 she, too, was hired at Santa Rosa Hospital, and worked there for ten years. She eventually received an RN degree from SAC and became a home health nurse. Gardener continued her career at Wilford Hall, and was employed there for twenty-five years.[6]

Mattie Mathis, Student, 1940s

Mathis, a student from Cuero, Texas, the oldest of five children, had three siblings besides herself who attended St. Philip's. Mathis said that when she came to St. Philip's, she did not know how to use the telephone. "There were persons in our hometown that had a telephone, but we didn't have one," she said.

Mattie Mathis' Story

Mathis, describing her experience at St. Philip's, said, "It was my first time away from home and I cried for a whole week until I finally got used to it. After a period of adjustment, I stuck it out and graduated in 1941. Then I went back home, married and moved back to San Antonio. We've been in this house since 1945 and my husband and I were able to help my sisters when they attended St. Philip's. All of my sisters got their start right here."

Mathis's aunt finished from Tillotson, but had gotten her start at St. Philip's before transferring. Her aunt was familiar with St. Philip's and advised her nieces to attend because she knew that it was affordable.

1940s: Life in the Dormitory

In the 1940s, St. Philip's was an all-black school with both boys and girls attending. The boys lived in a long one-story building. The majority of the girls in the dorm were from out of town and they all knew each other and were very close. Mathis lived on a long hall with little booths on either side of the hall. There would be a time of celebration when a classmate received a package from home, because they would all go to the girl's room and divide it there.

The kitchen was on the front end of the building and some of the girls that had finished the year before were the cooks. The library was on the first floor and there were laundry tubs with washing boards in the basement. The girls cooked the meals, which often was just grits and gravy. Some of the students said that it seemed there were grits and gravy every day.

The students saw Bowden daily because she also lived in the dormitory. They had a specific time to go down to breakfast and if they ran too much water, Bowden would say, "Cut off my water, please, you're wasting my water." For many years, Mathis and her sister kept up a correspondence with their out-of-town friends and, after more than fifty years, they continued to send cards to remember birthdays, though they discontinued writing letters. "They always talk to me on my birthday," said Mathis.[7]

Joyce Thompson, Student, 1940s

Joyce Thompson and Mattie Mathis are sisters and both attended St. Philip's. Thompson lived in Mathis's home while attending St. Philip's.

Joyce Thompson's Story

Joyce Thompson attended St. Philip's from 1947 to 1949. There were nine students in her graduating class. "St. Philip's, with a lot of students from smaller towns, was good for us, helped us to go on to something bigger, and gave us good preparation." She referred to St. Philip's days as "her best years."

Thompson and Dr. Frank Bryant were classmates. "We felt that our school was as good as a lot of the other schools because the teachers made us want to go and want to do. They had an interest in the students, really cared about us and really prepared us for college. When we transferred, the other schools accepted all of our credits."

"The teachers were very good and by 1947, the school was really moving on up. We had good times at St. Philip's. We went through a lot, couldn't go places, couldn't do things. But, we didn't worry about it because we had things going for us at school. There was a room where everybody went and socialized. We had nice little entertainment. Everybody was nice."[8]

Napolean Byrd

Napolean Byrd, father of Lanier Byrd, vice president for academic affairs, and a student in the 1940s, was interviewed at his home in San Antonio. He came to San Antonio after graduating from high school with plans to attend Prairie View College, but was drafted into the military and was not able to attend. Following his tour of duty in the armed services, he enrolled at St. Philip's. Three generations of the Byrd family attended and graduated from St. Philip's: Napolean Byrd (who graduated in 1950), his son Dr. Lanier Byrd, and Lanier Byrd's son, Shawn.

Recalling that Artemisia Bowden, Clarence Norris Sr., Stonewall Davis, Richard Kidd, and Lois White were faculty at the time he attended St. Philip's, Byrd also remembered that blacks used the leftover books that had been used by whites. "At the time, if there were not enough books for every student, the student simply did without a book. Sometimes, we'd have to walk five miles to school, if the buses weren't able to make those runs because of bad roads. There was just one building on the campus and there were barracks for the GIs," he recalled. Some of his classes were held in the barracks.

"It was a great help to me to be able to enter that school after being in the service and staying there for, well, I was there for a little better than a year," said Byrd.[9]

Sylvester Mitchell

We met Mitchell earlier as a student at St. Philip's in the 1930s. After a stint in the military, Mitchell entered Texas State University and after graduating from TSU, returned to San Antonio.

In 1948, after the war, St. Philip's began offering trade courses: body and fender, auto repair, electrical and radio. "St. Philip's has always grown and it was beginning to take off," said Mitchell. "When we first started,we didn't have to take math, but later on, I had to take the rest of the courses, after I finished the tailoring course over there. After they put these courses in, St. Philip's also got more instructors." Mitchell remembered that it was around this time that "Stonewall Jackson Davis came, and a fellow by the name of Tillmon, who taught government, Aspey in radio, Obey in shoe repair, Hawkins in electrical, Taylor in the tailoring department, and Malloy in sewing. Edith Boston was my English instructor. Mr. Turbon was one of her prodigies."

Recalling the instructors reminded Mitchell that "Turbon was a student at St. Philip's at the same time as I." When Turbon finished at St. Philip's, he entered Xavier in New Orleans and when he finished at Xavier, he returned to St. Philip's and worked at the institution until he retired. When Turbon returned, Mitchell came back to St. Philip's and enrolled in several courses under him.He recalled that Turbon believed that students "learn by examination and he would give an open book examination that was so complex, that if we had not studied, we were sure to fail, even with the open book."

Mitchell went on to study and graduate from Texas State University, along with some of the students that he had taught earlier. "I can say this about it, when you complete the courses that you take at St. Philip's, you're highly recognized [at] any four year school you go to. And, so many of the courses, you don't have to worry about what's going on because the subject matter you take at St. Philip's, when you go to a four year school, you were advanced in whatever you took. It's supposed to be one of the best junior colleges in the state, white, colored or whatever."[10]

Murray Slaughter

Murray Slaughter, who grew up in the neighborhood around St. Philip's, says that his footprints are under all the buildings there at St. Philip's, because, as a child, he and his friends played at the school all the time. At the time, there was just Johnston Hall and the church. Slaughter attended Wiley College, where he met Johnetta Slaughter from the social sciences department. She became his wife. "I just never thought about attending St. Philip's, " he said.

"Anyway, education was not a big thing in the black community when I was growing up," said Slaughter. "Money was tight and if anyone in the family was going to school, it would be the girls. If any money was left over, then the boys could go. Anyway, up to the 1920s, the only male student attending St. Philip's was Henry Stillwell."

While Bowden was known to be very generous in assistance to students needing help with tuition and board to attend St. Philip's, she was also creative in finding ways to pay for that help. Slaughter remembered that Miss Bowden's house was very large and there was an ice cream bar attached to her house. The neighborhood children could buy cones from her for five cents. A Mr. Mulkey tended a garden on Nevada Street that belonged to the college and abutted to his house. The college served meals to the students at that time and the garden provided a lot of the food.

"I don't remember Miss Bowden as a 'Sweet old lady,'" said Slaughter. "She was just Miss Bowden, President of the College. Teachers would come and then they would be gone because she couldn't pay them."[11]

Demonstrated Leadership: Faculty Interviews, 1940s

In this chapter, we meet faculty from the 1940s who worked at St. Philip's during Bowden's administration. A constant theme ran throughout their stories: love for St. Philip's and great respect for Miss Bowden.

Dean Hudgins, who interviewed for employment with Bowden, said when he visited St. Philip's College, he had

William Hudgins, Coach, Dean of Student Affairs

no intentions of working at there. But after interviewing with Miss Bowden, he ended up spending over three decades laboring for the school. In the process, he, too, became a legend, known and respected by students, faculty, and community alike.

William Hudgins, Dean of Student Affairs

During his tenure at St. Philip's College, Hudgins held several different positions: coach, dean of students, department chair, and instructor. When T. R. Williams became president, Hudgins was moved to vice president, he thinks "for between six months to a year." He retired as dean emeritus of the college. Hudgins was born in Mathews, Virginia, about forty miles from Hampton Institute. "But," he said, "I've been here so long, I guess I'm a Texan now. It took me five years to graduate from what was then called Hampton Institute, because at that time, we were poor and I had to take what is known as a work year. You work a year, make a little money, take about six hours, and it takes you five years to graduate. That was the way it was. Everybody had to work."

Hudgins came to St. Philip's from his position as coach and physical education instructor in the armed services. His first job out of the military was as an assistant football coach at Bishop College, then in Marshall, Texas. After working at Bishop for a year, Hudgins came to San Antonio. Richard Kidd was the business manager at the time at St. Philip's and it happened that Kidd was also a Hampton graduate. When Hudgins went by to see him, Kidd said, "Look Bill, how would you like to have a job working at St. Philip's? Miss Bowden is looking for somebody to run the gymnasium and set up a physical education program and I told her she had the right man in you."

When Hudgins agreed to speak with Bowden, Kidd arranged a meeting. But, Hudgins was thinking to himself, "I'll listen to Miss Bowden, but I'm not going to stay here." Describing that first meeting, Hudgins said that they met in this little office in this old building that doesn't exist anymore; they've torn it down. There were about three other buildings on the campus then and there were all these army barracks. They had an old building that they used for an administration building and upstairs was used for the girls' dormitory. "This was just like a little technical institute where they offered auto mechanics, electronics, tailoring, electricity, painting, and academics. Our meeting was the first time I'd ever seen Miss Bowden."

Miss Bowden talked to Hudgins, asked him where he was going, and Hudgins replied, "Well, Miss Bowden, some relatives in Pennsylvania told me about an opening in California and I'm headed that way. I have a wife and baby and I need a job." "Why don't you consider St. Philip's College?" she asked. "The pay is not going to be much, but if you stick with me, you can make it. A lot of benefits will come your way."

She promised Hudgins that one day St. Philip's would have a swimming pool, and Hudgins, who had grown up around the water and loved swimming, suddenly became interested.

When Miss Bowden said, "We can give you $2,700," he became really interested as he was only making $1,800 a year at Bishop College. "I know that sounds like a pittance, a small amount," said Hudgins, "but that was a lot of money at the time. Miss Bowden put Richard Kidd on me and before I knew it, I had decided to take that job with Miss Bowden," said Hudgins. He signed on the dotted line for $2,700. "Miss Bowden had me. Miss Bowden was a great talker, a remarkable lady and she knew what it would take for her to maintain the school."

Hudgins began coaching at St. Philip's, using veterans for his team. "One of the teachers there was trying to have a sports team using students but what I did was use veterans. We had a very good team of veterans but many of the veterans were as old as I was. I had veterans that were very good players, boys like John Mule Miles, Sonny boy Miles they called him, Clyde McNeil, and Jesse Jones. Clyde McNeil became a baseball player with the Brooklyn Dodgers. And that's how I got started at St. Philip's."

Both Miss Bowden and Hudgins took direct orders from the president of San Antonio college, who was over both colleges. "She was a product of segregation and so was I," said Hudgins. "She got us interested in her work by telling us that we could help to make St. Philip's a great place to grow and live. We could be an example for San Antonio, for the state and maybe the nation. She asked each of us to go to certain sections of the state, locally, within about a hundred miles or a little more and recruit students for St. Philip's College."

When recruiting, the faculty went in pairs. On one of his trips, Hudgins paired with Dean Watson and they went as far as Temple to recruit the high schools. As a new hire, Hudgins and others were sometimes asked to work during the summer without pay, in order to keep the school open. "We did a lot of free work to keep the school going," said Hudgins, "all because Miss Bowden got us interested in her work. If it had not been for Miss Bowden, there would be no St. Philip's today. I know because at one time, St. Philip's was in danger of closing," said Hudgins.

When St. Philip's became a member of the Union Junior College District, they would have an annual meeting of the Junior College Teachers Association. Hudgins recalled that the meeting in Dallas was the first time that blacks had ever been allowed to attend the meeting because the schools had not yet been integrated.The meeting was held at the still segregated Baker Hotel in Dallas. Hudgins drove Miss Bowden to the meeting along with faculty member and friend Esdale Malloy, home economics teacher.

Hudgins had an old car and he did not want to drive it to the meeting, and Miss Bowden's car was nice and new. Driving her to the meeting meant a free trip to Dallas for him. "It was like driving Miss Daisy," said Hudgins. Bowden and Malloy sat in the back seat while he drove. "Miss Bowden was a back seat driver," said Hudgins. "She would be talking to her friend, and stop midsentence and say, 'How fast are you going?'" Hudgins vividly remembered an incident that involved a car "kind of cutting across me and without thinking, I yelled, 'Man, what the hell are you doing cutting across me?' Miss Bowden said, 'Oh, do you curse?' I said, 'Oh, Miss Bowden, he was doing wrong. I didn't mean to do that; it just came out that way.' 'Well,' said Miss Bowden, 'Let's don't curse.'" When they reached Dallas, since they were not accepted at the hotels, Bowden went off to stay with her friend, instructing Hudgins, "You're going to stay over at the Men's 'Y.' You are to take the men over there, take my car and I don't want to see a dent on it when you come back."

Hudgins, who perceived Bowden as a learned, pious woman said, "The more I saw of her, the more respect I had for her. She could get things done when you would think it impossible. And one other thing about Miss Bowden, she didn't mind begging, you know, asking people for money. She wasn't ashamed."

Hudgins described her as knowing where the money was, the right people to meet, and the right buttons to punch. She knew where the people were who would probably give her help. "'I'll get the money,' she said, and she always did."[12]

Lois White, Faculty, English Instructor, 1940s

Lois White, who came to St. Philip's College as an English teacher in the mid-1940s, was hired by Bowden and worked under both Bowden and Norris.

Lois White, faculty

White, who expressed delight at being able to work at St. Philip's, said that when she came to St. Philip's in 1946, the war was just over and people were streaming into schools. "It is pretty hard for anyone to have any idea of what it was like seventy or eighty years ago," White said. "But, it was a time when people, blacks particularly, had three things in their lives: Church, school, and trying to make it up a little bit and that was all I heard coming from church people; education was the thing that was going to do it. And I think they were very wise, because at least they took something that in the end would mean more for them than anything else. Back then, they didn't talk about jobs as much as they talked about being of service to others and pulling other people along."

White came to San Antonio out of that kind of thinking. She said, "We were no exception. This was just the way it was. Miss Bowden would always say, 'Well, I know who you are.' She knew the kinds of things that we promulgated."

Describing social conditions at the time that she came to San Antonio, White recalled that in Texas, a lot of small towns did not have full scale high schools in every county, not even for white children. Children were sent to the closest town where there was a high school and that child would board there with someone, she recalled. White indicated that persons who could verify what she had just told us are deceased but if they were not, "they would tell you that they left Edna and they left other little towns and went to Houston or to Galveston, especially down there on the coast, to finish high school."

When White came to San Antonio, San Antonio College was on South Alamo, in the old German School, and St. Philip's had only one building, and that was Johnston Hall. White's description is printed just as she told it to us, for it is an eyewitness description of St. Philip's and SAC before they expanded. During the interview, White was a veritable repository of detailed knowledge about the time.

"They put up the little wooden buildings out there for the veterans. And, at one time, believe it or not, St. Philip's had a trailer camp for the veterans to live in, on what was the south side of the campus. And then, in '54, we got Bowden Hall, the first big building. San Antonio College was small, and we were small. After J. O. Loftin got a hold of it and they came up with this idea of the junior college expansion, then everything took off.

"But now, SAC didn't start with the church like St. Philip's did. And it had to catch on too, because remember you had the people, you had the colleges, you had Trinity. Trinity had moved down here from Waxahachie and I remember where Trinity was before it moved to its new campus—it was out on Cincinnati in what is the Peacock or military school. That was the setting for Trinity and they moved off of Cincinnati onto this, into the hills with their new building and all. So, they all got kind of upgraded. St. Philip's had a nursing component before San Antonio College did. After St. Philip's did so well, then SAC decided to embrace it.

"Miss Bowden hired me. Let me tell you, Miss Bowden was a polished woman and anybody who tells you that Miss Bowden went from door to door getting money for the school, I am going to say, 'That's a bald-faced lie.' That's their idea of what they thought Miss Bowden did, they didn't even know Miss Bowden, or the times from which she came. Because you see, Miss Bowden wasn't from here. She was a kind person, but there was nothing of the, well, I'll just let things roll over me. None of that! She was forceful in her own way. When you looked at her body you got force, not resignation.

"This was an Episcopal school. People who sent their girls here weren't rich, but they were people who lived comfortably in the community. When the church pulled out of the school, it left a vacuum, so that some years, Miss Bowden had to get money to run the school. She was able to take it for a while, but the real salvation came when this junior college district was established and took St. Philip's in.

"They took it in because of her. The very fact that they took it shows that she was definitely responsible for St. Philip's being what it became; because if she had not, they wouldn't have done it. They said, 'Now, we'll give you the school, you do what you want to.' Now I didn't hear them say that, that's what she told me."[13]

The Community Remembers Miss Bowden

Col. Roy Burley, 1940s

Burley, retired from military service, grew up in the shadow of the campus, across the street from St. Philip's College. While growing up, he considered the school a second home because, he said, "St. Philip's students were my first baby sitters." Though he did not attend St. Philip's, Burley, who retired from the military with the rank of colonel, had a family who had a relationship with St. Philip's that began before his lifetime, with his grandparents and great-grandparents. The family connection with St. Philip's began when his great-grandparents became friends with Miss Bowden before he was born. The relationship continued with his sister, who finished high school in 1938, went to St. Philip's, and graduated from there in 1940. Col. Burley had another connection to St. Philip's through his wife, Lillian Burley, who spent several years as an instructor in the evening division of the college.

On Bowden and the Community

Burley's grandmother lived across the street from the school and Bowden's sister lived across the street from his grandmother, facing the 500 block of Mittman Street. "Miss Bowden was the type of person I know personally could make do with almost nothing," he said. "And, she had such a love for that college that anything that could benefit the college, she would do. St. Philip's was, I guess you might call it, an industrial school for young black women; I guess they called them Negroes then. They were being trained to either work in somebody's kitchen or be a maid, you know."[14]

Butler Eddings, Custodial Staff

Custodial Staff, 1940s

Butler Eddings

St. Philip's has always been known for its loyalty among employees, including the custodial staff. Butler Eddings, a long-time, faithful employee who lived on the campus, served as head custodian, was known by name by faculty and students alike and was considered "one of the family." The 1964 annual edition of the *Echo* (the student yearbook) was dedicated to Eddings, who in 1964, had been with St. Philip's as a member of its staff since August 16, 1948. The tribute in the *Echo* paid to Eddings read:

> His faithfulness, versatility and honesty testify to his willingness to love and serve our school. We have come to know him as Mr. Fixit, Mr. President and Mr. Dean of the College. We have witnessed his long and hard work-days. We have witnessed his restlessness on forced vacations because of fatigue, and his inability to stay in bed when ordered by his doctor. We honor Butler Eddings publicly this year as we have honored him in our hearts through the years and as we shall continue to do when we leave our beloved school for further adventures in learning.[15]

Still a St. Philip's employee in the 1970s, he was remembered by Lanier Byrd, who recalled being a student at St. Philip's when Eddings served the college. When Byrd returned to St. Philip's as faculty, this same Eddings was still employed by the school. The family atmosphere extended not only to faculty, staff, and students, but extended to custodians as well. They were family, held in high esteem.

Lanier Byrd

"That little area, where the driveway is coming in, we had a custodian there who had been here for maybe fifty-something years. His name was Butler Eddings and he was the chief custodian for grounds and everything. He lived there. And, if any noise was on the campus late at night, he would come out of that little apartment he had down in there. He was always around.We knew all of the custodians, all of the grounds workers, those people would be permanently stationed here and were pretty much a part of our culture."[16]

Alzo Cole, a former student, remembers "Mr. Eddie": "I recall, when I went over to enter St. Philip's, Mr. Stonewall Davis gave me a working scholarship. I told Mr. Davis, 'I don't have no [*sic*] money to pay my tuition, I need a job to work my way through.' Mr. Davis took me over to Mr. Eddie [Butler Eddings]. He was the head custodian there at St. Philip's and Mr. Davis told him to give me a job to help me to work my way through St. Philip's. Mr. Eddie was a real fine fellow and he told me to work with him and clean the showers and help in the cafeteria and clean around. And I made enough money to pay for my tuition, buy my books and then had a little left over for spending."[17]

As an indication of the esteem in which he was held, Eddings was invited to be an honorary pallbearer at the funeral services for Miss Bowden. Eddings, too, was a member of the "longevity group," those faculty and staff who served the college and stayed the course, refusing to leave, even during difficult financial times. The foundation of St. Philip's College is built on such persons as Butler Eddings.

Bishop Gerald McAllister

McAllister, the son of Walter McAllister Sr., first president of the Board of Trustees, says that he is "about a fifth generation from San Antonio, since my forebears came here before there was a Texas." His great-great grandfather was mayor of San Antonio in the 1850s, and later became the county judge and "was county judge at the time that the red courthouse was built. My father was raised by a mother who had a strong sense of community and a strong feeling of owing things back to the community. She was one of the persons who organized the Parent-Teacher Association here in San Antonio, started many of the chapters, and organized them in many of the public schools in San Antonio. My grandmother was also the first state president of the PTA. I think a good bit of it rubbed off on her son," said McAllister, and, "as a consequence of that, he was very interested in education."

McAllister's grandmother was very influential in the field of education in San Antonio and a very close friend of Brackenridge, Bowden's friend and staunch supporter of St. Philip's College. It is pure speculation—but within the realm of possibility—that it was through Brackenridge's interest in education and through her friendship with Bishop McAllister's grandmother that she met Miss Bowden and developed her interest in the welfare of St. Philip's School. It may very well be also that McAllister's father met Miss Bowden through his mother, though others speculate that she may have met him just by knocking on doors while seeking donations for the school from the business district of the city.

Bishop McAllister's Story

McAllister first met Miss Bowden in the 1930s when he was "probably around fifteen or sixteen years old." Bowden was visiting his father's office to solicit money for St. Philip's and he says that he remembers the meeting very well for two reasons: "As a teen, my father and I were seldom on the same page, particularly when it came to political issues. I was very much a liberal humanitarian at that point in my life"; and secondly, "I was also pleased and surprised that she called him Walter. Not very many people did."

Though he did not know Bowden personally, McAllister was aware of her work, and he could tell, judging from his father's attitude toward her, that his father had great respect for Miss Bowden. Usually, he said, "people called my father Mr. McAllister or Mayor Mac, so hearing Miss Bowden call him Walter impressed me a great deal."

Through J. O. Loftin, who was, at the time, president of St. Philip's and San Antonio Junior College, McAllister's father became interested in the junior college system. "And really, it was out of a combination of his interest in education and his friendship with Miss Bowden that St. Philip's became a part of the junior college system. That really was an outgrowth of this friendship. When he saw what a good junior college could do for a community, that made him want to see St. Philip's become a part of the junior college system."[18]

McAllister, who subsequently joined the military, did not see Bowden again until after the war had ended and he had separated from the military. Following his tour in the military, McAllister became an Episcopal minister and joined a church where an acquaintance, Joe Brown, was the minister. Brown was in charge of St. Philip's Church at the time. At that time, St. Philip's Church was meeting in an un-airconditioned lodge hall on the second floor of G. J. Sutton's funeral home. "It was just unbearable," said McAllister.

"Joe Brown came down with hepatitis, could not take services and was confined to bed for several months; so, I took the service at St. Philip's during the time that he was ill. In my first service, there was a young fella named Dillard Robinson who was the crucifer for the service.[19] Dillard, probably eleven or twelve years old at the time, was really one of Miss Bowden's boys. She motivated people and pushed them in all kinds of good directions and Dillard went on to become dean of the Cathedral in Newark, New Jersey, which is one of the top jobs in the Episcopal Church."

McAllister attended seminary and continued on to become a bishop in the Episcopal Church. When he was ready to go to seminary, he had to give three letters of references, and he chose Miss Bowden to write one.

"I have always been grateful to her for that and felt like as much as anything, those three letters got me into seminary. I think they were curious to see who on earth this was, you know, to have a Negro woman, who was a college president, writing a letter of recommendation. I think the admissions committee at seminary said, 'we've just got to see this guy.' Anyway, I think that's how I got in."

During his time filling in for Minister Joe Brown, McAllister came to know Miss Bowden well, as she was one of a half-dozen people who were the leaders in the congregation. When St. Philip's moved into their first church, on the corner of Commerce and Grimes Street, McAllister led their services there when he came home from seminary during the summer. He described the building as "almost a house church."

McAllister, who had many opportunities for conversations and visits with Bowden because of their church affiliation, soon became aware of what a stalwart she was in the congregation. His respect for her grew and grew.[20]

Edith McAllister, Community Activist

Edith McAllister, sister-in-law of the bishop, whose husband also served as a chairman of the Board of Trustees of the Union Junior College District, is a community activist. She recalled seeing Bowden on some of her visits to her husband's office. When Walter Sr., her husband's father, became mayor, he could not continue in the position of chairman of the Board of Trustees, so her husband, Walter Jr., was appointed to the board in his stead. Her husband later became chairman of the board also, and he served, she thinks, for about eighteen years.

McAllister said of her husband, "The whole district was his love. That was what he put the most time and energy and effort and everything into."McAllister remembered that her father-in-law, who died in 1984, and Bowden were good friends, though she did not know how they met. She speculated that perhaps because of his position as chairman of the Board of Trustees and of the Junior College District and because his office at the bank was centrally located on the corner of Soledad and Commerce Streets and easy to find, that that's where Bowden met him.[21]

11 The Norris Years

I feel that you, above all applicants we have had in the past few years, have had that training and experience necessary to make a lasting contribution to your people through this institution. I urge your prayerful consideration of this matter, for somehow, I feel that the future of the institution may be affected by your decision.[1]

Clarence W. Norris Sr., Dean Emeritus

Nearing five decades spent at St. Philip's, and with retirement in the not too distant future, Bowden's search for a replacement led her to handpick Dr. Clarence Norris Sr. On June 8, 1943, Bowden sent a letter to Norris encouraging him to accept the position and explaining the reasons why she felt he should consider the position. Excerpts from Bowden's letter read:

> For several years, I have taken the utmost care in the selection of our Administrative personnel in view of the approaching close of my tenure of office. I have been anxious to bring young people with your qualifications into the work, who would be able to carry it on to higher attainments.[2]

Norris, who had given much thought to what the future financial security would be for his family if he accepted the offer of employment at the college, decided to take a chance. He had heard of St. Philip's history of not fully meeting its obligations to pay its teachers, but he surmised that with their recent affiliation with the school district, salaries would be more likely to be paid in a timely manner. With these thoughts in mind, he accepted the offer and, in 1943, left his position as State Supervisor of Adult Education, Negro Division, with the Works Progress Administration (WPA), to accept a teaching position in sociology, education, and Spanish, and the administrative position of assistant dean. At the time of his hire, Norris held a master's degree from the University of Michigan and was pursuing his doctorate degree at the University of Southern California. Early in the negotiations, Norris made it clear that he wanted to go to California for a part of each summer to continue his postgraduate studies for his doctorate.

Norris gradually assumed responsibility for administration of the college, freeing Bowden to devote additional time to fund-raising and public relations. When Norris was appointed dean of the college, he became an even more active participant in community social gatherings. Many persons in the neighborhood attended the church where he was a member, participated in the same functions, and frequented the same places. Moreover, he taught a Sunday school class that many in the community attended, thus adding to his influence.

For fifteen years, Norris served as dean of the faculty (1946 to 1954) and in 1954, when Bowden retired, he became dean of the college. The son of an ordained minister and teacher, Norris was born in Houston into a family of nine children. His father was a "strict disciplinarian" and some of the influence from his father can be seen in Norris's own strict enforcement of rules.

In his book, *Up From Poverty*, Norris explains that he spent a good deal of time during his first year becoming acquainted with Bowden, observing and analyzing the St. Philip's situation. From this vantage point, he was able to discover some of the problems in the school. One major problem he identified was the relationship between the SAISD and St. Philip's. The school district had been pres-

Clarence W. Norris Sr.

sured to accept St. Philip's and he likened their accepting St. Philip's to parents taking in an unwanted child.

Since St. Philip's was a financial liability, he understood SAISD's reluctance to take on what he described as a few old buildings with a small student body and very limited financial resources. After observing the situation for a year, Norris concluded that the only way that St. Philip's could survive was to have a steady and substantial increase in its enrollment. There was a total enrollment of 104 students when he arrived and one year later, enrollment had increased by only ten students.

Norris began an extensive campaign to recruit students from nearby towns, which included recruiting visits to Texas towns such as Victoria, Cuero, Port Lavaca, Yoakum, Gonzales, and Seguin. He described the results as "very meager." Not until the United States Government provided for veterans to attend the college at government expense did enrollment have a substantial increase. By 1945, enrollment had reached 230 students, double the number from the previous year. When St. Philip's celebrated its fiftieth anniversary in 1948, 483 students were enrolled, of which 75 percent (368) were veterans. Fifty-one students graduated that year. In 1955, when new laws regarding integration were enacted and St. Philip's opened its doors to all applicants regardless of race, out-of-town recruitment was discontinued. With the open door policy, enrollment of non-black students began a steady climb that, at this writing, has not abated.

Another important observation was the clash in personalities between Bowden and Loftin. Bowden, who had served as president of the college since its inception, had relinquished her title of president to Loftin and was now called Dean Bowden. Though the title of dean was a demotion for her, Bowden willingly accepted it in order to help the school, for she knew that without immediate financial assistance from SAISD or some other source, St. Philip's would cease to exist.

With her previous title and position, she dealt directly with the Board of Trustees, the Episcopal Diocese, the McAllister's, Eleanor Brackenridge, and other important persons in the community, such as the publisher of the newspaper, Frank Huntress. Norris noted that Loftin, as the former president of Texas College of Arts and Industries at Kingsville, Texas, and president of San Antonio College, had had limited experience with blacks in positions of power and probably none at all with black women in positions of power.

One of Loftin's chief complaints about Bowden was that, without first clearing it with him, she often went around him and contacted members of the Board of Trustees on various matters that he felt should have gone through him. She, on the other hand, saw no need to contact him first. Norris recalled one incident in which Dean Bowden and President Loftin had a misunderstanding and she became so angry with Loftin that she threatened to strike him. Norris, acting as mediator, brought calmness to the situation.

Clarence W. Norris Sr. and Others: Creation of the Junior College District

While St. Philip's had welcomed being under the SAISD banner, efforts were being put forth in the community to create a junior college district that would separate SAC and St. Philip's from the San Antonio Board of Education (governing body of SAISD). The measure had been brought to a vote earlier, in November 1941, and at that time the measure failed.

When Loftin and others began their efforts to secure the number of signatures needed to again place the measure on the ballot, Norris played a significant role in the campaign. He and faculty member Roger Lee contacted some of the black ministers in the community, who agreed to let members sign petitions at the close of the Sunday services. Norris personally presented several hundred more names to Loftin, who said, "You really saved my life."

With the necessary number of signatures secured, the measure was placed on the ballot and in October 1945, the measure passed, separating St. Philip's and SAC from the SAISD and creating the junior college district. At that point, Norris admitted to being more optimistic about his future with St. Philip's than he ever had before, for he felt that because of the voters' decision, a new day had begun for both St. Philip's and SAC.

Financial Stability for St. Philip's

For St. Philip's, being under the SAUJC with governance by the Board of Trustees also had its disadvantages. For one, the Board of Trustees was physically located on the campus of San Antonio College, a boon for SAC, but a negative for St. Philip's. Proximity provided opportunities for exposure to ideas, needs, and wants for SAC's faculty and staff, plus unlimited opportunities for social and business interaction. But for St. Philip's faculty and administration, being out of sight meant, most often, being out of mind, with limited opportunities for contact, few occasions for spontaneous conversation, almost no chance for social interaction or to indulge in small talk, and no opportunities to get to know the higher-ups.

Additionally, St. Philip's, an all-black school that depended solely upon black students for its enrollment, was located in a city where segregation was the law of the land. Numbers counted in appropriations, and with only a small black population and no opportunities for attracting students other than from the black population, the growth of the college was limited and likely to remain so.

The argument used by the district for inequities in funding was that, with its smaller population, it cost more per student to run St. Philip's than it did to operate SAC. Norris's stated opinion was that this "[l]egal separation of educational facilities slowed down the progress of St. Philip's."[3] As stated earlier, he felt that the legal separation, if allowed to continue, would hinder St. Philip's reaching its potential.

While St. Philip's shared in some, it did not share in all of the benefits of belonging to the Union Junior College District; in fact, the participation was not at the same level as San Antonio College. St. Philip's continued to be treated as a step-child, rather than as a colleague, equal with San Antonio College.

When St. Philip's became a public college, the school literally became the dumping ground for the district. If there were tables that couldn't be used, they were sent to St. Philip's. The same thing happened with unused desks, old books, and unsatisfactory copies of books. People were not willing to take St. Philip's seriously as an institution of higher education.

The advantages that accrued to the college, however, played a major role in the Class A classification awarded the college. As the facilities expanded, the opportunities for training increased, and as enrollment increased, the faculty increased, and instructors were needed to provide the training. A new initiative, called the Cooperative Employer Training Program, made significant opportunities available for student on-the-job training. Courses were taught in plumbing, carpentry, auto mechanics, and dry cleaning and pressing. A substantial plus was in gaining access to many of the supplies, facilities, salaries, and simple necessities that had been needed for a very long time.

However, the most immediate and profound advantage of coming under the Union Junior College District was relief from the ever-pressing financial worries of the past. Prior to St. Philip's joining the SAUJC District, neither Bowden nor the diocese were financially able to provide even the bare necessities needed and purchasing nonessentials was simply not an option. With the merger, progress was inevitable, for with it came the authority for the district to levy taxes. As a tax-supported institution, appropriations were anticipated for the construction of new buildings and repair of existing ones; teacher salaries were paid in a timely manner and other commitments that often had been paid if and when funds became available were now met before or as they came due. New land was purchased, allowing for expansion and growth of the physical plant and that provided impetus for growth in the student body. With the additional acreage added to the campus, new buildings were added as well, though construction did not begin immediately.

One of the much-needed additions was a new gymnasium, constructed in 1949.The new building housed two additional classrooms, faculty offices, and a basketball court with dressing rooms. Four years later, in 1953, a new two-story administration building was built containing science laboratories and classrooms on the first floor and space for a library, classrooms, and the business department on the second floor. During this phase of construction, a new student union building was erected that contained a cafeteria, book store, offices, lounge, and game room. The next year, in 1954, a swimming pool was added. Another great benefit was the ability to buy additional property and to call bond elections from which they raised enough funds to build a new physical plant. With the substantial increase realized in salaries, a new day began for St. Philip's.[4]

Another advantage that accrued to the college because of its affiliation with the SAUJC was that as the enrollment increased, opportunities for students to receive training increased and this increased the need for faculty to provide the training. As the faculty increased, the need for facilities increased. A new initiative, called the Cooperative Employer Training Program, made significant opportunities available for student on-the-job training. Courses were offered in plumbing, carpentry, auto mechanics, and dry cleaning and pressing.

In October 1945, when the voters approved the San Antonio Union Junior College District, a substantial gain was the access to many of the supplies, facilities, salaries, and simple necessities that had been needed for a very long time.

As a tax-supported institution, appropriations were anticipated for the construction of new buildings and repair of existing ones, teacher salaries were paid in a timely manner, and other commitments that often were paid if and whenever funds became available, were now met before or as they came due. New land was purchased, allowing for expansion and growth of the physical plant and that provided impetus for growth in the student body.

Under the Newly Elected Board of Trustees (SAUJC District)

When the citizens of San Antonio voted to place St. Philip's and SAC under the Board of Trustees, they also recognized the need to update the schools. A vote was passed in 1949 to issue $940,000 in bonds that would be used for purchase of a new site for San Antonio College and for construction of an Administration Building, Library, Science Building, and a Health Education Building for SAC. St. Philip's College was to receive repairs to the existing buildings and some new construction.

To become a part of the San Antonio Union Junior College District and be under the governance of the trustees, Bowden had to give up her title as president. When Loftin became president of St. Philip's College with its new designation, Branch of San Antonio College, Bowden assumed the title of dean of the college. Loftin held the position of presidency until 1956.

Dr. Waylon P. Moody

In 1956, Loftin and his wife were killed in an automobile accident and Waylon P. Moody, who had come to the district in 1947 as administrative assistant to the president, was named president, with responsibility for both St. Philip's and SAC. He was in office when the bond issue passed. Clarence Norris Jr. interviewed Moody, who felt that "after the district was created in 1945 and began in 1946 to operate as a publicly supported district, the district expanded and the schools grew. As indicated earlier, this was a whole new era for the colleges, because now they were tax supported. Better buildings could be built, better facilities could be provided and tuition and fees could be kept low."[5]

Establishing the Vocational Nursing Program

Bowden, with retirement looming and many other ideas on the horizon to put into play, assembled an advisory committee that met at her home in the spring of 1949 to discuss the establishment of a vocational nursing program at the college. This move set in motion a program destined to have a great influence on the enrollment of the college. Attending the first meeting was Sadie Brown, Director of Nursing Services at Bexar County Hospital, a representative from Santa Rosa Hospital and Baptist Hospital, Dr. Norris Sr., dean of the faculty at the college, and Bowden. They decided that the time was right to add vocational nursing to the curriculum, to seek an affiliation with a hospital, and begin a search for a qualified vocational nursing instructor. Their search led to Bertha M. Storey, and on August 16, 1949, the Minutes of the Regular Meeting of the Board of Trustees of the San Antonio Union Junior College District held on August 16, 1949, Item 2, read:

> Election of Teacher. Be it RESOLVED that the following named teacher, recommended by the President of the College, be and she is hereby elected teacher for

> the school year beginning September 1, 1949, subject to assignment and/or reassignment by the President of the College . . . written contract to be prepared and issued at a later date.

Storey[6] was elected by the Board of Trustees as St. Philip's first practical nursing teacher.

Bertha M. Storey

Storey attended Samuel Huston College, and earned an AB degree. She also attended Meharry Medical College in Tennessee (where she earned her RN degree), the Medical College of Virginia (where she earned a BS), and the University of Indiana, where she pursued graduate training. Her salary at St. Philip's was $3,000 for nine months and in addition to teaching, her additional responsibilities included coordination and supervision of the nursing program.

First Practical Nursing Class, St. Philip's College

Though the 1946–1947 St. Philip's College Catalog listed an offering of pre-medical, pre-nursing, and pre-dentistry courses, they were merely the basic subjects required for teacher training. It was not until 1950–1951 that the college offered practical nurse training leading to a certificate. On September 12, 1949, Storey taught the first practical nursing class at St. Philip's with twelve students, ages eighteen to forty-four, in the first class. Tuition was $41.00 for the semester. The class met six days a week for nine weeks, thirty-five hours each week. Members of the first class were:

> Banks, Irma; Calloway, Bertha; Daniel, Dorthula; Hollingsworth, Alma; Johnson, Mamie L.; Moncrief, Daisy; McVea, Robbie M.; Phillips, James Etta; Poole, Clara Etta; Reese, Mazzie H.; Smith, Dorothy; and Williams, Geneva.

Some members of the class had up to two years prior college training, while others had only completed ninth grade. When the nursing program began, Texas had not yet created a board to accredit schools offering training to nurses. This occurred in 1951, when the Texas Legislature passed a Vocational Nurse Act (House Bill 47, 52nd Legislature) that created a board to accredit the schools training vocational nurses and to examine and issue licenses to vocational nurses. Around that time, the name of the program at St. Philip's changed from practical nurse training to vocational nursing. The Vocational Nurse Examiners Board was created in September of 1951, to license nurses in Texas. On October 17, 1952, the Vocational Nursing Program at St. Philip's was accredited.

The Texas Board was abolished in 2003 and absorbed by the Texas Board of Nurse Examiners. Presently, the Vocational Nurses Program at St. Philip's College is approved and accredited by both the National Accrediting Groups for Allied Health and Nursing Programs and Texas Higher Education Coordinating Board.

Most of St. Philip's nursing students from Storey's class passed the State Board examinations on their first try, with above-average scores. Reportedly, Storey held drills, review sessions, and refresher courses to ensure that they passed. Clara Etta Brooks Poole Williams, member of the first graduating class, said this regarding her time in the program: "I graduated with honors and received a scholarship from Bexar County Tuberculosis Association to TSU in Houston for additional studies. My grade of 87 was equal to a 100+, based on how they graded us back then. I was hired at Santa Rosa Hospital to do clinical practice nursing and my hours was the 11:00 p.m. to 7:00 a.m. shift at $114.00 per month." Williams noted that when she graduated from high school in the early 1940s, she could not attend Santa Rosa's nursing program because it was not yet integrated; "but by 1949–1950, with assistance from Miss Bowden, it was made possible."[7]

Mrs. Ethel Taylor was employed in 1964 as coordinator-instructor of vocational nursing. She was succeeded by Peggy M. Powers in 1965. By 1965, the vocational nursing staff consisted of seven instructors, not including Powers. Under Powers, the nursing program continued to grow and by 1968, the program offered instructions for operating room technicians, ward clerks, and nurse's aides. An evening class in vocational nursing was added in 1969 as well as a program leading to an associate's degree in applied science as a medical record technician. In 1971, the evening program became a fifteen-month program and began offering associate's in applied science degrees in inhalation therapy, medical laboratory technician, and radiologic technology.

By 2011, the nursing program celebrated a class of seventy-one nursing graduates from the SPC campus and eighteen nursing graduates from the New Braunfels campus. The nursing program at St. Philip's produces the largest number of licensed vocational nurses in the state of Texas and is currently the only program in San Antonio that offers online vocational nursing courses.

Dr. Lanier Byrd

Faculty and Students during the Norris Era

By the beginning of the Norris era, longevity among the faculty had been established. Lanier Byrd, at his retirement in 2007, had served St. Philip's for slightly more than thirty-eight years. Byrd described what it was like to return to St. Philip's as faculty and to work under Dr. Norris:

"The first thing that I did coming back as a faculty member was to meet people who had taught me some years before," said Byrd. "They were still here. St. Philip's has that. People come here and they stay a long time and there's something else, for some reason, we know and remember the exact year they join the campus. For example, Carolyn Green came in 1954, Don Coleman came in 1961, Dean Hudgins was the longest—he came in 1949 and so did Mr. Turbon, who came later in the year. John Benjamin Franklin Willoughby Williams did the float, taught English, French and the little I know came from him. He was a real character here.

"When I address the public," said Dr. Byrd, "I tell them, there's a lot of love at St. Philip's. It's not an accident. It's just that when you hire good people, they bring other good people and that's where the love is shared. St. Philip's is known as The School That Love Built."[8]

Prof. Everett Turbon

Everett Turbon, Professor and Director of Counseling Emeritus

Everett Turbon, faculty under Dr. Norris, was a former student before joining the faculty. He enrolled at St. Philip's College at the age of sixteen years, at a time when St. Philip's was still run by the Episcopal Church. After completing bachelor's and master's degrees from Xavier and New York universities, respectively, he returned to his alma mater to be an instructor in mathematics, psychology, and sociology and was appointed as director of counseling and guidance. Turbon retired in 1984, with thirty-six years behind him and the distinction of being the longest tenured employee to serve in the Alamo Community College District (ACCD). He served for more than fifteen years as chairman of the United Way Committee at St. Philip's. As a board member of the San Antonio United

Way Agency for six years, he served also as vice president of the Executive Committee and as a member of the Allocation Committee of United Way. He was vice president of the Southwest Teachers Association, president and vice president of the Southwest District Teachers Association, a charter member and president of the Alamo American Cancer Society, and a member of the San Antonio Literacy Council.[9]

Mr. Turbon's wife, Sally, described him as the "go-to" person, meaning that students often came to their home in the wee hours of the morning after they had gone to bed, saying, "Mr. Turbon, you've got to come." They asked him to come to wherever they were having a party, if there was a disturbance. And, said Mrs. Turbon, "He would go." The students were confident that he could solve whatever the problem was, and they had no reservations about saying, "Mr. Turbon, you gotta come!"

Turbon's relationship to important members of the San Antonio community was equally as important as his relationship to his students. "Amy Freeman Lee worked with Turbon at St. Philip's before it was 'chic' to do so," Mrs. Turbon pointed out. "Turbon would call her on the phone and say, I need money for books, or I need money to send someone someplace, or I need money for shoes and she would send it. Turbon and Lee became such buddies that Turbon had only to call her secretary and tell her what he needed and he would get it. She really was a help to him." Amy Freeman Lee, born in Sequin, Texas, was a noted self-taught artist, specializing in watercolors. Active in the San Antonio community, Dr. Lee, who received an honorary doctorate from Incarnate Word, was chair of the Board of Directors for the college for many years.

For his contribution to the school as head counselor, as professor of psychology, as chair of the social sciences, and because of his work in the community, the ACCD voted unanimously in 1996 to name the student center in his honor.[10] The Turbon Student Center was dedicated on February 7, 1997.

Dr. Theodore W. Williams

Dr. Theodore W. Williams, Faculty

When he was hired in 1954,Theodore Williams was the only instructor in biology at the college and he shared the position of math instructor with Roger W. Lee. Miss Bowden retired shortly after he arrived. Williams, who rose in rank to become interim president of the college for a semester, returned to the classroom following his retirement. "I don't have too many areas that I was dissatisfied with," said Williams. "I enjoyed my time there."[11]

During the Norris administration, faculty would go on recruiting visits around the state to high schools, sometimes every two years. On one such recruiting tour in 1958, they traveled as far from San Antonio as La Grange, going through Columbus, Weldon, Smithfield, San Marcos, and New Braunfels enlisting students, before returning to San Antonio. In 1969 when the school changed deans, the recruiting pattern changed. The emphasis shifted to recruiting primarily from within the district. Rather than having instructors go on recruiting visits, the counseling department became involved, alternating each year.

The Faculty Speaks of Dr. Norris: Dean William Hudgins

Hudgins served the college for thirty-four years under three administrators—Bowden, Norris, and Murphy. He said this about Dr. Norris:

"Dr. Norris was a very collegiate, persistent type of person. He came from the University of Michigan, and then

Don Coleman, Registrar

he went to Southern Cal. He would go out to Southern California every summer of every year, until he got his doctorate. In every way, he was a protégé of Miss Bowden, carried on many of Miss Bowden's ways. Dr. Norris's daddy had been a preacher," Hudgins explained, "and a lot of that had passed on to him.

"In fact," said Hudgins, "it was Dr. Norris, who recommended me to be the dean of students. You know, he liked sports, he liked clean-minded people and he didn't like for you to curse or anything. He was from the old school. He was very effective, and you have to consider a lot of things when you say effective. You've got to consider the period when these people came along. Nowadays, a lot of people, presidents, would not tolerate things that people, including Dr. Norris had to put up with."[12]

Don Coleman, who worked very closely with Dr. Norris, described him as being from the old school. In many ways, his description of Norris was similar to Dean Hudgins's description. Coleman explained that what he meant by describing Dr. Norris as "old school" is that Dr. Norris observed the traditional values of the day. It was very clear from the interviews that Dr. Norris gave as much of himself as he demanded from others. He practiced what he preached.

Dr. Levi Jackson, Student, Faculty, Department Chair

Jackson grew up on the Eastside of San Antonio in a very strong family consisting of seven sisters and no brothers. He attended and graduated from Phyllis Wheatley High School where there were "supportive, inspiring role models all around." He received a scholarship to attend Morehouse College but did not go because he had no money to contribute to his expenses. His father was a charter member of Alpha Phi Alpha Fraternity and the Alphas offered him a $75 scholarship, "and, that was how I was able, in 1964, to go to St. Philip's."

As he remembered, St. Philip's in 1964, had one Hispanic student, one white instructor, and the remaining faculty and students were African Americans. Faculty thought nothing of telling students what they had to do because, with faculty, there was a sense of extended family.

"In research, they talk about situations where the teachers take over for the parents. It was here. Bill Hudgins would think nothing of telling us: 'Boy, take that hat off, put that shirt tail in.' We had to tuck our shirt tails in, we couldn't wear hats in class and we had to be respectful toward our instructors. That was our culture until the late 1980s. We were still a family, even when the hue of

Dr. Levi Jackson

the faculty slowly changed from black to brown to Anglo. Those were my formative years and I got my 'formation' right here at St. Philip's College."

After graduating from St. Philip's, Jackson attended Prairie View A&M where he received a bachelor's degree in electronics. In August, 1968, the year he graduated from Prairie View, while waiting to hear from the draft, Jackson received a call from Dean Watson, offering him a teaching position in the evening division at St. Philip's. Jackson had vowed that he would never teach. The United States was in the middle of the Vietnam War, so he decided that he would serve a few years in the military and then join IBM, the place to be for his major, electronics. Thinking that the assignment would be only temporary, he accepted the teaching position offered by Dean Watson and, in 1968, began his tenure under Dr. Norris. Each year at St. Philip's led to another and another, until Jackson, some twenty-five years later, found himself still doing what he vowed he'd never do—continuing to teach.

Jackson related an incident that ended with Dean Norris calling him in to his office to discuss his off-campus behavior. Newly hired and the youngest professor at the college, Jackson had attended a party at a friend's home one Saturday evening and while there, he drank a Schlitz beer. "Just having fun," he said. But on Monday morning, he was called into Dean Norris's office. "Son," said Dr. Norris, "Now that you're a Professor, you cannot go to parties drinking beer like that." "Don't know how he knew," said Jackson, "but the tentacles were there."

Somehow Norris learned that Jackson had drunk a beer at the party and he let Jackson know that even when away from St. Philip's, and on his own time, he was still representing the college. And, as far as Norris was concerned, drinking beer at parties was unacceptable for his faculty.[13]

Jackson retired in January 2009, after having been employed at St. Philip's for more than four decades. In March 2009, shortly following his retirement, Jackson passed away.

Dorothy McClinton

Dorothy McClinton, Chairman and Instructor in the Business Department

McClinton, a veteran faculty member whose tenure spanned more than three decades, worked under Dr. Norris for much of that time. Describing Dr. Norris as an innovative person from whom they all learned a great deal, she explained, "When we would have meetings, if we had questions he would not want us to just come to him and talk to him about it, instead he said, 'Put it in writing.' He taught us to use memos. If we had something that was important, 'Write it,' he said. We were not to just go to him with, 'I want so and so.' He would say, 'Put it in writing.'

"And," said McClinton, "we all learned how to write a lot of memos," so much so that when someone wanted to tell her something, she, too, learned to say, "Put it in writing. Let me see what you're saying." Sometimes when there were faculty meetings, the faculty would discuss problems with Dr. Norris, who would fill out additional information on how they could better solve the problem. Because he was an excellent administrator, Norris wanted things to be done exactly right, just as he had learned it, and just as he envisioned it. "Besides," said McClinton, "His suggestions really did help." Additionally, Norris started his faculty and staff saving money. "We all learned something about putting something aside for another day."[14]

Virginia Tatum, first a student, later a counselor, and finally campus minister, described Norris as orthodox. When asked what she meant by orthodox, she explained that the first thing that Dr. Norris asked was, "'Do you attend church, and if so, where?' And, that's how I ended up at New Light Baptist Church," said Tatum. Dr. Norris

Virginia Tatum

invited her (and others) to "Come to my Sunday school class [at New Light Church]." Tatum admits to being awestruck at the invite. "A dean, which would now be president, asking a little student from the woods, 'Come to my Sunday school class.' I thought I was Jesus Christ," she said. "The top guy had asked me to come to his Sunday school class. And if you think that I was not going to that Sunday school class, you would be wrong. Everyone he asked went to that Sunday school class."

One major difference between Bowden and Norris, as Tatum described them, is that Norris, being Baptist, took the spiritual side, while Bowden, an Episcopalian, was "kind of a people person." Tatum took that to mean that it would be all right with Miss Bowden if you took a little sip of champagne at the bar, but not Dr. Norris—no drinking, no smoking. "A true leader."[15]

A Family Perspective: Trusse Norris, Norris's Younger Son

Trusse Norris, the younger of Dr. Norris's two sons, grew up on Gibbs Street around St. Philip's. Prior to Gibbs, they lived on Burnet Street, and, though he was too young to remember that part of his life, he was told that they lived on Florida Street, over in Denver Heights, before moving to Gibbs Street. Dr. Clarence Norris Jr., Trusse's brother, was five years older than he.

Growing up under Dr. Clarence Norris Sr.

"The Norris's were a clan of educators, all of us, so far," said Trusse. Describing his family, Trusse said, "My dad was a disciplinarian and you would expect that, knowing his background. His parents' philosophy was 'spare the rod and spoil the child.' My dad had inklings of that. He didn't have the totality of that as much as his dad did, but he did believe that it was ok to use the rod.

"With Dad's faculty, everything had to be right; classes had to start on time, for example." He also remembered that his dad brought home a master plan of the college. "The college, at that time, was composed of two buildings: Johnston Hall and the gym, and we couldn't imagine the school going to Montana St. Imagine, the school

Trusse Norris

extending that far! [A distance of about three additional city blocks]." But Trusse was almost sure that the plans he saw had the school going to Montana Street.

It was a big deal when the gym was built at St. Philip's. He remembered that Wheatley High School gym was built about the same time, so it was a really big deal when St. Philip's got theirs.

Trusse described his dad as a social type in one way, but "in another was he was more a business social person. At one time, attending a conference in Fort Worth on a seminary campus in an integrated situation, his dad was introduced to making presentations using slides. "He really got jazzed up on what was, at the time, a new innovation—teaching lessons using slides—and he brought the idea of using slides to tell the story of Jesus, back to New Light Baptist Church where he was superintendent of the Sunday school. He wanted to expose his Sunday school class to slide presentations."[16]

A Job Well Done: Dr. Clarence W. Norris Jr., Older Son

Writing in his dissertation, "St. Philip's College," Clarence Norris Jr. described his father, Norris Sr., as an outstanding scholar-athlete and a quiet mediator. Other acquaintances and colleagues also described Dr. Norris as strong, calm, even-tempered, tactful, and resourceful, under very trying circumstances. Conversely, detractors viewed him as being too cautious. Despite the disparate views held of him, Dr. Norris viewed through the pages of history yields a picture of a quiet, gentle man, who though soft-spoken and even tempered, was administratively a giant of a man who more than capably filled Miss Bowden's shoes.

Dr. Clarence W. Norris Sr.: Another St. Philip's Legend Retires

On May 16, 1969, the Board of Trustees of the San Antonio Union Junior College District unanimously conferred upon Dr. Clarence Norris the title Dean Emeritus of St. Philip's College. By 1975 the Tech Building had been completed, and approximately 400 persons gathered to ceremonially confer the name "Norris Technical Center" on the building named in Dr. Norris's honor for the years of service he gave to St. Philip's College.[17] Norris, who served faithfully for thirty-one years, was dean of the college, professor of sociology, and chairman of the department of sociology. When he retired from administration in 1969, it was not a full retirement from work, only a break from management of the college. Immediately upon his retirement, Norris returned again to the classroom where he taught sociology until 1974, when he formally retired for a final time.

During his administration, many issues of great import to the community arose, but none as important as integrating the schools. Norris believed that St. Philip's not only could but should be kept open and brought up to par with SAC. As one of the leading opponents of the drive to close St. Philip's and allow all community college students to attend SAC, his decision to oppose the move proved to be shrewd and insightful, for in retrospect, the loss of St. Philip's contribution to the Eastside, to San Antonio, and to the nation, would be incalculable. In addition to his instructional and other duties, Norris was instrumental over the years in the increase in student body from slightly more than a hundred to an enrollment of over 5,000. Because of his contribution to the school and to the community, a building on the campus was named in his honor, to commemorate his leadership.

12 The Surprise Election of Garlington Jerome (G. J.) Sutton

BE IT ACCORDINGLY FOUND, DECLARED AND ORDERED on this 7th day of April, A.D. 1948, by the Board of Trustees for San Antonio Union Junior College District in Bexar County, Texas, that a majority of the electors voting at said election have cast their votes in favor of the election of Jesse N. Fletcher and G. J. Sutton, and such persons are hereby FOUND, DECLARED and ORDERED to have been elected to the office of Trustee for San Antonio Union Junior College District for a term of three years from and after April 3, 1948.[1]

Garlington Jerome Sutton, Trustee, SAUJC

Many improvements occurred under the Board of Trustees and additional changes were on the horizon. Electing Sutton as a member of the Board of Trustees of the San Antonio Union Junior College District, seen in retrospect, was a change that was vitally important to the growth and development of St. Philip's College. A staunch backer and promoter of St. Philip's, Sutton made it a priority to increase the resources devoted to the school.

He was known as G. J. to friends and foe alike. Early on he learned independence, and as one of fifteen children, soon learned how to fend for himself. His father, Samuel Johnson Sutton, was one of the first black teachers in Bexar County and served as principal of three high schools during his fifty-four year career in education. G. J.'s parents were determined that their children would be provided the best opportunities possible, and they made it a priority that all fifteen children earn a college degree. To do this, the children helped themselves and each other financially in order that all would have an opportunity to complete their education.

Sutton attended public school in San Antonio, Wiley College in Marshall, Texas, earned a bachelor's of science degree at Wilberforce University in Ohio, and later a degree in mortuary science at Cincinnati College. After his return to San Antonio in 1938, G. J. and his brother Samuel took over the family's business, Sutton and Sutton Funeral Home, the oldest black-owned mortuary in San Antonio. It is still in operation as of this writing.

From the 1939–1940 catalog edition of St. Philip's, we learned that while G. J. was the first Negro elected official of the Trustee Board of the college, his father had served as a member of the Board of Trustees of St. Philip's Junior College and Vocational Institute in the late 1930s, early 1940s. Following his tenure on the Trustee Board, G. J. was elected Texas State Representative, representing District 2 of San Antonio. G. J. served San Antonio in the Texas State Legislature until his death from a heart attack on his birthday in 1976. He was the first black official elected from Bexar County since Reconstruction.

During his tenure as a representative, G. J. proposed that "the state buy an office building in his district to save leasing money, to serve neglected citizens better and to enhance the city's efforts to revitalize the St. Paul Square neighborhood." While this did not happen in his lifetime, in 1982 a building in the city of San Antonio was renovated, named the G. J. Sutton State Office Complex, and dedicated in his honor. A three-story learning center building located on the campus of St. Philip's is also named in his honor and presently houses the administrative offices of the college.[2] G. J. left behind a legacy of hard work and love for the college and the community. He will be remembered by the college and community observers alike as not only a "mover and shaker" but also a true advocate for St. Philip's.

Garlington Jerome (G. J.) Sutton

Remembrances of G. J. Sutton

Dr. Norris Sr. often referred to G. J. as "[a] very dynamic leader from the Eastside of San Antonio who courageously and openly fought for racial equality in all areas of community life." Calling him "truly a man of conviction," Norris recalled that Sutton had called for closing St. Philip's, but only because he recognized that the physical facilities at St. Philip's were inferior to those at SAC. The motion did not pass for lack of a second.

Percy Sutton, Brother

Percy Sutton, the youngest of the family, was interviewed at his office at 125th Street and St. Nicholas Avenue in New York City in Harlem. When we visited him, immediately following his greeting to us, he set the parameters for the visit, announcing that he never gave interviews that lasted longer than thirty minutes. After about thirty minutes had passed, and as he continued telling us about growing up in San Antonio, we hastened to take our leave, pleased that he had agreed to an interview. Sutton invited us to keep our seats, assuring us that he had more to tell. And indeed he did, for after about one and a half hours had quickly passed, we were still being entertained. He regaled us with his stories, many of which had no bearing on the history of St. Philip's, but were so entertaining that we hated to leave. His sense of humor was evident throughout the interview and surfaced almost immediately as the interview began.

Attorney Sutton's Story

Sutton was born in San Antonio into a family of fifteen children; seven males and seven females, plus himself. He jokingly said he was born 105 years ago, and then corrected it to say, actually eighty-two years. His father, Samuel Johnson Sutton, was the principal of Douglas Junior High, the junior high school Sutton attended, and later was principal of the senior high school, Phyllis Wheatley, that he also attended. His father was born in 1862, three years before slavery ended. "They allowed him to stay on at the high school so that he could be present at my graduation," said Sutton.

He recalled that his father played a role in Bowden's coming to San Antonio by sponsoring her and by using the great influence that he had in educational circles. He also helped her financially, as did his brother G. J. and other members of the family through personal contributions. Sutton also recalled that there were a number of rich white people in San Antonio who helped financially, families like the Brackenridge's, and he recalled hearing some unnamed white persons say that "[t]hey didn't need another school on the Eastside for colored people." [3]

Dr. Theodore R. Williams—President, St. Philip's College

Williams, a member of the faculty during G. J.'s time on the Board of Trustees, noted that during that time, it was also pretty obvious that St. Philip's was not getting their fair share in the process. He expressed the thought that G. J. favored closing St. Philip's because he "pretty much wanted to do away with this dual education system." There was a segment of the black community who said,

"Let's close St. Philip's," and though G. J. was a full supporter of the college, he was among that faction. He was adamant about his position on closing St. Philip's.

Citing the building of the Bowden Building as an example, Williams said, "The Bowden Building opened in 1954 and when I tell you this, you get a pretty good picture of the reaction of the black community. The community didn't feel that the building that they were constructing would solve the problem or would be adequate enough to solve the problem because of unequal treatment. When the building opened in '54, it was not air-conditioned. Only the library and the administrative office were air-conditioned. They proposed to, and subsequently did, air-condition the building, but we went through a whole rigmarole before it was air-conditioned."[4]

Dean William Hudgins

When Hudgins came to San Antonio, one of the first persons he met was G. J. Sutton, whom he described as a very, very outspoken man, adamant about racism. In fact, he detested it. G. J. felt that St. Philip's was the stepchild to San Antonio College and he was always attacking the inferior facilities at St. Philip's. At the time, some blacks expressed the thought that St. Philip's wouldn't be anything if they didn't join the Alamo Community College District, and that for St. Philip's to grow, it had to be a part of a bigger program in order to generate public funds. If the school did not join the district, it would continue to be an independent junior college, struggling for existence. Other blacks felt strongly that St. Philip's should remain as it was.

One day, G. J., who felt that faculty pay scale at both colleges should be equalized, called Hudgins to his office and said, "Coach Hudgins, you're the coach. You ought to get more than $2,700; I think you should be paid $3,600." His pay was immediately raised to $3,600. Hudgins, who at the time had just left Bishop College where he earned $1,800, was elated to be earning $2,700 and now, because of G. J., he had just received a $900 raise. "I'll always remember G. J. Sutton for that," he said.[5]

Johnetta Slaughter, Professor Emeritus, Social Sciences

Slaughter came to St. Philip's as an adjunct instructor at the end of what she described as "kind of a political fight."

Johnetta Slaughter

One segment of the black population didn't want to see a lot of money put in St. Philip's because they thought there should be no division, just one school. The other faction favored bringing St. Philip's up to par with SAC. According to G. J., fixing St. Philip's would perpetuate segregation and he was in favor of integration. Slaughter, at the time a new member of the faculty at St. Philip's, did not know who among the faculty belonged to which faction, nor did she understand all about the divisions within the school. It was her opinion that the faculty was probably all in favor of putting money at St. Philip's. She knew that "G. J. was on the board and that he didn't really cotton to this idea of putting all this money at St. Philip's."

Slaughter had heard G. J. speak about how Miss Bowden was treated at the board meetings and, not one to bite his tongue, when he first attended a meeting and saw Miss Bowden sitting "somewhere way back, apart from the other people," he said, "No!" He told them that Miss Bowden had to "come up with everybody else." All the other administrators were up there and he wanted her up there too.

To this Slaughter said, "You might not like what he had to say, but he said whatever he wanted to say in terms of what he felt. In that, he and Ernest Stevenson, faculty member, were very much alike. They both were men of principle with a passion for their beliefs. Because G. J. would just come out and say whatever he thought, he was a thorn in the sides of the other board members."[6]

Dr. Jerome Weynand Remembers

In his capacity as reporter for the *Express News*, Weynand came in contact with G. J. often. He related an incident that occurred that gave insight into the passion that G. J. brought to his views. "At a meeting, held in Mr. Loftin's office at SAC, with the seven board members present, also several very quiet, and very nice NAACP members [National Association for the Advancement of Colored People], and G. J., small of stature, and quiet spoken. At that one particular meeting, a crowd assembled." Weynand, at the time, was covering the meeting as a newspaper reporter. The room quickly filled to beyond capacity, with standing room only, so the meeting adjourned to the upstairs library in McCreless Hall at San Antonio College.

"Loftin and G. J. got into a shouting match over some point and G. J. jumped up on the table. Loftin got red faced but stayed on the floor when Mr. Sutton jumped up on the table," Weynand related. "There was just no love lost between those two men for some reason." [7]

Community Perspectives on G. J. Sutton's Victory

The race for a seat on the Board of Trustees was usually a quiet race, with limited participation. According to Rev. Claude Black, there was a common coalition between the Mexicans (Mexican Americans) and the blacks, but the board race was always a very quiet race, with not many people participating. As a result, when Mr. Sutton won, it shocked the whole community because he was not expected to win that election. His place on the board was an unexpected political victory.[8]

Col. Roy Burley, retired military, said, "When G. J. was first elected to the board, I mean, that just threw this entire town into a tizzy. We had some prejudiced papers in those days. One of the papers had a picture in there that said, 'When you were asleep, look who got elected!'"[9]

13 Integrating the Schools: The 1950s

Mr. Sutton offered a motion to discontinue operation of the St. Philip's College as of August 31, 1952 and to enroll the students of St. Philip's Branch in the San Antonio College for the fall semester of next year. The President then called for a second to this motion but there was none offered. The President then announced that this motion had failed for lack of a second.[1]

Facing Reality

San Antonio's black community, weary of the desegregation rhetoric, voiced their sentiment that St. Philip's should be drastically improved and both St. Philip's and SAC opened to all students. The other option was to close St. Philip's and transfer the black students to SAC.

The Board of Trustees took the position that, rather than integrate the two schools, they would adhere to the "separate but equal" law of the state of Texas by maintaining separate facilities. The board proposed floating a bond issue to raise monies to improve both schools, arguing that St. Philip's would be brought up to par with San Antonio College. Even with the proposal, and in spite of the public rhetoric about "maintaining impartiality and equality," St. Philip's was to receive only about one-fourth of the proceeds of the bond issue, $625,000, while San Antonio College would receive the balance from the $2,500,000.

The amount that St. Philip's received was not enough to correct the inequities in the two schools, but the Board of Trustees countered with the argument that though the funding was unequal, the allocation was based on student enrollment. Some members of the community, who were strong supporters of closing St. Philip's, advocated for enrolling all of the students at San Antonio College. G. J. Sutton was among these supporters. Dean Norris, a strong proponent of the measure, favored keeping St. Philip's open.

The two colleagues, Norris and Sutton, political allies, friends, both of whom worked long and hard for St. Philip's cause, now found themselves on opposite sides of the controversy. Thus went the dialogue, not just between these two long-time friends, but also in the city itself.

During the course of the arguments for closing St. Philip's, it was noted that for twenty-plus years, from 1928 when the Johnston Memorial Building was completed, until 1949 when the gymnasium was erected, lack of funds had virtually halted construction on St. Philip's campus. During that time, no new buildings were constructed, nor were plans made for future construction. With so many years of failing to add to the campus or to make timely repairs on the existing buildings, many in the black community felt that it would take many years to put St. Philip's on par with SAC.

Heated discussions were held among faculty and students, both on and off St. Philip's campus, at San Antonio College and in the community. Many in San Antonio's white community favored a "wait and see" policy, while most blacks in San Antonio felt that more than enough time had been spent waiting for their status to improve. The anxiety and agitation coursing across the nation because of the segregation issue mirrored the angst felt amongst both races in San Antonio regarding the issue of integration. Many blacks, having served their country in integrated units in the military, were unwilling to tolerate a return to segregated conditions. Many whites, accustomed to being in positions of authority, were not yet ready to accept blacks as equals.

Walking a Fine Line

As the lone black member of the Board of Trustees discovered, it proved to be a lonely and difficult time, for Sutton found himself without an ally on the board. There were repercussions to be felt from attempting to please either camp, black or white. If he were too vocal, there could be consequences for St. Philip's from the white community; and, as a funeral director in the black community, his livelihood depended on the goodwill of the black population. Moreover, there was the problem of faculty and community groups, neither of whom supported his views on closing St. Philip's and actively worked against it. Dr. Norris was most notable among those against closing the school.

By his own admission, Sutton's business suffered because many black leaders were turned against him by influential members of the board. It appeared that the press was also against him. While the staff and faculty at St. Philip's opposed his position publicly, some staff members profited by receiving special job assignments. The college received a new athletic building that Sutton considered the result of his mounting the push to upgrade St. Philip's facilities.

Fodder for the Newspapers

Jerome Weynand, who later became president of both colleges, and who was working as a newspaper reporter with the *Express-News* during this time, remembered covering the Trustee Board, their board meetings, issues related to the bond proposal, and the problems that they encountered with integration. He also remembered "covering a lot of Mr. Sutton":

> G. J. would make a motion for something and there would be a counter motion, but Mr. Loftin, as administrator to board members, was the only member that G. J. ever crossed swords with. It was primarily that Mr. Sutton wanted to integrate without developing St. Philip's College. He thought it was a waste of money because we were going to integrate soon and the country was planning that way. Mr. Loftin knew it also and said, 'Just as soon as the State Board of Education tells me, we will work on that.'[2]
>
> G. J. wanted SAC integrated and no further monies spent on segregated schools, not on SAC and not on St. Philip's. Sutton said, 'Just end this segregation and start building new schools.' But, the state law did not permit this, the State Department of Education, TEA as it was called in those days, did not allow for that and I don't think the State Legislature allowed it either. It had to come finally from the Supreme Court.[3]

Despite dissenting urgings to the contrary from the black community and from G. J. Sutton, the board, with the exception of Sutton's lone dissenting vote, voted as a majority to keep St. Philip's open, resolving to "build a new St. Philip's" and, with the new construction, hoping to placate the black community.

William Hudgins, Dean of Students, Emeritus

Dean Hudgins recalled circumstances surrounding the acquisition of the pool at St. Philip's, noting that it took some time before they finally got a swimming pool at the college. One of Hudgins's students, who eventually became a lawyer, came over to St. Philip's and told him that he (the student) no longer wanted to go to SAC because he was told that "We would prefer that you go to St. Philip's College and take swimming." "I don't know who told him that," said Hudgins, "but I know that there were problems about blacks and whites using the same swimming pool. Unfortunately, that was the way it was in those days." [4]

Jerome Weynand: On Integration

According to Weynand, the district continued to follow the separate but equal doctrine "that was being followed not only here in San Antonio by the SAISD but also in other places. St. Philip's didn't have a swimming pool and SAC did, so they built a swimming pool at St. Philip's. A little ole dinky pool over there, really wasn't the nice one that SAC had. The library was not comparable at St. Philip's to the library at SAC but the students were driving that growth primarily at San Antonio College and St. Philip's too."

Weynand went on to say that using his reflections as a reporter, he believed that the board did not want to kill St. Philip's College but that "Mr. Loftin's desire was to continue building buildings, facilities, improving labs and the general campus at St. Philip's, while G. J. Sutton's desire was not to do that. Again, it can be summed up in the separate but equal doctrine. They wanted to nurture it, separate but equal."[5]

Hoping to placate the black community and avoid integration for another day, at a June 3, 1952 meeting of the Trustee Board, board member Fletcher motioned that the chairman of the Trustee Board appoint a committee to look into the cost of construction of a new administration and classroom building and the cost of other improvements that might be necessary to make St. Philip's a first-class junior college. In his argument justifying the motion, Fletcher cited the constitution of the state of Texas, saying that the constitution required the board to maintain separate and equal facilities for Negroes.

The Trustee Board Chair, as instructed, appointed a committee "to study the needs of SAC and St. Philip's." The chair further instructed the committee to report the findings to the board so that an amount could be determined for a bond issue that would be proposed. The committee met during the summer of 1952 to inspect the plants of both schools and then recommended that a fall election be held to issue over two million dollars in bonds. St. Philip's would receive $625,000 from the bonds toward its improvements and the remainder would go to SAC.

This committee was given the authority to determine the cost of purchasing whatever additional land St. Philip's needed so that the cost of the land could be included in the bond issue. When the president of the board called for a vote on the issuance of the bonds, G. J. Sutton cast the lone vote against the proposal.

As planned, an election was held in the fall of 1952 and the matter of issuing the bonds was put to the public for a vote. When the voters of San Antonio accepted the bond proposal, plans for construction at the two sites were immediately set into motion.

St. Philip's received funds for an administration building, classrooms, auditorium, audio-visual building, a student union building, and some additional land. It would be nearly two years later before St Philip's would receive a swimming pool.[6]

The 1950s, Continued

More was needed to correct the many disparities in the two campuses than the dollars received from the bond issue, particularly the dissimilarity reflected in the run-down buildings on St. Philip's campus. Besides the dilapidated condition of the campus, there were other inequities to be corrected—in expenditures for the two schools, course offerings, equipment, administrative positions, and in salaries. The inequities in administrative staff and salaries particularly rankled among the faculty and administrators.

Lanier Byrd, at that time a member of the science faculty, recalled the discrepancy in salaries and in other areas at St. Philip's that continued into the 1970s:"You'd go to a meeting and you were told what you were going to get and don't ask questions. I remember being so proud of Dean Hudgins, who would just speak right up. Dean Hudgins was always The Man. He was always tough in those meetings. He would tell them exactly what he thought, to the point. We heard stories that they'd threatened several times to fire him." During the time that G. J. Sutton was the State Representative, one Thursday or Friday afternoon the board put out a letter and after the faculty read it, Byrd described the climate as "almost like a riot. The faculty was walking up and down the hallways, just enraged. We could see where we could be on the pay scale and could see that we were all making about three or four thousand dollars less than we should have been making. Well, G. J. went over and told them that they would have to fix that immediately. They said they didn't have the money to do it, but they'd eventually get us on scale. G. J. said, 'Oh no, you're going to get them on scale right now.'"

Byrd talked about what it was like after his classes were over. "We were much smaller in those days, 3,000 or 4,000 students. Well, we left the campus and I will never forget going home. It was about twelve or one, my classes were over and I just got in my car and went jogging. I said, I make less, I'm going to have to do less work, you know. T. R. [Dr. T. R. Williams] said, 'Just settle down.' But, we just took off that day. We said, 'Classes are over, we're going home.' The next day, we were told we would be put on scale and paid retroactively.

"G. J. Sutton told them, fix this, or you'll never get another penny. He was over the state finance for funding for colleges at the community college level and when he said, 'You're not going to get a penny,' they didn't want to take a chance on that. Now, that is what I heard under cover. I remember my salary went up from $9,000 to $12,000. That was a lot of money in those days, and retroactive too, from the beginning of the year."[7]

It is fitting that Norris provided much of the leadership during integration, for he was the chief administrator of St. Philip's College when it developed from a school for black students only to an integrated college. He was instrumental in insuring that St. Philip's would not close because of whites and blacks attending school together. The period of apprehensiveness about integration occurred under his watch and, under his leadership, ended in the smooth, uneventful desegregation of St. Philip's.

14 Oral History Interviews, 1950s

St. Philip's was the school, I guess you would say, of default and one of the best things that ever happened to me. To go to St. Philip's College was the thing to do. It was a sound decision. I can't say enough about that. It was a place, a beginning point; it was a society on campus. You went to school there and spent the whole day.[1]

More than anything else, change was a mark of the 1950s, not only at St. Philip's, but also across the nation. It was a time when the United States was in great turmoil, particularly in the South, because of the Supreme Court mandate in *Brown v. Board of Education* to integrate the races. *Brown v. Board of Education* was the 1954 US Supreme Court decision that overturned the "separate but equal" doctrine that had made racial segregation legal in public facilities since 1896.[2]

But while other cities were reeling with discontent, San Antonio experienced a minimum of the discord evident on many campuses and in other large cities. In this chapter, we meet some of the students who attended St. Philip's immediately before and during the time of integration.

Students from the 1950s

Jeralyne Castleberry Williams

Jeralyne Williams, from East Texas, a place she described as, "not too far from Houston," came to San Antonio in the early 1940s. She entered St. Philip's in 1952 and graduated in 1954. Williams's hobby, interest, and passion is cultural awareness of the African American heritage of black Americans. "We really are a part of the fabric of the country and the city and I am deeply interested in the African American part in this country. We're not just a footnote in somebody's textbook; there is a story to be told about San Antonio and its African American heritage," she said.

Williams is a member of the African Historical and Genealogical Society, where the philosophy of African American as a part of American society is espoused. Williams, who also happens to be an author and well-known resource of San Antonio's African American history, is passionate about wanting others to know about black people and their history.

Williams arrived at St. Philip's just as San Antonio was going through a political upheaval involving the integration of San Antonio College and St. Philip's. Harry Burns, president of the National Association for the Advancement of Colored People (NAACP) and sponsor of the Youth Council of that group, was recruiting students to protest the lack of admittance of black students to SAC. He interviewed Williams and her mother about the possibility of her helping to integrate SAC, but because of her uneasiness with the situation, her mother, a single parent, shy about Williams's participation and not quite certain of what Burns told her, directed her daughter to St. Philip's.

Williams entered St. Philip's College with no real means of paying for her education until Stonewall Jackson Davis found her and offered a scholarship of about $35 to help pay her tuition. To earn the remainder that she needed, she worked as his student assistant, worked for Lois White in English, for her chemistry teacher, Roger Lee, and also worked for Dr. Norris. She still remembers classes under Bill Hudgins, her health and P. E. teacher. In fact, her memories of St. Philip's are still vivid and fond and she spoke in warm terms about how very good St. Philip's was to the students in lots of different ways, even though there were many other severe limitations.

Williams entered St. Philip's in 1952, when St. Philip's was an all-black school. It was a time, she recalled, that "there was the sense that certain members of the community did not send their children to St. Philip's." Williams said that she did not do as well as she should have; nonetheless, St. Philip's was the basis for her entry into the world outside of San Antonio.[3]

Lanier Byrd, Student, 1950s

Byrd, who earlier gave us insight into his experiences as a faculty member, also attended St. Philip's as a student. Byrd, a native of San Antonio, says he "met great role models" when he entered St. Philip's from high school. Since he was strapped financially with no resources to go elsewhere, he attended St. Philip's almost by default. After St. Philip's, however, he was able to continue his education at Prairie View University and he earned both a bachelor's and a master's degree there. When he returned to St. Philip's at a later time as a member of the faculty, he spent twenty-four years in the classroom. He spent a combined total of thirty-five years at St. Philip's serving as a member of the faculty, as a biology instructor and chair in the department of natural science, and as a member of the administrative team.

Byrd attended Jefferson High School, which he described as having a different exposure, with about three thousand whites and about twelve blacks. Each morning, the students assembled in the cafeteria and with the exception of a few instances, the black students did not see each other again until the end of the day. Only once did he have a class with one of the other black students.

"And did we have some bad experiences? Yes, we did. We had guys that would fight and call you names, but you learned to keep your mouth shut and go on. Just because they called you a name didn't mean anything." At Jefferson, Byrd joined the student government and participated in other activities on campus such as basketball and track. He described Jefferson as a college prep school with more positives than negatives but since the financial support was not there for him to attend another college, St. Philip's became his first choice.

Despite not having a choice of any other school over St. Philip's, it was one of the best decisions that Byrd made, for there he met Everett Turbon, William (Bill) Hudgins, T. R. Williams, and others who were successful and were great role models. Byrd adopted the attitude that if they could do it, he could do it too. When he finished St. Philip's, wanting to stay in San Antonio, he applied to St. Mary's University. His plan was to attend medical school and become a doctor, and while he considered St. Mary's an OK school, it did not have a premed program. In addition, he learned that the same instructor taught all the biology classes. After one year, he transferred to Prairie View in order to take advantage of more variety in instructors. Many of his friends were there and Prairie View had the good reputation of sending their students on to medical or graduate school. At Prairie View, which he described as another great move, he met professors with PhDs, other very important people, and as a result, he had a wonderful experience. At the time, John Murphy, later to become president of St. Philip's, was head of the graduate education program. "There were persons with PhDs from the finest institutions in Texas and from Notre Dame, Harvard, Princeton, plus great scientists like the Stubblefields, Dr. Collins, and Dr. Jewel Berry. You saw these great guys teaching and you said, Wow! I want to be like them."

In 1972, Byrd was offered the opportunity to teach at St. Philip's. He had finished all of the course work for his master's degree and all that he had left to do was to complete the actual research. Thus, he came to St. Philip's to teach biology and remained until his retirement. Under Byrd's watch, the department grew from biology only to include chemistry, physics, and geology, and subsequently to the department that is now called natural sciences. In 1975, at twenty-six years of age, Byrd was elected chair of the biology department. To be elected chair of the department at that age was an honor and a great experience and he said, "I could do the things I did because I had great mentors who worked with me and helped me.

"It just happened that they were looking around for somebody and opportunities for promotions were greater in those days. I was a very young kid and their choices were not that great." Byrd became a full professor in 1984 and though he is not positive, he thinks that at that time, he might have been the youngest full professor among the faculty. Byrd retired in 2007 as vice president of academic affairs. Dr. Byrd passed away unexpectedly in September 2009. His death was a great loss to St. Philip's and to the community.[4]

crops from plowed ground," said Littlefield-Tatum, "and I knew that because I've plowed ground and grown crops. So, when Miss Bowden said to me, 'look, this is a trade off, they're good to us, they respect us, we respect them,' then, it had meaning.

"Miss Bowden showed the students, 'You see what I'm doing, you see what we're doing for you. You don't go out and be a nobody. That doesn't speak well of St. Philip's.'" Littlefield-Tatum said, "I knew then when I looked at Miss Bowden, that someday I'd be a Miss Bowden. There was nothing that could stop me from that, and I ended up almost being a Miss Bowden."

Tatum went on to say that Miss Bowden knew that Dr. Norris, who at that time was the assistant dean, was going to respect authority, that he was going to be loyal to the students and to the community, because that was a part of his spiritual upbringing and beliefs and that he wasn't a very assertive person, but he was a loyal person. "I think that that was the one thing that she hired him for, his loyalty, because loyalty was high on her list," said Littlefield-Tatum.[6]

Alzo Cole and Martha McNeil

This sister and brother attended St. Philip's in the 1950s, working their way through. Both worked for Bowden, she as cook and he as Bowden's personal driver. During her last year at St. Peter Claver High School, one of the instructors suggested that after graduation, McNeil should consider St. Philip's. She visited the school, along with her parents and, according to McNeil, "We all fell in love with it."

McNeil lived in Bowden's house, across the street from the campus. Bowden had two rooms in the front of her home and McNeil lived in one of the rooms. A couple, nonstudents who worked in the community, rented the other part of the home. Mornings, after dressing and preparing for school, McNeil would help Bowden cook her breakfast. "She liked me and took me in as her daughter," said McNeil. "When she went out of town, she would give me a key to come in, prepare my breakfast and lunch. When I finished cleaning up, she trusted me to lock up her place and go back to my room."

Bowden frequently entertained persons like Dr. Norris and faculty member and friend Esdale Malloy, and she always had soft music playing in the background from her Victrola. Many afternoons and evenings, Bowden would go back to the college and spend time working there. McNeil described her as very fussy, someone who wanted things done just right. Food preparation had to meet her approval and then she'd compliment the students who worked for her, saying what nice jobs they'd done. When entertaining, one of her favorite foods was okra. "That's nice, that looks nice," she'd say, if the okra, for example, were washed, dried thoroughly, and cut very evenly. Her student workers learned not only academics from her, but were able to experience other things, such as dishes that were not the common foods they ate at home. "I learned a lot from her," said McNeil.

When McNeil left St. Philip's, Bowden paid her tuition at Prairie View, just as she had done for other students. McNeil wanted to go to Huston-Tillotson in Austin, but Bowden said, "Oh no, I want you to go to Prairie View. That is the college that I've selected for you and I'm going to pay your tuition."

Though at the time of the interview, more than fifty years had passed, McNeil still kept in touch with some of her friends from her days at St. Philip's. In fact, one friend from the early days of the 1950s, now living in Abilene, had visited McNeil the week prior to the interview.[7]

Alzo Cole, McNeil's brother and a minister in the city, also lived in one of Bowden's houses. While there, he worked as Bowden's driver for one year to help to pay his tuition. Though young, he had experience as a driver, having driven a fifteen-passenger school bus van for his brother, himself, and others in the area when he was still a high school student. He said that he was sixteen years old at the time.

Cole attended high school in Pleasanton, Texas, though he was born in Charlotte, Texas. He attended high school in Pleasanton because there weren't enough blacks in Charlotte to have a school exclusively for the black students to attend.

"This doesn't sound real, but the white school in Charlotte had us driving a van, my brother and myself, from Charlotte through Jourdanton to Pleasanton, picking up kids and transferring myself and my brother. You want to talk about busing; we bussed ourselves. I graduated from Lincoln High School in Pleasanton, Texas, at seventeen years old."

For Cole and his classmates, St. Philip's culture was enjoyable—as an athlete, he always had many friends. Cole described the campus life as having many fun things to do, for there were basketball games at home and away, banquets, talent shows, dances at Halloween, Christmas parties on the campus, and contests to elect the queen of St. Philip's. The freshman class would have a contest in which they would always try to outvote the sophomore class so that someone from the freshman class would be elected queen. Many of the activities were held in the main building, but equally as many were held in an area they called the breezeway. The cafeteria is now located where the breezeway was previously located. Cole, along with friends Robert McVey, Royce Ford, Junie Bown, Lewis Fields, and J. L. Sanders, were all on St. Philip's basketball team. Only Cole lived in the dormitory and then only for a short while before he moved out. The dormitory was eventually torn down and Bowden rented rooms to the students in a small house nearby that she owned.

To pay for his tuition, Cole's job was to keep Miss Bowden's lawn trimmed as well as drive as her chauffeur. "I wasn't too much of a yard boy, so she got tired of me not taking care of her yard and she said, 'I'm going to get me another yardman.' But, I continued to chauffer for her and she cooked and I ate meals with her."

St. Philip's had no means of providing transportation to the away games, so Coach Hudgins would use his car and a car belonging to one of the basketball players to transport the team to away games. "We rode the two cars to the games, with six persons in each car. St. Philip's was allowed to play St. Mary's B. Team, though we could not play the varsity team because of segregation." The remaining opponents were all black schools, such as Paul Quinn College.[8]

Nettie Hinton

Hinton, a community activist born in San Antonio, attended St. Philip's College from 1955 to 1957. One of her classmates, Hamice James, later became president of St. Philip's. Hinton grew up on the Eastside and lived there until she left San Antonio to work in Washington, DC, but when she retired, she came back home to where her family had lived since the 1870s. Hinton knew Miss Bowden personally.

Hinton had decided that she wanted to attend the University of Texas, but when she graduated from high school, the University of Texas undergraduate school was not yet integrated. During that time, Everett Turbon was a faculty member at St. Philip's and she knew him because he, too, was Catholic and they both attended St. Peter Claver Church. "It was just understood that the place I should be was at St. Philip's, for a number of reasons: One, Mr. Turbon was there and two, whether I knew it or not, it was probably the perfect place for me."

Hinton described growing up black in her community as "not a real world experience" because where she lived was a closed community that offered members everything that they needed. There was Commerce Street for the movies or to buy things; there were the schools, churches, and community stores; and while everything outside the community was segregated, residents didn't have to experience the daily separation between the races because their environment had what they needed. Even the library was across the street.

The community understood about segregation because examples were all around: downtown water fountains had "Whites Only" signs. Blacks were required to sit behind a line on the city buses and blacks sat in the balcony in the Majestic Theatre, which could only be reached by using the freight elevator. But, according to Hinton, the feeling in the black community was that those were things that came into their lives only occasionally because life was really full where they lived.

Hinton described St. Philip's as "a nice way station to be in while maturing." She graduated high school at sixteen, and afterwards attended St. Philip's. Faculty at St. Philip's at that time included Everett L. Turbon, Lois White, Theodore R. Williams, Carolyn Green, Coach William Hudgins, Stonewall Davis, and Mr. Leonidas Watson. Dr. Norris was president.

Some of Hinton's classmates were Constable Matthew "Nite" Marshall, Spott Barnett (the legendary saxophone player), Priscilla Preacher Armstead, and Gussie Milholland. All became well-known and well-respected members of the San Antonio Community.

The instructors at St. Philip's not only knew the students but they knew the students' parents and their neighbors. They may even have lived next door or down the street and were often a part of their students' lives outside of school, like Turbon, who saw Hinton regularly at mass or at some social occasion. Not everyone had plans to continue their education after St. Philip's and so the school operated on the premise that when the students left, they would be prepared for whatever they had chosen as their goal.

"The instructors were nurturing, demanding, in command of their subject matter, and were there to help you get where you wished to be," said Hinton. "Mr. Turbon, for example, could be a terrible taskmaster, but he did it with much sweetness and grace." Hinton described coming to St. Philip's to visit after she had graduated and was attending UT Austin. During spring break, she stopped at

St. Philip's to visit Mr. Turbon and happened to be wearing loafers and socks. Turbon said, "Dearie, we don't wear socks any longer. You are now a college student." So the next time she went back to St. Philip's and visited him, she dressed appropriately: hosiery, nice pumps with the appropriate attire, and proper demeanor and speech. Students learned a combination of academic preparation and finishing school at St. Philip's. "The lesson was there, but it was honey coated," she said.

Hinton recalled that Hamice James later became a minister and that he was always a sharp dresser, even then. James had been in the military before he entered St. Philip's. Hinton, who says that she knew Miss Bowden personally, nonetheless approached her with trepidation because, she said, Miss Bowden was an iconic figure whom she greatly respected because of her importance in the community. "The teachers in the black schools in San Antonio never had the most up-to-date text books, nor were the science laboratories cutting edge, nor were the kinds of infrastructure and building or materials to teach with the quality that other people in other parts of the school district had. But, those teachers gave their all and the schools graduated top black students."[9]

Hamice Roland James: Student, Faculty, Administrator, and President of the College

Hamice James, born in a small farming community near LaGrange, Texas, moved to San Antonio when he was thirteen years old, attended Douglas Middle School, and in 1947 graduated from Wheatley High School. His friends were going to schools such as Southern University in Houston and Fisk University in Nashville, Tennessee, and because his family was unable to pay for his education following high school, he refused to attend St. Philip's. With no money to pay his own way in college, he volunteered for and spent eight years in the military. At that time, the military was segregated and he joined the 24th Division, an all-black unit called the Buffalo Soldiers. Having had a change of heart about St. Philip's, when his tour of duty was completed, he got out of the military with plans to attend the college. James wrote Dr. Norris, asking about enrollment, and Dr. Norris, who did not have a secretary at the time, answered in his own handwriting, using pen and ink. "I intended to keep that letter for the rest of my life," said James.

At around twenty-five or twenty-six years old, James was older than the average St. Philip's student when he enrolled. His peers elected him class president in his freshman year and student government president in his sophomore year. After completing his associate's degree at St. Philip's, he earned a Bachelor of Business Administration degree and a master's degree in economics from St. Mary's University. Following graduation from St. Mary's, James worked days at the City Water Board as the first black hired in an administrative position and simultaneously, in the evening division at St. Philip's College under Dean Watson.

In January 1974, he resigned his position at the City Water Board and accepted a faculty position teaching business and economics at St. Philip's. Subsequently, he held positions at St. Philip's as Dean of Instructions, Vice President of Academic Affairs, a position in student advancement, and the position of Director of Business Services under Dr. Murphy and Dr. Jackson.

James, recalling the circumstances of the changes in leadership at St. Philip's, said, "When our president, Dr. Gloria Jackson was no longer president, they sent over a district person who had just gotten her PhD, and who was doing her practical work in the Chancellors' Office. The chancellor assigned her to replace Dr. Jackson and the turnover in the top senior management, from the chancellor on down, began to change so fast that we didn't know where we were from day to day."

When the office of chancellor changed, Ivory Nelson was the replacement. James described Nelson as "a go-getter." He went on to further describe Nelson as being responsible for much of the growth of the colleges and for the buildings. James thought that perhaps many people did not know that Nelson spoke before the legislature, made his case, and got millions of dollars for the schools, as he had done in previous jobs. "As long as Nelson was building the three colleges, we were OK," said James. The public can see physical buildings going up, but the public can't see what you're doing with curriculum.

"When you're here as chancellor for from three to five years, I guess you run out of steam and then you're gone. As long as Ivory was building and monies were going to the building of the three colleges, it was fine. After that, I don't know what happened."[10]

Frank Bryant, MD, student, 1950s

Bryant, another 1950s graduate of St. Philip's, attended the University of Texas Medical School and received his

Frank Bryant, MD

doctor of medicine degree from UT in Galveston, Texas. Following a stint in the military, Bryant returned to San Antonio in 1960 and built an office building on the east side of town. For more than forty years, he conducted a medical clinic there that provided medical care for thousands of patients. Bryant remains an example come true of the bishop's prediction regarding St. Philip's producing distinguished graduates. His years of community service and his list of professional and civic accomplishments is impressive. The list includes:

> Chairman, Board of Trustees, City Public Service Board; Director, ACCD Foundation; First African American President of the Bexar County Medical Society; Cofounder and first medical director of the Ella Austin Health Clinic; Co-developer of the East San Antonio Medical Center; Chairman, Texas State Board of Health; Chief of Staff, Santa Rosa Medical Center; First President of the C. A. Whittier Medical Society; President, Bexar County Chapter, Texas Academy of Family Physicians; Chairman, Board of Trustees, Second Baptist Church; Secretary/Treasurer, Board of Trustees, Texas Medical Foundation and Board member, Carver Cultural Center.

Bryant's untimely death in 1999 in an auto accident was a tragic loss for his family and the community. Gloria, his wife of more than four decades, said of him: "Frank was very dedicated to St. Philip's Junior College. He said that each of the instructors gave their very best, their utmost to the students." Bryant, influential across Bexar County and beyond, is a shining example of the leadership demonstrated by many of St. Philip's graduates.

In 2000, the Alamo Community College District Foundation established a nursing scholarship at St. Philip's in Bryant's honor. A colleague on the Foundation Board and in the medical profession, Dr. Ralph Wells, approached the Nix Health Care Foundation and suggested that the foundation pledge the first contribution to the scholarship. Gloria Bryant served on the ACCD Foundation Board as well.[11]

Ralph Wells, MD

Ralph Wells, specialist in gastroenterology, retired from active military duty in 1976 and joined San Antonio Medical Associates, a multispecialty, internal medicine group from which he retired a second time in 2008. He became interested in several Brackenridge High School students he met who were sitting on the bank of the San Antonio River, using the street lights to study. While speaking with them, he learned that they were there because they had discovered that the river bank was quiet and well lit, making it an ideal place to study. Through further conversation with the students, Wells learned that they had no place to study at home. Wishing to help in some way, he set up a scholarship fund for students from Brackenridge to attend the Alamo community college of their choice. Initially his idea was to raise funds privately; however, the fund was taken over by the King William Neighborhood Association and subsequently managed by the ACCD, who set up a tax structure and provided secure monitoring.

The idea of using the funds to provide a simulation laboratory arose out of a conversation that Wells had with Rev. Claude Black, who suggested that Bryant's contribution to San Antonio and to the Eastside should be honored. As their conversation continued, because of Bryant's strong ties to St. Philip's and to the Eastside of San Antonio, they targeted St. Philip's as a possible site for the laboratory. The Medical Education Technologies Incorporated (METI) first mannequin was purchased for the laboratory through the scholarship funds started by Wells.[12]

Joyce Turner-Ferrier, Coordinator, Patient Simulation Laboratory

Turner-Ferrier, who came to St. Philip's in January 2004, was, at the time of the interview, coordinator for patient simulation in the division of health sciences. A registered nurse, Turner-Ferrier trained with METI, one of the largest simulation manufacturers in the country. Named the Dr. Frank Bryant Jr. Memorial Patient Simulation Center at St. Philip's College, the simulation laboratory provides a state-of-the-art teaching environment that features customized and hands-on training in various aspects of health care. City Public Service generously contributed to the purchase of St. Philip's human patient simulator, which is a computer-controlled, programmable, life-size mannequin capable of exhibiting physiological symptoms and reacting to medicines and interventions like an actual person.

Turner-Ferrier, who was involved with the coordination and planning for the simulation center from its inception, met with the architects and planners in the early stages of the project. In her role as coordinator, Turner-Ferrier enthusiastically conducted tours for visitors to the center because, she said, "I feel very, very blessed to be able to say to the community, 'This is what you paid for, and because of you, this is what we have available for the students.'"

Offering courses from introductory to advanced refresher training programs, St. Philip's boasts of having the only patient simulator in the area available to train health care professionals and institutions in the various aspects of health care. Because realistic life-threatening situations can be simulated, students can engage in the practice of medicine without endangering the lives of patients, can gain experience in a risk-free environment, and can avoid costly mistakes.

When the matching funds committed by St. Philip's are added to the City Public Service investment, the training center alone is valued at more than a half million dollars. The center features mannequins by METI and Medical Plastics Laboratories Inc. (MPL) that simulate, look, and respond as human patients, but are controlled by computers. These life-sized mannequins can be programmed to exhibit real-life situations showing physiological symptoms of illnesses, reacting and responding as virtual humans. The center, with its state-of-the-art patient simulator, is unique in its customized, hands-on training and patient simulation technology.[13]

Theodore R. Williams, Instructor, Professor, Department Chair, and President, St. Philip's College

Williams was in the very first graduating class from Texas Southern in 1948, and continued his education at that institution, earning a master's degree in 1954. He completed further study at the University of Iowa, where, in 1956, he earned his doctorate. Williams did not attend St. Philip's as a student, but says that he worked at St. Philip's across six decades, from the 1950s to the 2000s.[14]

Williams began work at the post office in 1951 as a clerk, and worked there until he was hired at St. Philip's as an instructor in biology and math. "At the time, working at the post office was considered one of the best jobs because postal workers' salaries were more than teachers." When Williams began at St. Philip's, he was the only instructor in biology. Bowden retired from St. Philip's the year that Williams was hired by the college and he remembered that the first formal program that he attended at St. Philip's was for Miss Bowden in celebration of her fifty-two years of service. That was in November 1954.

After three years as an instructor, Williams was made an assistant professor. He served for four years as an assistant professor before being promoted to associate professor. Fourteen years passed and he was promoted to full professor, serving under Dr. Norris's leadership. "I actually made full professor the year that Dr. Norris stepped down from the deanship of the college," said Williams.

"Miss Bowden's home on Dakota, just East of Mittman Street in the 1600 block, was sold or given to the college and I believe that a part of the Norris Technical Building is located in the area where she lived." As she did with many of her students and faculty, Bowden encouraged Williams to continue his education, interceding with the Brackenridge Foundation to get a loan for him to start the PhD program at the University of Iowa. In 1956, Roland Martin, director of music, and Williams both began study for their doctorates at the University of Iowa.

One of the incentives that enticed Williams to come to St. Philip's was the new laboratory in the Bowden Building, which was new at the time. Bowden's office was on the first floor of the building. She was, Williams recalled, "just getting a little bit on the feeble side, but still, she would walk over to the campus from where she lived, which was about a block or a block and a half from the Bowden Building." Williams, who walked Miss Bowden home on many occasions, said that she always had a concern for where the college was, where the college had been, and where the college was going. He was impressed with the fact that she was acutely aware of all of those things, and yet could still see the progress being made.

When Williams arrived at St. Philip's, the Johnston Building was a three-story building with a section for administration, another section for classrooms, and another housing the girls' dormitory. That building was leveled in the fall of 1954. There were a number of army barrack- type buildings that housed the technical and vocational programs. Some of the stories that Williams related were told to him when he came to the college and concerned the years before St. Philip's was a part of the Union Junior College District. The stories referred to Miss Bowden as literally the savior of St. Philip's College and related that she actually stood on the street corners with a hat, collecting money that was used to keep St. Philip's open.

In reality, because Bowden was able to anticipate the benefits of becoming a part of the San Antonio Independent School District (and subsequently the Union Junior College) and because she could anticipate the support that the association with them would produce, she initiated the association with those institutions. Coming under the school district and becoming a part of the Union Junior College (as would later occur) negated the necessity to utilize measures such as traveling to northern cities accompanied by student musicians and speaking at fund-raising venues that she used prior to the merger to collect monies. Bowden was well aware that had St. Philip's remained as a part of the Episcopal Church only, it would have closed, and it is possible that she saw the merger as, if not the only way to keep the school open, then surely the best way.

Early in William's career at St. Philip's, the library moved from the Bishop Johnston Memorial Building to the second floor of the Bowden Administration Hall. While the site of the first library is unknown, the first librarian was Katherine Green (Durvan), beginning in1927.We thank Patricia Williams, who had a forty-year career at St. Philip's, much of it working in the library, for researching the information about the early history of the library, some of which she experienced.

The History of the Library at St. Philip's College

A letter of appeal, dated March 14, 1929, sent "To Whom it may Concern" from C. M. Chambers, mayor of San Antonio, solicited the library "Needs" and listed, among other things, 800 reference volumes for the library. Donations were to be made payable to St. Philip's Junior College and were to be sent to Ned McIlhenny, Frost National Bank, San Antonio, or to Miss A. Bowden, President, St. Philip's Junior College, San Antonio, Texas. By 1932–1933, the school had opened a library at 2120 Dakota Street with a collection of approximately twenty-five hundred volumes, thirty periodicals, and had a seating capacity of sixteen. The library was open daily from 8:00 a.m. to 9:00 p.m. and from 8:00 a.m. to 12 noon on Saturdays. St. Philip's 1934–35 catalogue records the library as located in the North Unit of the Johnston Memorial Building.

A May 17, 1936 publication entitled, "Facts You Should Know about St. Philip's Junior College and Vocational Institute, San Antonio, Texas," listed St. Philip's Library as having a collection of 5,500 volumes, of which 3,500 were accessioned, thirty-one were current magazines, two were daily newspapers, and four were Negro weekly newspapers in the Reading Room. Number twenty-two on the school's "want" list was the "immediate need for additional books for the library." Initially, use of the library was not free for high school students (day students), who paid $2.00 yearly for library fees. Day college students paid $3.00 yearly.

In September 1954, the library moved from the Bishop Johnston Memorial Building to the second floor of the Bowden Administration Hall, where it remained until August 1977. In August 1977, the library moved from the second floor of the Bowden Administration Hall to the third floor of the G. J. Sutton Learning Resource Center.

By 1995, St. Philip's library had organized an archives department to collect and maintain artifacts related to the history of the college. Mark G. Barnes Sr. was selected as the first Historical Services Coordinator of the archives department and served as coordinator until his retirement. Following Barnes's retirement, Patricia Wright Williams served as interim coordinator until August 2011, when she also retired. In 2010, Rebecca Barnard became the second coordinator of archives.

As a part of the bond issue of 2005, a new Learning Resource Center building was provided. In April 2009, the ribbon was cut, officially allowing entry into the ultramodern, three-story Learning Resource Center and on May 8, 2009, the new Learning Resource Center officially opened its doors to the students, faculty, public, and community. In 2009, library services were placed under the Division of Interdisciplinary Programs, with Dr. Karen Sides as the director.

Ola Robinson, Media Services/Library and Learning Resource Specialist

Ola Robinson, a classified audio-visual department employee, honed her skills in the library, where she began in 1977 as a student assistant. A versatile employee known for her work ethic, Robinson is skilled in many areas, having cross-trained in multiple positions during her thirty-five years at the college. Among the positions she held was secretary to the library coordinator and dean, work-study supervisor, responsible for pickup and delivery of equipment, videotaping, photography, and was assigned duties in circulation, reference, and purchasing.

Despite full-time employment while raising a family, Robinson continued with her education, earning certification as a Health Unit Coordinator from St. Philip's, an associate's of arts degree, also from St. Philip's, and a bachelor of arts in interdisciplinary studies/early childhood education from the University of Texas at San Antonio.

An interview with Georgene Bias offers insight into the growth of the library up through the later portion of the twentieth century.

Georgene Bias, SPC librarian

Georgene Bias, PhD, St. Philip's Librarian, 1959–1986

In 1959, when Dean Watson noticed library science credits on Georgene Bias' transcript from Prairie View College, he offered her Julia Taylor's position in the evening shift in the library. Taylor became ill and did not return to her position. At that time, books and about 300 periodicals for circulation were located on the second floor of the administration building. As the number of books and periodicals increased, the library outgrew its allotted space. The solution was to open a satellite library at Kelly Field. This proved to be a temporary solution as enrollment continued to increase, and the problems associated with insufficient space increased. To handle this, books were stored in boxes in a small room across the hallway from the library. Dr. Weynand, at that time president of SAC and St. Philip's, paid a visit to St. Philip's, and Bias invited him to accompany her across the hallway where she showed him the room with all the books stacked in boxes. She explained that this was because of space limitations. "That's when he put in for the new library," said Bias.

Bias, who worked in the field of education for twenty-seven years at St. Philip's, dedicated her life to the profession. In 1982, Dr. Bias received a doctorate degree in education from Nova University, Fort Lauderdale, Florida. She retired from St. Philip's with the rank of professor emeritus of the Learning Resource Center at St. Philip's.[15]

15 Learning to Adjust: Students and Faculty from the 1960s

The stories that follow tell of St. Philip's faculty from the 1960s. "The teachers were committed to excellence. It wasn't something that someone demanded of them; it was a history and heritage of excellence and a privilege and a pleasure and honor to serve," explained Olga Davis. The faculty was dedicated. The students felt as if, in turn, they could give nothing less. [1]

Olga Samples Davis, Student in the 1960s

Davis, who grew up in San Antonio, was introduced to St. Philip's as a child. Her mother, a member of St. Philip's faculty, played a starring role in some of the plays presented at the college. Davis attended Hampton Institute "right out of high school," but after Martin Luther King was shot, she received a mandate to come home. She then spent time at St. Philip's enrolling "in as many courses as I could before transferring to St. Mary's University" (in San Antonio).

Well known in the San Antonio and St. Philip's community for her writings, her poetry, and her plays, Davis is described by her fans as a bundle of talent. The community and faculty at St. Philip's enjoyed many performance of her plays performed in the campus theatre. Davis spoke of St. Philip's with great reverence, for she said, "St. Philip's was always in our community; always a jewel before anyone declared it such; always a jewel for us."

In her youth, Davis was a regular visitor to the St. Philip's campus because her mother, Browning Samples, taught at St. Philip's. Davis and her siblings were their "mothers' little cheerleaders, always on the front row." J. B. Williams was theatrical director at the time and Davis, seeing her mother on stage, became fascinated with theatre. "It was just such a wonderful experience," she said.

Davis spent thirty-one years in education and had this to say about it: "I had said that I would never in my lifetime be a teacher because it seemed that you worked all the time, thought about teaching all the time and it was endless. I wanted to have a job where things sometimes ended." But when her mother became ill, Davis thought that she would stay in San Antonio for a year. Thirty-one years later, she found herself still enjoying her time there and still not knowing what happened. At St. Philip's, she found a faculty committed to excellence and she

Olga Samples Davis

embraced them. "Faculty," she said, "felt it a privilege and an honor to serve.

"It was mesmerizing and captivating seeing that fire lit, that divine spark in a student," said Davis. "When it happened, it was over. You wanted more of it, you might try to run away from it, but it was something so glorious that you found a different level of goodness in yourself."[2]

Johnetta Slaughter, Professor Emeritus, Social Sciences

Slaughter, who began her career as an adjunct instructor at St. Philip's, rose to the rank of professor. She grew up in Texas, earned a bachelor's and a master's degree from Howard University in Washington, DC, and taught in the public schools in San Antonio before coming to St. Philip's. She said of the time: "I stayed at St. Philip's for twenty-three years and I've never regretted the change from the public schools." Slaughter served as chair of the department in social studies, and was teaching at St. Philip's when the veterans started coming. "That was in the fifties, and because of the vets, the school really began to grow. This was both exciting and stimulating."

When Slaughter moved to San Antonio, teaching jobs were difficult to find even with a master's degree, for segregation was the norm. Jobs available for black people were limited, for the city had just one high school and two middle schools, at the time called junior high schools. Slaughter's first teaching job at St. Philip's was as a part-time instructor in history. She recounted that in the late 1970s, the requirements had changed and students were no longer required to take history, government, and sociology. The administration in the vocational-technical areas felt that there was no need for their students to take social science courses since their students' focus was on finding jobs. Some faculty did not see the need for students to take anything other than whatever their particular technical-vocational trade was. This meant that the social sciences department began to experience great uncertainty in terms of enrollment.

During this time, Slaughter recalled, by accident, she attended a conference that another chairperson was supposed to have attended. It ended up being more than a stroke of luck for the conference was sponsored by the National Endowment for the Humanities. Slaughter was so inspired by what she learned at the conference that she brought the ideas back to her department at St. Philip's and her department developed courses that bridged the gap between vocational and academic students and gave both groups a common experience. Although the vocational students needed to learn the technical skills necessary for their trade, they were also going to have to interact with people. A humanities course would assist them in getting along with other people and help them to understand other cultures.

Slaughter's department wrote a grant and received funding from the National Endowment for the Humanities to develop a program that included a multicultural fair. The fair stimulated great interest in the humanities, "but people were very conscious of their territory and we met a lot of resistance," said Slaughter.

Marye Gilford offered to help because she felt that the students in her department needed the kind of experiences being offered by Slaughter and her department and that gave them, as she put it, "a crack in the door." "We weren't successful overnight," said Slaughter, "But because we were eventually successful with that, we developed another course based on Texas history called 'A Sense of Place. ' That course reflected the diversity of Texas's history. We expanded the department to include urban studies, world civilization and geography and later expanded the courses to include the behavioral sciences. We became very busy; there was never a dull moment." Slaughter's leadership included serving as president of the faculty senate, chair of the college's Black Heritage Committee, serving as a member of the Bexar County Historical Commission, Eastside Boys and Girls Club Advisory, the San Antonio Commission on Literacy, and the San Antonio branch of the NAACP.

Because the requirements for teaching in the vocational and academic areas were different, an issue developed between some of the academic faculty and the vocational faculty. Some in the academic department felt that they had to have degrees and take additional studies in order to get promoted, while persons in the vocational technical areas could teach without having earned a degree. The issue was that some who did not have degrees were promoted to assistant professor and that was resented by those who had degrees. There may have been the feeling among some of the day faculty that they were well-versed in their discipline, while a part- time instructor might work at another profession during the day and was not necessarily a teacher, except in the evenings. This caused resentment on the part of some faculty.

"Day faculty could not cover both day and evening," said Slaughter, "and St. Philip's could not operate simply because people didn't like who was teaching in the evening. The college was going through growing pains and adjusting to the new realities of what would be expected and what would be required."

Slaughter, who became full-time faculty at St. Philip's in the 1970s, retired in 2002. In recognition of her many years of tireless service to her community and her students, Slaughter was honored in 1990 as "Teacher of the Year" by the Alamo Community College District. She was recognized by the Texas Legislature as an "Unsung Hero" because her life was seen as proof that "one woman can make a difference through her tireless dedication to her fellow Texans." Mrs. Slaughter passed away on August 30, 2006. [3] Her fellow sociology instructor, Dr. Paul Renger, a longtime friend, said, "She always made me feel so welcome. She will be missed."

George Clark, Instructor, San Antonio's First Black Master Plumber, 1960s

Clark, a native of San Antonio, is a member of the O'Neil family. He makes a boast about his family that few African Americans can match since he can trace his family history back to the eighteenth century. Clark attended Brackenridge Elementary School, finished Douglas High School, and graduated from Tuskegee University. At Tuskegee, he studied plumbing with the intention of coming to San Antonio and opening a business, and in 1941, he realized his dream and opened his own plumbing business.

While training at Tuskegee, Clark met Dr. George Washington Carver and often shared meals with him. Clark met Miss Bowden in the 1930s, came to know her well, and spent many evenings sitting on her porch, discussing with her the future of St. Philip's. On several of these occasions, they were joined by Bowden's brother Henry when he came from Atlanta to San Antonio for a visit. Clark taught the first course in plumbing offered at St. Philip's.

"I'd always heard the name Miss Bowden, and St. Philip's School, and in fact, that was all you heard back there in those days. They would have social affairs over there and sometimes Miss Bowden would invite me over to entertain the girls. I came in contact with her often after I started the business because I would go there and do the plumbing."

In the evening, when Bowden and Clark sat on the porch of her two-story home, they sometimes talked for two or three hours at a time, discussing the future of St. Philip's. Clark thinks that she may well have been in her sixties or seventies at the time. "She was wondering what was going to happen to St. Philip's after she expired. She didn't know where it was going, but I had a vision for a vocational educational school and eventually they did offer vocational studies. As time passed, they also founded a vocational school at Kelly Air Force Base."

Clark said that he organized the first plumbing classes at St. Philip's, which he taught at night for fifteen years while working in the industry during the day. Some of his students followed the trade and are doing quite well. "Some of them followed the trade while some of them wanted to learn the trade just to go out and add to the bootlegging crew. You know how that goes!" Around 1960, Clark and Leonidas Watson, from the evening division of St. Philip's, along with Fogarty and Caldwell, two businessmen from the community, went to Austin to visit the State Plumbing Board to garner support for offering courses in plumbing. While Dr. Nail and Dr. Moody were concerned that there might be difficulties with the plumbing union, the State Plumbing Board was encouraging. As it happened, their concerns were unfounded and Clark was able to begin teaching classes in plumbing at St. Philip's without difficulty.

"We used to have classes under the trees sometimes and that's the truth. When the weather got bad, they moved us into that long building that they had down the side of the campus there. That's how we got started." During that time, St. Philip's also offered vocational classes in auto mechanics, upholstery, and welding. After Clark started the plumbing business, he would go downtown to San Antonio Machine and Supply Company on the corner of Center and Cherry Streets to buy the supplies Bowden needed for the school, because according to Clark, the owner was generous in his support of the school.

Clark said that when he started his plumbing business, "people used to ask me if I knew what I was doing. I'd say; 'Yes, I know what I'm doing. I'm training my competitor, that's what I'm doing.'"[4]

Mrs. Ivory Lee, Cafeteria Manager, 1960s

In 1967, when Ivory Lee came to work at St. Philip's in food service, her aunt was supervisor of the cafeteria department. Her aunt was also the mother of Hamice James, president of St. Philip's in the 1990s. When the cafeteria manager, Stella Hawkins, had to be hospitalized from a fall that resulted in broken ribs, her aunt was promoted to manager. Lee, unemployed at the time, came to work in the cafeteria for three weeks while Hawkins recuperated and was happy to work until Hawkins returned. Each time that she decided to leave, her aunt convinced her not to, so she stayed and stayed until finally twenty-five years had passed. Lee eventually became manager.

When Lee's aunt left the manager's position and Lee became manager, she worked under St. Philip's supervision for about two months until the Handy Andy company bid on the contract to manage the cafeteria. When Handy Andy's bid was accepted, Lee managed the cafeteria under Handy Andy's supervision for the next twelve years. There were numerous other companies who handled the food contract that she worked under, recalls Lee, naming ARA Food Service, Charter Food Service, Fast and Good Service, and Marriott. "There were at least six different food services, some I can't recall," she said.

Opening the cafeteria on time was important to Lee, who had to do the work of the other employees when they did not show up in the mornings. That could include preparing the food, readying the cafeteria for opening, and waiting on the customers. Nonetheless, it was "a happy time, working in the cafeteria," said Lee. An early riser, Lee preferred getting up early and she really liked working in the cafeteria. She enjoyed talking to and serving people, something she did for so long that it became a part of her and that made her happy. In the early days, the employees made the food "from scratch." From scratch meant that everything was prepared on the premises; nothing was brought pre-prepared. Lee had this to say:

"When Hawkins was manager, she would always bake a peach cobbler. Everybody wanted her peach cobbler. That was one happy time. Even the students were nice to me! I used to make biscuits every morning. Scratch biscuits. Wasn't no canned biscuits. Scratch! We did a lot of cooking from scratch. Twelve or thirteen years ago, even the chicken fried steak was made from scratch. We had to batter and fry all of that. Greens, pork bones, we cooked all of that.

"Katherine Morgan, from the music department, would say, 'give me some bones.' She loved those bones. She was nice, always with a smile. I've helped a lot of these kids, and I call all of them my children. They would say to me, 'I don't have a dime, can you let me have it [the food]?' I'd say, 'yes, bring me my money tomorrow though,' and they would. A lot of them called me Mama, Grandma, or Mom."

Ivory Lee

Lee referred to the students as "good, but devilish." Every morning in the cafeteria, they would put around thirty chili dogs on the cafeteria line, she recalled. The students would have a long line coming through the cafeteria and they would pass everyone either a hot dog or a donut and "then they'd get out of line and leave! But, that was all a part of being young," said Lee. Every now and then, Lee would see one or two of the students in the community and she remarked that they all seemed to be doing well. "I haven't seen one yet that's been in trouble; there might be some out there, but I haven't seen one. They're out doing great things for themselves."

The science building, which is now on the far end of the street, had not yet been built. The Norris building was built about three or four years after Lee arrived. "Tailoring, automotives, shop, electrical, all of that stuff, they offered it here. You could come to the Eastside to St. Philip's to get anything that you wanted done. But they moved it out west, south, and northwest and so we have limited things that you can get here now. Automotive is the only thing that's left."

At age seventy-eight, Lee was still working in the cafeteria, but because of the increase in paperwork and the strenuous nature of the physical work, she no longer wanted to manage the cafeteria. She did, however, consent to continue working the cash register and closing at night, much like her duties when she first began. Lee spent thirty-eight years employed at St. Philip's and she made this concluding statement: "St. Philip's has really grown and in my book, it's number one and always will be. I met a lot of wonderful people at St. Philip's and I had some wonderful times." Lee said, perhaps jokingly, perhaps not, "I should have been president. St. Philip's is my family. A lot of people ask me, why don't you retire? And I say, retire, for what? No, I'll just stay here until I feel like leaving." And she did. Lee retired in 2005 and in November of that year, she passed away. [5]

John Coleman, Art Student, 1960s

Though the art department was in its infancy in the 1960s, even then its mission was to train students to become masters of their craft. John Coleman, a student in the 1960s, was born in Saluda, South Carolina. He came to San Antonio with the US Army. Following a tour of military duty in Vietnam, he was discharged and decided to settle in San Antonio. In 1969, he enrolled at St. Philip's College and attended night school under Dr. Watson, using the GI Bill to pay his tuition. Coleman began his study as a business major, until he met John Quincy Adams, an instructor at what was then called the S. W. Craft Center, in downtown San Antonio.

When Coleman first enrolled at the college, Katherine Morgan was over the fine arts department at St. Philip's and she told him that she was planning to start a class in the visual arts. She invited him to bring her sketches of his work and after looking over his artwork and recognizing his talent, Morgan encouraged him to pursue a career in art at St. Philip's. She noted at the time that St. Philip's did not have a location either for classes or for art students to work. She asked him if he would mind going to the S. W. Craft Center for classes. There he met Terry Puckett, who became one of his teachers at the Craft Center.

Attending classes at the S. W. Craft Center was a new experience that he described as "very artistic." There he had his first exposure to drawing with a live model, and with one who happened not to be African American. Other new experiences included field trips to the San Antonio Missions and an opportunity to meet a Chilean sculptor, Guzman, an instructor at the Craft Center, who encouraged Coleman to try his hand at sculpting. Coleman found sculpting interesting but was more influenced by Robert Blake, an African American artist who painted African American subjects. At that time, Coleman, a self-taught wildlife artist, changed his subjects and tried his hand painting African Americans and their way of life, after his exposure to Blake's African American art, a subject with which he was very familiar.

Coleman, a retired civil servant, went on to win numerous awards. His paintings are prominently displayed in the homes of national celebrities and mentioned in at least three published books on arts. [6]

Solomon Wells, Student

Wells, an accomplished San Antonio artist, held in high esteem because of his art, is the sole interviewee who completed high school at St. Philip's. Born in Waelder, Texas, Wells was the youngest of nine children born to Rev. Solomon Wells Sr. and Annie Bilton Wells. Both his parents were deceased by the time he was ten years old; nonetheless, he was able to begin high school in Waelder, Texas, before moving to San Antonio in the mid-1940s. At that time, he had brothers and sisters living on the West Side of San Antonio with whom he lived for a short while. Soon after moving to San Antonio, Wells joined the military. After finishing his tour of military duty, he went back to high school, attended St. Philip's in the evening, and earned his GED. Wells enrolled at St. Philip's College, with a major in art, completed his art degree in 1958, and enrolled at the University of Texas in San Antonio. "I've had shows at the Witte Museum," said Wells. He also started Bob's Smoke House, a local restaurant, with his brother.

Wells, who had heard of St. Philip's before he came to San Antonio, had not heard of Miss Bowden, perhaps because she retired before he arrived. He knew Dr. Norris, who he described as a very fine man, and a very fine dean. "Dr. Norris would come by the classroom, talk to us, and give us ideas. He was a very well educated man, religious too. I remember one of my classmates, Shirley Gibson, and I went on to marry her."

Wells, whose memories of his days at St. Philip's remain strong, said he often thinks back to St. Philip's, and still remembers some of his instructors from the 1950s: Dr. Williams taught science, Professor Turbon taught psychology and American history, and Mr. Lee taught mathematics. Wells, who called himself "a super student," said that he always studied, always did his homework, and always worked very hard, spending four or five hours at a time in the museum.

In 2008, Wells entered the San Antonio Art League and Museum competition/exhibition and won first place for his oil painting, "The Cotton Picker." In February 2009, Wells entered the Veterans Arts and Crafts Show and Competition and won third place for an oil painting, "The Domino Players," and two ribbons for prints. His painting "LaCubi" won a flag and toured the United States. [7]

Dorothy McClinton, Professor Emeritus

McClinton, former chair of the business department, joined St. Philip's faculty in 1964, working under Dean Watson, and taught typing. At the time, Dr. Norris was the dean of the college and he told McClinton that teachers were needed in the business area. She went to see Dean Watson about a job and was hired on the spot. At the time, there were only two full-time faculty in the business department: Morris, chair of the department, and McClinton.

"When the business teacher resigned, the chair left word for them to put me in her position," said McClinton, who claimed not to have known what a chair was supposed to do. "But, I quickly found out," she said. The department continued to grow until, when she left, business was one of the largest departments. The business faculty at SPC decided that faculty in the business department at SAC could get almost anything they wanted before the department at St. Philip's was considered and since McClinton was friendly with the department chair at SAC, they would talk. McClinton would say, "Oh, you're getting so and so, well, let me check for St. Philip's." Because they had already gotten the items at SAC, McClinton would say, "'Well, since you already have so and so,' then shortly thereafter, St. Philip's would get the item. After SAC got what they wanted, they would willingly get the items for St. Philip's," she said. [8]

Don Coleman, Faculty, Vice President Emeritus of Student Affairs

Don Coleman came to St. Philip's in 1961 as chair of the mathematics department. Along the way, he taught math in the evening division, became registrar in 1967, and vice president of student affairs in 1982, succeeding Bill Hudgins. He retired in 1994 as vice president of student affairs, having served St. Philips for thirty-three years.

Coleman began his career at St. Philip's teaching part time in the evening division. The following information is from an interview held with Coleman in which he shared some of his earliest memories of working at St. Philip's. At the time of his hire, the college was preparing for a Southern Association meeting and they needed a math teacher. T. R. Williams and Roger Lee were teaching mathematics and Coleman, who was teaching part time in the evening division, then moved into the day faculty full time and as department chair. Enrollment numbered around 600 students at the time, and with the small enrollment, every spring there were rumors that the school would close.

Most of the students were from the cities of San Antonio, Gonzales, and Seguin. In the 1960s, when the veterans began arriving, there was a noticeable shift of the student body toward a more adult enrollment. Around the latter part of the 1970s, as the population shifted again, younger people began coming in larger numbers and the veteran population began to wane. This was the result of veterans benefits expiring.

Around 1970, the Norris Technical Center was built, and the college had an influx of Vietnam veterans who were taking advantage of the benefits offered by the government. Excitement was high as the enrollment went up to about 2,000 students.

During the 1950s and 1960s, when St. Philip's classes tended to be small, freshman level courses were always full, but by the time students were in sophomore level classes, enrollment would decrease, particularly in mathematics. Very few students actually completed their degrees and many transferred, particularly those in the evening division. Many attended for only one or two courses.

"Dr. Norris was from the old school," said Coleman, "and by that I mean, that he had certain things that he wanted the instructors to do. I guess he was typical of administrators for that period." Coleman described a culture in which the faculty was expected to sign in and out daily. T. R. Williams, who we met earlier as a member of the faculty, described a similar experience with signing in and out. He recalled an instance when, as he was leaving, he stopped to talk with the dean of the college. Because he failed to sign out, he received a written reprimand.

There were also expectations of how the faculty would dress and Coleman said that faculty met those expectations "right up to the 60s." As an example, the students couldn't wear T-shirts, the girls had to wear hose, women had to wear dresses or skirts, and the male faculty members had to wear ties. Around the late 1960s or 1970s, times began to change and, as times began to change, students and faculty members rebelled. Women began to wear pantsuits, and male students began wearing untucked T-shirts. Then, when students began wearing jeans and sneakers, the dress code completely changed. Faculty members were no longer required to wear ties. A lot of them still did, but there was no longer a written dress code.

Change began in other areas as well. Coleman, who held the post of registrar under Norris, along with his staff, used permanent record cards, keeping their records with pencil and paper. Then they migrated to punch cards. There was a period when electronic accounting machines were used, before the department moved to online terminals and computers. "They were called 'dumb terminals,'" said Coleman, "because all we could do was access the main frame, which was kept at the district location. We couldn't do programming on it and that's why they were called dumb terminals."

The registrar's office began using online registration, which was a tremendous help, and soon afterwards their department progressed to online transcripts. Before that, they posted grades by machine to a permanent record card. During the 1980s, because of the student unrest on social issues such as race, gay rights, and AIDS across the country, for security purposes, and for protection of the records, Coleman's department converted all student records to microfilm. Later, the office changed over to online record-keeping and transcripts and the process greatly improved. Then as telephone registration began, Coleman and his staff copied all of the records, back to year one, with duplicates, so that in addition to microfilm, there was also a hard permanent record card.

Change came when Dr. Murphy came on board. Besides his being less demanding of how faculty and staff dressed, there was a noticeable change in attitudes in the community and across the country, as far as dress was concerned. Before Dr. Murphy came to the campus as president, St. Philip's had no long-range plans, except during the time of the Southern Association Self Studies, said Coleman.

In the 1960s, the faculty was predominantly African American, with one or two Anglos. The school continued to have a small black student enrollment. In the 1990s, when the veterans and their children started enrolling, the population changed again and was about 50 percent Hispanic, with about 30 percent Anglo, and about 20 percent black. Coleman retired in 1995, having faithfully served the college for nearly thirty-four years. [9]

The Texas Coordinating Board: THECB

In 1965, the Texas Legislature created the Coordinating Board (THECB) to provide leadership and coordination for the Texas Higher Education System. According to Lanier Byrd, prior to 1965, there were no rules governing community colleges. The policies and handbooks presently in use had not been written. "In fact," said Byrd, "THECB did not really put its hands on the community colleges until about that time and since we didn't have a policy within the district, we grew up with the rules. The rules meant that whatever the four-year schools were doing in their first two years, that's what community colleges could do in their first two years. Community colleges were called junior colleges at that time."

The first policy manual, *What's What*, was written in the late 1970s. There have only been two policy manuals. Byrd credits himself, along with Linda Griffin, from the THECB, with the idea that "anatomy and physiology has three semesters that students could get credit for, that, but didn't see the need. I'm glad I did because now as we're involved in so many complex Allied Health areas, you see the need is there. You see the different types and forms of anatomy and physiology that is available to students."

By the late 1960s, Hudgins, who came to SPC under Miss Bowden, was now ready to hand over coaching to someone younger. He hired Elwood Overton Plummer to be the second men's basketball coach at St. Philip's College. Coach Plummer came to the college experienced in basketball, having played the game throughout his high school and college career. Born in San Antonio, Plummer graduated from Phyllis Wheatley High School, where he played on the varsity team and led Wheatley to become an all-district basketball team. Plummer enrolled in SAC in 1962 on a basketball scholarship earned at Wheatley, made all-conference for two years, and graduated in 1964. Following graduation from SAC, Plummer attended Jackson State College in Mississippi for two years, also on a basketball scholarship, lettering both years. While a member of the Jackson State team, his team was nicknamed the "Super Seven," and he earned the title "Best Outside Shooter" in the South Western Athletic Conference.

In 1966, when Plummer graduated from Jackson State,

he spent one month coaching at his alma mater, Wheatley High School, before moving to St. Philip's to assume the newly vacated position of head coach for men's basketball. Coach Hudgins vacated the head coach position to become dean of students at St. Philip's. Plummer held the position of head coach for men's basketball from1966 to 1969 at SPC, while also teaching classes in physical education, health, and serving as head coach for men's track. In 1969, he was recruited and accepted the position of assistant basketball coach at Jackson State. [10]

When Coach Plummer left in 1970, Clyde Clack came on board as head basketball coach at St. Philip's. As his obituary read, Coach Clack was known affectionately by many names: "Coach Clack" to those who played for him, "CC" to his close friends and family, "Uncle CC" to his nieces and nephews, "Mr. Clack" to students from his principal and vice-principal days, and "Dad" to his two sons. [11] When Coach Clack passed away, some of his students and colleagues from more than forty years earlier came from Lynchburg, Virginia, to bid him a fond farewell. In January 1972, Kenneth Pulliams was hired by Dean of Student Affairs Hudgins to replace Clyde Clack, who transferred to Sam Houston High School as head basketball coach.

Dr. Norris was dean (president) of St. Philip's College at the time and when he retired at the end of Pulliams's first year, Dr. John Murphy came on board. "I was most appreciative that Mr. Hudgins selected me, for he had taught me swimming during the summer in the swimming pool at St. Philip's," said Pulliams. Coach Pulliams followed Coach Clack as the fourth coach for men's basketball at St. Philip's.

Coach Pulliams grew up on the Eastside, attended schools in the SAISD, and graduated from Brackenridge High School and Prairie View. He received a BS degree in health, physical education, and biology from Prairie View A&M University, with a certification in all levels in science, health, physical education, recreation, and dance. Pulliams earned an MS degree in education, with certification in counseling and guidance and health.

One of Pulliams's duties as coach was to attend an annual coaches meeting where he said, "We would review, discuss the library and decide where there were changes, and recommendations. That committee would report back to the college. Many times the college president would go with the coach and when he couldn't go, usually, he would send Mr. Hudgins, so it was Dean Hudgins and myself for fifteen years, traveling to the various colleges, to discuss, schedule, vote, and return to our respective campuses and report the findings to our college president."[12]

Patricia Wright Williams

Patricia Wright Williams, from Austin, Texas, came to St. Philip's in 1969 as a student, right out of high school. She received a scholarship to St. Philip's, lived with a relative the first year, and then rented a room across from the campus, living in one of the houses on the college's approved list. Williams, who majored in business administration, graduated in 1974.

Dr. Norris, who helped Williams to find employment as a work study student for himself, Darrington White, and Dr. Jeanine Foster, also helped her to find employment at the college following her graduation. Since the dean of the college, who was serving as president, did not have a secretary, both Williams and Betty Johnson worked for him and wherever else they were needed: sometimes in the president's office, sometimes in the registrar's office, and oftentimes in the library. There was a family atmosphere on campus and since the student body was small, the faculty was well-acquainted with each student and his or her circumstances.

As an example, on more than one occasion, when Williams's financial aid allotment arrived late, her business

Patricia Wright Williams

instructor, Armond Hathaway, learned of it and paid her tuition, ensuring that she would remain in school. Not only work-study students worked in multiple locations, but faculty also. Around that time, Georgene Bias, who later became librarian, worked as dean of women. Frank Madla, who became a member of the Texas legislature and served as a state senator, was an instructor. Julia Taylor, the librarian, taught Williams and Johnson that everything had to be in order before they could leave for the day. "The library is just like your home," she said. "You must tidy up before leaving at the end of each day, and when you come in you are ready to begin another day."

Johnson and Williams preserved many artifacts that later became the first contributions to the archives, saving programs, clippings, and photographs of activities around the campus, before there was an archives. When archives began, they donated these items to the history of the college. In 1978–1979, Pearl Conyers and Williams planned a series of "Fun Raisers, which was the beginning of Spirit Week." With the intent of fund-raising, there was a kissing booth, a fashion show, door contests with trophies for the winner, a talent show (held during Black History Month), a basketball game, and a dance featuring a live band. The "fun raisers" were also the precursor of the campus Fiesta. Williams was crowned Miss United Way in 1972, the first time St. Philip's had a contest for Miss United Way to raise scholarship funds. Williams was a member of the library staff before they were computerized, when books and materials were checked out manually. In August 2011, Williams retired, having served St. Philip's for forty years. [13]

TAPE—Texas Award for Performance Excellence

2010 Engagement Award

A Green Tie Affair, Spring 2011

Phi Theta Kappa Veterans Memorial ceremony, Fall 2011

Historical marker

AT&T award

Center for Learning Resources (CLR), 2009

Center for Health Professions (CHP)

Welcome Center, 2009

Culinary Arts Gala

Green Engineering

Asian Poetry Competition

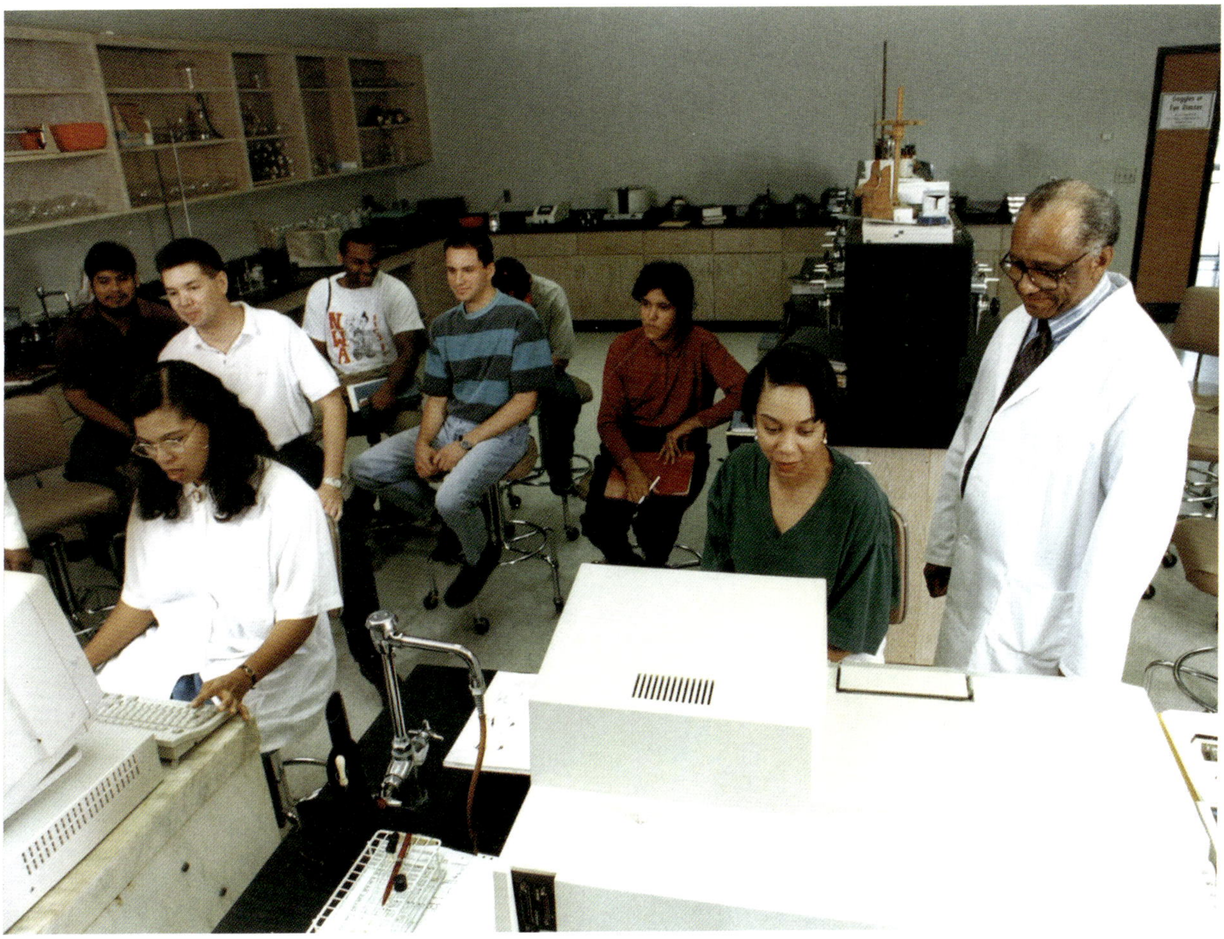

Classroom scene

2012 Master Teachers

Skills USA

SPC Library Grand Reopening, Spring 2011

16 The Evening Division

By the 1960s, the evening division, under Leonidas Watson, had become a very important component of the school. During Norris's tenure as dean, evening classes were especially welcomed because of their convenience for workers pursuing vocational or preprofessional training. Many instructors began in the evening division of the college before moving into the day section; however, other instructors elected to remain in the evening division of the college throughout their career.

Leonidas Watson: The Evening Division

For many students, the college experience consisted of working during the day and attending college in the evening. In fact, the St. Philip's College bulletin for 1944–1945 described an evening school division of the college "organized to provide educational opportunities for Negro youth and adults unable to attend school during the day." *The Tiger* newspaper mentions an evening division of St. Philip's College as having come into existence in 1946, shortly after the merger of San Antonio and St. Philip's Colleges into the San Antonio Union Junior College District. There is an even earlier mention of an evening school established in 1928, with an enrollment of five students; however, it was not until Leonidas Watson began as evening school dean that the division expanded. Norris also mentioned a summer school operation in 1929; however, these sessions were limited to teachers who needed to renew their teaching certificates or to complete additional college work.

Dean Leonidas Watson

Watson, who came to St. Philip's in 1954 as director of the evening division, led the division to its highest enrollment peak in the history of the school to that point. Certain factors influenced the growth in student population: World War II, the 1954 Supreme Court decision outlawing segregation, the expansion of the technical and vocational areas of the curriculum, and (according to Watson) the increased number of adults and war babies who came to St. Philip's to upgrade their skills so that they could qualify for promotions and better jobs. So influential was this growth that by the 1970s, the catalog listing of courses offered had grown to more than two hundred.

Watson spent more than twenty-seven years in service to the college as director of the evening division and as associate dean of the college. When he retired in February

Leonidas Watson

1981, St. Philip's named the Fine Arts Center in his honor for his years of service to the college. The district board of trustees conferred on Watson the title of Associate Dean Emeritus of St. Philip's College. A dedication service for the Watson Fine Arts Center was held in May 1981 with the late Dr. Prenza Woods, former minister of St. Paul United Methodist Church, as the keynote speaker.

Clarence Hill, Mathematics, Adjunct Faculty

When Clarence Hill came to St. Philip's, most of the buildings currently on the campus had not been built and according to him, the campus was small, housing only the Bowden Building and the gym. Hill recalled that "there might have been a few shops down there; but, all of the offices were in the Bowden Building. Dr. Murphy's office was there, Mr. Watson's office was there, and the Registrar's office was there." Hill began as a part-time instructor in 1968, and continued as adjunct faculty until he retired. Though recruited by Watson and offered a position in the day faculty, Hill did not accept, electing to continue with the evening faculty. "Many of us got started over here at St. Philip's through Mr. Watson," said Hill. "There was a shortage in evening instructors at the time. I don't know why I never took him up on becoming a full-time staff member."

The evening school culture differed from the day school in that the student body in the evening was a little older and somewhat more mature. Many of the evening school students worked during the day, attending school in the evening. Faculty in the evening division was limited to teaching two or three classes. One semester, Dean Watson said to Hill, "'Brother Hill, you've got to take another class.' 'I can't, Brother Watson, because you said that we can't,' replied Hill. 'Well, Brother Hill,' Watson laughed, 'I know what I said, but I also know that I can get a waiver for you.'"

Hill described the faculty as "almost like working in a high school." Teachers were required to take classroom attendance and Watson required that that attendance be turned in each evening, before the faculty could leave the school. Watson wanted to know who was present, who was absent from the class, and where everyone was. Between 9:15 p.m. and 9:30 p.m., Watson sent a runner to check all of the classrooms to see who was present. If the room was unoccupied, the runner was to mark down that room number and turn it in to Watson.

Because some of the faculty had taught at four-year schools that had academic freedom, they expected the same at St. Philip's, but Dean Watson said, "I don't care. If you're supposed to be teaching a class from 6:45 to 9:45, I want the class there from 6:45 to 9:45."

"Faculty that dismissed their classes at 7:30 and 8:00 didn't last long at St. Philip's," said Hill. Patricia Wright-Williams, who at the time was a work-study student for Dean Watson, echoed that she also recalled being told by Watson to run over to a specific classroom and see who was there. She recalled that sometimes instructors might take their class to a nearby restaurant and sometimes they failed to return, but woe to that instructor if Watson learned that the classroom was unoccupied.[1]

Browning McKinney Samples, Faculty Coordinator, Higher Education Achievement Program (HEAP)

Browning McKinney Samples, a former student who later became a faculty member, also began her tenure at St. Philip's in the evening division before transferring to the day faculty. Hired by Watson, Samples asked him, "What am I going to do over there?" "You're going to teach," he said. "Teach what?" she asked. He replied, "You're going to teach reading. You'd be surprised at the people who really don't know how to read." Samples replied, "Well, if they don't know how to read, they didn't come from my school, because when I taught them, I taught them the basics."

In its infancy, hiring practices at St. Philip's were informal. Mr. Watson spoke with Mrs. Samples one day and he invited her to "Just come on over here with me." "That was one of the best things that could have happened to me, because I met a lot of good people at St. Philip's and that's why I still pray for St. Philip's; I think it's most important. I want us to always have St. Philip's College because it was bought and paid for by people who really, really, made sacrifices to do so, to pay for it. We've had good leadership at St. Philip's."

Samples went on to describe some of the faculty who taught her as well as some who worked alongside her. "Lois White was my English teacher and boy, she was one of the best. She was wonderful in the classroom and she felt basically the same way that I learned to, later on. I have something that you need and you came here, you're paying for it, so you're going to get it. And she meant for you to get it and you got it!"[2]

Encouragement was the order of the day. Samples

described Roger Lee as "a good soul, a very gracious soul. There were other persons around here who would stop and talk to you and pat you on the back: 'How're you doing? OK, keep it up.' That meant keep on doing what you're doing and you knew you were doing the right thing."

Roger Lee was one of the first people Samples met in her science class. His laboratory was small; "there wasn't a lot going on, but whatever it was he was telling us, he made it so real and we appreciated it so much that it sounded like, I guess, like a little heaven. And that was really kind of basically the feeling and the impression that you got in everything that went on. And it was a little heaven too, because we knew what was on the outside."[3]

Dr. Levi Jackson, Faculty

Dr. Jackson began his teaching career at St. Philip's right out of college, working in the evening division under Dr. Watson. After receiving his bachelor's degree, he was undecided about what he wanted to do, except that he had vowed he would not teach. Jackson went so far as to say that he'd rather transport garbage than teach. One day, he was outside cutting his front lawn when he received a call from Leonidas Watson, who said, "This guy just quit, do you want to teach?" At the time, Jackson was waiting to get drafted, so he thought, why not? The call that came in August of 1968 was the beginning of his career at St. Philip's College.[4]

Lillian Burley, Instructor, Physical Education

Burley, married to community activist Roy Burley, who grew up in the neighborhood, contacted Dean Watson in 1970 for a position teaching physical education in the evening division. For the first year, her classes were held in the Catholic Building on New Braunfels. The next year, she was given classes in the gymnasium on campus, and in her last year, her classes moved to the Norris Building, because "the Sutton building was under construction. It was right by my room. Burley taught a class in personal hygiene, another in community health, and a required course in health and physical education."

Watson was sometimes described as tough, but Burley described him as "actually a very nice person, a very understanding man. You know some people can act tough and he could be like that." Burley's class was composed largely of veterans who had worked all day and who would nap in their cars until 6:45 p.m., and then come to class. "Even though they were sleepy, there was no fooling around, unlike teaching the day students and others who didn't know why they were in college," said Burley. "The veterans were attentive and discipline problems were nonexistent, for they were almost always there because they wanted to get a better job or a promotion."

Burley explained that she had little opportunity to get to know the other night school faculty because her classroom was initially off campus and later located behind a building. "You know, if you're off campus or somewhere behind a building as I was, you don't run into other people. Unlike today, where faculty convocations are held for all faculty and staff, I just knew where I was assigned and I came and I went. I would go straight to the office, get my test papers run off or pick up what I needed and when I'd go finish doing those things, I would go immediately to my class. That's why I didn't have any associates or know too much about what was going on on campus."

As evening adjunct faculty, Burley taught under Dean Watson for three years, but was not involved in activities outside of the classroom. After three years in the evening division, Burley resigned and moved to another military assignment with her family.[5]

When Watson came in 1954 as Director of the Evening Division, he was said to run the evening division with an iron fist. Yet each person interviewed spoke of him with great respect and admiration.

Bidding Adieu to St. Philip's "Savior"

An event of great significance occurred in the 1960s that was a great loss to St. Philip's. On Monday, August 18, 1969, following a long illness, Miss Artemisia Bowden, Dean Emeritus of St. Philip's College, died at Lutheran General Hospital. Described as a distinguished educator, philanthropist, widely-acclaimed humanitarian, versatile lady of letters, and able and ardent advocate of the maximum cultivation of one's talents, Bowden dedicated more than fifty years of her life to service to St. Philip's and to the San Antonio community.

Funeral services for Miss Artemisia Bowden were held Friday morning, August 22, 1969, at St. Mark's Episcopal Church in San Antonio. All of San Antonio mourned the loss of this great educator, for her enduring strength and dedication to furthering the education of all people endeared her to the hearts of all who knew her. None would deny that because of Miss Bowden, St. Philip's College exists today. Among her many accomplishments was the establishment of the nursing program at St. Philip's College. Additionally, she was primarily responsible for introducing a black nursing unit at Robert B. Green Hospital in San Antonio. She secured Lindbergh Park for black residents and established the East End Settlement House and the State Training School for Delinquent Negro Girls at Brady (now Crockett State School). She was also founder and president of the Negro Business and Professional Women's Club. For her lifetime of service, Bowden received many honors: Bowden Elementary School, San Antonio, was named in her honor; she was cited by the National Council of Negro Women as one of the ten most outstanding woman educators in the country; she was named by Zeta Phi Beta Sorority as woman of the year (1955); and the Bowden Building, St. Philip's College, was named in her honor.[6] Miss Bowden is interred in Corpus Christi, Texas.

17 The Murphy Years, 1969–1984

WHEREAS, Dr. C. W. Norris, who has served as Dean of St. Philip's College for teaching, and it becomes necessary to employ another person as Dean of the College
and
WHEREAS, the administration, having heretofore been Instructed by the Board to recommend a qualified replacement, recommends that Dr. John B. Murphy, BS, MS, PhD, be employed as Dean of St. Philip's College, effective July 1, 1969.[1]

The Late 1960s and the Early 1970s

When the community college came into being, its role was to meet the educational and vocational needs of the local community. While St. Philip's began as a junior college, it was miles ahead of the community college movement, for even as it was called a junior college, its stated intention from its inception was to equip the students using a course of study that provides the information he or she needs to solve life's problems.[2]

John Murphy, who succeeded Clarence Norris Sr. as Dean and Chief Administrator of St. Philip's College, noted that he had made his mind up years before coming to St. Philip's that he wanted to go into community college work and that is the course of study that he followed at the University of Texas. Murphy had also prepared himself with educational experience prior to coming to St. Philip's, working as a junior high school teacher, vocational agriculture teacher, county agricultural agent, science teacher, college professor, serving as chair of a department at North Carolina A&I State University, and serving as Chairman of the Education Department and Director of Teacher Education and Certification at Prairie View A&M College. When the opportunity presented, he was ready to assume the position of president of the college.

Shortly after he arrived, it became clear that in the years to come, he would need all of the preparation that he had gotten, for he quickly learned that he had to manage the school under what could only be called benign neglect. A colleague, who later also served as president of St. Philip's, had this to say: "John Murphy, from my point of view, was a miracle worker. He got nothing; he received virtually no outside help." Nonetheless, Murphy held the top position at St. Philip's for thirteen years.

John Brown Murphy's Story: Coming to St. Philip's College

In 1968, the year before Murphy arrived at St. Philip's, enrollment numbered about 1,500 students. During his first year as president, it went up a little, to about 1,700; not a great deal, but enough for Murphy to know that he was indeed well-prepared and ready for the position. Under his leadership, health careers and the vocational technical programs expanded to meet the needs of the community. Enrollment rose continually, so that by the last year Murphy was president, enrollment was just under 8,000 students. Student enrollment was unusually large because the benefits for veterans of the Vietnam War were coming to a close.

In 1981, the government began cutting the special benefit programs for veterans and, to take advantage of the programs before the benefits ran out, in 1982 a large number of veterans enrolled in classes. After that year, there was a drop in enrollment and, in fact, the enrollment went down for the next two or three years, to around 6,000, a drop of about 25 percent.

John Brown Murphy, President, SPC

Helpful Measures

At the same time, the college experienced a considerable build-up in the vocational-technical programs (auto mechanics and other departments), and that helped to increase the enrollment during those years of enrollment decline. The programs with the largest veterans' enrollment continued to be in the vocational-technical areas.

Faculty Relations

Around this time, Murphy began to experience problems with the evening division of the school, which could only be associated with growth. As the evening programs continued to develop and expand, an ever-increasing number of teachers were required. The evening division supplied many of the faculty needed by the day division of the college and, as Murphy explained, this presented a problem. In 1969, shortly after he arrived at St. Philip's, Murphy learned that the college was actually operating as two separate colleges: a day division and an evening division. Some of the teachers who taught full-time during the day were given part-time employment in the evening division to supplement their salaries.

This presented a problem because some department heads were given the opportunity to work as both day and evening faculty and others were not. As could be imagined, faculty not offered the opportunity to make the extra money resented the slight. As unsatisfactory as this was, the situation continued until the president of the colleges retired. The dean of the evening division fully controlled hiring teachers and administering them as part-time teachers. The practice did not stop until the new president of the college came on board.

Over the years, changes of importance came about gradually. Murphy contended that it was hard to pinpoint changes that took place on the basis of time because things just happened. One particularly important change that occurred while Murphy was dean brought a halt to the practice of choosing new faculty on the basis of personal friendship. Instead, hiring was based on qualifications and experience, without regard to race. "That worked out satisfactorily for me," said Murphy. "I think, on the whole, that I got along very well with the faculty."

Makeup of the Faculty

The new hiring policy resulted in a faculty integrated with Hispanics and Anglo Americans. Previously, for well over fifty years, the faculty and the student body had been totally black. "That sort of broke the ice against the discriminatory practices that existed before," Murphy explained, and "our faculty in the health careers fields became highly integrated with Hispanics and Anglos." The first Hispanic faculty hired came during Peggy Peterson's chairmanship of the Health Careers Department. The number of Hispanic students increased rapidly but there continued to be very few white students, particularly in academics. The majority of the whites that came were training for careers in the vocational and technical health fields.

Despite the fact that the Supreme Court decision of 1954 struck down discrimination, the first Hispanic student to graduate from St. Philip's did not occur until 1969, the year that Murphy came. "We got a lopsided enrollment picture between the academic departments and the vocational and technical departments," said Murphy, who was actually describing a lopsided racial picture. He explained that the concentration of students in the vocational-technical fields was overwhelmingly Hispanic and white. "We just didn't have many black students in the vocational departments."

Dealing with Social Issues

In the late 1960s and early 1970s, during Murphy's tenure, across the country student protests were launched on a variety of issues. St. Philip's, however, escaped much of the controversy. Murphy, who considered the time a period of development and growth, was pleased with the progress that took place, though there were a few negative incidents, not necessarily racial.

One such incident occurred in his first year. Some of the male students insisted on wearing hats to class so Murphy spoke to Bill Hudgins about it, and had Hudgins put pressure on the students to stop. When the students rebelled at the pressure, Hudgins said, "John, you don't need to let this bother you, just let them alone. They will change when the time comes for them to change. As long as the teachers allow them to wear their hats in class, I'm not going to bring any more pressure on them." Nothing more was said to the students, and from then on, it became a nonissue. The few students who insisted on wearing their hats in class either dropped out or stopped wearing their hats in class.

Mary Pierson Mackey

Dress Codes: Faculty and Administrators

Murphy observed that during this era, teachers in colleges and universities everywhere were more casual in their attire, seldom wearing ties or jackets. This was accepted as just the way it was. Previously at St. Philip's, particularly during the beginning of Murphy's administration, administrators wore jackets, following a dress code of sorts with a kind of unspoken rule; the department chairman did not. "Some women wore pants, some did not, and some you would never have seen with pants on," said Murphy, confirming what Coleman had said earlier about the culture of the school regarding dress codes. [3]

Mary Pierson Mackey, Supervisor, Housekeeping Staff

Mackey, a native of San Antonio, joined St. Philip's staff in August 1977, when St. Philip's was a part of the Union Junior College District. Having served under every president up to and including Loston (except Bowden and Norris), Mackey retired in January 2011. She gave thirty-four years of loyal service to the college.

When Mackey came to St. Philip's, she recalled the open area of the campus that stretched from Nevada Street to Walters Street, with parking on both sides, confirming the statements made by Ivory Lee from the cafeteria. The college offices were, at that time, located in a house across the street from the college. There was a small café inside often frequented by the students and staff. There were portable buildings and a fence enclosing the technical buildings. "We had both basketball and volleyball teams back then," said Mackey.

Mackey, who was hired as a maid, was promoted to supervisor in 1986. She enrolled as a student and received her associate's degree in restaurant management and hospitality, later also enrolling in a computer class. "The biggest change that I've noticed during this time is that the student ratio of Negro population as well as in the staff has fallen off from when I came," Mackey observed. [4]

Patricia Williams and Betty Johnson, Library Staff

Patricia Williams enrolled at St. Philip's College in 1969, following graduation from high school in Austin, Texas, her hometown. Williams graduated from St. Philip's in

Betty Johnson

1972 and was hired immediately to work mornings in the registrar's office and afternoons in the library. At that time, St. Philip's had a dean of women, Georgene Bias.

Williams, elected Alumni Association president, served in the position beginning in 1998. Because of her dedication and outstanding service to the Alumni Association, she was honored in November 2003 with the Distinguished Alumni Service Award.

Johnson came to the college in 1970 and retired in August 2010. During her more than forty years of service to the college, Johnson boasts of serving under every administrator of the college, with the exception of Miss Bowden, whom she did not meet. Calling her time at the college a labor of love, Johnson had this to say: "I will have been here, it will be forty-four years on March 5, 2010. The job that I do now is in the library and I love doing library work."

As was the case in the early years of St. Philip's, faculty and staff wore many hats simultaneously. And Johnson claimed that distinction. "When Dr. Murphy was without a secretary, I was the secretary in his office and I would be from the library to his office until he got a permanent secretary." Johnson retired in 2011 with forty-five years of loyal service and for a short time, returned to work as a part-time member of the library staff. [5]

Teresa Guajardo

St. Philip's had many staff and faculty who counted their years of service to the college in decades. Guajardo, another longtime employee of St. Philip's, began first as a student. She laughingly said, "I decided to check it out and I liked it. In fact, I liked it so much, I stayed thirty-six years! Forgot about my first plan to work at a hospital and stayed at St. Philip's College."

Guajardo, from Eagle Pass, Texas, came to St. Philip's in 1974. Earlier, she had joined the Marine Corps, not realizing they did not have a medical field. Following her discharge from the military, she ran into a friend in Eagle Pass with whom she had gone to high school and her friend suggested that if she was going to school, she should try St. Philip's College because "It's small, and it's nice." Because she had the GI Bill and because St. Philip's had a one-year medical technology program, she gave it a try.

Guajardo remembered St. Philip's in the 1970s as a small community college, "a nurturing type of institution where the numbers didn't matter. It was making that one student reach the level of maturity where you just worked with him or her until you found the right buttons that made 'em click, that made 'em want to learn more,

Teresa Guajardo

do more, be more. It was a tremendous push for education, for knowledge, for carrying the banner past just your degree and a job to make money. It was a mission of love, you know; the instructors, the staff, the closeness, so many things. We had many, many people who were on the go, that were on the ball and knew what we needed, and they were trying to teach us how to get it." Guajardo retired in 2010. [6]

Charles Anthony Bowers, Chair, Mathematics Department

Charles "Tony" Bowers came to SPC in the spring semester, 1972, evening division, under Dean Watson. He recalls the January 19 date because the night of his first class was the night that his daughter was born and he barely finished teaching in time to get to the hospital. Describing the campus when he came, he said, "The Norris building was new, barely five years old, the campus center was in place but without the cafeteria. The cafeteria was upstairs where culinary arts is now, and the administrative offices were in the Bowden building."His first class was held in a music room: "I had to move a piano around each week so that I could get to the blackboard. I worked around blackboards that were marked with music staffs. We made it work, though, and it was a very productive semester."

Bowers, who was teaching full-time during the day at a local high school, decided after two or three semesters that SPC was a nice place to work and there were good people at SPC. At the first opportunity, he approached Dr. Ling, who hired him. When Dr. Ling stepped aside as department chair, Bowers's peers elected him to the position and he served as chair for twelve years, stepping down in December 1995. During his tenure, Bowers was instrumental in keeping the department caught up with technology, and says that he started the computer science courses at SPC. Bowers was chair of the fine arts department for the school year 2003, and he agreed to help Regis Shepherd, who became chair, in any way that he could. [7]

Bowers was selected as St. Philip's Minnie Piper Professor for the school year 2010.

Dr. Gregory Hudspeth

Hudspeth, a lifelong resident of San Antonio, was introduced to St. Philip's at around seven years of age, when he took swimming classes under Coach Hudgins. Though he did not enroll in St. Philip's following high school graduation, Hudspeth says that he enrolled in classes each summer. D. T. Ling was the sole instructor teaching at St. Philip's in 2008 who was teaching at the college when Hudspeth began.

Dr. Gregory Hudspeth

Like many of his colleagues and predecessors, Hudspeth began his teaching career at St. Philip's as an adjunct faculty member. From 1975 to 1978, he taught part time and in 1978, was hired as a full-time faculty member. Hudspeth believed that his mission was to be a role model for black students, to ensure that they received a quality education at St. Philip's.

Hudspeth's teachers at St. Philip's inspired him such that when he became a faculty member and an administrator, he wanted to do the same, to be responsible for teaching all of the students. During his tenure, the college began an innovative program in the arts and sciences department called "First Time in College," where the goal was to identify 100 students with no regard to disciplines or majors, improve their retention rate, and encourage them to continue and to earn a four-year degree. [8]

C. L. Leonard and Hilario (Larry) Garcia started the First Time in College Program at St. Philip's. It began at Sam Houston High School with a group of activities called the Bridges Program. With the assistance of four instructors, they offered the classes to students at Sam Houston High School during a summer session, introducing them to tools to help them be successful in college. The college applied for and received a grant to continue the Bridges Program during the fall session, offering it to first-time college students. Bridges students took the same classes as other students, but the student development classes gave them a leg up, helping many students to do well on the college placement test. This program eventually became the First Time in College Program. [9]

Mary Gilford

Mary Gilford

Professor Mary Gilford came to St. Philip's in 1970, and retired in 1998 with the title chairperson emeritus. Gilford was hired by Leonidas Watson in the evening division as an adjunct instructor and she was subsequently promoted to chair of business information systems. The class that Watson hired Gilford to teach had already met twice without an instructor. With her background in accounting, Gilford began teaching in the evenings, then was named program director for real estate and accounting technology. With the title change, Gilford moved into a full-time day teaching position. Watson, who had a real estate license and was a broker, advised Gilford to take real estate courses, so that she could learn about the program and help it to grow and expand. With his extensive knowledge of real estate, he sponsored her at the state level and helped her to earn her broker's license. "It was all because of Mr. Watson, because he encouraged me," said Gilford.

Gilford, born in Hot Springs, Arkansas, moved to Pasadena, California, as a teenager and completed high school and one year of community college in Pasadena. She next earned a degree in business administration from Wiley College in Marshall, Texas. Gilford's ambition was to be a CPA and with that plan in mind, she attended the University of Texas at Austin. She was told at UT that she could not get the master's in public accounting because it required a CPA examination. Explaining that they had no record of a black CPA under which she could serve, and because of that could not place her, they advised her to go into teaching. "While at UT, I experienced many such instances of discrimination," said Gilford. "And that's how I got into the teaching field." She was the first black person to receive a master's in business administration in that field from UT Austin.

As department chair in the applied science department at St. Philip's, Gilford's duties included developing policy for unit chairmen. Department chairs were recommended by a majority of the teachers in the area in which they supervised and every three years, the members of the department would vote on whether or not they wanted the chair to continue. Gilford was well-liked, so when she was recommended and it went up through channels, she was always approved.

Gilford, who started in 1970, served for twenty-eight years at St. Philip's, and retired in August of 1998. "I loved my faculty, and I think my faculty loved me," said Gilford. "We are still good friends, meeting monthly for lunch." Following Mary Gilford's retirement, William "Bill" Lissenby became chair of the department and after about two and a half years, Janie Gonzales followed in his footsteps and became chair of the department. Mrs. Gilford passed away on July 20, 2012. [10]

Janie Gonzales, Faculty

During her tenure, Gonzales observed, experienced, and spearheaded many changes and developments within the business department. Gonzales was chairperson of the business information solutions department and a full professor. She joined the St. Philip's faculty in 1978. At that time, the department was called secretarial science and it was combined with business management arts, culinary arts, and accounting. Eventually, culinary arts split off and instructional technology (IT) and computer science became a part of the department. Gonzales, who at this writing, has been with the college for more than thirty years, was a very good resource for the history of the department.

The business information department presently consists of seven full-time faculty and fourteen adjunct members. Through 2011, the business information solutions department offered four major programs in which students may earn a two-year associate of applied science degree, a one-year certificate program, and a marketable skills achievement award. They are: accounting information systems, administrative computer technology, and business management and technology, Web developer. [11]

Dr. Elizabeth (Dolly) Hudspeth

Dr. Elizabeth (Dolly) Hudspeth

Continuing with faculty who served under Dr. Murphy, Elizabeth (Dolly) Hudspeth gave another look at the culture and a different perspective on serving at St. Philip's in the 1970s under Dr. Murphy. Called by her nickname, Dolly, Hudspeth is a native of San Antonio. She graduated from Wheatley High School and received a scholarship from the Brackenridge Foundation "to pay for the first two years of college, anywhere I wanted to go." She selected Huston-Tillotson College as her first choice and graduated second in her class. While she did not enroll in a degree program at St. Philip's College, Hudspeth did "take a class in government from Frank Madla, many years ago. It was a 7:00 a. m. class where I learned a little bit about government," she said.

At the time of the interview (2005), Hudspeth was beginning her twenty-eighth year at the college, having joined St. Philip's faculty in 1977 as a member of the English department. Under Murphy, she rose to the rank of professor of English in the English and speech department and was instrumental in starting, along with Dr. Burton Crow, the President's Lecture Series. At the time of this writing, Hudspeth has moved to Lakeview Community College, the newest college in the Alamo Community College District.

Hudspeth named her greatest contribution as her role in imparting to the students the same feeling of pride that her teachers gave to her and giving them the same sort of push that she was given. "If you can instill in students the feeling that they can achieve whatever they wish, the other things fall into place," she said. "I try to reach them as a human being first and then we get to the other things."

In 2003, Hudspeth was selected as a St. Philip's Piper Professor. Minnie Piper Professors are nominated by their college or university president's office. The winner receives a $5,000 award and the designation of Piper Professor. In 1958, the Minnie Piper Program began recognizing and honoring exceptional achievement in the teaching profession in colleges and universities in the state of Texas. Each year, Texas teachers compete for this award and since only ten persons across the state are selected for this prestigious award, it is an honor simply to be nominated. [12]

Becoming a Piper Professor recognizes superiority in teaching at the college or university level, and while receiving the award is an honor for the recipient, it also brings honor and credibility to the institution they serve. The nominees are recognized as having made special contributions to their profession, having had a special impact on their students, and having made significant contributions to their communities.

Because of the excellence exhibited by its teaching staff, St. Philip's College has had faculty to be honored as Piper Professors since the program began. The list that follows indicates the position faculty held at the college at the time they received the honor.

- Roger W. Lee, chairman, division of natural sciences, 1958
- Clarence W. Norris Sr. , professor of sociology, 1970
- Dolores C. Villarreal, associate professor/ chairman, medical clerical programs, 1979
- Hazelyn Lewis, associate professor of English, 1989
- Elizabeth (Dolly) Hudspeth, associate professor of English, 2003
- Charles Anthony (Tony) Bowers, chair, mathematics department, 2010

The Piper Professor program seeks nominations annually from all accredited institutions of higher education in the state for the award of being named a Piper Professor. A selection committee, whose job is to search for well-rounded, outgoing teachers devoted to their profession, reviews the applications and makes the selection. In addition to the $5,000 award, Piper Professors receive a gold pin and a certificate.

Since selection is by invitation only, St. Philip's is honored to have dedicated faculty whose outstanding scholarly achievements are recognized, not only statewide, but also nationally and internationally.

Olga Samples Davis, Faculty

Davis, who always found ways to be creative, even with severely limited resources available, related an incident with Dr. Murphy that provided insight into conditions at SPC in the 1970s.

"When Dr. Murphy cut back on our budget, I said, 'Sir, we've got to have a theatre season.' And he said, 'Well, you can have one if you pay for it.' Then he explained that there were amateur acting rights that had to be paid for, as well as property rights." Davis asked Dr. Murphy if there could be a theatre season if she raised the money. "And he said, 'Sure, but how are you going to get the play? That's a $300 venue or more!' 'I'll just write a play!'" said Davis.

Davis, who admits to not knowing what she was doing, left Murphy's office and said to herself, "I don't know how to write a play!" But, Davis had a mother who taught her that one can go to the library and learn how to do anything in life; that is, if one stays in the library long enough. So, Davis spent hours in the library and before long, she had learned how to write a play.

Davis's first play, called "Family Reunion," was sponsored by Amoco and the J. F. K Center for the Performing Arts. The play went on to the American College Theatre Festival Circuit. One of the judges helped to send it forward.

"Now," said Davis, "thirty-one years later, I'm getting the grandchildren and great grandchildren of my first students." Describing the culture when she came to work at the college, Davis said the setting was very open and loving. "Students were grateful to have you take the time to work with them and help them move beyond themselves in a situation. They wanted more, more, more and you could give them more, and more and more because they were so grateful. As teachers, we didn't mind exhausting ourselves," said Davis.

Now, even though circumstances have changed, Davis says that she lives for that "aha moment" and likes it best when the light goes on in her students' eyes and they see how it connects. "That is always best for me, the most rewarding moment and it keeps you going. It's a different kind of tough love we're giving now."[13]

Dr. William Conan Davis, Chairman, Department of Natural Sciences

Davis, who came to St. Philip's near the end of Dr. Murphy's tenure, is a renowned scientist who began his years of service at the college in 1983. Famous for his scientific discoveries, Davis described how he ended up at the college. "I was trying to unload some of the responsibilities that I had and even though I enjoyed my jobs, they were too much for me."Davis noted that by the time he had been in San Antonio for less than three months, he had three jobs and was very, very tired. When Dr. Lanier Byrd called him and told him of the opportunity to teach at St. Philip's, Davis knew that that was just what he wanted to do. His work at St. Philip's would mean that for the first time, he would have only one job to do at a time.

St. Philip's was not unknown to Davis, for his sister, who was over the social work department at the VA Hospital in Georgia, had told him about the school. Father Henry Bowden, Artemisia Bowden's brother, knew Davis's sister, and he also told Davis about the college in San Antonio that his sister was starting. Davis recalled that when he was a boy in his teens, he had an opportu-

William Conan Davis

nity through his sister to meet Miss Bowden; however, meeting her as a youngster did not have the impact that an encounter at a more mature age might have had.

Davis received his bachelor's degree from Talladega College, his MS degree from Tuskegee, and had a choice of schools to attend for a PhD.

"When Dr. George Washington Carver died, the Tuskegee Board of the Tuskegee Foundation needed black people to come back to colleges like Texas Southern or Dillard to teach science," said Davis, "so the board established a foundation where professional black scientists could practice science dedicated solely to pure research. Tuskegee was the only school in the US where a professional black could practice pure research. Employment with a big company as a chemist was the only other choice, but at that time, big companies were not hiring blacks as research scientists."

Blacks in the United States could earn a degree in education with a concentration in chemistry, and were expected to teach chemistry from that perspective, but programs that trained graduates to become professional scientists, dedicated purely to research, were not offered to blacks. With no opportunities to practice in the big laboratories, Tuskegee became a strong drawing point. Blacks came to Tuskegee not only for the opportunity to do pure research, but also for the opportunity to work with other black professional chemists and the option to work as a teacher of chemistry, if they desired.

Davis, recounting conditions he and other blacks faced in the 1950s as they strove to become pure scientists, noted that attempting simple things, such as traveling across the country, was a major undertaking, for accommodations in white-owned hotels were not accessible to blacks. Unable to find employment in the United States as a pure scientist, Davis elected to work in the Northwestern part of the country, where Dr. French, president of Washington State University, promised, "If you come to Washington State, and if you finish all the coursework, I will take you in industry." Davis went first to Washington State and then to Oregon, where he was hired as director of United Clinical Laboratories, a position he held for fifteen years.

Because in his later years he wanted to be in the classroom, when he became chairman of the department of natural sciences at St. Philip's, Davis taught classes in chemistry. By that time, he understood that there were areas to pursue other than research and that it was an honor and a privilege to teach the students. "Many students, not familiar with research, don't understand that it can be fun," Davis said. He also said that he was a bit disappointed at not having more African American students in his class. "I found no difference between the white, Hispanic, or African American students and I've been able to influence some of them regardless of race," he said. Davis, more prone to teach chemistry and physics rather than biology, always taught on the chemical side at St. Philip's.

Among Davis's achievements is his discovery of a process to make mashed potatoes instant, discovery of the sugar that makes ice cream creamier, and (with Lanier Byrd) the formula that makes Dasani water have a pleasant taste. According to the Fall-Spring 2009, *Palo Alto Review*, Davis and a team also discovered a wood sugar that is used to produce industrial glue. Another of his many discoveries is standardizing blood tests that make it possible to determine minute quantities of insulin and growth hormones. In January 2007, Davis was inducted into the Texas Science Hall of Fame, where he was honored as one of sixteen charter members.

Davis taught at St. Philip's for more than twenty-six years, while serving also as department chair and professor. In recognition of his years of service, in 2009 the ACCD Board of Trustees approved naming Dr. William Conan Davis professor emeritus of the natural science department. Additionally, in 2010, recognizing the years of service that Davis contributed to St. Philip's, and his lifelong commitment to the scientific community and the world, the Board of Trustees of the ACCD renamed the three-story Science Building on the campus of St. Philip's the "William C. Davis Science Building." Davis retired in August 2009 from teaching at St. Philip's, though he continues working and consulting on what appears to be a very promising fuel cell project. Despite his retirement, Davis was invited to continue using an office at the college where he is writing his memoirs, assisted by Dr. Jeannette Passty. [14]

Dr. Jeannette Nyda Passty, Associate Professor of English, St. Philip's College

Dr. Jeannette N. Passty

Jeannette Passty, who came to St. Philip's in 1988 as an adjunct instructor, is now an associate professor of English, editor-in-chief of SPC Press, and a deeply committed advocate for the college. Passty earned her PhD in English from the University of Southern California in Los Angeles in 1982. A consummate scholar, she has authored and presented more than "thirty papers in journals, literary studies, multicultural studies, and developmental education that were presented in academic departments and/or at conferences." In 2011, Passty presented a paper at the Institute of English Studies, School of Advanced Study, University of London in the United Kingdom on a "very popular British writer, journalist, critic and traveler, novelist and poet," Rose Macaulay.

She is also the editor-in-chief of SPC Press, a small college-sponsored press that produces books for children. The press began as a service learning project with the idea of promoting reading between parents and children, especially SPC students who are also parents. A special feature of the press is their visits to the communities to promote literacy.

The press's first publication came out shortly before Dr. Loston arrived and, as a welcome to the campus, the press presented her with a copy of the first children's book that they published.

Passty, who teaches five classes of developmental and college-level English, is a published author who earned the American Library Association's 1988–1989 outstanding Academic Book Award. She has been the recipient of many honors and awards for her excellence in teaching, including the St. Philip's College Teaching Excellence Award in 2003–2004. In 2003, Passty received the NISOD Medallion for Excellence in Teaching and Leadership from the University of Texas at Austin. In addition to her faculty duties, she serves on several committees at the college, including cochairing the Women's History Month Committee.

It was through the spearheading work and efforts of Passty that, in 2005, Gallery 100 in the Watson Fine Arts Center was renamed the Kathryn A. Walker Morgan Gallery. Because of Passty's renaming request, Dr. Runnels appointed a task force to establish the criteria. After the College Council considered her request to rename the gallery, a criteria for naming and renaming classrooms, labs, galleries, and studios was established. Runnels said at the time that renaming the gallery in remembrance of Morgan would be a lasting tribute to her contributions to St. Philip's and the many persons whose lives she touched.

In 2012, Passty was selected by St. Philip's College faculty senate members to be the nominee for the Minnie Stevens Piper Professor Award. [15]

Kathryn Walker Morgan

Kathryn Ann Walker Morgan, born in San Antonio in 1935, joined St. Philip's faculty in 1966, and became, in 1985, the first female dean of arts and sciences at the college. Morgan earned a bachelor's of music from Lincoln University in Jefferson City, Missouri, and a master's degree in music from University of Texas, San Antonio. She did further study at Our Lady of the Lake College in San Antonio and toward a doctorate in community college leadership at the University of Texas at Austin, Texas. A passionate supporter of the arts, and an ardent supporter of St. Philip's and the fine arts, Morgan was a dedicated educator and musician with many accomplishments. A sampling of her important contributions to St. Philip's and to the community is listed below:

- Developed the specifications for the Watson Fine Arts Center, while serving as dean of arts and sciences
- Established the San Antonio Symphony Residency Program
- Principal in establishment of the department of theatre and fine arts, to include music, art, dance, and theater; served as the first chair of the department of theatre and fine arts
- Developed and instituted the fine arts program leading to the associate in arts degree in music and art.
- Coordinated the Enrichment Series at St. Philip's: Arts Expo (1973–1974, campus arts festival)
- Established in 1994 the Kathryn Walker Morgan Scholarship Fund to assist St. Philip's students with their tuition

Kathryn W. Morgan

When Jeannette Passty was informed by Roland DuBay, executive director of institutional advancement that naming a building requires ACCD Board approval but the college president has the authority to name rooms within the building, she began a campaign to have a room named for Morgan. Because of the high esteem as an educator, musician, and arts advocate in which Morgan was held, in 2004, Jeannette Passty, Morgan's good friend, and goddaughter, wrote to Angie S. Runnels, then president of the college, requesting that Gallery 100 in the Watson Fine Arts Center be named in Morgan's honor. Passty was supported in her request by the faculty of the fine arts department, and chair of the fine arts department, Regis Shephard, along with a unanimous vote from the Women's History Month Program Advisory Committee.

As a tribute to her dedication to the arts, and in recognition of her twenty-eight years of service (1966 to 1994) to the college, students, faculty, and the community, on May 4, 2005, Gallery 100 on the first floor of the Watson Fine Arts Center was renamed the Kathryn A. Walker Morgan Gallery in her honor.

Morgan retired in 1994, and following her retirement, the Kathryn Walker Morgan Scholarship was established at St. Philip's to provide financial assistance for students attending the college. Morgan was a graduate school classmate of President Runnels at the University of Texas, Austin. A personal interview was scheduled with Mrs. Morgan but she became ill before the interview could be completed and she passed away soon thereafter.

Terry Puckett, a colleague who worked very closely with Morgan, had only the highest praise for her works, noting also that Morgan was responsible for Puckett's affiliation with St. Philip's. Puckett's association with Morgan and the college began in 1975 with a telephone call from Morgan, inviting her to interview for a position teaching an art class at the college. She did not know Morgan nor did she know the location of the college, but she accepted the position and, in 1975, began as the first teacher of an art appreciation class at St. Philip's. There was a problem however, for though the class quickly filled, there was no place in which to hold the sessions.

At the time, Puckett was teaching at the South West Craft Center, now the Southwest School of Art, and she asked the school for permission to hold St. Philip's art class there. The Craft Center not only allowed it, they offered it free of charge. Thus began a series of classes and labs with Puckett and instructors from the Craft Center teaching St. Philip's credit art classes. Puckett remembers that at the time, classes could be offered in whatever the instructor could make happen.

Terry Puckett and the Beginning of the Art Department at St. Philip's

At that time, the whole campus was different in terms of physical plant and campus layout. There was just an old concrete parking lot with a handicap ramp. The Sutton building didn't exist. The campus was unattractive with very few buildings, and entry to the art department was through the music building. As the program became more and more popular, Morgan and Puckett decided that they should start a real art department. More art appreciation classes and more lab classes were offered until they decided, "Something has to be done."

Because there needed to be an agreement between St. Philip's and the Craft Center regarding the space being utilized by St. Philip's students taking courses at the Craft Center, Morgan and Puckett invited the president, the deans, all persons at St. Philip's with decision-making powers, to come to the Craft Center to see the grounds. They planned a picnic, provided sandwiches and fruit, showed them around, and explained what they planned to do. They received the approval to continue holding classes and at that point, the Craft Center and St. Philip's College formed a contract that called for paying rent for the space that St. Philip's used.

Eventually, even though there were no facilities at St. Philip's, classes were moved to the college, where Puckett taught on the top of desks in the music building (now the student center). That area they utilized was renamed the Upper Deck (culinary department). It has again been renamed and is now called Artemisia. "Our little desks were attached to the seats. The elevator went up three stories, and you could only go out one way, and that was to exit into what was the old antique library stacks and into my classroom. We were in the library stacks for at least four or five years."

In 1982, Puckett was hired as full-time faculty. When the art department was built in the early 1990s, the department moved from one rented classroom at the Craft Center, to a large building on campus, with facilities that accommodated all sorts of things, except art exhibitions. Art exhibits were held in the lobby of the theatre and in the campus ministry building.

Puckett, who taught at St. Philip's for thirty-three years, twenty-five of which were full time, created and developed the first art distance learning class and art appreciation class for the St. Philip's campus. For ten years, she taught an Internet drawing class. During that time, she won the President's Award for creativity. Puckett retired from the classroom in 1999, though she continued to teach art and distance learning classes over the Internet. In fall 2008, she retired from teaching at St. Philip's altogether. [16]

Many of the students and the faculty talked about the dedication and the determination to see the students succeed that was prevalent at the college in the early years. None was demonstrated more clearly than the work that went into setting up and nurturing the art department to maturity.

The Higher Education Achievement Program, acronym HEAP, is another program that was designed to foster student success.

Higher Education Achievement Program (HEAP): An Exemplary Program

During the fall of 1972–1973, forty-three entering freshmen students at St. Philip's enrolled in a pilot program called HEAP. This federally-funded program, designed for that group of students whose educational profile reflected motivation and/or academic deficiencies and who were classified as "high risk" students when measured by traditional college methods, was one of three such programs in Texas and one of thirty programs in eleven Southern states. Dean Murphy appointed Browning Samples, formerly of the evening faculty and who by that time had joined the day faculty, to coordinate the HEAP.

HEAP offered training in English and basic mathematics with special emphasis on reading, and provided enriched opportunities to help students master the skills they were lacking. Realizing that the students enrolled in HEAP had a variety of performance levels and needs, the career choices, opportunities, and information made available to them were also varied. The idea was to raise the academic performance of underperforming students.

In addition to regular classroom activities, the curriculum included workshops, laboratory sessions, cultural activities and visits, enrichment activities, field trips to events, visits to community agencies, and discussions with civic leaders. Many of the returning veterans who took advantage of the opportunity for college also enrolled in HEAP.

HEAP staff in 1972–1973 consisted of Browning Samples, coordinator; Gerri Richardson and Virginia Tatum, counselors; Gloria Malone and Rita Randle, national teaching fellows; Beverly Dearborne and John Valle, teacher assistants; James Gross, teacher aide; and Norman Comet, instructional technologist. Maria Juarez was clerk typist.

In addition to administering the program, Samples and others counseled students who were behind academically, prepared them to be successful in college, and wrote educational prescriptions for the students to follow that were designed to develop the skills they lacked. Not only did the students benefit from HEAP, but there was also a faculty component. Twenty-nine faculty members in the fall and twenty-one faculty members in the spring received grants for further study through the program. Many of these students, appreciative of the attention given them, still speak reverentially of St. Philip's as family.

Like many in HEAP and others who were interviewed, John Gomez, a tech in the copy center, described St. Philip's as his family. Gomez is a perfect example of the esteem in which many of the students, faculty, and others hold for St. Philip's. In his case, it is particularly noteworthy, for though he has worked at the college for more than twenty years, he is a district employee and has never been on the college payroll. Gomez came to St. Philip's in the 1970s through the print shop under Dr. Murphy.

Kathryn (Kitty) Flores

Kathryn (Kitty) Flores, Administrative Assistant to the President

Noting that when she first arrived at St. Philip's, she was absolutely petrified going through the registration process, Flores says that probably the reason that she is still here is that when she arrived, she was welcomed with open arms. Mary Gilford and Grover Hodges, her typing teachers, both forced her to be conscientious and not use liquid paper to cover errors but to retype the material correctly. Hodges, who would even make her cry said, "One of these days you're going to thank us." "And I cannot tell you how many times I have thanked them. I am what I am today, as far as being a clerical person, because of their real interest in every single student." Gilford taught Flores's business English class, which was a part of her degree plan at the time and she says that she learned more in Gilford's English class than she learned in regular freshman English composition class.

Flores started out under Dean Murphy in the department of applied science and technology and worked for six months as a clerk typist for director Dr. Frank Williams. During that time, the Texas Education Agency funded occupational education and that department had a separate print shop and off-set printer, while the remainder of the college used mimeograph machines.

Flores worked for nine years in the secretarial science program division, working her way up with different titles: clerk typist, secretary one, and secretary two, but with different classifications. In 1983, she began in the president's office, under Dr. Gloria Jackson, and left for three years to work with Dr. Mitchell after he was transferred to the district as deputy chancellor (position now called the executive vice chancellor), and again with Mitchell when he was later transferred to Northwest Vista as president.

But circumstances change: according to Flores, Mitchell's time as president of Northwest Vista was brief though productive. As the first official president, he put together the academic plan for Northwest Vista: their capital plan, their physical building plan, all the background and the actual planning that went forward with the new regime. After three and a half years, Mitchell retired, her position reopened at St. Philip's, and Dr. Taylor, who was then president at St. Philip's, invited her to come back, a position she first declined. But, after six months at Northwest Vista, Flores realized that she really was more than a little interested in the position at St. Philip's.

From Dean Murphy to President Murphy: A Change in Title and Little Else

While it was business as usual on the academic side of the college, with programs, faculty, and staff moving right along with their duties, by the early 1980s, in the administrative arm of the school, change was fomenting, particularly in the position of chairman of the board of trustees. Leadership in that office tended to change, depending on the number of votes the leader could garner. Murphy voiced the opinion that when George Ozuna became chairman, it was obvious that he was intent on changing the complexion of the administration.

Around January 1982, the deans of the colleges, both SPC and SAC, were given the title of president. Murphy said that during the time he wore the mantle of president, "it was just a change of title, that's all, because I was doing the same things." Around June or July of the same year, following his assuming the title, the Board of Trustees called and asked him to resign as president. Even more puzzling was what happened the next day when the vice chancellor called and asked him to accept a position at the district office as his assistant. Murphy, who was planning to retire in two years, decided to accept the position of the vice chancellor's assistant because, he said, "I wasn't ready to retire." Expressing his frustration at the turn of events, Murphy said, "I accomplished nothing tangible while in the position of assistant vice chancellor." Dr. Murphy held the position of assistant to the vice chancellor for two years.

Successes in Office

Though Murphy was modestly reluctant when asked to talk about his accomplishments while in office, St. Philip's history would be incomplete without mention of some of his many "firsts" accomplished while he held the office of dean and then president. One of his most important undertakings was reorganization and enlargement of the vocational-technical programs, bringing St. Philip's programs in line with the needs of the community, particularly the military arm.

In the meantime, around the mid-1970s, the military was becoming a voluntary operation and as an inducement to the public to join the military, many new educational opportunities were planned, such as the College Assistance Program (CAP), where tuition assistance was paid by the military. Then there was the Service Members Opportunity College Program (SOC), which allowed military personnel to obtain a civilian education at educational institutions, including community colleges. To attract more students, St. Philip's began offering courses on the military bases. It was a win-win situation for both. For the troops, there was the convenience of on-base classes and ease of access, and for the college, the increase in the number of troops signing up for classes at SPC helped to swell the enrollment.

The programs offered in the health careers area grew faster and larger than any other program in the vocational-technical area. Murphy explained that these programs received state funding, and because there was a corresponding expansion in the number of hospital facilities in the city of San Antonio, this made a huge difference. The expansion of the hospitals in the city provided additional opportunities for employment and this, in turn, increased the interest in careers in the health field. It was a win-win situation for the college and the city. The health industry in the city grew and the health careers program at St. Philip's kept pace. With this parallel growth, the total student population under Murphy's watch increased by several thousand students.

"Another of my accomplishments was to expand and smooth out departmental structures. That wasn't something that you could put your finger on, it was subtle, particularly in the vocational areas," said Murphy. "We had to change the departmental chairmanships in order to modernize and upgrade the teaching program in those departments." We translated this to mean that some of the department chairmen who did not have a college degree were replaced by persons with a degree, which was probably necessary to gain membership in the American Association of Community Junior Colleges. St. Philip's became a member of the American Association of Community Junior Colleges under Dr. Murphy's presidency.

A Peer's Assessment

Perhaps most honest and true is an evaluation of Murphy that came unsolicited from a colleague who had no ax to grind and was simply making an estimation of the achievement of one colleague by another.

"John Murphy was given absolutely nothing; they never gave him any help; never gave him any support and he was president there ten or eleven years. By smoke and mirrors, he kept the place together, and that, from my point of view, is a major accomplishment. The place was run and kept in motion by people who had a set of unique experiences. These people came into academic life in the 1930s, 1940s, bussed the 1950s, and overcame God knows what kind of obstacles to get an education and get into college teaching. It's really amazing; it's mind boggling to think that you could coin a dozen of those people in one institution."

Dr. Murphy tendered his resignation from the district in August 1984. He passed away April 20, 2004.

When Dr. Murphy vacated the presidency, a period of unrest and dissension at the administrative level followed, as persons jockeyed for position in the race for the presidency of St. Philip's.

18

A Procession of Presidents, Era of Contention: The 1980s

While the Murphy years were marked by periods of quiet, sustained growth within the college, years of unrest waited in the wings. Immediately following Murphy's resignation, a search for a new president was launched, opening the door to a procession of presidents. This marked a time in the life of the college when the administrators' tenure was transitory.

The 1980s: Assessing the Time

As the unrest unfolded in the president's office, there was likewise disharmony within the Board of Trustees and chancellor's offices and even more to come. The period between Dr. Murphy's unplanned resignation from the presidency and the selection of his successor was a time of turmoil. The board, the faculty, the black community, each had their favorite candidate to replace Murphy. Amidst the controversy, a delegation of black religious, elected, and community leaders met with the district chancellor, voicing the sentiment of the black community that, because of its history, the top position at St. Philip's College should be filled by a black person. The selection committee argued additionally that "The individual selected should be knowledgeable in the history, traditions and background of the school, and have lived in the community for a number of years."[1]

Byron McClenney, chancellor of the district at the time, indicated that he had no problems with the requirement to have a black president as long as a qualified person was found. He described the search for Murphy's replacement as "very, very difficult. It really turned into just a brawl, there's no other way to describe it," he said, "and it took place behind the scenes in large measure, although at times it would erupt into the public arena." [2]

Theodore Williams, administrator and faculty member, possessed all of the qualifications, and many faculty and community members supported him for the position. The committee continued its search for a replacement and Williams, meanwhile, was appointed interim president of the college.

Theodore R. Williams, Interim President, St. Philip's College, 1982

Williams, who had held the posts of assistant dean, associate dean, and assistant associate dean (the post of assistant associate dean eventually became the vice president), said that for most of his tenure, he had had the responsibility of the faculty and he had excellent support from them. "I had been like the second in command here, over academic affairs and, in fact, I retired as vice president for academic affairs. Promotions came directly through me to the president and once we added a dean of arts and sciences and a dean of technical vocation that sort of changed just a little bit. But still, promotions went from them to me to the president."

When Williams began his tenure at the college, the three-story Johnston Memorial Building housed the administration building, a dormitory for girls, and classrooms. This building was leveled in the fall of 1954. The technical and vocational programs were taught in army barrack-type buildings.

Because of his long tenure at St. Philip's, Williams had participated in many changes and improvements, such as the revisions made in the electronics program. When he was chief academic affairs officer and chairman of the academic affairs council, managing classroom space was

T. R. Williams

a major task of his office. To handle the problem of lack of space, Williams said that he initiated the Monday–Wednesday, Tuesday–Thursday class schedule and also introduced the weekend-college concept. According to *The Tiger*, he was a very strong advocate for getting the gymnasium addition approved.[3] One of the things Williams was most pleased about was solving the problem between the academic faculty and the technical and vocational faculty. The tech-vocation people felt that the academic people looked down on them because they had less training. Only a bachelor's degree was required in some of the technical areas and in some cases, no degree was required. Williams brought them together so that there was just one faculty group.

He was also involved with faculty development, which he described as "an ongoing kind of thing." When he stepped down as vice president for academic affairs, Williams did not retire but continued to serve the college as an adjunct faculty member in the biology department.[4]

Selecting the President

After the college's Presidential Search Committee made their selection, they forwarded the names of three candidates for president of St. Philip's to the chancellor. The candidates were: Dr. Theodore Williams, interim president; Dr. Gloria Jackson, chairperson of St. Philip's business department; and Dr. Alberta Helen Smith, academic vice president of the State University of New York-Delhi. Williams, who met all of the criteria, was endorsed for the position by a delegation from the black community. The chancellor also recommended to the board that Williams be appointed as president of the college but when the time came to vote on the appointment, four of the seven trustees abstained. Since a majority vote, along with endorsement from the community and recommendation from the chancellor of the board was required before action could be taken on which candidate could be selected, Williams was not selected.[5] Not selecting Dr. Williams as president caused great angst and division among the faculty, as well as in the community. "Racist and petty politics" read the newspaper criticism of the decision. The article went on to report that after the board failed to act on McClenney's recommendation, the board went into executive session and when they returned, McClenney had changed his position.[6] He then recommended Dr. Gloria Jackson as interim president and with this vote, the board had the majority of the votes they needed in hand. The Board approved the recommendation. A few strokes of the pen later, Williams was out as interim and Gloria Jackson became the new interim president of St. Philip's College.

19 A Tumultuous, Progressive Time: The 1980s

The 1980s can only be described as politically chaotic, for within the district and within the city of San Antonio, there was great unrest. In fact, the struggle that took place on the board of the ACCD mirrored the political struggle that was taking place in the government of the city. Despite the goings-on in the city and even at the college itself, faculty and staff maintained calmness in the classrooms.

Dr. Gloria Jackson, President, 1982–1984

Gloria Jackson, who became interim president of St. Philip's College in December 1982, held the interim position for two months before becoming president in March 1983. She brought to the position twenty-nine years of experience in the field of education that included serving as chair of the business department at Alcorn A&M College and achieving the title of full professor. As Jackson explained, "I was qualified to be president." When Dr. Murphy retired and the position of president became open, Jackson applied. She had attended Prairie View A&M College and earned a bachelor's degree in home economics with additional hours in elementary education. Following graduation, she worked at Bastrop County with the title of Negro Home Demonstration Agent. "I believe that I was about the last one in Bastrop," she said.

While Jackson was at Bastrop, Dr. Evans at Prairie View recommended her husband to be manager of the college laundry at Alcorn and to teach laundry and dry cleaning as well. Confident that she could find a job, Jackson moved to Alcorn to be with her husband and she found employment first in the registrar's office, next in the business office, and later as an administrative assistant. Wanting to attend graduate school in business, Jackson enrolled at Alcorn to prepare for her master's. "It was a turbulent time in the state of Mississippi, and anything you wanted to do and could go out of Mississippi to do, the state helped you with out-of-state aid. The state of Mississippi helped a lot of black people in Mississippi attend some of the top universities outside of Mississippi." In fact, Jackson attended Indiana University, earning a master's degree, for which the state of Mississippi paid most of the cost. Additionally, they paid for several trips home during the summer for Jackson to visit her family.

Working with Mr. Watson

Jackson also worked in Navosota, Texas, close to College Station, near Hempstead and Prairie View. Leonidas Watson, working at that time as county agricultural agent in Navasota, later became dean of the evening school at St. Philip's and when Jackson returned to Texas, Watson was at St. Philip's, though she was not aware that he was there before she came.

In June 1973, when Jackson came to San Antonio looking for a job, she applied at both St. Philip's and at SAC. Watson and Armond Hathaway, department chairman of the business department at St. Philip's, convinced Jackson that with all her experience, she was needed most at St. Philip's. SAC was interested in hiring her because she knew machine shorthand, but by stepping down as head and returning to the classroom, Hathaway made sure that she became head of the business department at St. Philip's.

When Jackson was hired at St. Philip's, her rank changed from holding the title of full professor in a four-year institution to assistant professor in a two-year college. She again worked her way up to full professor and then, for several years, became Dr. Murphy's assistant, where she was placed in charge of testing personnel to be

Gloria Jackson

hired. In fact, Jackson remembered testing Kitty Flores, who later served as her secretary, and was secretary and assistant to several presidents of the college.

By the time Dr. Murphy left St. Philip's, Jackson had worked under and with him, had been chairman of the business department, had gained experience in several other positions, and felt ready to serve as president. At the time, there was a division on the Trustee Board with one faction wanting Dr. Williams to be president, and the other favoring Jackson. In December 1982, when Jackson was hired as interim president, she said, "There was a faction against me in the college, and I can understand that. They had their friends, their person that they wanted to serve as president. I worked as interim president for a short period and then I served as president through the beginning of January 1984. Then I left."

During Jackson's tenure as president, an incident occurred that actually resulted in her being removed from the office. According to Jackson, there was a board member who was against her all the way and he was determined to see that she was removed from the office of president. Around that same time, Palo Alto College was being established and the Board of Trustees launched a search for a president of that institution. According to Jackson, she was told that "It came to the point where the choice was vote to remove Jackson at St. Philip's and get your choice of president at Palo Alto." And, said Jackson, "when it came to a vote, that's what happened."

Jackson, who began at St. Philip's in the business department in 1973, progressed from instructor to department chair and then in 1982 became president of the college. In January 1985, Jackson went to the district and worked on special projects for Dr. McClenney as his special assistant. She also worked on the development of Palo Alto College and wrote the policy manual, *What's What*. In fact, she said, "He just turned me loose on that and other jobs. But, you know, sitting over there in the district, it was quiet, you'd go to work, you'd do your job, you'd go to lunch, you'd come back. I missed the students. I'd been hearing all that noise, up and down the halls, playing with students all my life and I just missed that."

While Jackson was working at the department, Max Castillo, president of San Antonio College, invited Jackson to come to SAC to be a part of the business department. With no females nor a black in the department, Jackson described herself at SAC as "what you'd call a 'twofer.'" She began at San Antonio College in September 1985 and worked there until October 1999. When her sister became ill, she decided to retire to care for her. "Chancellor Ramsey tried his best to get me to just take leave because he said, 'You know you'll want to come back. You could stay on leave until you're sixty-five, maybe longer than that if you want to.'" This was amusing to Jackson, who was already sixty-five at the time. "That was the nicest thing he'd said to me since I'd been there," she commented.

Jackson returned to SAC and taught classes until December. By that time, she had worked in education for fifty years. It was time for relaxation. Her leisure time was brief, however, for she soon began working on a project with St. Philip's and her church, St. Paul's United Methodist Church, restoring the Brackenridge House, one of the first educational institution for blacks in San Antonio. Jackson's role was to serve as project coordinator for the church. Mamie Williams, a now-deceased St. Philip's employee, had written a grant to restore the historical building and when Mamie passed away, Jackson accepted the position.

Most Memorable Administrative Moments

Placing persons in positions who were subsequently very successful in working with students constituted some of

Jackson's proudest moments. She attributed their success with students to their loyalty to the school and the desire to be the best at their positions as they could. Jackson felt that most of those under her brought that loyalty to their positions. "I look at the improvements, the renovations, the expansion of the college, and know that a lot of that planning was done when I was there. And as I think back," said Jackson, "I had several memorable moments, and the loyalty of the faculty really encouraged me. The faculty supported me and did everything they could to make the college go. Their personal dedication was most encouraging."

During her tenure, Dr. Jackson's major thrust was recruitment and retention of students. A newspaper writer alleged that she never really had a fair chance because from the moment of her arrival, Jackson met with a degree of uncooperativeness and disdain by certain administrative and faculty members. But Jackson's assessment of the time was that "As the top administrator, I worked with all of the programs, visited all of the departments, and they appreciated it. I enjoyed my time there and met some lovely people."[1]

Administrators, Faculty, and Staff in the Jackson Era

Dr. Elizabeth (Dolly) Hudspeth, English Department

When Dolly Hudspeth joined the faculty of the English Department, there were only two faculty members in the department who were not African American. Because she was so thankful to be at St. Philip's, she said that she didn't pay a lot of attention to what the administration did. The black community was struggling with who was going to be president of the college, Dr. T. R. Williams or Dr. Gloria Jackson. It appeared that the school was changing presidents every two or three years until the board stepped in and selected Dr. Jackson.

CL Leonard, Staff

Jackson hired CL, a staff member at St. Philip's from July 1984 to 2007. His "real" name is CL (pronounced as it is spelled), and that is what he uses as a first name. A retired military officer with twenty-five years of military service, Leonard is from Bastrop, Texas. "As for my name, that's another story. The military kept trying to give me a name for years," he said, "but my ID card, my driver's license and all legal documents with my name read CL Leonard, without the periods!"

Leonard came to St. Philip's as director of student development and special population and became director of counseling, a position he held for eleven years, working under Dr. Lyn Hill at South West Campus for five years, as assistant to the vice president and afterwards under Dr. Zaragoza. Ultimately, while serving under Dr. Runnels, CL became director of college partnerships, acting as an ambassador for the college in the community and as personal representative for the president.[2]

From 1985 to 2001, when there was again a significant growth in St. Philip's enrollment, Leonard estimated the increase to have added about 7,000 students. When Kelly Air Force Base closed, many persons from Kelly came to St. Philip's for training and during that eleven-year period, enrollment, which had begun to wane a bit from the Vietnam War, gradually began to increase. Enrollment steadily increased as more and more eighteen- and nineteen-year-old Caucasian and Hispanic students began enrolling at St. Philip's main campus. An even greater number of Hispanic and Caucasian students enrolled at the Southwest Campus. As the number of Caucasian and Hispanic faculty coming to St. Philip's increased, fewer and fewer African American students, administrators, and faculty applied to the school, electing to take advantage of the opportunity to enroll in schools heretofore unavailable to them.

Events in the 1980s

Describing events that occurred in the early 1980s, the statement was made by a person who declined to be identified, "that if that part of the history of St. Philip's were not told of what it was like at that time, then you're not getting the history of the college" and, in fact, the person suggested that those events were supposedly among the biggest stories in the San Antonio newspapers for a couple of years.

According to newspaper accounts, an internal audit was made of a program at St. Philip's that a faction of the board attempted to stop. A district audit uncovered possible mismanagement of school funds and falsification of student records in the restaurant management program, and allegations were made that the board directed the president to stop the audit. (Calling the president by the

Byron McClenney

name of "chancellor" had not yet begun.) Following the audit, the chairman of the business management department was suspended. In addition, as rumors of mismanagement, irregularities, nonrenewal of contracts and dismissals abounded, officials of the ACCD asked the district attorney to also investigate alleged wrongdoings in the auto body department of the college.

As this was happening, the president met with a representative of the Southern Association of Colleges and Schools, who happened to be in the city at the time. It was alleged that the chancellor accused the board of violating district policy by interfering too much in administrative activities. This including passing over the president's recommendation for the position of president of Palo Alto College and three other high-level administrative appointments. It was further reported that two board members allegedly also met with the Southern Association representative to give him the board's side of the story. The board members explained that they had only acted in cases when it felt that the administration had acted inappropriately or had failed to take action. Before the controversies ended, the district attorney became involved in some of the issues, the press had a field day, and the allegations provided the city with front page news for a good long time.

"That was a very, very turbulent period of time," said McClenney. "The City Council went through a huge upheaval; the way things are determined in San Antonio went through this huge upheaval; the college district went through this huge upheaval and the San Antonio Independent School District went through this huge upheaval." San Antonio went through that because people had been left out of the system for so long that it just could not continue. It was a time when both the African American community and the Hispanic population made their discontent known, declaring that they would no longer be ignored in this city. "'We will no longer be left out, we will be a part of the decision making process,' they said."

As president, McClenney stepped squarely into the middle of the discontent, noting that he thought that the white businessmen in the city, who were the leaders and decision makers, were trying to develop a strategy to deal with the disarray, but still maintain their power. McClenney, a native of San Antonio, said that he "goes way, way back in that community," not only because of his affiliations with the city, but because he said that he also had insight into the workings of the city. His contact with St. Philip's began in the late 1950s when he was a student at SAC and played in the basketball competition between St. Philip's and San Antonio College.

Fast-forward to 1981 when McClenney returned home to San Antonio after completing graduate work and working in several positions elsewhere. He accepted the position of president of the San Antonio Union Junior College District and soon found himself facing that "time of upheaval" that he had described earlier. When asked to explain what he meant by "a time of upheaval," he labeled what was happening in the city early in his administration as "a tumultuous time, with each faction attempting to gain control! The leadership among the board changed four times, but only involved two persons," he said, "and that is why the change in board leadership was so significant."

When an internal audit was conducted, irregularities in bookkeeping in the restaurant management program at St. Philip's came to light and accusations flew back and forth between the president and the board. At Southwest Campus, district equipment was reported missing and an internal audit revealed a lack of written accounting policies related to selling district property. This was followed by accusations of a cover up and a call for the chancellor's resignation by some members of the trustee board. At one point, McClenney sent a memo to the Board of Trustees expressing anger, sadness, and discouragement with the board's behavior, to which a member responded that if he did not like the way the board operated, he could pack his bags. In another instance, McClenney threatened to seek other employment if his contract was not extended, but the board ignored his threat.

Eventually, before his contract expired, McClenney was reassigned by the board to the position of executive director and president of the ACCD Foundation. In a "To Whom it May Concern" letter, the then-Chairman of the Board of Trustees complimented him on his accomplishments, specifically confirming that "He came to the ACCD at a time when the District was going through a very difficult period. . . . He has," said the writer, "accomplished a great deal in the time he has been in San Antonio." The correspondence went on to commend his relationship with the community at large, calling it outstanding, and said that his work with the community college associations and the Texas legislature had been most beneficial to the district.

"When I was there in the early '80s, most people were unaware of the terrific, wonderful mix of men and women, Blacks, Hispanics, Anglos, that St. Philip's had. It was the kind of model that you hope community colleges will be, in terms of all the people who live in an area of a city coming together on a college campus. There were strong and weak programs on each of the college campuses and my effort was to get them to look at the weak ones and to improve them. My work was to focus on how do we create two very strong colleges and have a foundation for creating a third one, which we eventually did. It became Palo Alto College."

During McClenney's tenure, the title "president" changed to "chancellor" and the name of the colleges changed from the San Antonio Union Junior College District (SAUJC) to become the Alamo Community College District (ACCD). "The change in names came at a time when we were redefining how the colleges would work, and that's when, in the early 1980s, we made the transition and named presidents of SAC and St. Philip's College. There were no huge shifts in duties, just a reflection of expectations," said McClenney. During this period of introspection, discussions were held on whether or not the system should be a multicampus or multicollege district.

Meanwhile, in spite of the uproar that the hi-jinks caused within the culinary department at St. Philip's and despite the discord within the board, the college continued to carry out its mission—to serve the students and provide them with an opportunity for a quality education. McClenney explained the results of the fallout from the discord going on within the board this way: "I think that the saving factor for the colleges in San Antonio over all these years of struggle with the board is that, below the level of president, things seem to continue to work. And that's the most important thing in terms of how the students were affected day by day. Thankfully, the politics of the Board were pretty much kept out of the classroom and the interaction between faculty and students."

Few persons can say with the utter confidence displayed by McClenney that "in five years, I absolutely accomplished everything I set out to accomplish"; nor can many persons point to such a magnitude of goals accomplished in as few years.

McClenney, who took credit for creating Palo Alto College, commented, "I got that done. That was not easy, but I set out to expand the college district boundaries and I did that. Now, everyone benefits because they have the county-wide tax base that they did not have. The city of San Antonio didn't even include the college during my time there, so we first got the expansion to the San Antonio city limits. Then we got the expansion to the county line. We got the state law changed to April where there would be a county-wide vote and then the later vote came and it expanded to the Bexar County line. Thirdly, we got the tax base put in place to support a multicollege district in a way that it needed to be supported."

McClenney went on to say, "Equally important was the process of creating equitable systems in that college district: the classification systems, the salary schedules, the policy manuals which said, 'it doesn't matter where you are in the Alamo Community College District, you're going to be treated equitably.' I will always feel good about those accomplishments."

A member of the support staff in the district verified that McClenney straightened out an out-of-control classification system and provided an avenue through which classified workers (clerical, custodians, maintenance technicians, and campus police officers) and professional staff could have a voice in the governance of the college district. The staffer went on to say that McClenney was the first administrator to recognize that the nonteaching staff had the right to express themselves and to offer input on issues that directly affected the staff.

McClenney's closing remarks in the interview summed up his tenure at the ACCD: "I'm finishing my thirty-second year as a community college president and I'm still having fun!"[3]

The Perspective of Several ACCD Board Members

Douglas Harlan and George Ozuna, influential members on the board of the ACCD during the 1980s, each brought to the board a great desire to make changes for the good of the community. Despite their wishes, they often found themselves embroiled in and on opposite sides of those issues. According to Ozuna, "The first six years were tough; I couldn't get anything approved. Any of my suggestions were squashed! But, slowly we chipped away. Six years later we had made quite a change."

Harlan had this to say about his becoming a member of the ACCD Board: "A lot of people felt that there was a need for a change of leadership on the board, so I was asked to run. I needed a companion to run with me because two people were needed to change the majority. Had I run alone and won, it would not have changed the majority of the board; so Gerardo Gonzales was asked and he accepted the request to run at the same time."

Douglas Harlan: Dealing with the Issues

When Harlan joined the Board of Trustees, he described conditions at St. Philip's as deplorable because there had been no preventative maintenance done in decades. The facilities were rotten and the attention given to support and improve the college was scant. "I don't know when the last building had been constructed," he said. "Morale was low and things were just not good. The president, Gloria Jackson, resigned and an interim president was appointed by the chancellor. The board had nothing to do with that appointment."

However, the board was very involved with the selection of the new president who replaced the interim. Seeking a person with talent, ability, energy, and the toughness to do what needed to be done for St. Philip's, the board selected Steve Mitchell from the slate of applicants to replace the interim. Harlan called him "a great choice."

Asked about his greatest accomplishments while on the board, Harlan said, "Well, I suppose my most enduring accomplishment, in terms of its affect on people, would be improvements to the physical plant at St. Philip's, the construction of Palo Alto College, and the recruitment of strong leadership for Palo Alto." While Harlan was modest in noting the things he did while interim chancellor, one change that he initiated had a major impact. Prior to his intervention, adjunct faculty could not, under any circumstances, qualify for health benefits. He said, "I single-handedly got that changed by working with the state leadership to say that any adjunct faculty who taught three courses could qualify for health benefits."

Harlan served the ACCD Board as trustee from 1984 to 1992 and was interim chancellor of the district from 1992 to 1993. During this time, he developed a master plan for new campuses to be built and also got land donated for Northwest Vista College.

Harlan's former board member and friend, Gerardo W. Gonzalez, described him as "a fierce advocate for community colleges and for excellence in teaching, administration, and public service." Dr. Harlan passed away on Friday, November 7, 2008.[4]

Gerardo Gonzalez, ACCD Trustee

Gonzalez, a native of San Antonio, graduate of St. Mary's University in San Antonio, and a local stockbroker, served on the ACCD trustee board for eleven years (1984–1995). While on the board, he held positions either as president of the board or chairman of the finance committee. Explaining how he became involved with St. Philip's, he noted, "I was invited to lunch by two San Antonio businessmen who recruited me to run for a seat on the ACCD Board of Trustees." Doug Harlan had agreed to run for the board, on the condition that they could recruit a second person to run with him, as this could swing the board's majority in a different direction. Giving an affirmative reply to the businessmen when they asked if he would be interested in running for the board, in the spring of 1984, Gonzalez and Doug Harlan successfully ran as a team and were elected to the ACCD Board. Gonzalez agreed to run for the seat held by Dan Martinez because he said that "the district needed enlightened leadership and not politics at the board level." He believed that he was the person that could bring that quality to the board.

At the meeting with Gonzalez, the businessmen explained that since the business community depended upon the college to educate and train the workforce, they were looking to find someone who could turn around what they perceived to be interference into matters at the college. "It is necessary to go back into the history of the college district to understand what was going on," said Gonzalez, "but it was front page stuff and it wasn't necessarily good."

He explained that at that time, St. Philip's employed more black professionals with degrees than any other San Antonio employer, with the possible exception of perhaps the federal government. Gonzalez continued, "the largely Anglo San Antonio business community felt that there was a lot of outside political leaders, elected and nonelected, who were messing with St. Philip's, trying to get people hired, trying to get people fired if they got upset with them, and trying to influence promotions and assignments within the college." The business community felt that this influence and interference at both SAC and St. Philip's from people in the community was impeding the educational mission of the institutions. They were very concerned, because they depended on the colleges to educate and train the workforce. Persons with the ability to influence who was hired, fired, and promoted at St. Philip's would have a great deal of power, so the business community was recruiting persons to run for the board who could change the situation.

A local newspaper, calling it "an unusual political move," reported that a bipartisan group of Republican and Democratic public officials had crossed party lines to support Harlan and Gonzalez in their run for the board. The article went on to refer to the faculty as demoralized and the quality and stability of the college jeopardized because of what they referred to as political infighting and empire building. Harlan and Gonzalez went on to win that election in what was, at that time, alleged to be the largest voter turnout in Bexar County Board of Trustee history.[5]

George Ozuna

Ozuna, a member of the ACCD Board of Trustees for twelve years representing the West Side of the city, served much of his time on the board during the same time as Harlan and Gonzalez. Ozuna, who credits Dean Watson with being his mentor, brought to the board a set of credentials that included many years of service to the San Antonio community. His term included several times being elected chairman of the ACCD Trustee Board. Ozuna said that his election as chairman occurred whenever he was able to garner enough votes. When his time on the board was over, the district's Board of Trustees placed his name on the Learning Resource Center at Palo Alto College. Ozuna served as a member of the ACCD Foundation as well and assisted in raising scholarship funds for students attending the Alamo Community Colleges. He called his work raising scholarships "one of the more rewarding efforts of my career."

Each chairman and board member had his own way of proceeding and Ozuna, an engineer by profession, said that his way was to respond scientifically. He noted that "after the first six years, from 1980 on, everything changed. The board set policy on employment and gave blanket approval on payments made. They were seeking responsible persons, so they formed committees and said there had to be integrity in every department. They set up a police department for security for each campus."[6]

During Ozuna's term, the board acquired the campus at East Kelly, which at the time, consisted of a number of dilapidated buildings. "But, we felt that we could use East Kelly and besides, there was a need for it. It turned out to be a multimillion-dollar gift from the government. As I recall, we had first dibs on it and it was either the school district or us and we took it. There was an inquiry and opposition to our accepting it, but the majority said, 'take it,' and we did. Look at it now!" East Kelly became Southwest Campus of St. Philip's College.

In the 1980s, while Ozuna, Harlan, and Gonzalez were on the board, a situation was developing at St. Philip's that was described as a serious crossroads in its history as an institution of higher learning. The college, which in its history had experienced many periods of sustained unrest, now found itself embroiled in yet another controversy over the top administrative position. The chancellor, who was at the time Dr. McClenney, named Kay Moore, his assistant, as acting president at St. Philip's. Unfavorable conditions persisted at the college: declining enrollment, a program under investigation, internal unrest, and a new college branch in the district likely to offer competition for students. Such was the state of affairs in the St. Philip's College community in the 1980s.

A New Leader

When the St. Philip's faculty and staff returned from the 1984 Christmas holiday for the second semester in January 1985, it was to a change in leadership, to a new president, and with many questions. Dr. Jackson, who had held the position since March 1983, had been reassigned and on December 18, 1984, just before the Christmas holiday, Dr. McClenney made the surprise announcement that his assistant, Kay Moore, would be the acting president of St. Philip's, replacing Jackson. Citing that he had been directed by the board to make a change in the leadership of the college, he gave declining enrollment as the biggest concern. Jackson was reassigned to the district as McClenney's special assistant.

Dr. Kay Moore, Interim President, St. Philip's College, 1985

Moore, who had served as McClenney's assistant since July 1982, was appointed interim president in December 1984 and began her new post on January 8, 1985. She earned a doctorate in educational administration from the University of Texas at Austin, a master's degree from Texas Christian University, and a bachelor's degree from Trinity University. Moore held prior positions that included director of the women's programs at San Antonio College, a program that served more than 3,000 women yearly, chairperson of the Mayor's Commission on the Status of Women, was a member of Target 90 Goals for San Antonio Board of Trustees, and member of the national executive boards of the American Association of Women in Community and Junior Colleges and the National Council on Research and Planning.

One of Moore's first moves was to hold a faculty convocation at which she answered questions, vowed to establish priorities, and to pursue funding opportunities that would make it possible to achieve excellence in the goals set by the faculty and administrators. This move helped to quell some of the many faculty and staff anxieties.

According to a January 18, 1985 publication from the Alamo Community College District that gave an update on St. Philip's, during the convocation, Moore provided answers and indicated her intent to be an advocate for the college. She shared her plans to move the college forward and to assist individuals and programs to achieve their goals. Showing that she was familiar with the unique characteristics of St. Philip's, during the meeting, Moore outlined some of the rare qualifications of the institution and how its strengths could be used to meet the goals and expectations of the faculty, administration, and the community. This, too, was seen as a step in the right direction.

Early in Moore's tenure, the college participated in a self-study and was visited by the Southern Association of Colleges and Schools. Other projects included finalization of the college's master plan and planning and budgeting for the 1985–1986 academic year. But before Moore could implement her plans for the college, her term as interim was over, she was transferred to Southwest Campus, and the search for a permanent president began.

20 Poised for Change

Unbeknownst to me, at the time of the appointment, there were strong undercurrents. The chancellor called me in Hawaii following the board meeting and said that I'd been appointed and that there had been a modest disturbance about this. But, I was not to worry. The next day, I received a phone call from a person in San Antonio who said, "You know, I don't know you personally, but I don't want you to take this job."[1]

St. Philip's College in the 1980s

Despite protests, Stephen Mitchell was selected as the seventh president of St. Philip's College. There were seventy-eight applicants from which the eight-member search committee, which included three black members, culled the list, ending with ten applicants. From the ten, the search committee made a choice of six applicants and Chancellor McClenney selected three finalists from the six candidates for personal interviews by the trustees. Of the three candidates, all Anglo, Stephen Mitchell was selected. Several black leaders spoke to the board, urging the trustees to reopen the selection process and seriously consider hiring a black professional. A local newspaper referred to Dr. Mitchell's appointment as "insensitive and a callous disregard of the black community's demands."[2]

Nonetheless, Mitchell became president of the college and held the position until 1992, when he moved to the ACCD as deputy chancellor.

Dr. Stephen Mitchell, President, St. Philip's College, 1985–1992

With St. Philip's having a history in the district of being treated as a "stepchild," many faculty and community credit Mitchell and his presidency with being responsible for St. Philip's becoming a fully-fledged member of the ACCD family and with being the force needed to affect change at the college.

Mitchell began his academic life as a faculty member in political science at Washington State University. Prior to coming to St. Philip's, he spent ten years in the classroom and another fifteen to seventeen years in administration. When he went to the University of Hawaii in 1973, Mitchell, as an Anglo, had his first experience as a minority person. He described his interviews with the search committee for St. Philip's as "very good," because the committee was very clear about what they felt the "wants" were at St. Philip's. The college interested Mitchell for a variety of reasons: he had looked at other places in California, Florida, and Texas, and had been to San Antonio a couple of times for conferences and decided that there were a lot of things about Texas that he liked. After applying, Mitchell was given the courtesy of an interview and on the second interview, was hired.

One day, before leaving Hawaii for Texas, Mitchell received a telephone call from Texas, from someone he did not know and had not spoken with before, who said, "This job ought to be for a black person and it would be better if you wouldn't take this job." Mitchell's reply was "Unless the board or the chancellor tells me not to, I intend to accept the position, since I really have been given to understand that that's not the case. In any event, I'm going to come." "And," said Mitchell, "that was the only negative phone call that I got. I received lots of positive ones, including people who called me and said, 'Please don't pay attention to these things.' So I came, and from the day I got here until today, I have never had a cross word from anybody in the black or white commu-

Dr. Stephen Mitchell

nity about the inappropriateness of my being president of St. Philip's College. People could not have been nicer; they were more than willing to wait and see what would happen."[3]

When Mitchell met with the board, the trustees were very open about the status of the college, informing him that St. Philip's had been "the stepchild, for God knows how long." Mitchell explained, "Two or three members of the board, primarily Gerry Gonzalez and Doug Harlan, said: 'We're looking for an advocate for St. Philip's College, someone who will turn this place around. Here it sits, junky buildings, crappy campus, blah, blah, blah and we want someone to help us at this level.'" Mitchell, on the other hand, learned that one reason no one wanted to go to St. Philip's was that the district offices were on SAC's campus, and the chancellor was always there looking down the gun barrel at SAC faculty and programs.

Once he arrived in San Antonio, Mitchell said that he and the faculty at St. Philip's enjoyed a cordial relationship. "In fact," he went on to say, "If I had problems, they were below my consciousness. The arts and sciences faculty was black and Anglo with a small fraction of Hispanic people. In the technology field, the makeup of the faculty was partially Anglo and Hispanic."

While the college seemed, at times, to be in a state of flux with regard to its enrollment, the faculty and staff brought a stabilizing effect to the college because of their constancy. One such employee, Kitty Flores, began her thirty-year-plus career as a part-time student while a full-time employee. "I've been here almost thirty years, and will just die here. That's my plan," she laughingly said.

Receiving the Historically Black College and University (HBCU) Designation

"We received the HBCU designation while I was president," said Mitchell, "because we applied for and got that designation. I don't know how much we ended up with every year, but we're still looking at HBCU money. Having that designation made it, I think, probably more attractive to persons and to the faculty members."

During the 1980s, Gaynell Gainer, SPC program director for radiologic technology under Mitchell, was asked to make a site visit to Tuskegee Institute (now University) to evaluate their radiology program. While serving as a member of the Joint Review Committee on Education in Radiologic Technology (JRCERT), Gainer made a site visit to Tuskegee Institute to evaluate the radiology program and as a part of the evaluation, looked at Tuskegee's financial records in the department of allied health. She noticed that the institute was receiving funds for students needing remediation, special assistance, and tutoring in radiology courses and asked the source of the funds they were receiving. When Gainer learned that the funds came as a result of their historically black college designation, she became really interested, thinking of the possibilities for St. Philip's.

Anxious to return to San Antonio and look into the possibilities for St. Philip's, Gaynor says that when she did, she excitedly met with Dr. Mitchell and asked if St. Philip's could consider pursuing the historically black designation. Mitchell contacted the board, set in motion the process for the application, and successfully received the historically black description along with the attendant funds. At this writing, St. Philip's is still the only community college in the nation with the designation of Historically Black and Hispanic Serving Institution.

Another major accomplishment that Mitchell scored in the artistic sense during his tenure was to bring the San Antonio Symphony to St. Philip's College as a "Thank you, Community." He insisted on construction of the Watson Fine Arts Center and that it be a facility of which St. Philip's and the community could be proud. This incurred the wrath of those who felt that before a theatre was built, St. Philip's should have a gymnasium. In defense, Mitchell said that he tried to use the facilities of the college as a bridge to the community. As the school grew and more and more people visited the campus, Mitchell began to believe that he had succeeded in building that bridge.

"We used to do a helluva job recruiting students," said Mitchell. Perhaps they did, for from a population of 6,000, they realized 2,500 to 3,000 new students every year. "We tried to make black students feel comfortable at St. Philip's College," Mitchell continued, "and people who had a choice when they came, who could have gone anywhere, basically, chose St. Philip's College overwhelmingly." St. Philip's College was a very welcoming place for students to come, as evidenced by their enrollment figures. The school offered tutoring and according to Mitchell, "did it seriously, before anybody in town did it."

When Mitchell came to St. Philip's, he estimated that the school had about 120 reading disabled students. And at the end of three years there were over 900. "Now does that mean that we recruited over 900 disabled students?" he asked rhetorically. No, it meant that there were always that many learning disabled students, but during his tenure, St. Philip's went to the trouble of trying to identify them, offered them help, and got them remediated.

When asked to come talk to schools all over the country about what they were doing at St. Philip's College, Mitchell would reply, "I don't want to come talk to you, you come look at what we've done!" Queried about his accomplishments, Mitchell had this to say: "I felt good about the fact that we showed the way nationally in student remediation, particularly in technological applications and student remediation. We were at the cutting edge. I told the faculty at St. Philip's and I told others, we can demonstrate it to you in terms of statistics and data. We take students in a failure mood and we get them to feed on others."[4] Following are excerpts from interviews with faculty and staff who served under President Mitchell.

Faculty and Staff under Stephen Mitchell

Gaynell Gainer, MS, RT (R), and Professor Emeritus

Gaynell Gainer

Gainer, who grew up in San Antonio, received her undergraduate degree from the University of the Incarnate Word (then Incarnate Word College). Gainer recalled that she was hired in 1970 at St. Philip's at a salary of $600 per month to set up the radiology program, which she initiated and developed, the details of which follow. She was employed by the college for thirty-five years and held the position of program director of radiography diagnostic imaging.

The nursing program was already in place, as was a surgical tech program. Peggy Powers (Peterson) who, as program director for nursing, had a dream to offer allied health programs and radiologic technology, became the first allied health course activated. In the early days of the program, the program director was responsible for student selection. From the time of her hire, Gainer had only three months to plan, set up the program, and write the curriculum. She worked diligently to be ready for classes to begin in the fall semester of 1970. In order to begin classes, a laboratory was required, or a room that could be set up with lead-lined walls or something concrete for demonstration of the radiographic procedures.

Gainer learned that there was a one-story industrial building on the south end of the campus where the shop programs, air conditioning, automotive, and other trades programs were held. She secured space in the area in which she had three rooms constructed into a classroom, a dark room, and an x-ray room for practicum. Practicum is now called clinical education. In the meantime, while the lab was being set up, Gainer was granted permission to conduct classes at San Antonio College. The radiographic program began in the fall of 1970 with fourteen students. By the twelfth day, eight students had met the criteria. The program began with no classroom space of their own at St. Philips, no equipment, and no text books. By the year 2005, the program had grown to averaging around fifty students per semester. Gainer learned that there was a general x-ray unit that was not being used at San Antonio College and she secured permission to use it. The first radiography class to graduate from St. Philip's consisted of eight students and was held in 1972.

Since its inception, the program has had four medical directors offering advice to the program, all of whom were radiologists employed in the field. John Braxton, in massage therapy, was the first president of the radiography club, then called the Rad Tech Club. The top students to earn associate's degrees in the first radiography class were Richard Casanova from Seguin and Ernest Galvan from Austin, Texas.

Gainer had many firsts in her thirty-five year career at St. Philip's. Among others, she was a charter member of the St. Philip's faculty senate, a charter member of the Educational alliance, the first black president of the Texas Society of Radiologic Technology and the first black officer in the Texas Junior College Teachers Association. Gainer retired from St. Philip's in 2005.[5]

Julia Briggs, Director, Department of Information and Communications

Briggs began employment at St. Philip's in 1986 under Dr. Mitchell and she shared with us the following history of IT. In 1989, Texas passed a law mandating that all students had to pass the Texas Academic Skills Program (TASP) test in order to take college-level courses. With the state mandate, all entering students had to be tested to assess if they had the skills to handle college-level work and if they did not, they had to be remediated. St. Philip's, and to some extent the district, decided that students in developmental classes had to take three hours of classroom instruction as well. Students in developmental reading, English, and mathematics were required to take three hours of lecture with one hour laboratory and one hour mandatory computer lab.

At the time, St. Philip's purchased 120 IBM computers and put together a network to support these developmental students and found that after two years, the developmental students would complete their remediation and return on their own to the computer lab. Since the college did not have computer labs for students in college-level courses, the president said, "We can't get these students excited about being in college and then take away the tools." Because of this, the college opened additional labs that were to serve all students, developmental or college level.

As computer usage across the nation exploded, Dr. Taylor, who was by then President of SPC, created a department for instructional technology that focused on computer labs and equipment and the use of software in classrooms. The focus was to ensure that all students could have access to the technology and in addition, faculty would have access to the tools they needed, including Internet access. Developmental classes were given preferential treatment in signing up for classes. Since the licensing examination for nurses went online in the 1990s, that group became the second group to receive preferential sign-up laboratory privileges. The department began offering workshops on how to use Word and Power Point. Macros and other quick steps were developed for additional help for the students, even mobile labs. At this point, campus computer usage truly exploded.

During the early 1990s, IBM, who was working with SPC to get and keep the technology working properly, began learning more about SPC, its mission and its successes in the developmental classes. IBM selected St. Philip's as one of ten colleges across the United States and Canada to become a technology transfer center, training primarily other community colleges and some four-year colleges how to use technology to support academic programs.

Because of the success St. Philip's was having in its developmental education classes, the college worked with IBM to develop a product that was built at SPC and sold nationwide. SPC was compensated by IBM with new equipment and software and thus became first in the district to have Microsoft Office Suite. Briggs and her staff were continuously on the road, for SPC's role was to train not just colleagues in this region and in Texas, but also to help train colleagues in New Mexico, Louisiana, Arkansas, and Oklahoma.

While the innovation center at SPC began as a part of instructional technology, by the school year 1995–1996 the educational support services and the technology portion became separate entities. Presently, IBM no longer makes PCS and all of the new technology comes through innovation centers. The innovation center at SPC began as a part of instructional technology under Dr. Briggs. The center at SPC has since spun off into the Instructional Innovation Center (IIC).

The IT department at St. Philip's has the responsibility for all the computers throughout the college on MLK and Southwest campuses, Randolph-Lackland, Truck Driving School, some off-campus locations, all software used by the college, and responsibility for all the telephones and the college website. Its responsibility includes taking care of about 4,000 computers and over 1,000 telephones.[6]

Luis A. Lopez, Director, Instructional and Professional Development

Lopez, employed by the college since 1988, has at this writing been with the college for twenty-three years. Presently holding the position of director of instructional and professional development, he began in fall 2007 as an instructor, progressing from assistant to associate to professor. He became a tenured employee in 1997. The majority of Lopez's employment has been as a faculty member in the computer information systems department program, teaching courses from introduction to computers and applications to programming and Web development. Lopez has been a part of the department of instructional and professional development from its infancy, serving as the first director of the instructional innovation center.

Instructional Innovation Center (IIC)

The instructional innovation program began in 1997, initially with Luis Lopez and a multimedia specialist. Within a few months, a faculty member was added and by spring of 1998 the program had grown to four, adding Dr. Sides as instructional designer, Bess Porter, and a specialist in multimedia.

The instructional innovation program began initially to promote professional growth and professional development opportunities for faculty, as well as to provide professional development opportunities to support and empower staff. Teaching faculty how to instruct and become more proficient at using the Internet has been and is an integral part of the mission of the center. The mission of IIC is aligned with the mission of the Alamo Colleges' Strategic Goal IV–Capacity to Serve.

With two locations, MLK Campus and Southwest Campus, many opportunities are provided for faculty and staff to receive the support they need to succeed, including providing resources and opportunities to grow as well as providing educational workshops. Blackboard Vista Certification, Faculty Development Institute, Distance Learning Showcase, and Administrative Professionals Workshop are further examples of opportunities provided for faculty and staff learning.

Master Teacher Certification Program

The Master Teacher Program, offered through the IIC, began in fall 1998 in response to a desire to improve teaching skills. Open to both experienced and new faculty, the program has been wildly successful since its inception. Teachers entering the program are able to fine-tune their teaching skills using technology and the Internet. The IIC brochure boasts that "quality experiences are provided to allow faculty to actively engage in reflective and creative exercises to improve their own teaching." Opportunities are provided for faculty to dialog about teaching, about the role of the teacher, and about the role of the student. Because of the popularity of the program and to accommodate the need, from its inception, additional sections were added.

The faculty and staff have now grown to eleven full time and three part time. Classes are completed online within a Blackboard Vista course.

Blackboard Vista (BBV) Certification

Blackboard Vista is the standard learning management system for online classes at the Alamo Colleges. Blackboard Vista enables faculty to incorporate online discussions, e-mail, assignment drop box, assessments, Web links, and other online tools into their classes. Faculty must successfully complete the six-week Blackboard Vista Certification training online in order to use BBV for online or hybrid courses. From Luis Lopez and a brochure from the Instructional Innovation Center, we learned that President Loston made this a requirement in 2008.

Mary Gilford taught business technology in the applied science area. In the 1970s, applied science began offering courses in culinary arts as a program within business technology. Because of their rapid growth and expansion, culinary arts felt that they should be separated and their courses offered apart from business technology. Additionally, there was the perception that as long as they were with business technology, it would be difficult for them to reach their full potential.

Dr. Mitchell, concerned about culinary arts and wanting to know how Gilford felt about it, invited her to come to his office to discuss the matter. Gilford, sympathetic with culinary arts, asked him when he was going to do it. "As far as I'm concerned, to this day, I believe that detaching culinary arts from business technology was the best decision that Dr. Mitchell made. I think about the accomplishments that they've made, all the awards they've received, and I know that was a good decision," said Gilford.

Tourism, Hospitality, and Culinary Arts (THCA) Department

By 2007, with nine full-time faculty, five full-time staff and the third-largest culinary arts department enrollment in the applied science and technology division at the college, the program could boast of having 525 students and a waiting list. For many years, St. Philip's offered the only culinary arts program in the San Antonio metropolitan area. Not only has the department been recognized for its accomplishments, but St. Philip's instructors and students in the program have also been recognized for their skills, and for being the recipients of many culinary awards.

From 1970 to the 1990s, programs related to restaurant and hotel management, food service operations, chef's apprenticeship, and dietetic technology were listed under business technology careers or business management programs. As programs were added, they continued to be listed with the business technology careers programs until the department of hospitality operations was established. In 1993, an associate of applied science (AAS) in culinary arts degree was established, and was accredited by the American Culinary Federation Educational Institute Accrediting Commission. When the program separated from the business management department, the name was changed to hospitality management. In 1996, the culinary arts department changed its name to the department of tourism, hospitality, and culinary arts, to better reflect its mission. Students enrolled in the program may earn a one-year certificate of completion.

What's Cooking in Artemisia's?

In 2009, the Upper Deck, a restaurant component of the THCA department, was renamed and began operation as Artemisia. Named for the school's first president, Arte-

Dedication plaque for Artemisia's

misia Bowden, the restaurant features groups of students who collaborate to prepare, coordinate, and serve meals of various styles and cuisines. Their tempting invitation reads: *Venture up the stairs in the Campus Center and see what our students are preparing for you!*

The students prepare gourmet meals in the restaurant-classroom that rivals fine dining at any upscale restaurant. Reservations for dining in the restaurant are required. Twice a year, the students prepare and serve a culinary feast called the Culinary Gala Dinner that consists of five or six courses, complete with sorbet to cleanse the palate between courses. Students in the program are held to very high standards by the program faculty, as exemplified by the requirement to earn a grade of B or better in their "hands-on" cooking classes before they may progress to the next level. Students earning less than a B must repeat the course. Their top graduates have attained prestigious positions at some of the finer restaurants, hotels, and businesses in San Antonio and beyond, including the Hilton Palacio, the Four Seasons Hotel in Austin, HEB Central Market, and the Marriott River Center Hotel.

Awards Earned and Received

In August 2008, the department of culinary arts and department of restaurant management (under department of tourism, hospitality, and culinary arts) was awarded exemplary status by the American Culinary Federation Foundation Accrediting Commission, the largest organization of professional chefs in North America. St. Philip's College is one of the first twenty-five schools worldwide to receive this status and the only nonprofit community college in Texas to receive the award.

The culinary arts program has made its mark in the San Antonio community and beyond. In September 2003, the Texas Higher Education Coordinating Board (THECB), who oversees and assesses the state of higher education in Texas, awarded St. Philip's culinary arts program the designation "Exemplary Program among Community and Technical Colleges."

In 2006, Chef Will Thornton, program director for the culinary arts and restaurant management program and culinary arts was selected as TCA (Texas Chef's Association) Chef of the Year at the annual convention of the Texas Chef's Association. He was first selected as the 2006 local San Antonio chapter's Chef of the Year, which qualified him to become eligible to compete for the title of Texas's Chef of the Year. Mary Kunz, department chair of tourism, hospitality, and culinary arts, was honored in 2003 by the San Antonio Dietetic Association (SADA) for her outstanding commitment to education, to her students, and to the community through the dietetic technology program at St. Philip's. Kunz was recognized in 2010 by the college for twenty-five years of service to the St. Philip's community.

Rani Duprey, a St. Philip's College student majoring in culinary arts, was selected in 2004 as the Junior Chef of the Year. Before winning, she competed with six other Texas finalists, four of whom were prior gold medal winners in culinary competitions. Each finalist was rated on his or her professionalism and dedication to the culinary arts. According to Kunz, "this was the first time a San Antonio student chef had received this honor."

Mary Kunz, Chairperson, Department of Tourism, Hospitality, and Culinary Arts

Mary Kunz, who began as full-time tenure track faculty in 1984 under Dr. Mitchell, dreams of some day offering a bachelor's degree in culinary arts at St. Philip's. Because there are currently no programs in South Texas leading to the degree as of this writing, St. Philip's could logically expand its culinary arts program to offer a bachelor's degree in the field. While, at this writing, an associate's degree is the highest degree offered by the culinary arts department, students may also earn a one-year certificate. The program prepares students to take their place in hospitality, one of the major industries supplying San Antonio's economy, by equipping them with the knowledge and skills necessary for success in the industry. Because of this preparation, the prospects for employment for culinary arts graduates are very positive.

The mission of the culinary arts program is to prepare students to work in hotels, restaurants, country clubs, and retirement centers, as caterers, and in other venues that deal with food. During each semester, the students plan and prepare meals, from the exotic to the traditional, often with an ethnic theme. They gain experience by serving full course meals to the public three or four times a week in Artemisia's, all at a very reasonable price and all of which are nearly always sold-out. With nine full-time faculty and five full-time staff, the department offers associate's degrees in culinary arts, baking and pastry arts, hotel management, restaurant management, and hospitality event management.

Kunz, who at this writing has been with St. Philip's for twenty-five years, grew up in Ohio. Following high school, she worked in the restaurant industry for twelve years before earning her bachelor's degree. A registered clinical dietician, she also earned a master's degree. Kunz credits three individuals at St. Philip's with being instrumental in furthering her career; women that she described as being very strong and professional, whom she admired because of their contribution and commitments to the college: Mary Gilford, Peggy Peterson, and Maritha Burmeister. Gilford served as chair of the business department for many years, Peterson was supervisor of nursing education, and Burmeister was longtime director of institutional planning and research. She felt that each had "a little bit of Artemisia Bowden" in them.[7]

Faculty Opinions

Many of the faculty had complimentary things to say about Dr. Mitchell: they approved of his administration, credited him with putting St. Philip's on the map, gave him credit for making great improvements at the college, and commended him for St. Philip's getting the Watson Fine Arts Center.

"The community didn't want Mitchell because he was Anglo and St. Philip's, in their opinion, was supposed to be a black school," said a member of the faculty. Then too, Mitchell would fight with the Faculty Senate. "The senate, the committees, many faculty fought him because they wanted more classrooms. One person, who used to be a counselor who was sort of like an activist, fought him because he didn't want the grassy knoll areas," said a member of the staff. He quoted Mitchell as having said "point blank, 'Look, I'm not going to have this place looking like a prison or some industrial complex.' Mitchell's vision was to have the school look like a college campus and he fought the different powers at St. Philip's to achieve it." "Ivory Nelson and Stephen Mitchell worked hand in hand getting money, getting the bond passed so they could do things for St. Philip's and SAC," said another. "Stephen Mitchell was at the right place at the right time."

Mitchell served as president of St. Philip's College from 1985 until 1992, after which time he was reassigned and accepted the position of deputy chancellor at the Alamo Community College District. When he resigned from the presidency, St. Philip's found itself facing the search for yet another new administrator. The search culminated with the hiring of Byron Skinner.

Dr. Byron R. Skinner

The search for another president for St. Philip's led to Dr. Byron Skinner who, in 1992, became the eighth president to lead the college in the school's ninety-four-year history. Skinner brought to the position not only years of administrative experience, but also years of experience as a college president. Prior to coming to St. Philip's, Skinner had served as president of Palo Alto College in the ACCD, president of San Jose City College at San Jose, California, and president of the Augusta campus of the University of Maine.

In addition, Skinner held positions as administrative dean, vice president of academic affairs, area dean, behavioral and social sciences, and director of social sciences division in California. He had classroom experience as well, was the author of several books, and wrote and published in professional journals.

The community, dozens of elected officials, and representatives from area churches and community organi-

Dr. Byron R. Skinner

zations, along with ACCD Trustee Donald McClure of District 2, where St. Philip's is located, warmly embraced Dr. Skinner. McClure's encouraging welcome to Skinner noted that "Dr. Skinner will give strong leadership to the college and enhance the strong tradition of education and community service of which we are all proud to be a part." His prior experience as college president and the other administrative positions he held played a significant role in his meeting the goals that he espoused for his leadership role at St. Philip's.[8]

Jeanette Passty, member of St. Philip's English Department Faculty, writing in the *Palo Alto Review*, praised Dr. Skinner for creating an environment that nurtured faculty research and publication. "He led us by his own exemplary quest for excellence in exploring new territory," said Passty. "His bold and brilliant research documented, to our everlasting benefit, the correspondence and the mutually supportive friendship of our founder, Artemisia Bowden, and Mary McLeod Bethune, who visited our campus, attended our graduations, and inspired our future."[9]

Dr. Skinner's tenure, however, was short-lived, for in 1993, after a short term in office, he too, vacated the presidency. He was replaced by Hamice James, who said, "I was looking to work with Byron for a couple of years and then I was going to think about retiring. Dr. Skinner was a real good historian; he wrote books! I admired him, he was a good man." But, this was not to be. Shortly following his retirement, Dr. Skinner passed away in 2010.

Rev. Hamice James

Rev. Hamice James: Resident to President, 1993–1995

The ninth president of St. Philip's College grew up across the street from the campus, never dreaming that he would one day be its president and chief administrator. It is hardly surprising that he was selected, however, for as Rev. James said, "St. Philip's was a part of my history." His ties to St. Philip's began when he was a youngster, playing on St. Philip's campus. "I saw the WWII veterans come and it expanded just with old barracks, all the way up."

James, who assumed the interim presidency in August 1993, talked about how, from his perspective, he became president. "One day, without my prior knowledge that they were coming, two board members and the chancellor appeared at my office and they asked me 'How would you like to become president of St. Philip's?' They just sprung this on me," said James. "I had not sought the office. In fact, I was completely surprised at the offer. And," he recalled, "I told them, I have some requests and preferences myself and I proceeded to tell them three points that I wanted. "'Do I tell you now,' I asked, 'or do I wait until after the board meets?' 'No, tell us now,'" they said.

James indicated to the board members visiting him that he wanted to receive the same salary as his predecessors. "I don't want the responsibility for nothing; at least give me the same salary as my predecessors. And I want that in writing," he said. His second request was that the clock be stopped on the early retirement package being offered by the board. The package was seldom offered and since he didn't know when or whether it would come around again, he wanted to take advantage of the good incentive features in the package. The board agreed. The next request he said "was just a joke." "I kind of know my way around at St. Philip's, been here a long time, I know when I'm in trouble, so, I said, 'You don't have to call me, I'll call you.'" Though he was sure that would not be accepted, he threw that in anyway.

James said that one of the reasons he went into education was to assist students in any way he could. "And," he continued, "We went through the two years, which was a lot of work and I guess it was a lot of patience and a lot of damage control. We tried to get the college back into some kind of order, some kind of acceptability of each other. We were then, as blacks, getting very thin. I established the diversity committee and kind of got that going. We knew we couldn't get on the calendar for two years and I didn't have two years left. They finally got on there and I'm glad to see it."

James hired Julius Gordon as his assistant to take over the student affairs area and according to James, Gordon did a good job while he was there. James had a few problems with the students that he attributed to being older than they, but, he said that he was from the old school and wanted to do things in the manner that he knew worked before. "I was very grateful for Julius, because he was more lenient to most of the students. I approved of how Gordon worked things out and how he worked under my supervision."

Gordon, born in Victoria, about twenty miles from San Antonio, learned about St. Philip's through some of his high school friends. He visited St. Philip's College on a high school tour, but was never enrolled in the school as a student. Gordon was associate dean at the University of Houston for seventeen years, and upon his retirement, moved his family to San Antonio.

James expressed the feeling that some of the relationships that he had during his time as president were false but some of his accomplishments at St. Philip's became the real relationships that he had during that time. "We knew that we had to keep going and keep close to our purpose, what we were there for," said James, "and we had good community contacts."

James, who knew that he was planning to leave the college in two years, said "What we could do, we did. At the time, an early incentive retirement program was being offered and many of the older people were taking advantage of the program, including Courtenay Hopkins, dean of applied science." James's thought was that he would probably have to hire personnel to get the loyalty that he wanted and needed and he wanted to leave at least half the vacancies for the new president to fill.

"And, I successfully did that, but the new president got rid of people I moved to permanent positions. In other words," said James, "I saw the need to have permanency in those positions, especially the dean of applied science, so I put David Brimley in there and then Rose Thomas as vice president of academic affairs. And I agree that they didn't have the credentials. I didn't have them myself, but . . . I think they were good, hard, honest workers."

True to his word, two years after assuming the position of president, having served St. Philip's College a total of twenty-one years, Hamice James retired from the presidency of St. Philip's College and was succeeded by Dr. Charles Taylor. "I was ready to go," said James. "It was time."[10]

Following James's retirement, with the new administration, one of his prime appointments was short-lived. Rose Thomas, vice president of academic affairs, was reassigned. In 1999, the Rose R. Thomas writing center was opened and named in her honor. The center, located in the Norris Technical Building, is designed to help writers at all levels improve by offering such services as one-on-one tutoring. Tutorial assistance is available daily, Monday through Friday, in a low stress, informal, instructional setting. The center is open to all students as well as to the community to help them to improve their writing. Thomas passed away in August 1998.

21 Keeping Watch: The 1990s

Nearing the end of the twentieth century, and weary of the turmoil, St. Philip's was again poised and ready for new leadership. Having lived through numerous changes in administration, scandals and unrest on the campus, scandals on the trustee board, and seasons of wins and losses, the college was primed and ready for a long and lasting relationship with its president.

St. Philip's Welcomes a New President, Dr. Charles Taylor, 1995–1999

Rev. James's replacement, Dr. Charles Taylor, came to St. Philip's from Battle Creek, Michigan, "having been lured to San Antonio because of a college that puts students first and has as its slogan, 'A Point of Pride in the Community.'"

Taylor, who embarked on a career in education during his undergraduate years at the University of Maryland, based his philosophy on helping students to further their lives. He was described in St. Philip's school newspaper as a team player and Chancellor Ramsey, who selected him for the position, was looking for a team player who could easily work with his team and work in sync with the other college presidents in the district.

Following a period of rapid change, when four of the five previous administrators served two years or less, the community, faculty, and staff warmly welcomed Dr. Taylor to lead St. Philip's even as they anticipated an era of permanence with his appointment. The community perceived him as a candidate who could bring to the position the stability that the college needed. There were several other reasons that he was so well received in the black community:

- Taylor was well-prepared education-wise, having earned a doctorate in educational administration and supervision from Loyola University of Chicago, a master's degree in education from Johns Hopkins University, and a bachelor's degree in sociology from the University of Maryland, Baltimore County.
- With his previously held administrative appointments in Michigan, Illinois, and Maryland, the community was proud to have a well-qualified black man as president.
- His teaching experience in the department of counseling, psychology, and higher education at Loyola University of Chicago and his experience as an assistant professor in education at Chicago State University suggested that he was well grounded in education. To members of the community and the faculty, who urged the board to hire a black chief executive for the position, these qualifications made him a good fit.
- Taylor was an African American male and many in the community felt that the history of the college, coupled with its location in the black community, dictated a moral obligation to select a qualified black person for the position.

An administrator since 1976, Taylor's first managerial position was as an assistant dean at Loyola University of Chicago. After serving in that position for ten years, Taylor became dean at Chicago State, where he was also an assistant professor in curriculum and instruction. Continuing his administrative rise, Taylor became vice president of student services at Kellogg Community College, Battle Creek, Michigan. There his responsibilities

Dr. Charles Taylor

included enrollment, retention service, and student development.

A local newspaper quoted Taylor as saying that his philosophy of lending students a helping hand has been the prime driving force in his life, his way of giving back to the community.

Faculty and Staff under Dr. Taylor

Almost without exception, faculty, staff, and students interviewed who served under Taylor spoke with a sense of pride regarding St. Philip's and Taylor's administration. When interviews with persons from the 1930s forward were compared to interviews with persons from the 2000s, many used the same terms to describe the school's culture: dedication, respect, pride, and a sense of family. One can speculate that this harmony of thought was an influencing factor that contributed to St. Philip's longevity, to the sense of loyalty that continually surfaced, and to the schools evolving into the great institution that it has become.

Dr. Elizabeth (Dolly) Hudspeth

Hudspeth, having served under each administration from Murphy to Runnels, reflected in this portion of the interview on her feelings about working under Dr. Taylor:

"Dr. Taylor was a man for the season and he seemed to be good for St. Philip's at that time in the sense that he was a strong black male." Reflecting that the faculty grew under his leadership, Hudspeth said that when Taylor came in, that was the first time that she actually heard the push for more students: "6:00 classes, 7:30 classes, more students. We would spread the table to get students. It seemed to me, that that was when we started growing by numbers."[1]

Dr. Lanier Byrd, Vice President of Academic Affairs

Byrd, promoted to vice president in 1966, remembered that by 1996, St. Philip's had between 5,900 and 6,000 students. In an effort to increase enrollment and "Because I knew something about building programs in college," Byrd said, "we got rid of Monday, Wednesday classes. We just told faculty, 'No More.' We said, 'We're going to have Monday, Wednesday, and Friday class.' So, we made the times flow: Monday, Wednesday, Friday and Tuesday, Thursday. Before that, students found that they couldn't get scheduled right because classes held only on Monday and Wednesday conflicted with the normal flow. We ran early bird classes, meaning that they started at 6:00 a.m." Byrd taught the first four early bird classes, four classes in a row. "I had a heart attack that semester and I blame it on those early classes," he said. "But, I wanted to let them see, I was doing it, they could do it, too!" The classes were popular, because if one wished, classes could be taken prior to going to work at 8:00 a.m. But afternoon classes were another story. No one wanted to see a class after twelve o'clock!

The problem, as Byrd described it, was that the classes weren't scheduled because "No one wanted to teach a class at 2:00 p.m. and no one wanted the class to make." This presented an infrastructure problem that prevented the school from growing larger. To circumvent this issue, faculty was forced into classes at 1:00, 2:00, and 3:00 p.m. "We wouldn't allow sections only at ten o'clock. If we ran

Dr. Lanier Byrd

classes at ten, we could satisfy everyone in the day at ten. But, we said no, we'll run sections all day and then if we need extras, we'll add them at one, two, or three. That way, when students said, 'there's nothing left in the day and I really need the class,' then they took it at one or two. And if they really couldn't, they wouldn't. Having off-campus sites helped with the problem as well."[2]

Rebecca Sanchez, Faculty Chair, Allied Health Department

At the time of the interview, Rebecca Sanchez, a St. Philip's College veteran, had worked at the college for twenty-three years and experienced working under many of its presidents. She also observed the extensive growth of the school. While Sanchez was never enrolled in St. Philip's as a student, and even though she could not claim alumni status, she influenced some of her relatives to attend. "In fact, my brother graduated from the LVN program in my department," she said.

When Sanchez came to St. Philip's, she recalled that there were twenty-six full-time faculty, but only three Hispanics on the allied health faculty, despite the student body being predominantly Hispanic and older. Peggy Peterson was a member of the faculty, as was Virginia Tatum, and since the counselors would each have their own department, students and faculty were never in doubt to which counselor they should go. The concept, which was a good one, facilitated ease of keeping counselors advised of changes needing to be made. It was like a family that Sanchez described as "feeling embraced."

At the time of this writing, Sanchez had eight very dedicated, responsible program directors in the allied health department, each with student advisors housed nearby, all anxious to do their jobs well. Because they cared so much for their programs and took such pride in them, Sanchez described situations in which she could get stats from them at any time. This theme of feeling privileged to be employed at St. Philip's College resonated throughout the interviews, not only in allied health, but other departments, as indicated by the interviews that follow.[3]

Dr. Karen Sides, Professional Staff, 1997

Dr. Sides came to St. Philip's from a university in another state in 1997, in response to a St. Philip's newspaper advertisement. As a professional staff member in the Instructional Innovation Center, she also taught art appreciation in the evenings as an adjunct faculty member. Sides, in charge of professional development of faculty and staff at the college, said, "I loved it because it gave me an opportunity to practice what I teach."

At the beginning of the fall semester in 2007, Sides was promoted as assistant to President Loston. Then in 2010, at the beginning of the new fall semester, Sides received another promotion and became dean of interdisciplinary programs.

When Sides came to St. Philip's, the college was beginning its centennial year. During her first week of employment, she was tapped as a member of the centennial committee. She credits the experience of observing the more than 100 events offered during the centennial with giving her a sense of how fortunate she and others are to be here and an understanding of how many people suffered greatly, and worked hard to make this a possibility. "If more individuals understood this, it would change some things," she observed, "particularly because of the love, the appreciation, and the doors they've opened for us. Miss Bowden is still here and there are times when I am very frustrated and can hear her voice telling me to get my act together."

Sides experienced an incident that she says made her appreciate what she has and that influenced her to do even more: "My class was held in the evening. The oldest person in class was seventy-three years. On the first day of class, the students introduced themselves and this seventy-three-year-old student said that she was going to school to show her grandchildren what for: 'I've lived in this neighborhood all my life,' the grandmother said. 'Always made my children and my grandchildren go to school and now my grandkids are running around like wild Indians. They told me, You never went to school, grandma. So here I am. I'm here so that they can't use that excuse anymore.'"

When queried about changes she would like to see, Dr. Sides made this suggestion: "I would like to see growth managed in a way that we not lose sight of why we're here."[4]

As a professional staff member in the Instructional Innovation Center, one of Sides's duties was to supervise employees, one of whom was Sharon Crockett-Bell. Crockett-Bell was hired by Dr. Charles Taylor to coordinate the dual credit program. The second coordinator of St. Philip's dual credit program, she was given the charge to build the program, which began in 1995. She found that the charge was not difficult to accomplish for the program was offered at no cost to the high school students. Having their high school pay for their books was also a boon for the students, and they earned college credit simultaneously while enrolled in high school before graduating.

Dr. Sharon Crockett-Bell

Dr. Crockett-Bell, who grew up in San Antonio, attended elementary and middle school when San Antonio's schools were segregated. An honor student throughout her school years, Bell walked to St. Philip's during the summers and learned to swim under Dean Hudgins. Attending St. Philip's was a family affair, for her mother, uncle, nephew, niece, daughter, and cousin are all St. Philip's alumni. Crockett-Bell was a transient St. Philip's student, attending evenings and summers while enrolled at UTSA. At the time of this writing, she is in her fifteenth year of employment at the college.

The dual credit program Crockett-Bell was asked to coordinate had been started by Joannis Flatley in 1995, as mentioned above, and its first coordinator had been Jim West. As the second coordinator of this program, which was important to the college's mission and goals, Crockett-Bell was given the charge to build enrollment in the program. The demand for the program's offerings grew, encouraged by the involvement of the participating high schools, which provided the students' textbooks at no charge and offered high school credits for the courses that were also receiving college credit. Students could thus get a head start on their college educations without paying any tuition fees. In one year, the number of students enrolled in the program doubled.

In 2007, President Adena Loston established the return of the Homecoming Celebration. Crockett-Bell was instructed to plan three days of fun for everyone, young or old. "We'll blame Crockett-Bell if something goes wrong," said Loston. "It won't," promised Crockett-Bell, and true to her word, the dance, the dinner, the worship service, everything, took place without a hitch. Everyone had a wonderful time and Loston was so pleased that, at the end of the dinner dance, she presented Crockett-Bell with a beautiful bouquet of red roses.

In 2008, Loston put forth the idea of a Heritage Committee composed of one representative from the seven divisions of the college. As the chairperson of the Heritage Committee, Crockett-Bell serves ex officio on each the four anniversary committees: Women's History, Black History, Spanish Heritage Committee, and the School's Anniversary.

Homecoming

Homecoming at St. Philip's, held annually, provides an opportunity to promote the college's programs, celebrate its accomplishments, and see old friends. When, in the late 1990s, Dr. Charles Taylor reinstated the Alumni Association, which had been dormant for a number of years, he also instructed Patricia Williams and Betty Johnson to contact alumni graduates and invite them to visit the campus for a reception, a program, and campus tours. In addition to dues, alumni were asked to contribute funds that would be given to the students as a scholarship.

The alumni responded positively, plans were made, and officers were elected. Because there were alumni and others who did not graduate from the school, who wished to be a part of the association, the group voted to add "friends" to the group. Each year thereafter, an essay contest was held among the students and the winner received a $500 scholarship, later increased to $1,000. One of the activities of the association was to place the first brick on the Heritage Tree. The brick was donated by the Alumni Association in memory of Artemisia Bowden.

Each year, a free Blue and White Dinner Dance is held, and a homecoming king and queen are crowned, who represent SPC at events and activities on campus. The king and queen each receive a $1,000 scholarship. In 2011, Loston promoted Crockett-Bell to the office of institutional advancement and development.[5]

Concern for Students

The theme of "looking out" for students surfaced in most of the faculty and staff interviews. Randall Dawson, who began at St. Philip's as an instructor in physical education and as intramural coordinator, came to St. Philip's in 1997 under Dr. Taylor. During the interview, Dawson—who teaches foundations of kinesiology, first aid, and a softball class— stated that what he liked best about his position was "being involved with students, staying active, and seeing students do things they enjoy doing." Dawson, who works closely with students in his role as student advisor, has served under three administrators: Taylor, Runnels, and Loston.

Randall Dawson

Dawson came to St. Philip's with hopes of starting collegiate basketball and was initially successful. For a short while, there was a basketball team but not long after he arrived, the team was discontinued for financial reasons. St. Philip's athletic program, which included the men's basketball and women's volleyball teams, was discontinued in 1988. The director of student activities, meeting with the student representative assembly, explained that the program was eliminated because of budget cuts. During 1977 to 1980, the teams were supported by various departments who used money from their budgets to provide the support needed for the teams. When, sometime in 1985, the state began cutting their support, that made it almost impossible to continue the sports programs. Despite the loss of the sports teams, Dawson had nothing but praise for the college itself. "The college is family oriented; that's the nice thing about St. Philip's, the family atmosphere that exists," said Dawson. "I can go talk to whomever because everyone seems to have the goal of helping students. The department does a good job of staying current and viable with courses that the public and the students want." Dawson became kinesiology program director in August 2008, chair of early childhood, clinical services, and physical health in January 2010, and chair of allied health in July 2011.[6]

The theme of being a college family, with students at the center, seemed to flow from the top down. Following are other staff and faculty who worked under Dr. Taylor.

Gool Castleberry and the Women's Volleyball Team

Gool Castleberry, chairperson of the kinesiology department, was born in Quetta, Pakistan, to an Indian mother and a British citizen father. Castleberry, who graduated first in her college and first in her university in India, earned two gold medals from her schools and as a reward for her scholarship, two trips abroad from her father: one around Europe and England and one to America and Canada. On her trip to America, she came to Denton, Texas, where her cousin lived and became fascinated with the educational system, decided she liked the flexibility of the American system, and decided to study here. She had to complete an additional year for her bachelor's degree to be recognized in the United States because of the differences in educational requirements, so she enrolled in the school system in the United States. After completing her degree, she heard that St. Philip's was hiring and she visited the college, where she met Dean Hudgins, who hired her. In 1975, she began at St. Philip's and, as of 2012, remains employed there.

Castleberry remembered working seven days a week teaching seven classes a day, coaching after class, and attending games on the weekends. "Lots of hard work, and long hours and the extra duties offered no extra pay." Under Castleberry, the volleyball team was invited to attend the National Volleyball finals, against Miami Dade College. For five consecutive years, St. Philip's Volleyball Team went to the nationals and finished in the top five teams in the nation each year. The first year, the team came in second in the nation. Along the way, the team received many invitations to play teams that did not normally play junior colleges. Coach Castleberry took the team to Japan for a month, where they learned not only important lessons about volleyball, but also lessons about the Japanese culture, particularly discipline. The athletes learned their lessons well and put what they learned into practice when they came home. Seeing the Japanese teams run their practice inspired the St. Philip's athletes to organize practices on their own.

When the athletic programs ended at St. Philip's, Castleberry started the Alamo Volleyball Association to allow her athletes to have an opportunity to gain more experience. "I focused on creating future leaders, not just good athletes, through their interest in volleyball," said Castleberry, who continues, at this writing, to teach first aid and health classes in the department.[7]

SPC Women's Volleyball team

Hilario (Larry) Garcia, Counseling Department

Garcia, originally from Beeville, Texas, came to San Antonio following a stint in the military. At the time of the interview, he had been employed in the counseling department at St. Philip's for six years. Garcia, who incorporates music into his specialty, conducts research on voice, sound, and music, and when he is not teaching, does consulting using voice, sound, and music.

Hilario (Larry) Garcia drove from Beeville once a weekend for twenty-plus years, never dreaming that he would someday wind up right across the freeway from where he was previously employed. Garcia came to the college in 1998, was hired by Dr. Taylor, and has served under Dr. Angie Runnels, Dr. Patricia Candia, and Dr. Adena Loston.

Garcia's students range in age from seventeen to sixty and represent many races and ethnic groups. Students in his early morning psychology classes tend to be younger while the night classes, those meeting from 6:45 p.m. to 9:30 p.m., are made up of more mature, older students. The two populations are entirely different and seem to model the night students from the 1970s. Like the night students from the 1970s, Garcia's night students are motivated to learn more, do not miss class, and are never late, while many students in the early morning classes arrive late. Because of his dedication to his students, in January

2005 Garcia received the 2004–2005 Teaching Excellence Award.

Along with CL Leonard, Garcia started a program called (at the time) the Bridges Program. Working with four instructors, Garcia and Leonard offered the program to students at Sam Houston High School during a summer session, introducing them to tools to help them become successful in college. Because of the success of the program, the college applied for and received a grant to continue the Bridges Program, which later became the First Time in College Program.

Rita Castro, Learning Resource Center

Employed at St. Philip's College since 1994, Castro, at the time of the interview, was interim dean and librarian. Though she was never enrolled at St. Philip's as a student, Castro attended several of the other colleges in the ACCD and enrolled in a class at Southwest Campus. At that time, Southwest Campus was still a part of San Antonio College.

Castro described St. Philip's as "the best-kept secret in San Antonio." For one, St. Philip's library has a variety of information formats, books, and audio visual materials for the visual learner or the auditory learner, covers programs from business to health, and does a great job of providing information on a variety of topics. Secondly, because of its superior collection, over the years Castro observed that SPC rarely has to borrow from other libraries. Each year other libraries borrow more materials from St. Philip's than St. Philip's borrows from others. SPC librarians make a concerted effort to consult with faculty and students for input into what information would be most helpful to them that they would like to see provided in the library.

Under her leadership, students traveled at least once to Corpus Christi where, as a part of their community service cultural awareness, they participated in the annual beach cleanup. The students traveled to an orphanage in Piedras Negras to take clothing and food. Since some of the students had never been out of San Antonio, visiting Piedras Negras afforded them an opportunity to cross the border and travel out of the country.

The students participated in the Mitchell Lake Project, a successful rejuvenation of an environment that had been laid waste, was revived, and is now thriving with life, which is considered a feather in St. Philip's cap. At this writing, Castro has served under five of St. Philip's presidents: Taylor, Hayes, Runnels, Candia, and Loston.[8]

Vernard Grice, who came to SPC under Dr. Charles Taylor, was program manager in continuing education for eight years at the college. Under continuing education, his division developed courses that they forecasted would be needed by industry, ensuring that the courses offered provided the training needed by professionals to maintain their certification. Grice's job was to sell education to businesses and industry.

A Pivotal Role for St. Philip's

When Kelly Air Force Base in San Antonio closed, St. Philip's provided an essential service to the thousands of employees out of work who had been employed by Kelly, some for more than thirty years. St. Philip's assumed the role of counselor, helping employees adjust to Kelly's closing. Liz Amaya-Alarcon was one such offsite counselor/coordinator at Southwest Campus. She began working with St. Philip's in 1996 at Kelly AFB.

When Kelly Air Force Base closed, Amaya-Alarcon and her team at St. Philip's helped the employees to transition into a short-term training program, which administered tests and taught them the registration process that applied to any college in the ACCD. In addition to providing needed counseling for Kelly employees to get enrolled in the college and help them through the registration process, once the students were ready to graduate, the team worked with the workforce centers to match the students' capabilities.

Since many of the former Kelly employees had experience in aircraft, Southwest Campus provided additional and extensive training solely for the Kelly employees through a grant funded by the Alamo Work Force Development. Southwest Campus performed training for Boeing employees affected by Kelly's closing, and Dr. Zaragoza at Southwest Campus provided a link between the companies interested in having a similar type of training.

Always forward-looking, in the late 1980s St. Philip's staff noticed that a sizable number of students who enrolled came from the North East section of the city. In the 1990s, when politicians in the North East area of San Antonio requested that St. Philip's open a satellite campus in their area, St. Philip's and Dr. Taylor (president at the time) found the request very tempting. The request (from Universal City, Schertz, Kirby, Cibolo, Live Oak, and Selma) to locate a St. Philip's campus in the North East area of the city was looked upon favorably.

St. Philip's College Expands to the Northeast Campus

Dr. Taylor responded proactively to the politician's request and rented space on I-35N at Toepperwein in the Oak Village shopping area. According to Dr. Debbie Hamilton, the first North East Campus employee, the initial startup funds came from Taylor's presidential discretionary budget. The site, known as the Northeast Learning Center on Toepperwein, an extension of St. Philip's College, developed into two classrooms, a computer lab, and a small intake office with two full-time employees and four temporary employees. St. Philip's began offering back-to-back classes, serving just over 500 students. The college continued operating in that location from 1996 to August 2001.

The response to the classes offered was so positive that space soon became a problem that could only be solved by moving from the Toepperwein location. In 2000, ACCD Chancellor Robert Ramsey was prodded by the North East community, in particular the North East Partnership (mayors and elected officials from the ten Metrocom cities), who suggested that though additional classrooms, an additional computer lab, and a break room for students had been added to the first location, an even larger center was needed than St. Philip's was able to deliver. The Alamo Community College District (ACCD), aware of the potential, responded in June 2000 by buying and renovating property at 7990 Pat Booker Road and invited San Antonio College to partner with St. Philip's in the new larger facility.

The first joint effort between the two colleges began in spring 2001 in the Pat Booker location. The school was renamed Northeast Campus, dropping the name "Learning Center." Meanwhile, St. Philip's continued to offer classes through the spring and summer of 2001 in the original location on Toepperwein but by fall semester of 2001, St. Philip's closed that location, anticipating the cooperation between the joint operation conducted by St. Philip's and SAC. The lease at Toepperwein was not renewed and everyone was placed under one location, including the 387 students enrolled. Classes were held at the renovated property at 7990 Pat Booker Road until fall 2006.

After the ACCD purchased another site on Pat Booker Road (8300), a former grocery store was renovated and classes held there while a new permanent 284 acre site was constructed to accommodate the double digit growth that was occurring. By fall 2001, the student population had grown to about 1,500 students.

In 2007, the ACCD authorized another name change, from Northeast Campus to Northeast Lakeview College. Fall of 2008 saw the new campus opened with five new buildings and by fall 2009, nine buildings had been constructed and occupied with more than 5,000 students. Northeast Lakeview College, serving St. Philip's and SAC students, along with a small stream of North East students, was advised by the Southern Association to simplify their process and only serve one sister college, resulting in Lakeview transitioning out St. Philip's students.

According to Hamilton, though some felt that Lakeview was trying to get rid of their St. Philip's heritage, the rationale behind choosing to continue with SAC over St. Philip's was that the majority of the students enrolled at Lakeview were San Antonio College students. Ending the enrollment of St. Philip's students impacted around 1,800 St. Philip's students, as opposed to impacting 2,800 students at SAC. Lakeview declared that they followed the path that negatively impacted the least number of students.

In January 2007, the Board of Trustees fully authorized Northeast Lakeview College as an entity independent of St. Philip's and in fall 2009, the joint association of St. Philip's and SAC at Northeast Campus ended. This does not mean that students who attend St. Philip's do not attend Lakeview, for "With the implementation of Banner, students can register for any of the Alamo Colleges without additional paperwork."[9] Banner is a higher education software system used by the Alamo Colleges to integrate human resources, students, financial aid, and finance processes. Banner numbers replace Social Security numbers as a means of identification in the Alamo Community College system.

Debbie Hamilton, hired by St. Philip's College in August 1999, was offsite coordinator for the Northeast Campus, and the first employee in the district to be hired at Lakeview. In the vice president position since 2004, Dr. Hamilton's journey was a series of promotions, title changes, and role expansions that kept pace with the growth of the campus.

"I like to make the distinction of Northeast Lakeview being a St. Philip's initiative," said Hamilton, "because the initial startup of the campus, which grew into a college, was not a district initiative. It was a St. Philip's College initiative and I want to be sure that we don't lose that piece." Hamilton's title, at this writing, is vice president, student success.

In 1999, Taylor, president of St. Philip's College since 1995 and following a very successful tenure, resigned from the presidency. The presence of this dynamic leader was keenly missed both by St. Philip's and by the community.

A newspaper article quoted ACCD Chancellor Robert Ramsay as having said, regarding Dr. Taylor's leaving the district: "Dr. Taylor came to San Antonio having never before served as a college president and he did an excellent job during his term here, got experience, and became ready to go out and assume greater responsibilities."[10]

Donald McClure, the first African American elected president of the ACCD Board of Trustees, credited Dr. Taylor with not only bringing the college back to the community but with opening it up to the community as well. Vernard Grice echoed this feeling, adding that Dr. Taylor not only brought the college to the community and the community to the college but he made them one and the same. St. Philip's and the Eastside community were finally getting the recognition they deserved.

St. Philip's College celebrated its 100th anniversary during Dr. Taylor's tenure, while also witnessing double-digit growth in enrollment. The *Express-News* wrote, "Since Taylor joined St. Philip's, San Antonio's historically African American college, the institution jumped in 1999 from having one program rated exemplary by the Texas Higher Education Coordinating Board to twenty-one programs, the highest percentage of any community college in the state."[11]

Dr. Homer M. Hayes

Dr. Homer M. (Butch) Hayes, President, St. Philip's College, 1999

Hayes followed Dr. Charles Taylor as interim president of St. Philip's College. Already a twenty-three-year veteran of the Alamo Community College District, Hayes brought with him a wealth of experience, having come to St. Philip's from the position of dean of workforce development for the ACCD. His practical experience included positions as dean of occupational, technical, and continuing education at San Antonio College from 1989 to 1996. From January 1987 to December 1988, Hayes served in a similar capacity at Palo Alto College. He also held the position of associate professor at San Antonio College and before that, served in various administrative positions with the Peace Corps.

With a PhD in curriculum and instruction from the University of Texas at Austin, Hayes came to the position of president well-prepared academically. In addition to his doctorate, Hayes held a master's degree in business education and a bachelor's degree in business administration from Northern Illinois University.

Dr. Ramsay, chancellor of Alamo Community College District, praised Dr. Hayes for his vast and thorough knowledge of community college administration, saying, "His knowledge of our community and the college district makes him an ideal candidate to guide St. Philip's while a presidential search is conducted."[12]

Hayes came well-prepared for the position; however, his tenure with St. Philip's was brief, for a few months after the national search for a president of the college began, it was over. Dr. Angie Runnels was named the new president of St. Philip's College.

22 A New Year, A New Place: The 2000s

I've never seen, nor have I ever heard of, a community college that was as well positioned in the community as this one is, nor one that has the support of the community that St. Philip's has.[1]

Dr. Angie Stokes Runnels

In 2000, when Angie Stokes Runnels took the reins of St. Philip's College, replacing Homer Hayes, she had this to say of the decision: "St. Philip's selected me, and I am eternally grateful for their decision." Conversely, St. Philip's was fortunate to have been led by Runnels, for she was well-suited for the position and she wore well the mantle of president. During the interviews, several faculty and staff compared Runnels with Artemisia Bowden, noting the similarities in their personalities and management styles.

Imminently qualified to fill the position of president, Runnels brought to the office a background of experience at the district level and in community college work. Prior to coming to San Antonio, she held positions as interim president at North Lake College in Irving, Texas, and as executive district director of educational partnerships at Dallas County Community College. In her position at Dallas County Community College, Runnels became well-versed in the importance of building alliances in the community. Runnels's experience in building relationships served her well in her tenure as president of St. Philip's.

Runnels was well-prepared educationally also, for she held a doctorate in educational administration from the University of Texas at Austin, a master's in education from East Texas State University, and a bachelor's in English from Butler College. Furthermore, Runnels was no stranger to the classroom. Her practical experience included elementary, high school, and community college teaching.

Dr. Angie Runnels, President, St. Philip's College, 2000–2006

Angie Runnels served as president of St. Philip's College for six years. During the interview with her, she noted that when St. Philip's selected her from a group of candidates, she came with a pretty good sense of the history of St. Philip's and the opportunities the college offered. It was also a college that was very similar to colleges that she had worked in, thus she felt very comfortable with the idea of leadership of a college in the ACCD.

Runnels understood and appreciated the unique characteristics the college possessed, particularly its position in and the support it receives from the community. "This college had a very different beginning," said Runnels, "and, as it developed and became St. Philip's College as we know it today, it did so in a community unlike development we see in community colleges." Runnels knew that the community had grown up with the college and she knew that the college had grown up simultaneously with the community. She understood that intrinsic to her role was the nurturing and growing of the association between the two entities.

When St. Philip's began as a college, a large part of its mission was to provide training where none was available—training that, at the time, was seen as necessary for

Dr. Angie Stokes Runnels, SPC President, 2000–2006

Negro children. Now, with the passage of time, St. Philip's has become a driving force in the community and broadened its mission to include and embrace any and all ethnic groups. The college provides an educational opportunity for success for any person who chooses to come.

Runnels explained the scope and range of today's mission, saying, "It has many ways by which it fulfills today's mission. Our policy is open door, but along with it, we offer tremendous support. It is expectations, in terms of the criteria to enter programs, and while all of that feeds the mission, ultimately, the college says, if you can come here, if you can find your way and select us, we're not only going to give you an opportunity, we'll support you to the point that you can be successful." St. Philip's faculty and staff understand and adhere to that mission, as evidenced by those whose tenure is counted in decades of service. They value the institution and appreciate the vision and the opportunity to be a part of such a mission.

When asked to comment on St. Philip's role today and its responsibility to black students, Runnels noted that "The college probably has no obligation because of how it started, but there is a moral sensitivity, a very conscious, deliberate commitment to provide educational opportunities for African Americans." Runnels went on to speak of the responsibility that the college has to the community that includes African Americans. "It might even feel, and I think it does, a special commitment to the African American community," she said. "We see many of our people, both young people and old who are accepting higher education and we need to encourage and give them an opportunity and support to do that. So, in that regard, the college does put forth a special effort to attract and keep African Americans."

When St. Philip's began, an all-black faculty and an all-black administration served an all-black population, but in the 100 ensuing years, the changes that transpired produced a different faculty, a different administration and a student body of a different complexion that dictated concerns that differed from the stresses that Bowden and her faculty and administration experienced. There are mandates from the ACCD that set out what its members can and cannot do, and St. Philip's position as a member of the district dictates that it will follow the mandates. Explaining the change, Runnels outlined some of the restrictions: "Unlike yesteryears, a school cannot receive state funds and be restrictive in whom they admit. As an open-door institution, the school cannot regulate who comes; we say the policy is open door and anyone can come."

Runnels reflected that St. Philip's efforts are always to help any and all students be successful who select St. Philip's and then to extend that effort to recruiting others. But with a population of students in the city at less than 20 percent African American, it would be difficult for St. Philip's to have a majority population of African American students in any one discipline.

St. Philip's: An Uncommon Institution

St. Philip's College is the only institution in the nation with the dual designation of African American and Hispanic Serving, thus it holds a special place among community colleges. What is also exceptional about St. Philip's is that there is no question that the community owns it. With the increase in enrollment across the state and the growth in the district, the ACCD became the second-largest community college district in the state and the tenth-largest community college in the nation.

Even with its incredible growth, for fifty years, only one bond issue passed. The open admissions policy in the ACCD allows any high school graduate to enroll at any of the colleges in the district, the state of Texas provides no financial assistance to community colleges for the construction of facilities. The Alamo Community College District Bond Election undated Fact Sheet issued in 2004 by the Alamo Community College District (ACCD) informed the public of key facts about ACCD "in response to recommendations from a citizens' committee for a $450 million capital improvements program and the calling of a bond election."

In 2002, as the district was experiencing the highest enrollment ever, proposals were considered for a bond issue to deal with the increasing enrollment. Many citizens agreed that there was a dire need for the bond issue. The population in Bexar County had increased more than 40 percent in twenty years and the number of students increased by almost 10,000. This growth in population fueled an obvious need for increased educational attainment. The justification was put forth that supplying that need would produce a skilled labor force and a healthy economic future for the city of San Antonio. Moreover, the projections for future growth pointed to an even greater need to expand the present facilities, as well as a need to increase construction of new facilities.

Even as the situation was argued, local news sources reported that several trustees of the ACCD Board were involved in attempts to influence the bidding procedures for construction projects in the district. Subsequently, it was revealed that city council persons, individuals who were or had been ACCD Board chairmen, several trustees, architects bidding on ACCD Board projects, and persons from the community were implicated in the events. At least nine individuals were indicted, including a school principal, senior board trustee, former board president and chair, board employees, city council persons, and individuals from the community.

Meetings were held in the community and on the campuses to develop strategies that could lead to consensus and passage of a bond proposal. Despite the fact that the ACCD had had only one bond election (1987) in the past fifty years, concern was expressed that winning approval for passage of the bond election might be difficult to achieve because of the scandals occurring at the time.

Since the outcome of the scandals led to several indictments as well as prison terms for some, to deal with the bad press that resulted, the district appointed a Citizens Committee and charged them with the responsibility of developing a recommendation to the ACCD Board of Trustees regarding a capital improvement plan and bond proposal for the colleges in the district. The district was experiencing the highest enrollment ever, a factor that the Citizens Committee took note of when recommending the bond issue. They further recommended that a citizens' bond oversight committee be appointed to ensure that the plans as set forth by the college presidents and endorsed by the committee were implemented.

Subsequently, a Blue Ribbon Commission was appointed in the spring of 2002 to (1) study the improvements and repairs needed at the existing campuses of the ACCD, (2) look at the construction of a new college to accommodate the fast-growing population in Northeast Bexar County, and (3) study the feasibility of floating a $430 million bond issue to fund the improvements and construction. Even so, when the bond issue was put to a vote, the measure failed.

The Board of Trustees recognized that the district had experienced dramatic growth in the number of students served and that an increase in the numbers of students served was likely to continue. Because of this, a solution had to be found to deal with the inadequate classrooms and laboratories and additional space needed. In 2004, the ACCD Board of Trustees again called for an election for a bond issue. A Citizen's Bond Committee was formed, chaired by Jackie Van De Walle, chair of the ACCD Foundation Board. The Bond Committee met for several months to evaluate the need in the district and was given the responsibility of developing recommendations regarding a capital improvement plan bond proposal for the district's colleges. The plan, to be presented to the ACCD Board of Trustees, would ultimately be presented to the citizens of San Antonio.

The committee was made up of more than 100 business leaders and others appointed from the community. They looked at enrollment data and projections, met with community groups, and held public hearings about the bond issue, all in an effort to arrive at a recommendation. The presidents of the five colleges in the ACCD—Palo Alto College, St. Philip's College, San Antonio College, Northwest Vista College, and Northeast Lakeview College—developed a plan for improvement of the district and the Bond Committee agreed to accept the recommendation of the college presidents without change. The committee concluded that the need for additional space was justified and they recommended improvements for all of the colleges, to include renovation of existing buildings, construction of new facilities, and upgrading telecommunications to provide the space needed to accommodate the anticipated growth in the district.

The committee further recommended that the board

adopt the plans and place the Bond Election for $450 million (up from $430 million) on the November 2005 ballot. They recommended that plans for assembling an oversight committee be implemented and that the oversight committee be given the duty to ensure that the capital improvement plans from the presidents were carried out.

The ACCD Board took the position that in order to keep pace with the growth in the county and to continue to provide the educational services needed just to maintain the progress already made, steps had to be taken to raise monies needed to build new facilities and renovate and improve existing ones. They announced that since the state does not provide financial assistance to community colleges for the construction of facilities, another source of revenue had to be found, and the only way to raise the monies in the amount needed was to issue bonds.

The chancellor reported in the college district's newsletter that student enrollment had grown by 41 percent in the previous six years, which added to the need for more space and additional classrooms. He cited the need for expanded facilities to accommodate future economic growth in the area, as well as to meet the future educational attainment needs of the population. The committee recommended to the board that a bond issue be floated and when the board accepted the recommendation, they also set into motion a $450 million bond proposal to meet the needs of the growing enrollment.

At the same time, the trustees tacked on a proposal that the nursing and allied health careers programs be moved from St. Philip's and SAC to the North West quadrant of the city. They left the final site to be determined. Students in the program would continue to take their requisite courses at the community college of their choice, but when they were accepted into the programs, they would be required to continue their training at the new location, wherever it was.

Two outside consulting firms, as well as the ACCD, analyzed possible sites and after many presentations, discussions, and questions from the public, in a split vote, the board voted to move the nursing and allied health programs from the existing campuses of SAC and SPC to the South Texas Medical Center Complex.

A huge public outcry ensued at this proposal. The issue was so divisive that the board scheduled town meetings to be held in the various parts of the city that allowed citizens to be heard regarding the issue. Powerful groups within the city on both sides of the issue launched campaigns to save or defeat the proposal to move the programs.

The issue of relocation reopened old wounds for some individuals in the black community who had long believed that new projects were located away from the underserved portions of the inner city. Valid and convincing arguments on behalf of the institution were put forth by both sides and included press conferences called to report issues regarding moving the programs. There was no question that persons in the community, including a county commissioner, were totally committed to helping St. Philip's in the fight.

The Eastside demonstrated just how much ownership of the college meant to the community by turning out in force to protest the decision by the ACCD Board to move the nursing school from St. Philip's campus. Opponents of the move argued that those hardest hit by the move would be the less affluent members of the community from the less affluent parts of the city, namely the East and West sides. Transportation to the medical school area was seen as a major issue. Some in favor of the move argued that the proximity to the health care institutions at the medical center and the opportunity to interact with other students would override the travel inconvenience.

Proponents of the move argued that, even though a waiting list was kept, hundreds of qualified applicants were turned away from St. Philip's and SAC each semester because of lack of space. A further argument for the move was the shift in the population center of the city to the northwest side of town. Meanwhile, the community mobilized in opposition to moving the nursing and allied health programs. To hear the voice of the communities, the ACCD Board of Trustees scheduled a series of special public hearing meetings at which attendees could sign up to speak. Powerful groups and individuals, accustomed to having their voices heard, spoke in opposition to the move. Communities Organized for Public Service, Metro Alliance, Community of Churches for Social Action, several state representatives, including State Representative Ruth Jones McClendon (whose husband was a member of the ACCD Trustee Board), well-known physicians in the community, and faculty members from SAC and SPC all signed up and spoke in opposition to the move.

Great pressure was mounted on the ACCD Board of Trustees by community groups, business leaders, and local elected officials, some of whom wanted the campus built in the inner city and others who wanted it moved to the Northwest side of town in the South Texas Medical Center. Each group urged the board to carefully consider their decision to move the nursing and allied health programs away from SAC and SPC. At a regular board meeting, Chancellor J. Terence Kelly had made his preference clear in his support for the medical center location.

A state senator, commenting on the importance of the bond issue, noted that the only negative heard about the bond was the portion that dealt with the allied health and nursing facility. Otherwise, if that part were taken care of, the bond issue had a very good chance of passing.

The Capital Improvement Program (CIP)

In November 2005, voters in Bexar County received the $450 million bond proposal designed to meet the needs of the increased enrollment in the Alamo Community College District. Statistics placed an increase in student enrollment from 36,000 per semester in 1998 to 50,000 students in 2004. Moreover, enrollment in ACCD was projected to rise by the year 2010 by nearly 20,000 additional students. To accommodate this unprecedented growth along with the projected increased in enrollment, new facilities would be needed if the district were to be able to continue to provide the quality education the community had come to expect.

The committee, mindful of the costs and needs of the taxpayers of Bexar County, also noted that while the district had continued to grow, funds to handle the continued growth had not been appropriated, and the only way to keep pace with the needs of existing and future student demand was through issuing bonds. The committee acknowledged that without a bond issue, the district would be hampered in their efforts to meet the needs of the additional student population. Because of the critical role that the ACCD plays in meeting the training needs of the workforce in San Antonio and surrounding areas, the committee was forced to examine the critical need for additional facilities and labs, particularly for the health profession, and specifically for nursing and allied health.

Because of the lack of adequate facilities in which to accommodate them, each year students in those areas of the health field were turned away, even though a waiting list was maintained. Another area of critical need in the area of workforce training was in bioscience and manufacturing.

The CIP committee met weekly, with some of their meetings open to the public. In addition, two meetings were held in which the committee received comments and input from the taxpayers. They held meetings with and received presentations from administrators and presidents of the colleges in the district and made site visits to the colleges to better understand their needs. Since the state of Texas does not provide support for the construction of facilities, passage of the bond issue was critical.

Julius Gordon, Staff

Julius Gordon, director of student services, is a long-term employee who served under Loston. Gordon also held the position of coordinator for the Capital Improvement Program. As coordinator of capital improvement, he was in charge of all construction and renovation projects at St. Philip's College. In conjunction with his construction position, he automatically became a member of the Citizen's Oversight Committee for the CIP program. The Oversight Committee was formed by the district to oversee the project, and to ask hard questions such as "What are you doing and why are you doing it this way?" The Oversight Committee was selected by and reported to members of the trustee board.

When put to a vote, in November 2005 the bond proposal passed and each of the colleges in the district received monies from the $450 million package. Over two

Julius Gordon, Director of Student Services and Coordinator of CIP

million dollars of St. Philip's share was allocated for a new diesel lab at Southwest Campus.

Tommy Adkisson, County Commissioner, Precinct 4

Former State Representative Adkisson, an attorney, has been county commissioner for Precinct Four in San Antonio since November 1998. He attended classes at St. Philip's during the summers of 1967 and 1968. During the 2007 Homecoming Get Re-Acquainted Mixer, Commissioner Adkisson was among the honorees, and received an official 2007 Homecoming Medallion.

Continually demonstrating his understanding and appreciation of the value of St. Philip's to its community, Adkisson placed his support firmly behind many of the school's projects, including the one to relocate the nursing and allied health campus at St. Philip's College. Noting that all of the colleges in the ACCD would be winners in the bond proposal, he went on record in this fight indicating that keeping the nursing and allied health campus at St. Philip's College would be an enhancement. Adkisson cited one of his reasons for determining St. Philip's to be the best site for the campus as "ease of access to St. Philip's by the great populace that seeks health education." He went on to say that St. Philip's location does not invite its students to travel a great distance and struggle with traffic congestion.

SPC's portion of the $450 million ACCD bond was $67.5 million, of which $30.8 was earmarked for the nursing and allied health complex. In November 2005, the issue was again put to a vote and the San Antonio community passed the multimillion dollar bond issue. The bond project was designed to build a new community college in the North East, provide new facilities for each of the four existing community colleges, and provide greatly expanded learning opportunities, particularly in the area of health careers. The proposal to move the nursing school was voted down.

Commenting on the results, Runnels had this to say: "The community is the voice that the board didn't hear early—heard late. And, as I go back to it, never have I seen or heard a community that would take on an organization on behalf of, or in support of or in opposition to." She continued, "Now, I understand that this community can take on a position in opposition to this college and be just as strong as they were in support of it. A unique feature of this college is that the community has a role in it and when they believe that harm is going to come to the college, the community becomes very active. This college has penetrated the community far beyond those of us who are African American."

Faculty and Academic Programs

Runnels observed that St. Philip's does what is not always done for community college academic programs, and that is "to outline for students an academic program where academics as a major is identified." If a student wants to major in English at St. Philip's, a pattern of study is developed for that student, all done online, and this is not generally done in community colleges. The transfer guides and the articulation agreement are online, so that any student going on to the university can look specifically at that university and look at the curricula comparison of what will transfer, for example, between St. Philip's and A&M. The Transfer Program at St. Philip's can be attributed to the ideas of one person, Pearl Conyers.

The Transfer Program and Pearl Conyers

As the October 2004 issue of the *Counseling Department Newsletter* stated, "It is with painstaking excellence that Ms. Pearl Conyers developed the St. Philip's College (SPC) Transfer Center." The Transfer Center at St. Philip's became a "model" for transfer centers throughout the Alamo Community College District. Conyers, who at this interview has been with the college for forty years, came to SPC in 1971. In fact, she still recalls the date, August 9. Though she did not receive a degree from SPC, she did attend for one semester, taking history classes. From the time of her hire, she has witnessed many changes, including seeing the first Hispanic hired in an administrative role.

History of the Transfer Center

Because there was, at times, a problem with classes transferring between the four-year colleges and two-year institutions, Conyers came up with the idea of a transfer center, making St. Philip's the first college in the district to have such an entity. As a counselor, she wanted to give her students more information about what would transfer between the colleges, since there was no guarantee

Pearl Conyers, developer of SPC Transfer Center

courses offered would transfer. Conyers made a list of all the courses taught at St. Philip's and sent this information to the four-year colleges and universities in the surrounding area, requesting course equivalents. Then, dreaming of an office where students could go that was dedicated solely to transfer information and working with fellow counselor, Johnny Walker, the two developed and implemented the career center, the forerunner of the transfer center. After discussion with several others, Conyers developed a plan for St. Philip's students to ensure that they would not take courses that would nqot transfer into the major that they were studying. She began by collecting prior SPC catalogues.

St. Philip's has derived many benefits from Conyers's ideas. The first program that she chaired was Spirit Week, four days of activities designed to build school spirit. At the time, SPC had a basketball team and Conyers and Patricia Williams banded together saying, "We can have our own spirit week." They solicited persons to form a committee made up of persons who were experts in their particular area, namely, Olga Davis, speech expert, and Kathryn Morgan, music expert. During the late 1980s, Conyers founded Black Students Educational Network, open to students who wanted to enhance their education. St. Philip's intercessory prayer group in the 1980s was another of her creations. In 2008, Conyers and instructor Cynthia Cortez put together the first Hispanic Mother-Daughter Conference to promote communication between mothers and daughters. Door prizes and two scholarships were given away.

St. Philip's President Runnels observed that this college district is committed to hiring faculty, and developing full-time, tenured track faculty to ensure that students receive the courses they need. With all of the courses offered, St. Philip's is superior to many colleges in the number of faculty actually hired. Though she was already on staff when Runnels came, Conyers exemplifies that employee, for she is committed to helping students to achieve the best possible fit in the courses they attempt.[2]

What's Lacking?

Yet, with all of the support services and opportunities available, St. Philip's has not yet developed to the point that a degree can be earned without coming to the campus. "We're getting close in one of our allied health areas and in some of the general academics," Runnel said. "But you still have to come [to the campus] for something. Not all of our student support services nor all of our testing can be done off campus, but we're close. A student could take a course, even a few courses, but before that student could complete a program, it would be necessary to visit the campus."

Though St. Philip's passed the century mark and, in the process, underwent vast changes, its values, its focus, its moral fiber, and its emphasis on providing quality service to its students and to the community remains steadfast. These attributes have not altered from the strong foundation set in place by Bishop Johnston and by Miss Artemisia Bowden.

Runnels: Most Important Contribution

While Runnels admitted that it was much too early for her to judge, she thought that she could chance an opinion that the organization is focused and refocused on service to students. She used the opportunity given her to select staff and faculty to help with that focus and she selected and invited persons to join her administration who she felt would fit into what the college is doing. Runnels selected employees who could really make a difference in the lives of the students, and she considered their attitude as well as their academics.

To ensure that there would be a good fit in the organization, Runnels interviewed her entire faculty before hiring them, just to be sure they would fit, regardless of their preparation.

Runnel's goal was to ensure as nearly as possible that faculty would be a good fit for the organization, regardless of race. Her concern was less with the ethnic background and more about being committed to the organization. Because Runnels displayed such great attention to detail in hiring employees for the college, she felt very comfortable that St. Philip's was staffed with a cadre of dedicated employees who remained true to its mission.

She went on to say, "We've had some challenges when people have simply not been willing to shift to what it is that we do and what we consider most important." Invoking the name of Miss Bowden, Runnels went on to say that as a result of some deliberateness on the part of the administration, "We've really kind of moved to where I think she looks down and smiles and says, 'You're on the right track there now' and that's in service to this organization.

"We're at a good place, we really are, and it's the result of lots of people working in the interest of the institution."[3]

Faculty and Programs under Runnels

Dr. Burton C. Crow

Dr. Burton C. Crow

Crow, who grew up in Dallas and Fort Worth, came to San Antonio and St. Philip's in 1986. He was employed at the college for twenty-three years and retired in 2010. During his full-time employment, from January 1987 to 1990, he was over continuing education, then, in 1990, became director of advising and assessment, a new position created in response to the Texas Academic Skills Program. Crow served nine years in the director position until he was asked to become acting vice president for student affairs, a position he held for about a year before becoming director of admission and records. He moved to the position of dean of enrollment management, a position he held through August 2010. Crow retired from full-time employment at SPC in August 2010 and continued his employment at St. Philip's in a part-time position in the Learning Resource Center for a short time before fully retiring.[4]

During his tenure, Dr. Crow served as co-chair and member of the President's Lecture Series Committee. At least one performance of the lecture series is held on or near Juneteenth, the oldest known celebration commemorating the ending of slavery in the United States.

History of the President's Lecture Series

In 2002, Angie Runnels selected Dollie Hudspeth and Karen Sides to be co-chairs of the inaugural President's Lecture Series Committee. Both accepted enthusiastically and, for the next five years, worked tirelessly to support this new program. To begin with, they decided on a series of approximately five lectures per year: two in the fall, two in the spring, and one in summer. Dr. Hudspeth and Dr. Sides shared with us an account of the origin of the series.

Co-chairs Hudspeth and Sides submitted a list of names of potential committee members to Dr. Runnels for her approval, and when she agreed with the list and gave her approval of the selection, the co-chairs and their committee began work on a plan for the 2002–2003 inaugural series. The committee decided that each lecture should consist of two presentations: one in the morning for day students and an evening session for night students and the broader community. The lectures were to be developed around a theme that was academic in nature as well as inspirational and motivating to the students. This free to the public forum was and continues to be well attended by St. Philip's students, faculty, staff, and community.

Inaugural Lecture Series Committee Members	
Dollie Hudspeth, chair	Karen Sides, Co-Chair

Committee Members	
Olga Samples Davis	Rosalinda DeHoyos
Julius Gordon	Paul Martin
Donna Stetz	Richard Tietz

Funded through the president's office by the President's Lecture Series grants, the series began with a $25,000 budget to defray costs. As the years passed, the committee began working with a speakers bureau to identify prominent essayists, authors, scholars, entertainers, actors, and others guests to visit the college and make a presentation on their area of expertise.[5] The lectures are always well attended by faculty, students, and community and with standing room only; the concluding lecture for 2011 was no exception.

In recognition of their lecture series presentation and as their gift to the college, a stone, reflecting a gift of at least $500, is placed at the base of the heritage tree in the Heritage Room to commemorate the gift of the presenters' services. A very popular part of the series is the visit the presenters make to classes that are relevant to his or her topic. The class visit, usually held following the presentation, includes an interactive question and answer period with the students.

If the presenter has written a book that goes along with their lecture, the committee will secure a consignment of the book to be placed in the campus bookstore. Time permitting, books are signed by the author as they are sold in the lobby of the Watson Fine Arts Theatre. The President's Lecture Series is one of the premier presentations offered by the college.

Dr. Gregory Hudspeth

Gregory Hudspeth, another longtime employee of SPC, has served the college for twenty-seven years. He has held during his tenure, among others, the prestigious position of vice president for academic affairs. Hudspeth witnessed during his time many activities on campus that he described as defining moments in the life of St. Philip's. Specifically, two of the most memorable moments occurred when Jesse Jackson and Rosalind Carter visited the campus. At the time, Mrs. Carter was the First Lady of the United States and Jesse Jackson was playing a pivotal role in the civil rights movement.

Hudspeth gave his assessment of what it was like to serve under Runnels: "Dr. Runnels was a wonderful person to work with because her leadership was clear and precise. I didn't have to wonder; I knew what she was thinking. Because of the clarity of her administration, this has been a very positive environment for me in which to work . . . it becomes my charge to make sure that I express that same clarity to the people who are working with me. As administrators, we should not view others as people working for us but people working with us. We're all part of this field and we need to work together to get the job done."

Hudspeth was instrumental in the development and implementation of the First Time in College Program as well as the Honors College. Both were Runnel's ideas and evolved from the planning process. His assessment of the faculty echoed what Runnels had to say about the quality of the faculty. He singled out English, math, social and behavioral Sciences, and chemistry departments, noting that the administration had really done well with regards to hiring persons in those departments. Because they were able to think outside of the box, they found persons who practiced good scholarship and that helped the administration improve the quality of education offered. "That's important for us, because we're aiming to move from being thought of as a vocational school only to an academic environment offering vocational subjects," said Hudspeth, "and the goal is to bring in people that are able to help us meet that goal."[6]

Tracy Shelton, Associate Director of Records

Shelton, who came to the college in 2002, has been with the ACCD for twenty-five years. She worked previously at San Antonio College. Shelton and others in her office act as custodians of student data, maintaining data and filing student records. She has constant contact with students, a job she loves, even with the usual challenges of personnel, money, and equipment.

In her position, between the many different students that she sees, Shelton describes typical students: some are more savvy than others, some need a lot of encouragement and nurturing, and some are quick to complain about having to use the computer to register. "Why can't we just register for the classes? We didn't do it like this before," some students complain.

Despite the hesitation on the part of some students, Shelton noted that there has been an increase in Web registration, which she says more than doubled in two years. Even so, not all registration is done on the Web. There is Web and telephone registration and there is also a period when one-on-one personal contact registration is done because of the necessity to maintain human contact.[7]

John Gomez

Dr. Runnels was the first female president under which Gomez served, and he compared her to "being rather like Miss Bowden." In his opinion, she moved the school along and did a lot for St. Philip's. During Runnels's administration, the college acquired new copiers. With the new technology, faculty and staff learned from Gomez that it was not necessary to come to the print shop to fill out a form or to bring in the originals. Everything was done using the technology. Faculty and staff e-mailed their jobs to the print area and Gomez and staff returned it using the technology.[8]

DJan (Jan) Aggrey, Faculty, Business Department

St. Philip's students have an opportunity to interact with local, national, and international faculty on a daily basis. Jan Aggrey, a member of the international faculty who grew up in Ghana, moved to Canada at the age of seventeen to continue his education. After almost twenty-seven years in Canada, Aggrey moved his family to Texas. He was introduced to St. Philip's College through Dr. Sandra Mayo, former chair of the arts and sciences department.

Aggrey, a Microsoft program instructor, teaches his students about PCs: how to build computers, how to troubleshoot and maintain them, introduction to the basic knowledge of hardware, and to operating systems. A new IT program director, his goal is to get across to students where they are, how far they can go, and to have them become qualified as certified technicians. Aggrey says that he "gets the jitters when his students come to class in flip-flops and a cap," because he expects his students to treat his classroom like a workplace and to come to school dressed as though they're going to work. "I want to give them the assurance that the avenue that they take is one avenue that can take them to places well beyond their imagination," said Aggrey.

Concluding that even though the college cannot yet do a four-year course, Aggrey feels that students that graduate from St. Philip's have really excelled and that gives the instructor the zest to do a little bit more and to see that their efforts have been successful. "This is not the end," he tells his students, "this is just the means to an end." Students that go through Aggrey's class soon learn that the journey is just beginning.[9]

Diana Garza, Executive Secretary

Garza, from San Antonio, is from a family of fifteen children, ten brothers, and four sisters, many of whom, including herself, were military. Garza, activated into the military after 9/11, was sent to guard duty at Ft. Sam Houston in San Antonio. She retired from the military in 2007 and decided to come to St. Philip's because of her very favorable "over the telephone" experiences.[10]

John Westerbeck, Coordinator of Veterans Affairs, Air Force Retiree

Westerbeck, who came to St. Philip's in October 2000, is responsible for establishing student eligibility for all forms of VA educational benefits and ensuring that students receive those benefits.

A graduate of Southwest Texas State University (now Texas State University) and a former Texas State staff member, Westerbeck spent four years as a financial aid officer at Texas State before coming to St. Philip's. He learned about St. Philip's from his youngest daughter, who attended a number of colleges, including St. Philip's. She recommended St. Philip's to him over all the other schools that she attended because of the personal attention that she received while there.

When Westerbeck arrived at the Veterans Affairs Office in the late 1990s, he described the office as "an absolute dump. Nothing had been done to the office for at least ten years. They started with furniture that they'd gotten from the VA or probably from S. W. Campus a long, long time ago." With support from Dr. Runnels and Dr. Candia, he successfully renovated the area and, though the process was a year in the making, the end result was being able to work in a first-class professional environment. In 2009, the office moved into a new location in the Welcome Center.

The Office of Veterans Affairs

The Office of Veterans Affairs works specifically with veterans, dependent spouses, children, and (in some instances) members still on active duty. The office serves a number of different categories of students, the largest group having gained their eligibility by serving on active duty. While the veterans are discouraged from using their GI Bill while on active duty, it is explained to them that because the GI Bill will only cover tuition and fees, it is wiser to wait until they are no longer on active duty because then they will receive additional benefits, an important factor for returning veterans who come with the expectation that their schooling will be paid.

The veteran's office is one of the first places retirees and veterans seek when they come to SPC. There, they receive full briefings on their benefits when they separate from the service. Even so, Westerbeck and staff will travel to talk with any group that requests their services.[11]

St. Philip's College Veterans Outreach and Transition Center

Already a veteran-friendly place, SPC has plans to become even more welcoming to its more than 1,000 veteran students. Presently, SPC has service offerings at Lackland Air Force Base, Randolph Air Force Base, Fort Sam Houston, and the Mobility Project at the Center for the Intrepid. Plans are in the works to partner with the city of San Antonio to renovate the Eastside Good Samaritan Hospital, which was the first black hospital in San Antonio. The old hospital is located about a mile from the MLK Campus in an economically depressed neighborhood with substandard housing. When complete, the building will become a Veterans Outreach and Transition Center, providing services to both veterans and their families, job support, and transitional services that may be needed by the veteran, including counseling and job training.

With $2,000,000 in funding provided by the city of San Antonio for renovation and land acquisition, and SPC providing the operational personnel needed to support the center, it is anticipated that this project will service over 2,300 individuals per year with no financial impact on the operational budget of the Alamo Colleges. The project will contribute to historic preservation for the Eastside community.

Student Perspectives

Raymont Donyale (Donny) Penn, Student, 2005

Not only did faculty and staff speak in glowing terms of the school, but students did as well. Donny Penn, a first-year student at the time of the interview, was, as he put it, "in a race against time, trying to get out of school as quickly as possible." St. Philip's, for him, was a great starting point for going on, a good learning experience before attending a four-year university.

When Donny attended St. Philip's in 1995, he was just out of high school. He confessed to being "not quite set on school," so he didn't complete the first semester. Ten years later, at the time of the interview, he was twenty-eight years old, had made the decision to come back to school, and now he is set to focus on his plans to earn a degree in nursing. Donny now has a wife and three children, and his wife is also in the RN program at St. Philip's.

Donny, a work-study student in the department of student life, assists John Martin and Julius Gordon, administrators in the department of student life, in putting on different programs for the students. Closer in age to the students than Gordon or Martin, Donny bridges the gap with the younger students and with the efforts of the college to retain them. He elected to attend St. Philip's because it is located in the area where he went to high school, because of close proximity to his home, and because he identifies with students at SPC, who have some of the same concerns as he.

But, he suggested, St. Philip's could do more outreach for African American men. Having attended Girard High School, which is right down the street from the college, he was critical of the fact that, at that time, no one around his age came to his school to let the students know that St. Philip's was interested in them as potential students. Student life is working on a mentoring program to address outreach for African American males. One such program they developed is called African American Male Mentors.[12]

John Martin, under whom Donny worked in Student Life, has been associate director of the program since 2000. Originally from Houston, Texas, he moved to San Antonio in 1988 to attend UTSA. Associate director of student life since 2000, Martin is charged with the responsibility for all extracurricular student activities, and, In fact, student life has the responsibility of approving all extracurricular activities on campus, whether or not they sponsor the activity.

One of the largest and most important activities sponsored by student life is Culture Fest, which celebrated its sixteenth anniversary in 2012. The Culture Fest "originated from the president's office in about 2005, then switched to the department of student life where it remains to the present," said Martin. The originators of the Culture Fest were Patricia Williams, Pearl Conyers, Mark Barnes, and Eddie Harris. The Culture Fest began as a "two-day event Fun Raiser," and is now the college's official Fiesta event, supported financially by a grant from the Fiesta Commission as a Participating Member Organization (PMO) based on the availability of funds.

Several years ago, when Fiesta week coincided with Easter, the event changed from Friday to Saturday to Thursday to Friday and "it stuck," says Martin. Now the event is always held the Thursday before Good Friday and the Battle of Flowers. Chef Will Thornton had the idea for a Culinary Arts Rib Cook-Off and for the past seven years, this has become a successful Fiesta event in the Culture Fest. The number of participants have grown to fifteen or more with high- profile judges, identified by the president's office, to judge the ribs.

Another popular event sponsored by student life and a part of the Heritage Commission activity is Juneteenth. Student life sponsors an array of clubs and organizations on campus designed to meet the needs of students. Following are a number of currently active student organizations and clubs on campus:

Anime Club (Japanese cartooning)
Diagnostic Imaging
Early Childhood Studies
Future Latino Leaders for Change
Histology Club
Invasive Cardiovascular
Le Patissier Association
LVN to ADN
Phi Theta Kappa
Physical Therapy Assistants
Respiratory Care
Science Club
Society of Sonography Students
Vocational Nursing Student Association

One of the more important events held on campus is the yearly African American Male Initiative. On December 14, 2004, Dr. Angie Runnels assembled a committee to address the issue of the declining enrollment of male students, particularly African American males. The goal of the committee was to increase African American male enrollment to 20 percent of the total student enrollment. Committee participants were Charles Guenther, Levi Jackson, James Wright, Eddie Harris, Mark Barnes, Vernard Grice, and John Martin. In 2008, an event addressing the importance of college-age students getting involved in the presidential election was held on St. Philip's campus. Called "Decision 2008," Rock the Vote informed the students of the value of becoming involved in the presidential election and of having their voices heard in elections.[13]

In the school year 2010–2011, SPC participated with Delta Sigma Theta Inc. EMBODI Program, Northeast Lakeview College Minority Male Initiative, and SPC Men of Color Conference in a collaborative partnership.

Early Childhood and Family Studies (ECFS) and SPC Child Development Center

Early in 2001, St. Philip's approved a new program, early childhood and family studies. Under program director and assistant professor, Pamela Ray, with more than 400 alumni, the early childhood studies program is one of the ten most popular majors in the college. Always on the move, in January 2011, St. Philip's College began enrolling students in the first online early childhood studies associate's degree program from an accredited community college in San Antonio.

The two-year program in the allied health department, designed to prepare early childhood professionals to earn an associate's of applied science degree, began with twelve students enrolled. The Child Development Associate National Credential (CDA) may also be earned by students through the allied health department. The program uses the SPC Child Development Center as a laboratory, utilizing research-based practices to prepare students for a variety of jobs in the early child care and education profession.

Having the use of a laboratory allows students to integrate classroom instruction with firsthand clinical experiences. As a clinical training site, the center provides supervised practicum experience for the students through working with children. Students completing the early childhood studies program either enter the workforce or are prepared to transfer to a university to pursue a bachelor's degree. The program's motto, *Make a Difference in the Life of a Child,* the program's vision is to be the best accredited program in the nation.

The Child Development Center (CDC), opened in 2000, was constructed in part with funds received from a Department of Housing and Urban Development (HUD) grant written by Mamye Bailey Williams (now deceased). Williams was, at that time, ACCD director of public funding administration and was often referred to as the college's "Million Dollar Baby" because of her ability to raise funds.

Early Childhood and Family Studies (ECFS) and SPC Child Development Center

The primary purpose of the CDC, with the capacity to serve fifty-seven children, is first to serve students, then faculty, and (space permitting) the community. The center accepts children from twelve months to five years and is open Monday through Friday, from 7:00 a.m. to 6:00 p.m. The children receive breakfast, lunch, and an USDA-approved snack. Rates for children of students are based on grade point average (GPA). Students whose grades fall below 2.5 pay the full rate set by the ACCD. The Kimmelman Scholarship and Temple Beth El subsidizes students' child care funding.

The child care center serves a dual purpose on the campus, fulfilling the role of a laboratory for occupational therapy (OTA), physical therapy, licensed vocational nurses (LVN), and LVN to ADN programs.

In 2002, the child and families studies program began pairing with nursing, allied health programs, and local health and human services to host Child Check. A community service project, Child Check offers free health and developmental screenings for children from birth to three years old in the San Antonio area.

Then, in 2004, the advisory committee approved a name change for the program, from child and families studies to early childhood studies. In 2009, the name was revised again to early childhood and family studies, meant to reflect an instructional unit that prepares students to work with families as well as with children.

In 2005, the National Association for the Education of Young Children (NAEYC), the nation's leading organization of early childhood professionals, awarded the SPC Child Development Center accreditation, recognizing them for their commitment to reaching the highest professional standards in the field. The program was awarded a $750,000 five-year grant, under the US Department of Health and Human Services (HHS)–Office of Head Start (OHS), Higher Education Grant (HEG). The program was reaccredited in 2010 by the NAEYC. Reaccreditation is an indication of the program's continued dedication to excellence and is further recognition by the organization that the program exceeds the highest professional standards in the industry. The Child Development Center received 100 or 100 plus in each area of testing. The accreditation period runs from May 6, 2010 through June 1, 2015.

In 2005, the program celebrated the first group of students to graduate with an AAS degree. Students may now earn an AAS degree as well as a technical certificate. The program has been approved, since 2008, to offer additional AAS degrees with specializations in language and literacy, and leadership accreditation.

There are lessons to be learned outside of the classroom as well as in a classroom setting. Continuing opportunities for new experiences abound at St. Philip's College, such as the opportunity provided for students to visit other countries. A student enrolled in the occupational therapy assistant program excitedly pointed out that this was her first opportunity to travel abroad.

Occupational Therapy Assistant (OTA) Students

During the summer of 2008, six students from the OTA program traveled to Guatemala for an eight-day visit and to participate in an internship honing their occupational therapy skills.

Larry Duran, faculty member in OTA, arranged the visit with students ranging in age from twenty-one to over forty, and included one student who is a member of the United States Armed Forces. Some students travel long distances each day to take advantage of the OTA training at the college, and some travel as much as eighty-five minutes each way, twice a week. One student lives in a neighboring town about forty miles away and travels to San Antonio twice a week, spending more than an hour in travel time each way.

Over the course of the eight days spent in Guatamala, the students gained a wealth of experience that included the following procedures:

- Preparing patient treatment plans
- Screening the children for health problems
- Developing activity plans that addressed areas in which the children were not as advanced as they should be
- Rearranging the facilities to make them more functional and user friendly.

The students were exposed to learning not associated with textbooks, such as an appreciation for how others live. As an example, they stayed in a hotel with just the basic amenities, and experienced having to wait an hour for hot water.

The occupational therapist assistant program (OTA) is offered to the community through the department of allied health at St. Philip's College. The program first enrolled students in 1971 and in 1973 the first students graduated from the program with an associate of applied science (AAS) degree. The program is the second-oldest OTA program in Texas and the oldest to offer an AAS degree. While the inaugural program graduated eight students, the 2009 graduating class had twenty two students.

St. Philip's Great Loss

After serving as president of St. Philip's College for just over six years, Dr. Angie Runnels, for health reasons, resigned her position as president. Having brought to the position of the presidency an understanding of what St. Philip's needed and required from its top administrator to steer its course in the twenty-first century, the great loss of her leadership to the college was incalculable. Runnels's faculty and staff were complimentary of her administration, expressing the feeling that she was doing a great job, and that she brought to the office of the president a certain grace and dignity that she coupled with skill in dealing with difficult situations. Her decisions throughout her administration were tempered with a love for the school, they said. When, on May 2, 2008, the college learned that she had passed away, the feeling expressed among faculty and staff alike was that her leaving was premature; they were not ready to see her go. A memorial service was

Dr. Patricia Candia, interim President 2006–2007

held for her in the Heritage Room at the college on May 8, 2008, and was attended by a host of dignitaries from around the city. She continues to be missed.

Dr. Patricia Candia

On August 1, 2006, Patricia Candia, vice president of student affairs, was selected to fill the position of interim president. Candia began her career at St. Philip's in 1982, the year before she graduated from high school, when she enrolled in the early admissions program, from which she received college credit but no high school credit. Candia worked in the psychology department, became manager of the tutoring department, and worked another seven to eight years as director of student life, all experiences that were of immense help as she began her new presidential position. "When students had a concern, whether it was in an area within student affairs, records, counseling, or testing, we worked with them and tried to do what we could to help them out," said Candia.

Candia attended SPC for two years, completing the courses she needed to transfer to UTSA. Following UTSA, Candia continued her education at Incarnate Word, earned a master's degree, and went on to Texas A&M, where she earned a doctorate of philosophy degree. At age forty, Candia was the youngest person and the first Hispanic to serve as president of St. Philip's College. Describing herself as a student advocate, Candia said that the best part of her job was "trying to ensure that students receive the best experience that they can get at St. Philip's." As interim president, she continued with this philosophy. Some of the programs that she inherited to oversee were:

- The $67 million capital improvement program to build the learning resource center, the health careers center, the new welcome center at the MLK campus, and the diesel lab and additional parking at Southwest Campus.
- The Quality Enhancement Plan (whose focus and goal for SPC students was to demonstrate critical thinking skills through student engagement activities and provide faculty opportunities to enhance student learning by formally integrating critical thinking skill development into the curriculum).
- Development of Learning Communities (small groups of students that take their first semester classes together to build retention alliances).
- Continuation of the Achieving the Dream Program (a learning program where students are challenged to interpret and understand historical events in the context of today's events).

While Dr. Candia's term as interim president showed great promise, her term was brief; in January 2007, trustees for the Alamo Community College District announced that a new president had been selected for St. Philip's College.[14]

23 A Brand New Leader and a Brand New Day

On March 1, 2007, St. Philip's College welcomed its fourteenth president. Bold headlines in the *San Antonio Express-News* announced her arrival, describing her as "lured" from NASA to St. Philip's. Denver McClendon, chair, Alamo Community College District Board of Trustees, summed up the appointment of Dr. Adena Laverne Williams Loston with these words: "She is undoubtedly the appropriate selection."[1]

Dr. Adena Loston, President, St. Philip's College

President Loston came to St. Philip's from the National Aeronautics and Space Administration's Flight Center in Virginia, where she held the position of Director of Education and Special Assistant for Suborbital and Special Orbital Projects Directorate for the Goddard Space Flight Center, Wallops Flight Facility. She was also Chief Education Officer for the National Aeronautics and Space Administration at IT headquarters in Washington, DC. She grew up in Vicksburg, Mississippi, in the 1950s, where she attended Freedom Schools taught by "Freedom Riders" from the North. During this era of the fight for civil rights for blacks, she was exposed to teachers who helped to shape her core values and beliefs.

Like many of her predecessors, including Artemisia Bowden, Loston grew up in a home led by parents who had great expectations for their children and who held strong religious beliefs. A regular participant in church from a young age, Loston views her spiritual educationas equally important as the education she received in public school. Loston was reared by parents who taught their children to remain economically independent; thus, she and all four of her siblings were encouraged to learn a vocational skill and also to earn a college degree. Their father believed in Booker T. Washington and emphasized the value of learning a skill or a trade, something that you could do with your hands and also to give back to the community. Their mother believed in W. E. B. DuBois, and required that they each earn a college degree. Loston satisfied the requirements of both parents by earning an undergraduate degree in business education and also learning to be a seamstress.

Becoming a seamstress provided a similarity in history with the young black girls whose roots were planted in the sewing class out of which St. Philip's College grew. Loston could not have known that her preparation would bring her, some fifty years later, to lead the very institution from which those young black girls began their education. Her preparation, rooted in the skills and discipline she learned as a seamstress early in her career, is much like the college she now leads, for both she and the college succeeded because of hard work, discipline, and determination.

Loston received a bachelor's of science degree in 1973 from a Historically Black College (Alcorn A&M College, now Alcorn State University), a master's degree in business education from Bowling Green State University in 1974, and a doctor of philosophy degree in educational administration and supervision from Bowling Green State University in 1979. She continued her education through the Institution for Educational Management at Harvard in 1996, the Presidents Roundtable at Oxford University in 2001, and the professional development program at Wharton School of Business, University of Pennsylvania, in 2005. In 2005, Loston was awarded an honorary doctorate of science from Wiley College. She has served for over thirty years in various positions in higher education.

Dr. Adena W. Loston

Throughout her professional career, Loston blazed a trail for her race in the positions she held, serving as the first or only black in the position. Her selection as president of St. Philip's marks the first time that she followed another African American in a professional position. St. Philip's College, on a journey to greatness, presently engaged in strategic planning, facilities master planning, various renovation projects, and Good 2 Great principles, now finds itself with the master of her craft at the helm.

During her career, Loston received numerous educational and professional awards and recognition for excellence, including, in 2010, the Amazing Energy Award given to her from CPS Energy during Black History Month. During her tenure as Chief Education Officer at NASA, she was the highest-ranking African American female in the agency. She was the second president of San Jacinto College South in Houston and the first African American college president in that district, a position she held from 1997 to 2002. Other positions throughout her career include instructor, Arkansas State University; associate professor at Georgia State University; dean of professional programs and dean of vocational education, budgets, and facilities, Santa Monica College in California; and adjunct instructor at Texas Southern University and the University of Houston-Downtown.

Loston's experience as a member of the faculty and then as an administrator equipped her well to meet the needs of the diverse community that she now serves. Because she is the product of a Historically Black College and is familiar with community college work, Loston feels comfortable with providing leadership at St. Philip's.

In September 2010, Loston received a Federal appointment from Arne Duncan, United States Secretary of Education, as an advisory board member of the Historically Black Colleges and Universities (HBCU) Capital Financing Advisory Board. As one of several representatives of public HBCUs on the board, which includes presidents, chancellors, and CEOs, they collectively advise the secretary and other prominent persons connected to the White House and to businesses in the nation. Loston is the only community college representative.

Dr. Loston is as at home with clergy members as she is with educators. When the Episcopal Diocese of West Texas met in San Antonio for a council meeting, the late Rev. Richard Thayer, interim rector of St. Philip's Episcopal Church, invited her to speak to members of the diocese on behalf of the college. The first African American female to address the diocese at its council meeting, Loston's address included a historical overview of St. Philip's College. She reminded everyone of the long association and close historical ties between St. Philip's Episcopal Church and the college, and the important role the Episcopal Church played in the March 1898 founding of the college. As a result of the meeting between Thayer, the members of the diocese, and Loston, there was a renewal of the once close association between the church and the college.

In his address to the Council of the Diocese, Dr. Thayer made mention of St. Philip's 110th anniversary, celebrated in March 2008. Noting the significance of the anniversary, he reminded the congregation that the memories and knowledge of the affiliation of St. Philip's College with St. Philip's Church is hazy, if known at all. Thayer continued: "People need to know the stories that inspire, because there are precious few, and I want people to know who Mrs. [*sic*] Bowden was."[2] Rev. G. Richard Thayer III was awarded the honorary associate of arts degree at the 120th commencement in December 2008. Five honorary degrees have been awarded (see recipients in the following list, in order received):

- Actor Ossie Davis, brother of the science department's Dr. William Davis
- Rev. Richard Thayer III
- Honorable State Representative Ruth Jones McClendon
- Dr. Martha J. Kanter, US Department of Education, Under Secretary of Education
- Dr. William Davis, brother to Ossie Davis

Bishop Gary Lillibridge has expressed recognition of the important work that the college, led by Loston, is doing in the community. In his position as current bishop of the West Texas Diocese, Lillibridge formally announced that the diocese was establishing a scholarship to further support student success at St. Philip's College.

While Loston considers the presidency of St. Philip's College her assigned ministry, it is an assignment in which she is firmly anchored. She approaches her position as president of the college with the same modus operandi that she showed in learning her skills, perfecting her craft, and earning her degrees. In the years since Loston assumed the presidency, numerous San Antonio organizations have recognized her for her work and awarded an impressive number of well-deserved honors for her service to the community, as well as for her labors for the college.

With Loston, the college embarked on a journey of self-improvement to enhance and improve performance. Under her leadership, a committee was formed to determine where improvement was needed, determine which areas most needed improvement, and discover the best way to achieve that goal. Defining St. Philip's goals was the first step. A key goal of the college was to focus on leading learning, accountability, and transparency, and student empowerment. The college focused on three ideas to implement: (1) understanding the purpose, (2) collaborative institutional culture, and (3) focus on results.

To begin with, Loston planned a Good to Great Retreat, with more than eighty persons in attendance representing the college. Her strategy was to include everyone that had the ability to influence how the college was allocating resources. The attendees first identified the college's accomplishments through the appreciative inquiry process. The initial planning for the Centers of Excellence in Science and Mathematics was identified as an area of accomplishment. The Centers are a cooperative effort between several entities (the college, businesses, teachers, and community) to respond to the needs of business for workers trained for careers in science, technology, engineering, and mathematics (STEM).

Another accomplishment was the $10.2 million newly renovated Centers for Mathematics and Science that opened at Southwest Campus.[3] New degree programs were launched that included:

- Associate of applied science in power generation and alternative energy
- Associate of arts in statistics
- Associate of science in earth science and natural energy resources
- Associate of science degree in biotechnology

Another accomplishment was the "Agreements made with the University of the Incarnate Word that will lead to a bachelor's degree in meteorology and environmental science."

Acutely aware of the need for STEM field majors, since 2007, Loston has instituted the summer math and science academies on campus and they have continuously expanded. Summer 2012 is no exception. An academy is planned for summer 2012 that will expose students to math and science in action, hear math and science professionals speak, and become involved in projects taught by certified math and science teachers.

Mathematics and science professionals are planned as guest speakers, with a free lunch to be provided. Partnerships are planned with the University of Texas Health Science Center and the University of Texas at San Antonio. Good to Great strategic planning will be implemented.

The Volunteer Income Tax Assistance Center (VITA)

Under Loston's leadership, SPC offers an income tax assistance program that services more than 2,000 individuals yearly. The program has grown over time to generate more than $7.3 million dollars yearly in returns for the community. SPC has become the number one VITA site in the ACCD.

A summer academy for children ages four and five is held through the division of continuing education for the community. Several programs offered by the college achieved the honor and distinction of exemplary. They are: respiratory care technology, culinary arts, and occupational therapy assistant.

The Inaugural Scholarship Golf Tournament at St. Philip's College

During the first week of March 2009, three very important events took place at SPC. The college celebrated its 111th anniversary. Adena Loston began her third year as president, and to mark these milestones, she established a golf tournament to raise scholarship funds to support the diverse needs of the students. With nearly 80 percent of students relying on financial aid or scholarships to help them to achieve their educational goals and dreams, it would have been difficult to find a more fitting goal for the tournament. Loston's dream come true was that the tournament would become an annual event. In 2010, AT&T joined SPC as a corporate friend, benefactor, and name sponsor for the event.

The first tournament, held on March 3, 2009, was hosted by Loston at the Pecan Valley Golf Course where she welcomed her guests with a luncheon, recognition of the sponsors, a raffle, and a silent auction. This very successful event was destined to become a much touted and greatly anticipated annual affair. The tournament included 107 golfers who raised $145,406 in scholarship funds. SPC, with an enrollment of more than 11,000 credit students and 8,000 continuing education students, welcomed the funds raised, for they provided over 200 scholarships.

Dr. Michael Chavez and Dr. Dreand Johnson served as co-chairs of the event. Serving as committee members were Dr. Benjamin Kraft, Jorge Trevino, Matari Jones-Gunter, Sharon Crockett-Bell, Paul Borrego, and George Johnson. The year 2009 brought landmark achievements for SPC. Some of the noteworthy events that occurred were:

SPC was ranked number one in the state for awarding the most degrees and certificates to at-risk students in critical fields (science, technology, engineering, and mathematics).[4]

SPC culinary arts program was rated exemplary by the American Culinary Federation. SPC is the only nonproprietary institution in the state with this designation. Only twenty-five institutions in the world hold this honor.[5]

SPC was named "Military Friendly" in *GI Jobs* magazine's 2010 list of Military-Friendly Schools.[6]

SPC is highly rated in the *Hispanic Outlook in Higher Education* magazine's 2008 Top 50 list of community colleges awarding the most degrees to Hispanic students and the Top 20 list among Hispanic faculty members.[7]

In 2009, SPC ranked first statewide among its community college peers with the highest Licensed Vocational Nurse (LVN) pass rate in programs with 100 or more graduates per year.[8]

SPC Occupational Therapy Assistant (OTA) students experienced 100 percent pass rate during spring 2009 testing, exceeding US averages by 16 percent.[9]

SPC programs rated exemplary in a Texas Higher Education Coordinating Board evaluation: culinary arts, respiratory therapy, physical therapy assistant.[10]

SPC ranked above the national average among other large colleges on:
- Quality of support given students to help them succeed at the college
- The quality of relationships with administrative personnel and offices
- Students acquiring job- or work-related knowledge and skills
- Satisfaction with financial aid advising, academic advising, tutoring services, and skills lab.[11]

St. Philip's Receives a $2 Million Stimulus Funding Grant

In May 2010, at a joint news conference with the city of San Antonio and UTSA, St. Philip's College announced a grant of $2 million through the federal stimulus program, Department of Energy, to be used for a solar energy installation at Southwest Campus. With this grant, which comes from the Texas Comptroller of Public Accounts, the college plans to install a 400-kilowatt grid solar energy system on Building 1 of the Southwest Campus.

Applying for a Baldridge Award and the Texas Award for Performance Excellence (TAPE)

During Loston's tenure, the district and St. Philip's became involved in a national program that recognizes businesses and institutions with the highest award for national recognition of excellence in performance that a US organization can receive. Called the Malcolm Baldrige National Quality Award, it is named for Malcolm Baldrige, secretary of commerce from 1981 to 1987, whose excellence in management resulted in improved efficiency and effectiveness at the government level. The Baldrige is a much sought after award that identifies businesses and institutions as having made a commitment to excellence and to sustained and continued improvement.

Institutions involved in the Baldrige Award program commit to the Seven Baldrige Criteria Categories. These are core values involving (1) leadership; (2) strategic planning; (3) student, stakeholder, and market focus; (4) measurement, analysis, and knowledge management; (5) focus on the workforce; (6) operations; and (7) results.

The Baldrige program is a national program that involves self-assessment, provides the framework for understanding performance management, and examines the institution's progress toward its goals. The criteria provides a common language that is understood by the institutions involved in the process based on best practices among organizations and provides a system by which institutions can measure their performance.

The Texas Award for Performance Excellence (TAPE), is given by the state to recognize excellence. Areas addressed by TAPE are:

- Student learning outcomes
- Customer satisfaction and engagement
- Product and service outcomes, and process efficiency
- Workforce satisfaction and engagement
- Budgetary, financial, and market results
- Social responsibility

St. Philip's College was recognized in 2010 at the "Engagement Level" for the TAPE Award. In 2011, St. Philip's was again recognized at the "Achievement Level for Organizational Excellence" toward the TAPE award. Chancellor Leslie announced plans for the district to engage in the Baldrige journey along with colleges by applying to become a new TAPE applicant. Noting that the quest for performance excellence involves everyone if it is to be successful, he challenged the district to participate with the colleges, though separately.

School year 2009–2012, Grants and Scholarships
- SPC received a $700,000 Nursing Grant from the Higher Education Coordinating Board (THECB)
- Received a $100,000 AT&T donation for workforce development scholarships
- Received $50,000 scholarship donation from HEB during ribbon cutting for new MLK facilities
- Received an $80,000 work-study and mentoring grant from THECB
- Received a $10,000 Big Read Grant from the National Endowment for the Arts
- Received a $10,000 grant from Lowe's for collaboration with the Merced Housing Texas
- Received a first year grant of $1.5 million mandatory Historic Black College and University (HBCU) funding-five year allocation.
- Received $10,000 Volunteer Income Tax Assistance (VITA) grant through Kellogg Foundation
- Generated $4,075 for student scholarships through SPC's Good to Great Planning Retreat
- Alumni Scholarship Dance, 70s Soul Train, raised $4,500 for student scholarships

Awarded eleven $1,000 scholarships for the Women in Technology program
Raised nearly $2,000 at the Women's History Luncheon for the Alumni and Friends Scholarship Fund
Awarded eleven $1,000 scholarships for the Women in Technology program

Not only did the college receive many honors, Loston also was the recipient of many honors from the community and from organizations.

Honors Conferred upon Loston
Exceptional Achievement Award–Goddard Space Flight Center (NASA)
La Prensa Foundation Outstanding Women in Action Education Award
Inducted into the San Antonio Women's Hall of Fame
Inducted into the Educator's Hall of Fame National Sorority of Psi Delta Kappa Inc.
CPS Amazing Energy Award
Juneteenth Award for President's Lecture Series Program
Appointed to Advisory Committee for Capital Financing by US Secretary of Education
Awarded Phi Theta Kappa Shirley B. Gordon International Award of Distinction. Loston is the first African American to receive this award twice.[2]

When Dr. Loston came to SPC, Phi Theta Kappa had not received stars for its accomplishments. Now, because of the more than 1,000 service hours generated during the semester, the chapter has five stars. A Veterans Monument Project, generated by this chapter, was designed and installed on the campus green at SPC in November 2011 to honor military veterans in all five branches of the military. St. Philip's branch of Phi Theta Kappa, the official honor society for two-year colleges, is recognized by the American Association of Community Colleges. It was in the top 100 Phi Theta Kappa chapters in the Hallmark Awards competition.

Phi Theta Kappa Membership is based on superior academic achievement and is conferred only by invitation of Psi Kappa Chapter of St. Philip's College. To be eligible, students must have completed at least twelve college hours with a minimum cumulative 3.5 grade point average. Phi Theta Kappa membership is recognized as the official honor society for two-year colleges by the American Association of Community Colleges. The chapter provided 910 service hours during the spring semester.

Psi Kappa Chapter at SPC nominated Dr. Loston for the 2011 Shirley B. Gordon Award of Distinction, which is only presented to college presidents and CEOs. One of only nine presidents recognized nationally, Loston was presented with the award at the 2011 Annual Phi Theta Kappa Convention held in Seattle.

A Moving Experience

Just as the problems and difficulties Loston faced shortly after her arrival were challenging, many of the accomplishments achieved were uplifting. Perhaps none was more inspiring than the ribbon cutting and dedication that signaled the official entry into the three new buildings that resulted from the bond issue of 2005: the Welcome Center; the Center for Health Professions, and the Center for Learning Resources. At 10:00 a.m. on April 29, 2009, what began under Angie Runnels's watch, and continued with oversight by Patricia Candia, became a reality and was welcomed into being by Adena Loston, with the blessings of Mayor Phil Hardberger, County Commissioner Tommy Adkisson, City Councilwoman Sheila McNeil, Chancellor Leslie, and many other dignitaries from around the city.

During the ribbon-cutting ceremony, Loston gave credit to the residents of the community for their support and "unwavering belief in the power of education and training to transform lives and communities," while acknowledging that without the community, the vision would not have come to fruition. St. Philip's received in total $67 million in bond construction dollars. A total of $49 million was allocated to construct its multipurpose academic complex, designed by architects Saldana & Associates and Pfluger Associates and managed by Parsons with Skanska USA Building Inc. as construction manager. The newly constructed buildings, furnished with state-of-the-art equipment, also included a new Diesel Technology Center and Lab constructed on St. Philip's College's Southwest Campus. The Diesel Technology Center was dedicated April 16, 2009.

The three new buildings, occupied in June 2009, included new parking facilities and new tennis courts as a part of the construction. In addition, an auxiliary central plant that provides cooling and electrical service to the new consolidated building was a part of the bond package.

Center for Health Professions (CHP)

The Center for Health Professions (CHP) that resulted from the bond issue is the most advanced medical training facility east of the Medical Center. Built to resemble a small hospital, the three-story building includes laboratories, classrooms, and a camera system incorporated into the learning structure that monitors students' reactions to re-created medical emergencies. The classrooms and laboratories replicate various departments found throughout health care facilities in the city. Loston instructed faculty and staff with "no discernible difference between what students experience here and what they experience in the workforce."

Additionally, the center supports career programs such as vocational nursing, surgical technology, radiology and diagnostic imaging, physical therapy assistant, respiratory therapy, occupational therapy assistant, medical assistant, health information systems, histology, and medical transcription. Both the physical therapy assistant and respiratory thery assistant programs at St. Philip's College are rated exemplary by the Texas Higher Education Coordinating Board.

Considered one of the most high-tech medical facilities in the city, CHP contains 113,000 square feet and was built at a cost of $30.8 million. It features high-demand instructional programs such as vocational nursing, invasive cardiovascular technology, and surgical technology. CHP houses the Frank Bryant Jr. Human Patient Simulation Center, which boasts of a complete radiology system, two surgical suites with supporting scrub and sterilization areas, a multifunctional skills lab, four specialty-care simulation rooms, a twelve-bed clinic, and an eight-bed general hospital suite with a fully-operational nursing station.

With all of its modern technology, CHP had a humble beginning. Bertha Storey started the first medical program at SPC, called health careers in its early days. Peggy Peterson was one of the first faculty hired to work with her to develop the LVN program. Allied health came into being in the late 1960s and the radiology program—radiographic technology and OT, occupational therapy assistant, and physical therapy assistant program—began in the early 1970s. Peterson, over nursing and allied health, was called "supervisor" of health careers. According to William David Bentley, Peterson was strictly in an administrative position. In the fall of 1985, nursing and allied health became one department and Bentley was elected the first chair, serving from 1985 to 1992. In 1992, Bruce Fisher became department chair, serving until 1996. In 1996, Fisher returned to teaching full time, and was recommended by the respiratory care faculty group to be the program director.

The respiratory care program terminated in 1972 because it was not accredited, and without accreditation, the program could not continue. In 1975, the program restarted as a one-year certificate program under Robert William Hamilton, a cardio-pulmonary specialist who had just separated from the Air Force. A registered therapist, Hamilton had worked in respiratory care prior to joining the military. The program received its full accreditation as a one-year certificate program in the fall

The Center for Health Professions

of 1976 with the graduates being eligible to take a certified respiratory therapist technician exam. When, in 1980, Hamilton became too ill to work, Bentley became program director and Bruce Fisher came on board as clinical coordinator. The program trained up to thirty students and graduated twenty-five to twenty-eight students a year. Around spring of 1981, Michael Carpenter was hired as full-time faculty.

Respiratory care began a two-year program in 1975. The program has grown to accept between twenty-five to thirty students, graduating between seventeen to twenty students yearly. Understanding that the accrediting agency was phasing out one-year programs, requiring them to be minimally an associate degree program, the allied health director worked with the advisory committee of the program to convert to a two-year program. They put together a proposal and invited program directors of the hospitals to accompany them to make a presentation to the Coordinating Board with the help of an advisory committee from the community. Examples of the questions asked by the coordinating board were: How do you know if the hospitals are willing to pay more for a more advanced training person? Are they willing, basically, to spend more money?

According to Bentley, "The director of respiratory care at University Hospital, who voluntarily answered the questions, spoke up and gave the employer's viewpoint, and why they would pay more. He explained that patient safety and competency in that safety was the big thing." Before Bentley and those accompanying him even left the room, they were advised, "We are recommending approval. You've been approved as a two-year advanced associate degree program." [13]

The two-year program began in fall of 1997, with twenty-four students and great support from the community, much like the kind of support they had from the director at the University Hospital who assisted them in receiving their two-year certification. The two-year program is fully accredited and all of the major medical facilities in San Antonio, including long-term care facilities, hire St. Philip's graduates. Students are required to apply for a state license to practice through the Texas Department of State Health Services and they receive their full-time license from the state when they pass their national certification examination. St. Philip's has had a 100 percent pass rate for the last several years.

Bentley, full professor in allied health at SPC, with the program for thirty-five years and now retired, was full-time faculty from August 1976 to July 2011. Now adjunct faculty, he rose to the rank of associate dean in the applied science division. During that time, he was also over continuing education, including all the military bases and various locations of high schools, middle schools, and other places that offer extended courses or services. Much like the early days of the school, Bentley taught one course part-time for the program while serving as full-time associate dean. Rebecca Sanchez preceded the current department chair, Randall Dawson.

The Center for Learning Resources, the Welcome Center, and Diesel Technology Center and Lab

The Center for Learning Resources (CLR), including the collection at Southwest Campus, houses approximately 143,726 volumes. Built at a cost of $18,900,000, the CLR is home to a collection that includes more than 1,000 periodicals and online databases and serves as the hub for students to study and access research materials from books, periodicals, computer-based resources, and the Internet. The center provides numerous individual and group study rooms, a spacious exhibit area, and an expanded archives unit including music CDs, audio books, and DVDs that may be viewed in the TV/DVD viewing room. The center's newest feature, the media production rooms, offers the latest in technology to students for class projects. Multimedia resources are available in a fully-functional darkroom with viewing and editing equipment for both audio and video media.

Reuben Guerrero, Interim Coordinator, Media Services

Ruben Guerrero in the media services department, at the time of this writing, has been with SPC for the past nineteen years. He joined the college in 1993 under President Hamice James. A graduate of SAC and Southwest State University, while he did not attend SPC, he has close relatives who did; namely, his father, who earned two associate degrees, and his two sisters.

In the early 1980s, Milton Burrell officially started the media services department. At that time, it was a part of the library. Media services is now a three-person department, consisting of Ola Robinson, learning resources specialist five, and Patrick Evans, the official photographer for SPC. With her knowledge of Banner, Robinson provides information to order equipment and process orders.

The Center for Learning Resources

The Welcome Center

Evans, in addition to being the official photographer, handles the audio visual and sound, provides information on how to print and process film, provides videos, and can print flyers or posters to archives.

While these services are currently not available to the community, the department will help classes edit film shot to present to the class. Media services will also provide assistance to other campuses and to district offices for special events on request. An example of a service that could be provided is an oversized copy of a scholarship check. Photographs can also be provided to Public Relations for funerals for persons who have been employed by the college long enough to have a history.

The Welcome Center

Constructed at a cost of $18 million, the Welcome Center is the first stop and gateway for all incoming students seeking admission to St. Philip's College. As a comprehensive one-stop model, the center provides all of the necessary services in one location where students may receive advisement, register, be assessed, and pay their tuition. Students may receive assistance in all aspects of the admission and enrollment processes, including assessment, bursar's services, counseling, dual credit, financial aid, GED registration, testing, veterans' affairs, and international student resources.

Diesel Technology Center and Lab

Included in the bond issue was a new $4.7 million Diesel Technology Center, located at Southwest Campus containing two buildings: an 11,000 square foot Diesel Technology Lab ($2.2 million) and a 10,000 square foot classroom building. There are ten instructional diesel technology bays housed within a one-story, pre-engineered metal building. Classrooms, faculty offices, a hydraulics laboratory, trainer classroom, high-bay diesel mechanics instructional areas, and other related support spaces are included in the improvements to the building. The diesel technology program offered at Southwest Campus provides an opportunity for students to earn a one-year certificate or a two-year degree. Classes are offered in diesel service management, theory and skills of refrigeration, electronic and mechanical fuel injection, chassis maintenance, vehicle inspection, tune-up, engine overhaul, transmission repair, brake service, and handling of hazardous waste.

Faculty and Staff under Loston

From its inception, St. Philip's College has boasted of having a dedicated host of faculty and staff. A testimony from one of the newer administrators gave insight into why. "When you come on this campus, you will always be treated with respect. Even if we disagree, we agree to disagree in a manner that is respectful of each other," said Erick Akins, who came to St. Philip's in August 2009.[14]

As dean of continuing education and workforce development, Akins heads a department of the college that offers a bridge from the noncredit to the academic side of the institution. Continuing education and workforce development is described often as an introduction to the campus for individuals who are coming onto the college campus, some for the first time.

Through workforce development and continuing education, the college offers contract training, which can be customized to the needs of a business. In fact, offering customized training is one of the distinctive characteristics of the department. A hallmark of Akins and his team is that they work with students and businesses in the community to ensure that the needs of the businesses are met.

Businesses needing staff to be trained as well as individuals wishing to take courses for personal development and enrichment are accommodated through a variety of technical- and workforce-related classes. These classes are held at either Southwest Campus or the main campus on Martin Luther King Drive. Those not seeking a degree will not receive college credit for the courses; however, they may receive continuing education credits (CEUs) and will gain valuable knowledge and skill.

The college's commitment to serve its community extends not only to businesses but to its senior citizens as well. Through workforce development and continuing education, the college offers courses designed to enhance the lives of its Silver Seniors, defined as adults aged fifty-five and above. Called Silver Circle Enrichment Classes, seniors may choose from a variety of classes, many that are offered at no cost or a nominal fee. As an indication of their commitment to pleasing senior members of the community as well as businesses, Dean Akins and his staff have accommodated many requests, even one for belly dancing.

Classes offered run the gamut from cooking for health challenges, such as diabetes and heart disease, to jewelry making 101 or help in choosing the right computer. Not all classes are held on campus; some may even be held at a location more convenient for attendees through their off-campus programs and services. This accommodation exemplifies the depth of commitment that the college has to providing quality training and education through continuing education, workforce development, and the Academy of Professional Development and Training (APDT). The vision of workforce development and continuing education is "to become the preferred provider" for training the workforce in San Antonio and surrounding communities, and for providing professional development and the community services needed in the areas they serve.

Meet Dean Erick Akins

Akins, who grew up in Chicago, has, at the time of this writing, been living in San Antonio for twenty-eight years. From a family of eight, he is the first male in his family to graduate from high school. Being a member of his high school band afforded him an opportunity to attend Southern University in Louisiana, where he again played in the marching band and where he earned a degree in music. Akins came to San Antonio through attending graduate school at Trinity University, and with a background of workforce experience and years of teaching and working in grant writing, he applied and was hired at St. Philip's in 2009.

Because of the ever-changing needs of San Antonio's

workforce and the technical skills that are needed by both new and experienced employees, the department tries to satisfy those needs by providing credit and noncredit classes along with the flexibility of on- and off-campus classes, and weekend, weekday, and evening sessions. Their motto is that they will provide training anytime, anywhere! Some areas of training offered through continuing education are: aircraft technology, air conditioning and refrigeration, automotive body repair, diesel mechanics, homebuilding, plumbing, precision metal and welding, forklift operator, drafting, and electrical and power transmission.

In 2011, when Akins transferred to grant writing, Maureen Cartledge became dean of continuing education and workforce development.

The Academy of Health Career Training (AHCT)

Within the division of workforce development and continuing education, there is a division called the academy of health career training (AHCT) that is a provider of health career and hospitality training programs. The AHCT is often the first stop on campus for individuals entering the health care field. Basic training classes are offered at the MLK Campus in San Antonio and the Central Texas Technology Center (CTTC) in New Braunfels. In addition to the entry-level courses, AHCT offers classes for health care professionals needing to update their licenses and continuing education classes for professionals needing to earn hours to maintain their certifications. As with the aforementioned classes, course offerings and off-campus locations abound.

Programs Instituted under Loston

While St. Philip's has many reasons to celebrate, there are none more important than those realized in the last decade. During its 113th anniversary celebration, St. Philip's held a reception to show its grateful appreciation to AT&T for their magnanimous gift of twenty-five pieces of original artwork given in November 2010. (See appendix for featured artists and their works.) The beautiful artwork is prominently displayed and housed permanently in the Center for Learning Resources, the Welcome Center, and the Center for Health Professions at the college. The three beautiful new buildings that were built as a part of the college's Capital Improvement Project and dedicated in 2009 are a fitting home for AT&T's generous and wonderful gift.

AT&T's generosity to St. Philip's has been ongoing. As a part of the 112th anniversary celebration, AT&T presented to the college a gift of $100,000, aimed at workforce preparation, through the Alamo Community College District Foundation. Michelle Thomas, assistant vice president for external affairs at AT&T, presented the scholarships to President Loston.

Julian Castro, mayor of San Antonio, Denver McClen-

SPC Administrators and AT&T representatives at the presentation of a scholorship check from AT&T

don, ACCD Board, and many other dignitaries from the community were in attendance at this very special occasion. Thomas, speaking for AT&T, indicated that the impetus for the contribution came about because of AT&T's admiration for St. Philip's Presidential Scholarships.

Presidential Scholarships

President Loston established the Presidential Scholarship in 2008 as a platform to recognize outstanding scholastic achievement and to recognize the students' commitment to community service. To be eligible to apply for the scholarship, students must have achieved a 4.0 overall GPA, be enrolled as a full-time student, commit to thirty hours of community service per semester, and undergo an interview and application process. Since inception of the award, eleven outstanding students have received a total of $33,000. Students receive $3,000 each, $1,500 each spring and fall semester. The Scholarship Gold Tournament helps to fund the Presidential Scholarships. Since its inception, honorees have contributed more than 350 hours of community service to organizations in the city of San Antonio. The 2008–2011 recipients of the Presidential Scholarship are listed in the chart below.

In fall of 2012, this scholarship opportunity was expanded to include a project management component, where students could demonstrate leadership skills and the addition of receiving a transfer scholarship up to $900, if the student graduated from St. Philip's College. In 2009, Loston redirected scholarship funds for all students.

Student Engagement Grant (SEG)

The 2007 academic year was eventful. Among other events, the Student Engagement Grant (SEG) was designed and put into place. In 2008, the nine-member SEG Committee was formed, chaired by Mary Kunz, department of tourism, hospitality, and culinary arts, and co-chaired by Regis Shepherd, chair, fine arts department (now deceased). Members of the committee were: Tammy Anderson, Diego Bernal, Burton Crow, Vernard Grice, John Martin, and Jorge Trevino. The SEG was put into place to support special curricular and co-curricular initiatives where student participation is critical. Students are expected to give back on the campus in exchange for the scholarship support.

Examples of such initiatives are: college choir, sports teams, academic programs in need of enrollment, and new instructional offerings that can attract new students. The SEG application states that activity and student participation in the initiatives must be tied in to the overall mission and goals of the college. Guidelines by the committee for SEG states that it is to "stimulate development of special college initiatives; support recruitment; increase enrollment in targeted programs; and improve student retention by providing financial support and increasing opportunities for student engagement."[15]

The department chairs were asked to review and make recommendations as to how scholarship funds could be allocated to students, beginning in fall of 2009. Thus, the concept of the "Student Engagement Grant" was conceived. Their proposal to engage students was adopted by the president's SEG Council and students.

The SEG scholarship grants are available to part- or full-time students who have a minimum GPA of 2.5 or higher who demonstrate commitment to the special initiative funded by the Student Engagement Grant. These scholarships are based upon merit, not financial need, and are funded in the amount of $1,250 for full-time students ($750 for tuition/fees and $500 for book vouchers per term) and $750 for part-time students ($500 for tuition/fees and $250 for books). Students may apply for a second term if they maintain academic standards and continue to support the initiative. As of 2012, over $280,000 in SEG and presidential scholarships have been allocated to 189 students.

Presidential Scholarship Students

2008	2009	2010	2011
Thomas Espinosa	Johnell Gould	Normalinda Trevino	Normalinda Trevino
Ava Delgado	Doris L. James	Rachel Pounders	Nicholas Wong
Jana Penniston	John Chavez	Nicholas Wong	Laurie Ann Garcia
	Carlos Escajeda		Kimberly Lischke
			Liliana Solis

College Celebrations

Three of the many celebrations held at the college annually are: Women's History Month, Hispanic History Month, and Black History Month.

Women's History Month at SPC

When Dorothy Pickett learned of the Women's History Week national celebration, she gathered a committee and planned a St. Philip's Women's History Week program. The first Women's History Week celebration was held at St. Philip's from March 7–11, 1988. Pickett, a pioneer in many areas, was campus minister at the time. She said, "People are doing this nationally and we should do something here." She invited Johnetta Slaughter and Sandra Moore-Pope to join her. Later, Olga Samples Davis and Jeannette Passty also joined her. "We didn't need our names on it," said Davis, "and once it got started, people got behind it and the program just evolved." They sat down with Pickett, began talking and dreaming, and eventually, when Moore left, Davis and Passty ran the Women's History Program for a number of years. Nationally and locally, Women's History Week developed into Women's History Month.

Women's History Luncheon

The inaugural Women's History Luncheon, founded by Pearl Conyers, was held in the Heritage Room on March 7, 1997 with the theme "Celebrating Women." From its inception, women attendees were invited to wear heels, pearls, and dresses befitting ladies of distinction. From the beginning, the luncheon was a success.

Hispanic History Month

The month-long celebration of Hispanic history was revived in 2008, when Felipe Lopez took note of the fact that despite the fact that St. Philip's is a Hispanic serving institution that lately serves more Hispanic students than any other ethnic group, she could not recall a program held at St. Philip's to observe the occasion.

Noting that Hispanic History Month is celebrated nationally, Lopez approached Dr. Loston, who recommended that St. Philip's begin planning such a celebration for Hispanic History Month. Beginning in 2008, Hispanic History Month celebration was again held at St. Philip's. To mark the occasion, St. Philip's College began with a lineup of free events and since that time, has continued annually with a series of events free and open to students, faculty, and the community. All events are education-oriented, and appropriate and welcoming for families.

The 2008 committee chairpersons and committee who revitalized Hispanic month are in the following list.

Hispanic Heritage Month Committee Members
Felipa Lopez, chairperson
Dr. Sharon Crockett-Bell, co-chairperson
Mark Barnes
Rafael Brisita
Cynthia DeLeon
Miguel Delgado
Eddie Harris
Gina Herrera-Jasso
Alfred Landeros
Cecilia Martinez
Joe Quiroz
Jorge Trevino
Yolanda Vargas
Melissa Vasquez
Freddie Zepeda

The 2011 Hispanic History Month celebration opened in the Kathryn Morgan Gallery on St. Philip's campus with artist Cesar Martinez, a native of Laredo, Texas. A 2011 exhibition of recent works by Martinez, entitled "Batos y mas," began with a reception and ran from September 15, 2011 to October 15, 2011. Martinez's work addresses the concerns and issues of contemporary Chicano culture. The 2011 Hispanic History Month celebration included El Mercado, an outdoor fund-raising event held on the main campus green to support student organizations, and an event featuring the Latin Army Band.

Other activities for 2011 that celebrated Hispanic History Month at St. Philip's main campus included the Best-Tasting Salsa Scholarship Competition, where local high school chefs tried their hand at preparing the best-tasting salsa. A visual art exhibition, "One American Spirit—Unity, Strength, Leadership," was held in the college's newest display space at the Center for Learning Resources. Southwest Campus presented a lunch hour event featuring an all-female mariachi ensemble.

Leadership under Loston

Loston established three standing committees: the facilities committee, the marketing committee, and the heritage committee, which is charged with preserving the significance of our heritage.

Despite Loston's exemplary leadership, her tenure has not been trouble free. Shortly after her arrival, she learned of what could only be described as "very serious problems" in the associate degree nursing program. Chancellor Leslie described her introduction to the problems as "A baptism by fire."

In 1997, St. Philip's began offering a program called LVN to ADN mobility. After four semesters, the program allowed students enrolled in the program to earn an associate of applied science degree in nursing. Upon successfully meeting all the requirements, eligible students could apply for and take the National Council Licensure Examination for Registered Nurses (NCLEX-RN) and receive their RN degree. The program was fully accredited by the Texas Board of Nursing and the Coordinating Board.

Between 2004 and 2006, however, there was great concern for the program at St. Philip's and by 2007, the rate of passing the nursing examination in the ADN mobility evening program had dropped to between 69.5 and 71 percent. Since 80 percent was the required passing rate, as a consequence of falling below that number, the Texas Board of Nursing Examiners changed the status of the program from full approval to conditional approval "until the end of the 2008 examination year, that is, until September 30, 2008 or until such time that the graduates from the last two cohorts of admitted students who test in 2007 and 2008 and the program, demonstrate a pass rate for first time test takers of at least 80 percent on the NCLEX-RN® examination."

Because of the conditional approval rating, the college was not allowed to accept new students into the ADN mobility program (the only program affected), until the passing rate improved. After learning of the troubles within the ADN program, Loston held a press conference at which she stated that the program was not meeting the needs of the students. Noting also that St. Philip's had not come to grips with the issues, and citing outdated curriculum and lax attention to the problem, Loston and the Board of Trustees took immediate action to resolve the issues and to steer the program back on track.

With district approval, measures were instituted to correct the problems, including offering free tutoring and assistance to currently enrolled students to help them to improve their test scores and to assist in the program recovery. Free tutoring opportunities extended not only to students currently enrolled but also to students who had completed the program since it began but had not received their license. Loston created a new position, dean of allied health programs, and hired Dr. Christopher Pate to oversee the programs and to ensure that the students received proper training. The measures were successful, and by 2009 the program was restored to full approval. Students were again allowed to enroll in the LVN to ADN mobility program.

Dr. Christopher Pate, Dean, Center for Health Professions

Dean Pate, who came to St. Philip's following a career in the Army Medical Service Corps, grew up as an "Air Force brat," and served a short tour as an enlisted medical lab tech before getting out of the military early and completing his degree. After earning his degree, Pate returned to military service as a commissioned officer and spent his adult life in the Army. The military services afforded him an opportunity to travel all over the world and to experience many different cultures, lands, and foods.

During his twenty-five-year tour of military duty, Pate served in health care administration and health sciences education and, he observed, "It seemed to be a natural fit, coming from the military environment of health care education and administration to the program of instruction and the environment at St. Philip's." There were programs that had challenges at St. Philip's. The college needed a leader in health science education and Pate was eager to take on the challenge. Pate was very interested in St. Philip's programs and agreed with the directions they wanted to go with the programs.[16]

But scarcely had Pate assumed his new position at St. Philip's before he found himself facing the Texas Board of Nursing to discuss the insufficiencies in the RN program. The RN side was a relatively new program, he explained, and for many reasons, it failed. Some of the reasons for its failure are in the following list.

The RN program failed to meet the standard 80 percent per year licensure requirements pass rate, on average, that the program must meet

There was a lot of overlap between the two programs that should have been very clearly broken off

The RN program was insufficiently staffed, with not enough resources

Nurses in the RN program were stretched so thin that they could not properly manage the program in accordance with the requirements of the Board of Nursing certification

Nurses in the RN program were working more hours than they should have, which left them little time to perform many required duties that needed to be accomplished

Given the enormity and seriousness of the situation, Pate had no choice but to take immediate and drastic measures to repair the problems. Some of the measures taken included revising the curriculum, assigning a new director, and paying more attention to conditions such as the class syllabus, which had previously not been addressed for lack of time. Clinical placement was another area that had been stretched very thin. The nurses were working hours that could only be described as off the charts. This meant that sometimes nurses were out on training sites for an entire week, resulting in the inability to attend required meetings. One aspect of repairing the problem meant bringing nurses' work hours more in line with work load policy.

When Pate resigned from the program in 2010, Rose Mary Spruill was hired from within the program and assumed the position of interim dean of health sciences.

First nursing class

Rose Mary Spruill, Director of the Vocational Nursing Program

Spruill, who joined St. Philip's faculty in 2001, was not a stranger to St. Philip's for she had attended the college in 1977, earning a vocational nursing certificate. At the time, St. Philip's did not have a registered nursing program and St. Philip's students wishing to become RNs had to enroll elsewhere. Following graduation, Spruill went to San Antonio College to pursue a registered nursing license but acknowledged that attending St. Philip's gave her roots in the sense of where she wanted to go and what she wanted to do. "It set a pathway for me," she said. "Besides, I think the instructors saw something in us and gave us a lot of encouragement. They were nurturing, caring, and diligent about making sure that students made something of themselves. My program director of the LVN program, Ella Flowers, told me 'This is not going to be your last step. You're going to RN school.'"[17] Sure enough, that next January, greatly inspired by Flowers, Spruill started RN school.

Spruill became a student at the University of the Incarnate Word, received a BSN degree, continued on with her training, and earned a dual master's in nursing and nursing health care education. At the time of this writing, Spruill, while holding the position of dean of health sciences, is pursuing a PhD program in nursing through Capella University.

St. Philip's Nursing Program

From its inception in 1949, when St. Philip's established its first health care program with twelve students, the vocational nursing program has evolved into the associate degree nursing mobility (ADN) program and the RN certification. The ADN program began in 1998 on the occasion of the school's centennial celebration, and had two locations: MLK campus and the Central Texas Technology Center in New Braunfels, Texas. In 2009, a pilot program began for high school students from Edison and Floresville High Schools, under the Health Professions Academy with Dr. Rich Butler as chair. This program, led by the LVN staff and directed by the then-vocational nursing program director, Rose Spruill, provides a tuition-free, early college experience for high school students.

When the program began in 1998, its objective was to facilitate the transition of working nurses from LVN (licensed vocational nurse) to RN (registered nurse) certification. Through offering in-depth, intensive, eight-week courses, the LVN to ADN mobility program can now be completed in four semesters by combining classroom and laboratory lectures with real-world, supervised clinical experience. Students must complete twenty-eight credit hours of general education courses and thirty-two credit hours of nursing education courses. Those students who successfully complete the program are eligible to apply for the National Council Licensure Examination for Registered Nurses (NCLEX- RN).

As one of the oldest nursing programs in the state of Texas and one that is always in the forefront of education, the nursing program at St. Philip's participates in the College Tech Prep Program. The College Tech Prep Program provides an opportunity for high school students to begin earning college credits while in high school and then to complete the program at a community college. St. Philip's has a College Tech Prep pilot program in Floresville and a pilot program at Edison High School in San Antonio, with ten students enrolled in each program.

More than 90 percent of graduates in the LVN program go on to seek employment in a variety of medical treatment facilities, including long-term care, acute care, ambulatory care, and home health care. Approximately 50 percent of Tech Prep graduates continue their education beyond vocational nursing training by completing prerequisites in preparation for entering an RN school. The goal in attending the program is to obtain either an associate's degree or a bachelor's.

The new Center for Health Professions at St. Philip's acts as the gateway for implementation of the nursing education department's philosophy: health care must be administered in a holistic manner that empowers the client to continually strive toward a healthy adaptation to their ever-changing environment.

Allied health has two departments: one focused on diagnostic and basic health services and the other focused on early childhood, physical health, and other clinical services. The child development center is also a part of the allied health department, while nursing is composed of the registered nursing program, the associate's degree in nursing program, and the LVN program.

Solving the problem in the LVN/ADN program was not the only problem Loston faced. Early in her tenure, Loston was faced with a series of difficulties that had the potential of having serious consequences as well as benefits for the college. Foremost among them was the issue of single and individual accreditation, a consideration affecting the entire district.

Accreditation: Individual or Single

When Denver McClendon proposed that some thought be given to single accreditation versus individual accreditation, even the names given to the proposal seemed to be contradictory. Once again, the community and the college united.

At a meeting of the ACCD Board held in June 2009, Board Chairman Denver McClendon proposed that consideration be given to single accreditation for the district. Single accreditation, as it relates to the community college, is the opposite of individual accreditation. Individual accreditation, the model under which the district operated at the time, allowed each college to meet its own accreditation standards, while under single accreditation, the proposed model would have all of the colleges in the district be accredited under one umbrella.

When Chancellor Leslie came to the district in 2006, he was purported to have made attempts to merge institutions and consolidate operations in at least two of the colleges he led prior to coming to the ACCD. Shortly after his arrival at the district, rumors began circulating that the five colleges in the district would merge into a single accredited system. While it did not occur, the rumors resurfaced when McClendon proposed looking at single accreditation as a cost savings measure. The board denied the claims. Despite the denials, the board took the steps of subsequently mandating that the colleges use a common logo and common marketing, established cross-college councils to foster cooperation between the colleges, and gave the go-ahead to look at having a common curriculum among the colleges. With each college having programs unique to that college, loss of individuality was of great concern. In fact, it seemed almost a certainty.

Chairman McClendon appointed Chancellor Leslie to organize a committee to study the benefits, disadvantages, savings, and costs of moving to single accreditation and how the colleges would be affected. One of the major consequences of adopting single accreditation for St. Philip's was the potential loss of its HBCU status and loss of the funds that accompanied the designation.

With consent from the Board of Trustees, the chancellor appointed individuals from the community to serve on an Accreditation Review Committee. The appointees represented the five colleges in the district, the community, and the student body. The committee, jointly chaired by Dr. Jackie Claunch, president, Northwest Vista College, and Jeff Hunt, San Antonio College, chair, theatre and speech communications, held their first meeting in July 2009.

At the first meeting, Chancellor Leslie clarified board expectations and charged the committee with the task of collecting and examining data related to the two distinct models: individual accreditation and single accreditation. After first taking note of the advantages, disadvantages, costs, and savings of each model, the committee was to report back to the board with a summary of the data collected.

The committee was not required to make recommendations to the board regarding the selection of one model over the other, only to bring a report of their data to the trustees by December 2009, so that consideration could be given to costs before the budget was approved. They were given a list of thirteen questions on which to base their findings. Other measures proposed by the board that appeared to favor single accreditation were discussions on consolidating admissions, registration, student financial services, continuing education, teaching certification programs, and printing and copying services.

Most faculty and staff at the four colleges (St. Philip's, San Antonio College, Palo Alto, and Northwest Vista) vigorously opposed the merger. Not only was there the potential for major losses to the colleges, there was also no guarantee that the district would benefit from combining them. Northeast Lakeview, the newest school among them, was working diligently to achieve its accreditation, and while it was concluded that single accreditation might aid Lakeview with its accreditation, there was no assurance that single accreditation would speed up the process.

The separation, meanwhile, would save the district about $235,000 yearly. Additionally, to become singly accredited, the Southern Association of Colleges and Schools (SACS) required each of the colleges to have their bookkeeping system separated from the other colleges and to provide a stand-alone audit.

Another problem that surfaced was that Lakeview could not offer their students federal financial aid. To get around this problem, Lakeview students enrolled at both St. Philip's and SAC while attending classes at Lakeview. The Southern Association, however, did not approve of this policy. Another very large concern to each of the schools was the possibility of loss of the special programs offered by the individual colleges. Following is a summary of the reasons voiced for and against the merger.

Reasons for Merging the Colleges

- Operations could be streamlined and the standards of the entire district could be raised
- Merging could be a cost-saving measure
- The merger might possibly facilitate Northeast Lakeview College receiving their accreditation from SACS
- There could be increased collaboration between colleges through process alignment and common outcomes

Reasons Not to Consolidate

- Potential loss of individual histories and established cultures of individual colleges
- Loss of HBCU status and resulting loss of eligibility for Title III federal funding for St. Philip's, a potential loss of $5 to $7 million annually
- Forfeiture of the ability to apply for Title V funds by the other colleges, an annual potential loss of over $1,000,000 yearly, if St. Philip's appealed and won the HBCU designation
- SACS accreditation for this newly consolidated institution would have to be secured

While most faculty and staff agreed on the benefits of collaboration, process alignment, and common outcomes, there was deep concern about the potential loss of flexibility at the colleges and concern about their ability to affect programs and innovations that improved student results. The time required to develop district-wide processes to satisfy SACS criteria for single accreditation was likely to be costly, in terms of time and money.

While it was speculated that the single model of accreditation would be less costly than accrediting each college individually over the next ten years, there was the possibility that the total expenses would eliminate any savings. Additionally, since an "institution" (in this case, ACCD as a whole), could not receive both Title III and Title V funding, the other colleges in the district would be unable to apply for Title V grants, even if St. Philip's appealed to retain HBCU status and won the appeal. The potential loss to the other colleges could be as much as $1,000,000 annually in federal grant monies. The likely loss to St. Philip's of its HBCU status might mean a loss of between $5,000,000 to $7,000,000 annually from Title III funds and Title V funding. St. Philip's had the right to appeal the potential loss of its HBCU status but there was no assurance its HBCU status could be regained on appeal.

Since each college in the district is a Hispanic Serving Institution (HSI) and three of the colleges are eligible for federal grants based on their HSI designations, if St. Philip's were granted the appeal, the district would then have to choose between being an HBCU and an HSI. If the appeal lost, the colleges could retain their HSI status.

At the January 2010 meeting of the board, Dr. Loston outlined the benefits and subsequent losses that would accrue to St. Philip's should Title III funding be lost. This included the Center of Excellence in Mathematics and Center of Excellence in Science, Campus Construction, and Project Administration, costs of operating the SPC Freshmen Center, Welcome Center, academic support, instructional technology and instructional innovation. The cost to the college would be approximately $7,401,506 yearly.

Much like a mother hen protecting her brood, the community rose up in support of each college maintaining their individual accreditation. The ACCD Board scheduled numerous meetings giving individuals, community groups, faculty, students, and organizations attending the meetings opportunities to be heard. All desiring to speak were required to register beforehand and were limited to two minutes in order that all could be heard.

The community, faculty, students, individuals, be they African Americans, Hispanics, or Anglos, all spoke with one voice, and were unanimous in their opinion: individual accreditation must be maintained. Additionally, several members of the Trustee Board hinted that they, too, might be in favor of remaining individually accredited.

After five months of review and fact finding, the Accreditation Committee reported their findings to Chancellor Leslie, who then made a recommendation to the board. With unanimous support from the faculty, student body, and community, and citing the counterproductivity and potential loss of grant funding, Leslie reported that because the potential loss of grant funding would be counterproductive to fulfilling the mission and services to students, "I recommend that the colleges remain as a family of individually accredited institution." Leslie's recommendation to the board and the board's unanimous verbal acceptance of his recommendation was met with thunderous applause from the packed audience. [18]

Southwest Campus

Southwest Campus, located at 800 Quintana Road on what was once East Kelly Air Force Base, opened on January 13, 1975. While it is located in the southwest quadrant of the city, its purpose is to serve the needs of the entire city of San Antonio and nearby towns. A major element of St. Philip's College, Southwest Campus plays a vital role in the growth and development of the college. Southwest Campus provides academic and technical courses for credit, continuing education noncredit courses designed to increase vocational skills and provide personal enrichment, and occupational, technical, and general education.

Southwest Campus became an official campus of St. Philip's during Dr. Mitchell's tenure as president and though it had been an extension of the college since 1975, it was not until 1987 that the designation became official. Prior to 1987, Southwest Campus operated as an extension of the Alamo Community College District. In 1987, Southwest Campus was designated an official part of St. Philip's College.

The campus houses three main buildings as training sites for the technical and industrial trades and other workforce development specialized training programs.

Pablo Pena, a former graduate of St. Philip's, was born on the West Side of San Antonio. At the time of the interview, Pena had been associated with St. Philip's for twenty-five years. "I always worked hard," he said, "took the trade in high school and started working on cars behind my house until I graduated." Following high school, Pena worked for the Cadillac dealership for one year. At that time, in the late 1950s, the industry was paying $3 an hour, flat rate, and he was making 40 percent of that $3. Once he became proficient, he said, "I can make a hundred for them, I think I can make this hundred dollars for me."

When the Edgewood School District called him about a job and sent him to the university to get a vocation degree, he taught in the district for two years before leaving for Burbank High School, where he taught for ten years. During those years, Pena said he "took the national championship of the entire United States in Auto Body Repair."

Pena came to St. Philip's as an instructor: "Took over the department in 1981 and worked this department from nothing to what it is right now. They used to say that I was from the old school, and I'm still from the old school but the things is, I've had my own business for forty-three years and 90 percent of the persons (employees) I have,

SPC Southwest Campus

I trained in this program, starting with my son and my daughter. If I didn't feel that it was right, I wouldn't be doing that for my son and my daughter."[19]

Pena says that when he started, he did not have the equipment that he has now and his program was called a hobby shop. "But my hobby shop produced students on the job in 90 percent of the big shops in San Antonio and about 60 percent of the insurance companies," he said. "And many of my students that I trained have their own shops."

Pena said that when he began teaching at St. Philip's, he made his own tools. "In fact, before we had a frame machine, we used to pull them between beams, the old way," he said.[20] Declaring that he used to bring a lot of his materials from his shop and give them to the school to keep the students going, he spoke of being a firm believer in teaching students from the ground up. "The only place you start at the top is digging a ditch," he said.

At one time, Pena said that he had nearly 300 students and seven full-time instructors, all from industry. He taught all aspects of a body shop business, starting from estimating, framework, paint work, body work, and upholstery. His students were taught productivity because "If you can't produce for a person, he's not going to make it and he's not going to pay you." At the time of the interview, the program had just gotten the beautiful spray room that he had been asking for for fifteen years. "But," he said, "if you know how to do your job, you don't need the fancy equipment. It's like putting on a suit compared to a tuxedo. It will serve the same purpose."

Southwest Campus is home to the Middle College Program, the Phoenix Program, four programs called the Alamo Area Academies, Allied Construction, Multi-Modal Transportation, Repair and Manufacturing, and Women in Nontraditional Occupations (WINTO).

The Middle College Program

The Middle College Program, modeled after a New York high school alternative program, is a collaboration between Southwest Campus and various school districts in the San Antonio area. The program prepares high school students to achieve academic, personal, and economic success by providing stimulating hands-on learning experiences and real-world speakers inside and outside the classroom to explore careers in industrial and technology programs. Worksite visits may be included in order to gain a realistic perspective of how various skills are utilized in the workplace.

WINTO: Women in Nontraditional Occupations Program

Following a twenty-seven-year military career and a short stint with the city of San Antonio, James H. Wright, from Delaware, left full-time city employment to work part time under Dr. Zaragoza at St. Philip's Southwest Campus. Soon after, Wright became a full-time SPC employee and served the college for more than fifteen years.

In 2009, James Wright, director of Middle College Programs, having just completed a four-year term as State Director-Postsecondary Division, Texas Skills USA, reflected on some of the things he had learned and accomplished in the position. Examining the statistics on the number of women across the nation engaged in occupations traditionally held by men such as welding, homebuilding, automotive, and diesel, Wright noted that the percentage of women employed in those positions was drastically lower than the number of men. (The Department of Labor labels such occupations nontraditional when the percentage of women or men in a particular field is 25 percent or less.) He concluded that an initiative needed to be undertaken to increase the number of females in the nontraditional occupational programs offered at SPC and to assist them to gain entry into the workforce in those occupations.

With the low percentage of women at St. Philip's enrolled in the technical programs, Wright saw a recruitment opportunity; an opportunity to offer support for those already enrolled in the program and an opportunity to improve the graduation rate. He began working on ideas that culminated in the first WINTO Conference, noting that the time was right for a conference to be held at Southwest Campus to which local secondary and postsecondary students would be invited. Assisted by Laurie Rodriguez, Wright assembled a committee that planned the first conference, which included an education/career fair. The first WINTO Conference at Southwest Campus was held on March 31, 2010, and was held in conjunction with Women's History Month. Rated very successful, more than 200 students attended.

Guest speakers for the first conference were Sandra Hawkins, Southwest Research Institute Senior Research Engineer, and Beverly Beavers-Lyle, US Department of Labor Regional Administrator for the Women's Bureau and Field Operations Manager of all ten regional offices.

National Skills USA /Texas-College/Postsecondary Division Leadership and Skills Championships and Conference

Southwest Campus hosts and sponsors the conference that provides opportunities for students to demonstrate their technical knowledge in technical, skilled, and service occupations and their leadership skills. At the conference, students practice and compete to become world-class workers and responsible American citizens. Southwest Campus has hosted the State Conference, now a three-day event showcasing some of the best trade, technical, and skilled services, including allied health occupations, architectural drafting, welding, diesel technology, cosmetology, automotive technology, nurse assisting, aircraft technology, robotics, collision technology, public speaking, dental assisting, and RV news anchor.

The Phoenix Program

The Phoenix Program (formerly Project Phoenix) began in spring 1997 as a joint education partnership between the ACCD–St. Philip's College, San Antonio Independent School District (SAISD), and the San Antonio business community. Eighty students (all volunteers), all interested in technical occupations and all from among the eight high schools within SAISD, initially enrolled in the program. The program presently serves up to 100 students. SAISD teachers are assigned to Southwest Campus to teach the high school classes and students attend dual-credit classes taught by Southwest Campus instructors.

During their junior year, students are provided opportunities to rotate through an exploratory program to experience and explore all the industrial and technical programs offered by St. Philip's College–Southwest Campus. Students must meet the requirements set forth by the Texas Education Agency (TEA) to earn their high school diploma, including successful completion of the Texas Assessment of Knowledge and Skills (TAKS) test.

The Alamo Area Academies

An innovative training and educational partnership, the academies are designed to provide education, experience, and job opportunities for high school students. They offer a two- year program that allows students to enroll in their home high school during their junior and senior years, while taking approximately half of their classes at the community college. Upon graduation, the student will have earned twenty-seven to thirty-five college semester hours and a Level I Certificate of Completion from the community college along with their high school diploma, all at no cost to the student.

In 2008, Loston conceived the idea of Centers of Excellence to "increase student enrollment, engagement, and success in Science, Technology, Engineering, and Math (STEM) degree programs." Included in the power generation and alternative energy portion of the program is a house with the largest noncommercial solar array in San Antonio and a large wind turbine, which helps to defray the cost of operating campus facilities. Wind turbines, fuel cells, and solar cells are used to study devices that generate electrical power through alternative sources of energy.

Students are trained and certified in the installation, repair, and maintenance of alternative energy systems. As a means of reaching the goal of increasing student enrollment, innovative partnerships are created with local school districts, regional higher education institutions, businesses, and industry. The goal is to create a larger, more diverse, and well-developed STEM workforce. Funding for the programs was provided by the Department of Education, through the College Cost Reduction and Access Act (CCRAA) and Title III.

On April 26, 2011, a "Green Tie Affair Program" was held at Southwest Campus complete with ribbon cutting, student presentations, and tours celebrating the grand opening of the centers. The Center for Excellence for Mathematics includes a professional teaching and learning center, a math advancement institute, math for alternative energy, and math for allied health. The Center of Excellence for Science provides state-of-the-art settings to address national initiatives aimed at increasing the participation in science and mathematics career fields' labs. Five new associate degree programs will be offered, each designed to attract, generate, and retain state-of-the-art high-wage business and employment opportunities for the community: biotechnology, chemical research assistant, environmental science, earth sciences, and natural energy resources.

Dancing with the Stars

Not everything that takes place at the presidential level of the college is educational, nor is everything staid and stodgy. In fact, some things are downright fun. SPC's president donned a "fittingly appropriate" costume and participated as a contestant in the San Antonio Area Foundation gala, "Renaissance Dancing with the Stars." The fun-filled evening, which benefited the San Antonio Area African American Community Fund, was an "organized effort to raise grant-making dollars that are governed and administered by community residents from the San Antonio area for the purpose of improving the opportunities and lives of African Americans." The invitation to this event, held at the Grand Hyatt Hotel in late summer around the end of August, describes it as an evening to inspire the San Antonio area to invest in a living legacy in support of the African American community.

President Loston, who came in second in the contest, said, tongue in cheek, "I can't accept this. I can't take a second-place trophy back to the campus, not with St. Philip's history of always being first."[21]

24 Conclusion

One hundred plus years after it began St. Philip's has come full circle. This institution, after a roller coaster ride that encompassed more than one hundred years, has embarked upon an exciting new journey where the sky is the limit.

What was begun by Bishop James Steptoe Johnston in the nineteenth century was persisted in the twentieth century by the perseverence of Dr. Artemisia Bowden, who inspired a cadre of dedicated leaders to follow her lead. Even as she retired from daily duties, she would not allow St. Philip's to lose its momentum but continued to have her say until she could no longer participate because of ill health. Dr. Norris, Murphy, Williams, Mitchell, Jackson, Taylor, and others in the twentieth century guided the school as it continued to flourish. In the twenty-first century, Dr. Angie Stokes Runnels carried the torch and under her leadership, the college grew. Now led by Dr. Adena Loston, the movement continues, and under her watch, St. Philip's College is making its mark.

When Runnels resigned, she was well into her sixth year as president. She kept a picture of Miss Bowden on a wall in her office and it is likely that Miss Bowden was pleased to be there, for from its position, it is easy to believe that she continued to keep watch over her most prized possession, St. Philip's College. Runnels was deeply involved at St. Philip's and well on the road to longevity and success in her own career, but fate intervened and because of ill health, she was forced to resign. When, in 2008, illness claimed her life, St. Philip's again lost an able leader, one who was dedicated to the mission. St. Philip's mourned the loss of all its leaders but, as it has from the beginning, St. Philip's continued to forge ahead.

A Closer Look

From its humble beginning as a totally segregated, black-only college, St. Philip's is now a facility with blacks in the minority, Hispanics in the majority, and whites as the fastest-growing population. Its history includes a period when, in the not too distant past, the topic of discussion was whether to close the college. But the Eastside community, aware of the school's importance to its children, to the community, and to those in the future who would come, would not see it shuttered. St. Philip's College, having grown up side by side with the community is, after all, an integral part of the Eastside's existence.

There have been many onslaughts to St. Philip's existence and there are compelling reasons that St. Philip's continues to survive each one. Besides being an essential part of the neighborhood, a prime reason has to be Bishop James Steptoe Johnston, who along with Bowden, "the Savior of St. Philip's," laid a sound and solid foundation for the school. He persevered to the end of his life in his quest to establish the school, and following his death, Bishop Capers, Bowden, and others seized the opportunity and dedicated themselves to St. Philip's College. For Bowden, St. Philip's was her life.

Another equally compelling reason that St. Philip's continues to thrive has to be the committed leaders who followed in those able leaders' footsteps. Between Artemisia Bowden, first president, and Adena Loston, current president, there is a cadre of devoted leaders who, if one is to believe the testimonies of the students, faculty, staff, and community, were unswerving in their intent to see St. Philip's College continue. They succeeded beyond their wildest aspirations.

There are similarities between the leaders of St. Philip's College that go beyond their labors for the school. Three black women leaders were singled out for mention because the school was originally a school for young black women and, because the similarities between Artemisia Bowden, Angie Runnels, and Adena Loston are striking. It may well be said that all of the persons who wore the mantle of president had much in common, but for the sake of brevity, mention will be made of only the three leaders selected: Artemisia Bowden, Angie Runnels, and Adena Loston.

All three can be described by the following traits:

Effective leaders, with singleness of purpose, particularly in regard to St. Philip's College
An enduring commitment to service with strong support for faculty, staff, students, and community
Belief in the position that St. Philip's is "family"
A history of solid familial support and strong religious ties
Fathers who gave their daughters a sense that "You can do anything"
Working with a supportive faculty, committed to the ideal of making St. Philip's great
An attitude that exhibited, whether or not it had been done before, I Will Do This

This Eastside community continues to struggle with the issue of maintaining St. Philip's identity while embracing all who come. Should all the colleges come under one umbrella, loss of identity will become more of an issue. The history of this college is unique and must be preserved for generations to come, and knowing and understanding its roots are vital to its survival.

A further reason for its survival is the college itself, what it stands for and the services it provides. From its inception, this institution emphasized service to its students and to the community. The college affirms its purpose in its mission statement, which reads:

> The College takes pride in its individual attention to students . . . places value on a student-centered culture . . . and is described as valuing a strong connection to our neighborhood communities.[1]

St. Philip's fulfills its commitment to its students and to the community, which it serves by doing what is necessary to carry out its mission. With nineteen departments offering classes, St. Philip's provides something for everyone, from GED preparation to honors classes, and from campus-based continuing education classes to distance learning courses taught on the Internet. Included in this something for everyone is free tuition for senior citizens (aged sixty-five and older) taking noncredit classes.

The passing of the bond issue in 2005 that earlier had been rejected is an indication of how strongly the citizens of San Antonio affirm the value of the institution. With the passing of the bond issue, improvements were funded that included the opening of Northeast Lakeview College, a new campus located on the Northeast Side, five new buildings for St. Philip's with state-of-the-art equipment, and new construction for each college in the district.

St. Philip's is "among the oldest and most diverse of community colleges in the nation" and remains one of the fastest growing in Texas with tentacles reaching far and wide, a far cry from its humble beginning. From six little black girls to a multi-campus enrollment that is projected to surpass 12,000 in the very near future, this school proudly wears the distinction of being the only school in the nation with the designation "A Historically Black and Hispanic Serving Institution."

Name Changes for St. Philip's College: 1898–2009

From its inception, the name of the institution reflected the changing instructional needs the school attempted to fulfill. (*Source:* College Catalogues: St. Philip's College.)

1898 St. Philip's Saturday Evening Sewing Class
1898 St. Philip's Vocational Day School
1900 St. Philip's Industrial School
1902 St. Philip's Industrial School for Girls
1903 St. Philip's Grammar and Industrial School
1906 St. Philip's Normal, Grammar, and Industrial School
1918 St. Philip's Normal and Industrial School
1927 St. Philip's Junior College and Industrial School
1939 St. Philip's Junior College and Vocational Institute
1942 St. Philip's Junior College, a Branch of San Antonio College
1946 St. Philip's College, San Antonio Union Junior College District
1948 St. Philip's Junior College
2009 (March) Alamo Colleges, St. Philip's College

Time Marches on: Resolution 5-2012, Recognition of Dr. Artemisia Bowden

Artemisia Bowden is now under consideration by the Historical Commission of the Diocese of West Texas to be added to the Liturgical Calendar.

The commission, making note of the "high priority of the Church in this day," wrote:

> THEREFORE BE IT RESOLVED that this 108th meeting of the Diocesan Council meeting in convention in McAllen, Texas propose that Dr. Artemisia Bowden be recognized in the Calendar of the Church Year as well as Holy Women, Holy Men; and, BE IT FURTHER RESOLVED that this 77th General Convention propose an additional commemoration for inclusion in the Calendar of the Church Year and authorize for trial use for the triennium 2012-15, a day commemorating the "dedicated dreamer" Diocese of West Texas educator, Dr. Artemisia Bowden.[2]

The commission went on to speak of the "high priority that racial reconciliation remains in this day," making it a high priority to honor her life.

Denver McClendon

Denver McClendon, Former Chairman, Board of ACCD Trustees

The Board of Trustees played and continues to play a major role in the operation of St. Philip's. Here we meet Denver McClendon, who served as chairman of the Board of Trustees beginning in 2003.

A retired military officer with twenty-six years of service, McClendon grew up in Atlanta and graduated from Tennessee State University in Nashville. He was selected by the Board of Trustees in July 2003, from a group of three or four persons, to fill the unexpired term vacated by Donald McClure. McClendon successfully ran for election in May 2004 and won the election to the Board of Trustees. In June 2008, his peers elected him chairman of the Board of Trustees. He was reelected in 2010 by voters as a member to a second six-year term.

According to McClendon, Johnetta Slaughter, former chair of the department of social studies at SPC and Donald McClure, member of the board, were instrumental in his first becoming involved with the Board of the Alamo Community District. The Trustee Board was, at the time, experiencing a problem with credibility and, since this was also his big concern, he consented to become involved. The primary concern was with members of the board doing what was right for the colleges without regard for their own agenda. "I think we have worked tirelessly to do that," said McClendon, "so much so that the community now has confidence in the board and feels that we are going to do what is right for the colleges."

When McClendon joined the Trustee Board of the ACCD, issues of great importance were being decided. Some of the issues were:

- Should the nursing programs at St. Philip's and at San Antonio College be moved to the medical school area?
- Would the bond issue pass?
- How should the colleges deal with the issue of individual accreditation versus the issue of single accreditation? The district was faced with a completion average rate that averaged less than the statewide average of completion and there was the need to immediately improve the rate of student success, and to improve the percentage of students entering college in the district and completing their education.
- Should the cost of textbooks be lowered, since in some cases, the costs of textbooks to students could cost more than the cost of tuition?

"The issues were a wake-up call for all of us," said McClendon. Since the trustees were representing the taxpayers of Bexar County, it was their responsibility to ensure that a return on the taxpayers' investment be provided. Despite budget cuts and being forced to do more with less, the board's responsibility is to show that they can perform efficiently.

As chairman, McClendon and the board addressed the issues he outlined, but they by no means declare the issues solved. "But," he said, "We're doing a better job now and concentrating more on student success and academic success than we have in the past, and that's going to pay off."[3]

Dr. Stephen Mitchell, past president of St. Philip's, said some years ago, "There is more reason to be proud of the school today than there was twenty years ago."

Even so, the school's success cannot be attributed to what any one person did that caused the community to embrace the college as they did. The fact is, the college has become a part of the Eastside community. That is important. It is important to the college and it is important to the community. It is true that the college, its offerings, and its influence have improved with time. Back then, twenty years earlier, Mitchell expressed the fact that "St. Philip's is a good school that lots of black people go to," but then went on to say, "lots of other people go there as well and over time, it will become an institution with appeal to the general public, rather than being a good school for black people."

These prophetic words have come true. St. Philip's is not just a good school, and it is no longer a school for black people. It has become a great school, and because it is a great school, it is one that blacks and many other groups are selecting in record numbers.

The story does not end here. The students, staff, and administrators continue daily to live out the St. Philip's story. Bishop Capers predicted nearly a century ago that St. Philip's would someday be a great institution of learning. His prediction is now a reality, a dream come true.

Appendix A

Presidents of St. Philip's College, 1898–2012

Bishop J. S. Johnston
Founding Bishop, 1898

Ms. Artemisia Bowden
1902–1954

Dr. Clarence W. Norris
President, 1954–1969

Dr. John B. Murphy
President, 1969–1982

Dr. T. R. Williams
Interim President, 1982

Dr. Gloria Jackson
President, 1982–1984

Dr. Kay Moore
Interim President. 1985

Dr. Stephen R. Mitchell
President, 1985–1992

Dr. Byron R. Skinner
President, 1992–1993

Mr. Hamice James
Interim President, 1993–1995

Dr. Charles A. Taylor
President, 1995–2000

Dr. Homer (Butch) Hayes
Interim President, 2000

Dr. Angie S. Runnels
President, 2000–2006

Dr. Patricia (Patti) Candia
Interim President, 2006–2007

Dr. Adena Loston
President, 2007–Present

Appendix B

Administrators of St. Philip's College, 1898–2012

Years	Administrative Position			
1898–1902	*Administrator* Bishop Johnston			
1902–1916	*Administrators* Bishop Johnston	*Adminstrator* Artemisia Bowden		
1932–1938	*President* Artemisia Bowden	*Dean* James L. Hawkins		
1939–1940	*President* Artemisia Bowden	*College Director* Alphonso B. Johnson		
1943–1944	*President* Artemisia Bowden	*Director of Studies* James W. Brown		
1944–1945	*Dean* Artemisia Bowden	*Registrar* Alma J. Morgan	*Assistant Dean* Clarence W. Norris	
1945–1947	*Dean* Artemisia Bowden	*Assistant Dean* Clarence W. Norris		
1947–1954	*President* J. O. Loftin	*Dean* Artemisia Bowden	*Dean of Faculty* Clarence W. Norris	
1954–1955	*Dean Emeritus* Artemisia Bowden	*Dean of College* Clarence W. Norris		
1955–1961	*Dean Emeritus* Artemisia Bowden	*Dean of College* Clarence W. Norris	*Dir. Evening Division* Leonidas Watson	
1961–1969	*Dean-Registrar* Clarence W. Norris	*Dir. Evening Division* Leonidas Watson		
1969–1973	*Dean of College* John B. Murphy	*Dir. Evening Division* Leonidas Watson		
1973–1975	*Dean* John B. Murphy	*Associate Dean* Theodore W. Williams	*Dir. Evening Division* *Leonidas Watson*	
1975–1981	*Dean* John B. Murphy	*Associate Dean* Theodore W. Williams	*Dir. Evening Division* Leonidas Watson	*Dir. Southwest Center* James Dye

Years	Administrative Position				
1981–1983	*Dean* John B. Murphy	*Associate Dean* Theodore W. Williams	*Dir. Evening Division* Alfonso Cervantes	*Dir. Southwest Center* James Dye	
1983–1985	*President* Gloria M. Jackson	*VP of Academic Affairs* Theodore W. Williams	*VP of Student Services* Don A. Coleman	*Dir. Southwest Center* James Dye	
1985–1986	*President* Kay Moore (acting)	*VP of Academic Affairs* Theodore W. Williams	*VP of Student Services* Don A. Coleman	*Dir. Southwest Center* James Dye	
1986–1987	*President* Gloria M. Jackson	*VP of Academic Affairs* Theodore W. Williams	*VP of Student Services* Don A. Coleman	*Dir. Southwest Center* James Dye	
1987–1989	*President* Stephen R. Mitchell	*VP of Student Services* Don A. Coleman			
1989–1992	*President* Stephen R. Mitchell	*VP of Academic Affairs* Hamice R. James	*VP of Student Affairs* Don A. Coleman	*Assoc. Dean, SW Campus* William McCoy	
1992–1993	*President* Bryon Skinner	*VP of Academic Affairs* Hamice R. James	*VP of Student Affairs* Don A. Coleman		
1993–1995	*President* Hamice R. James (interim)	*VP of Academic Affairs* Rose Thomas	*VP of Student Affairs* Rose Thomas	*Dean, SW Campus* Linda A. Rodriguez	
1995–1996	*President* Charles A. Taylor	*VP of Academic Affairs* Rose Thomas			
1996–1999	*President* Charles A. Taylor	*VP of Academic Affairs* Lanier Byrd	*VP of Student Affairs* Lynn Hills	*Dean, Continuing Ed* Alvoid R. Bennett	*Dean, SW Campus* Frederick Zaragoza
1999–2000	*President* Homer M. Hayes (interim)	*VP of Academic Affairs* Lanier Byrd	*VP of Student Affairs* Lynn Hills	*Dean, Continuing Ed* Alvoid R. Bennett	*Dean, SW Campus* Frederick Zaragoza
2000–2002	*President* Angie S. Runnels	*VP of Academic Affairs* Lanier Byrd	*VP of Student Affairs* Lynn Hills	*Dean, Continuing Ed* Alvoid R. Bennett	*VP, SW Campus* Frederick Zaragoza
2002–2004	*President* Angie S. Runnels	*VP of Academic Affairs* Lanier Byrd	*VP of Student Affairs* Patricia Candia	*Dean, Continuing Ed* Alvoid R. Bennett	*VP, SW Campus* Frederick Zaragoza
2004–2006	*President* Angie S. Runnels	*VP of Academic Affairs* Lanier Byrd	*VP of Student Affairs* Patricia Candia	*Dean, Continuing Ed* Alvoid R. Bennett	*VP, SW Campus* none listed
2006–2007	*President* Patricia Candia (interim)	*VP of Academic Affairs* Lanier Byrd	*VP of Student Affairs* none listed	*Dean, Continuing Ed* Alvoid R. Bennett	*VP, SW Campus* Jorge Trevino
2007–2008	*President* Adena W. Loston	*VP of Academic Affairs* Lanier Byrd	*VP of Student Affairs* Patricia Candia	*Dean, Continuing Ed* Alvoid R. Bennett	
2008–2009	*President* Adena W. Loston	*VP of Academic Affairs* Ruth Dalrymple	*VP of Student Affairs* Patricia Candia	*Dean, Continuing Ed* Vernard Grice	
2009–2010	*President* Adena W. Loston	*VP of Academic Affairs* Ruth Dalrymple	*VP of Student Success* Ruth Dalrymple	*Dean, Continuing Ed* Vernard Grice	*Dean, SW Campus* Maureen Cartledge
2010–2011	*President* Adena W. Loston	*VP of Academic Affairs* Ruth Dalrymple	*VP of Student Success* Ruth Dalrymple	*Dean, Continuing Ed* Vernard Grice	*Dean, SW Campus* Maureen Cartledge
2011–2012	*President* Adena W. Loston	*VP of Academic Affairs* Ruth Dalrymple	*VP of Student Success* Sherie Lang	*Dean, Continuing Ed* Erick Akins/Art Hall	*Dean, SW Campus* Maureen Cartledge

Appendix C

Letter and Signatures

Diocese of West Texas
RT. REV. WILLIAM THEODOTUS CAPERS, D. D., BISHOP
EPISCOPAL RESIDENCE
108 WEST FRENCH PLACE
San Antonio, Texas

May 31, 1928.

To the Board of Trustees
of St. Philip's Junior College.
~~Bishop W. T. Capers, Pres.~~
Rev. Rolfe P. Crum, ~~Vice Pres.~~
H. H. Ochs
Ned McIlhenny
John E. Mitchell
Dr. F. G. Oppenheimer
E. H. Kifer
Albert Steves, Jr.
Geo. T. Allensworth
Col. W. S. Hendrick
Herman Horner

Gentlemen:

Under Canon 9, Section 1, of the Canons of the Diocese of West Texas, the control of St. Philip's Normal and Industrial School for Negro Girls is committed to the Bishop of the Diocese. Acting under this Canon I have changed the character of this school by accepting from the Department of Education of the state of Texas the grade for it of Junior College. By accepting this grade, the name of the school has been changed from its former name to that of St. Philip's Junior College. Under my authority I have invited you to become sharers with me in the control of this college. And in asking you to become partners with me in this great enterprise, I wish, by this official communication, to give to each and to all of you the full powers of a duly appointed and authorized Board of Trustees. I shall not presume to take any action in reference to the conduct of St. Philip's Junior College other than at meetings that are duly authorized and called under the bylaws of our Board. I shall not undertake under any circumstances to over-ride, or to nullify any action of this Board through my personal influence as the Bishop of the Diocese, but to the contrary, I shall gladly and willingly follow the leadership of the majority of the Board when such action is taken at its duly appointed meetings. With the consent of the Board of Trustees, I shall act as President of the Board and will ask the Rev. Rolfe P. Crum to accept the position as Vice-President of the Board with the understanding that during my absence at any time he will have the power to call meetings of the Board for the discharge of business, and that I shall not expect such action taken during my absence to be referred to me for my approval. I deem it quite necessary that the Board should be empowered to act independently of my presence and that I should be regarded simply as a member of the Board and that my absence should count only as that of a member of the Board. I earnestly advise that at this meeting the Board be duly organized into departments and that proper bylaws be drafted for its direction.

I wish to take this opportunity to say that the Board must realize its responsibilities in the government of St. Philip's Junior College. Among such responsibilities being that of handling all fin-

To the Board of Trustees
of St. Philip's Junior College

-2-

ancial matters; of adopting a budget which can be reasonably met; that all items of income and expenditure should pass under the scrutiny of the Board; that all teachers and other employees of the school should be selected by the Board in conference with the President of the College, Miss Artemesia Bowden. Her experience, of course, should make her advice of the greatest possible value to the Board in selecting the faculty and where it is possible we should give her nominations preference, but at the same time we should carefully examine the credentials of every applicant.

I think that in general I have covered what you might expect of me in indicating what is to be the authority of the Board and what are to be its responsibilities and duties. It gives me great joy to face the future of St. Philip's Junior College with such an able body of men as my full partners in this noble enterprise, and I honestly believe that, under God's blessing, a great institution for the advancement of Christian character and higher education for the people of the negro race will be built up through our labors.

Faithfully and gratefully yours,

Wm Theodotus Capers

William Theodotus Capers,
President of the Board of Trustees
of St. Philip's Junior College.

1st Can the SA Bd of Ed
Cooperate with the present
Bd of Trustees – [illegible]
Basis

2nd Can the school Bd
lease the property & take
over the management &
operation of the Jr College
leaving the vocational
dept under the Bd
of Trustees, not less than 2 [illegible]

3rd Will it be necessary
for the School [illegible] Bd
to purchase the property
in order to operate the
school

175

ST. PHILIP'S JUNIOR COLLEGE

SAN ANTONIO, TEXAS

May 18, 1931.

The Trustee Board
St. Philip's Junior College
San Antonio, Texas.

Gentlemen:

We, the undersigned citizens of San Antonio, wish to take this means to petition the Trustee Board of St. Philip's Junior College to take under advisement the following request concerning the operation of St. Philip's Junior College.

In view of the fact that the Negro citizens do not have a municipal junior college, nor any form of junior college training for our youth other than St. Philip's Junior College, we, some of the representative citizens, do hereby petition the trustees of said institution to offer to the San Antonio Board of Education the supervision and direction of the curricula of the school.

We further petition the trustees that, in consideration of the service this institution is rendering to our group and the recognition that has been given by accrediting agencies, that St. Philip's Junior College coordinate with the San Antonio public school system in supplying junior college training for our youth and thereby making permanent this training for our boys and girls.

We feel that St. Philip's deserves the opportunity to serve in this much needed capacity and trust that you will see fit to recommend same. We shall be pleased to meet with your committee concerning same.

Respectfully submitted,

M. Sampson Brooks
J. W. Warren
G. L. Curry
J. H. Talley
J. W. Weakley
T. D. Young
C. H. Stapleau
J. J. Taylor

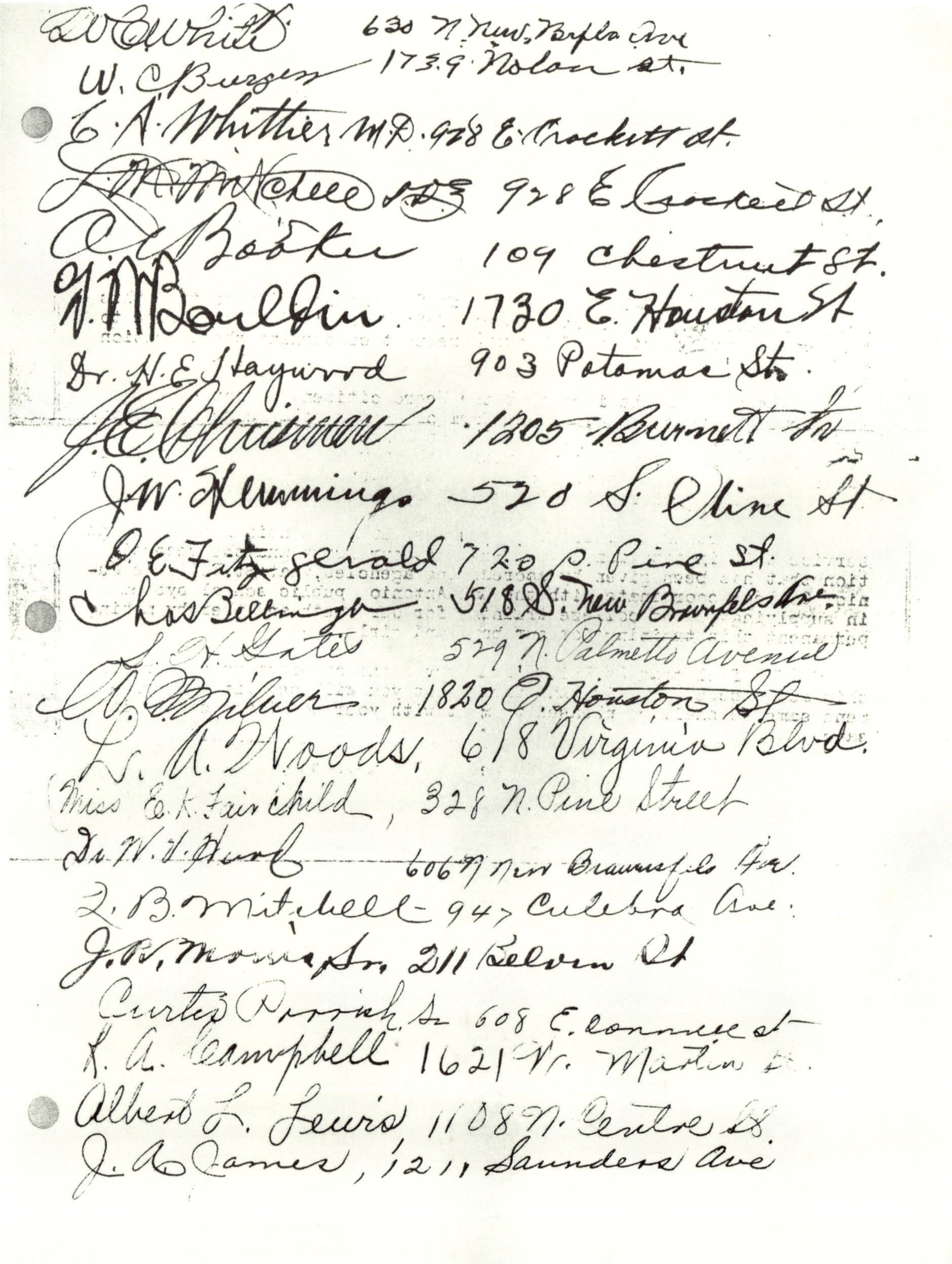
L. W. White 630 N. New Brfls Ave
W. C. Burgess 1739 Nolan St.
E. A. Whittier M.D. 928 E. Crockett St.
L. M. McGhee D.D.S. 928 E. Crockett St.
A. C. Booker 109 Chestnut St.
J. T. Bouldin 1730 E. Houston St
Dr. H. E. Haywood 903 Potomac St.
J. E. Chrisman 1205 Burnett St
J. W. Hemmings 520 S. Cline St
D. E. Fitzgerald 720 S. Pine St.
Chas Bellinger 518 S. New Braunfels Ave.
S. J. Gates 529 N. Palmetto Avenue
A. Milner 1820 E. Houston St
L. A. Woods, 618 Virginia Blvd.
Miss E. K. Fairchild, 328 N. Pine Street
Dr. W. L. Hurd 606 N New Braunfels Av.
L. B. Mitchell 947 Culebra Ave.
J. B. Morris Sr. 211 Belvin St
Curtis Parrish Jr. 608 E. Commerce St
R. A. Campbell 1621 N. Martin St.
Albert L. Lewis 1108 N. Centre St.
J. A. James, 1211 Saunders Ave

Appendix D

AT&T Artists

AT&T Art Donation at St. Philip's College		
Art Piece	**Date**	**Artist**
Trilogy I, II, & III	May, 1976	Dozier Bell
Instruction	1940	Thomas Hart Benton
Edge of Town	1938	Thomas Hart Benton
Pear	1973	Hector Borla
Iris Triptych	1978	Bernard Chaet
Gemini	1975	Peter Cumba
Darragh's Pond	1975	Robert Dash
Untitled	1978	Roy De Carava
Untitled	1978	Roy De Carava
Growth and Development	1974	Robert Goodnough
Musky II	1984	William Griffith
Kelp Flats-I	1978	Peter Holbrook
Black Elk	1988	Wesley Kimmer
Dunes at Ano Nuevo # 22	1980	Peter Loftus
Mooncraters		Lowell Nesbitt
Hook	1972	Lucus Samaras
Ribbon	1972	Lucus Samaras
Hermaphroditus Series # 1 North	1990	Sharon Sprung

Appendix E

Interviewees, Oral History Project

Adams, Audrae
Adkisson, Tommy
Aggrey, DJan
Akins, Erick
Alarcon, Elizabeth Amaya
Alexander, Veola
Barnett, Vernon (Spot)
Bentley, Dr. William David
Bernal, Diego
Bias, Georgene
Black, Claude
Bowden, Richard Perry Mallard
Bowers, Charles Anthony (Tony)
Briggs, Dr. Julia
Bryant, Gloria
Burley, Lillian
Burley, Roy
Byrd, Lanier
Byrd, Napolean
Candia, Dr. Patricia
Castleberry, Gool
Castro, Rita
Clack, Aurelia (for Coach Clack)
Clark, George
Cole, Rev. Alzo
Coleman, Don
Coleman, John
Conyers, Pearl
Crayton, Tommy
Crockett-Bell, Sharon
Crow, Dr. Burton
Davis, Dr. Milbrew
Davis, Dr. William
Davis, Olga Samples
Davis, Shirley
Dawson, Randall
Fisher, Bruce
Flores, Katherine
Gainer, Gaynell
Garcia, Hilario (Larry)
Gardener, Madelyn
Garza Diana
Gilford, Mary
Gomez, John
Gonzales, Janie
Gonzalez, Gerardo S.
Gordon, Julius
Grice, Vernard
Guajardo, Teresa
Guerrero, Ruben
Hall, Rose McCann
Hamilton, Dr. Debbie
Harlan, Dr. Douglas
Harris, Eddie
Hays, Hazel
Hill, Clarence
Hinton, Nettie
Hudgins, William
Hudspeth, Dr. Elizabeth (Dolly)
Hudspeth, Dr. Gregory
Jackson, Dr. Gloria
Jackson, Dr. Levi
James, Rev. Hamice
Johnson, Betty
Kraft, Dr. Benjamin
Kunz, Mary
Lee, Ivory
Leonard, C. L.
Leslie, Dr. Chancellor Bruce
Lopez, Luis
Loston, Dr. Adena
Mackey Pierson Mar
Martin, John
Mathis, Mattie
McAllister, Bishop Gerald
McAllister, Edith
McClendon, Denver
McClenney, Dr. Byron
McClenney, Kay
McClinton, Dorothy
McNeil, Martha
Miles, John (Mules)
Mitchell, Dr. Stephen
Mitchell, Sylvester (Deceased)
Murphy, Dr. John
Musquiz, George
Norris, Lucille
Norris, Trusse
Oppenheimer, Sue
Ozuna, George
Passty, Jeanette
Pate, Dr. Christopher
Pena, Pablo
Penn, Raymont (Donny)
Plummer, Coach Elwood
Puckett, Terry Gay
Pulliams, Kenneth
Robinson, Ola
Runnels, Dr. Angie (Deceased)
Samples, Browning
Sanchez, Rebecca
Sanford, Mrs. Serilia McCann
Shelton, Tracy
Sides, Dr. Karen
Slaughter, John Etta

Slaughter, Murray
Spruill, Rose Mary
Stevenson, Henrietta.
Sutton, Atty. Percy
Tatum, Virginia
Taylor, Georgia
Thompson, Joyce
Toliver, Sherry
Trevino, Jorge
Turbon, Sally
Turner-Ferrier, Joyce (J. T.)
Vincik, Charles (Chuck)
Warner, Vernice
Wells, Ralph, M.D.,
Wells, Solomon
Westerbeck, John
Weynand, Dr. Jerome
White, Lois
Wiemers, Susan K.
Williams, Clara Etta
Williams, Dr. T. R
Williams, Jerelyne
Williams, Patricia Wright
Wright, James

Appendix F

History of the College President's Lecture Series

History of the St. Philip's College President's Lecture Series		
Date	**Lecturer**	**Lecture**
10/17/2002	Dr. Osvaldo Barreneche	Causes Searching for Meanings: The Process of Independence in Latin America
3/25/2003	Dr. Larry Hufford & Sister Martha Ann Kirk	Is Peace Possibe in These Volatile Times?
6/19/2003	Dr. George Wright	Is There Still a Need for Juneteenth Celebrations?
1/29/2004	Farooka Gauhari	Searching for Saleem: An Afgan Woman's Odyssey
3/30/2004	Ossie Davis	With Ossie and Ruby: In This Life Together
6/18/2004	Francis Bok	Escape from Slavery: The True Story of My Ten Years in Captivity and My Journey to Freedom in America
10/28/2004	Chris Hedges	The Mythology of War: Reflections of a Veteran War Correspondent
3/24/2005	Harry Wu	In the Mouth of the Dragon: U.S./China Relations in the 21st Century
6/17/2005	Nontombi Naomi Tutu	Truth and Reconciliation: Healing the Wounds of Racism
10/11/2005	Richard Rodriguez	On Being Brown: Mixture in America
3/23/2006	Winona LaDuke	American Indian Economic and Environmental Concerns
6/19/2006	Ron Kirk	Perspective of the Juneteenth Celebration
10/10/2006	Maria Hinojosa	Her Career in Radio and Television
3/20/2007	Steve Curwood	The Good News about Global Warming
6/21/2007	Roya Hakakian	Armed and Innocent: Children Soldiers of War
11/8/2007	Fernando Reyes	His Professional Journey as a Successful Entrepreneur
2/27/2008	Dr. Willis Mackey	Black History Month
3/27/2008	Enrique Morones	U.S. Border and Beyond: A Debate on Immigration Reform
6/19/2008	Donna Wyant Howell	What Really Happened During Slavery!
11/4/2008	Bruce E. Miller	Port San Antonio
2/18/2009	Dr. Belle Wheelan	One Woman's Story from the Eastside of San Antonio
3/26/2009	Aaron Tuley	The Climate Project
6/18/2009	Kathyrn Woods	Sojourner Truth
9/21/2009	Tim O'Brien	The Things They Carried
2/12/2010	Robert Darden	Black Gospel Music
6/17/2010	Guy Peartree	Frederick Douglass: A Timeless Champion of Human Rights in 1859
11/30/2010	Julian Castro	The Café College
3/9/2011	Nontombi Naomi Tutu	Building Gender Coalitions Across Racial Lines
6/16/2011	Hezekiah Watkins & Patricia Baskerville Dilworth	1961 Mississippi Freedom Riders
10/27/2011	William P. McManus & Victor Rivas Rivers	Domestic Violence: It is Everyone's Issue
2/9/2012	Jim Lucas	Classic Addresses of Dr. Martin Luther King
6/26/2012	Kevin Powell	Barack Obama, Dr. King, and the Future of Civil Rights

Notes

Preface

1. Henry Hampton and Steve Fayer, *Voices of Freedom: An Oral History of the Civil Rights Movement from the 1950s through the 1980s* (London: Vintage, 1991).

2. Kwame Anthony Appiah and Henry Louis Gates Jr., *The Encyclopedia of the African and the African American Experience* (New York: Basic Civitas Books).

3. Stokely Carmichael, civil rights activist, and onetime chairman of the Student Nonviolent Coordinating Committee (SNCC).

4. Gwendolyn Etter-Lewis, *My Soul Is My Own* (New York: Routledge, 1993).

Introduction

1. Nettie Hinton, interview by Marie P. Thurston, April 13, 2004, Oral History Collection, Archives, St. Philip's College, San Antonio, Texas. (Henceforth, the archives from the Oral History Collection will be cited in notes as OHC.)

Chapter 1: 1898 and Before

1. Daniel Alexander Payne, *History of the African Methodist Episcopal Church* (New York: Arno Press, 1969).

2. Milbrew Davis and Shirley Davis, interview by Marie P. Thurston, May 21, 2003, OHC.

3. Clarence Norris Jr., "St. Philip's College: A Case Study of a Historically Black Two-Year College," PhD dissertation, University of Southern California, 61.

4. Michael Heintze, *Private Black Colleges in Texas, 1865–1954* (College Station: Texas A&M University Press, 1985). Edward A. Jones, *A Candle in the Dark: A History of Morehouse College* (Valley Forge, PA: Judson Press, 1967).

5. Heintze, *Private Black Colleges in Texas*, 55.

6. Bishop Capers, letter to Grace Lindley, November 26, 1940. Copy in archives, Diocese of West Texas.

7. Bishop Gerald McAllister, interview by Marie P. Thurston, May 30, 2003, OHC. The crucifer is the person appointed to carry the church's processional cross during processions at the beginning and end of the service.

8. According to Rev. Milbrew Davis, "St. Philip's [Church] was organized at the request of a group of Negroes who had been members of the St. James African Methodist Episcopal Church in San Antonio." Davis, *History of St. Philip's Episcopal Church, San Antonio, Texas 1895–1985* (Trader Publications, 1986), 77.

9. *Journal of the Thirtieth Annual Convocation*, Western Texas and the First Council of the Diocese of West Texas, San Antonio, May 10–15, 1904, Appendix I, 52.

10. *Journal of the First Annual Council of the Protestant Episcopal Church in the Diocese of West Texas*, May 10–14, 1905, Appendix K, 61.

11. Norris, "St. Philip's College," 64.

12. Ibid.

13. *Journal of the Twenty-Sixth Annual Convocation, Protestant Episcopal Church*, Missionary District of Western Texas, San Antonio, May 16–20, 1900, 24.

14. Ibid.

15. *The Journal of the Twenty-Seventh Annual Convocation*, Missionary District of Western Texas, St. Mark's Church, San Antonio, May 8–12, 1901, 21.

16. Ibid., 34.

17. Norris, "St. Philip's College," The first graduation, 61.

18. *Twenty-Eighth Annual Convocation*, Missionary District of Western Texas, San Antonio, May 7–12, 1902, Appendix K, 42.

19. Ibid.

Chapter 2: Coming to Texas

1. Letter to Artemisia Bowden from Bishop Johnston with offer of employment, travel instructions, and train fare to San Antonio. (All letters quoted in this book, unless otherwise noted, are from the St. Philip's College Archives.)

2. See table in chapter 24 for chronology of name changes for St. Philip's College.

3. Carleton J. Hayden, "Issue Dedicated to Artemisia Bowden: Educator and Uplifter of Black Youth 1879–1969," *Linkage*, No. 8, September 1987.

4. Ibid.

5. A hod is a v-shaped tray on the end of a long pole, usually carried on the shoulder, used to carry loads such as bricks, mortar, and other building materials.

6. Dr. Harry F. Greene, Dean of Prairie View State College, TX, Letter to Bishop William T. Capers, San Antonio, TX (date unknown).

Chapter 3: Artemisia Bowden and St. Philip's Industrial School

1. Journal of the Thirtieth Annual Convocation, Appendix One, May 10, 1904, 52.

2. Clarence W. Norris, "St. Philips's College: A Case Study of a Historically Black Two-Year College," PhD dissertation, University of Southern California, 1975, 64.

3. Bowden wrote: Miss Hill has spent much time teaching gardening. The little ones took great pleasure in sowing the seeds and watching their growth and it not only gave them an idea how it should be done, but helped the cooking school." Journal of the First Annual Council of the Protestant Episcopal Church in the Diocese of West Texas, Appendix K, May 9, 1905.

4. Personal interview, Sylvester Mitchell, interview by Marie P. Thurston, November, 2002, transcript, St. Philip's Archives.

5. Ibid.

6. St. Philip's Grammar and Industrial School Catalog, vol. 4, no. 1, 1903–1904.

7. Journal of the Sixth Annual Council, Protestant Episcopal Church, San Antonio, May 18–22, 1910, Appendix J, 58.

8. Journal of the Third Annual Council, Protestant Episcopal Church, Diocese of West Texas, San Antonio, May 1–5, 1907, Appendix K, 70–71.

9. Ibid., Bishop's Address, 42.

10. Journal of the Fifth Annual Council, Diocese of West Texas, May 9–16, 1909. Bishop's Address, 44.

11. Journal of the Sixth Annual Council, Appendix J, 62.

12. Catalogue of St. Philip's Normal, Grammar and Industrial School, Twelfth Annual Session, 1910–1911, 9.

13. Personal interview, Georgia Taylor, interview by Marie P. Thurston, November, 2002, transcript, St. Philip's Archives.

Chapter 4: The Industrial Side of Education at St. Philip's School

1. Clarence W. Norris Jr., "St. Philip's College: A Case Study of a Historically Black Two-Year College," PhD Dissertation, University of Southern California, 1975, 62.

2. Juan Williams and Dwayne Ashley, *I'll Find a Way or Make One: A Tribute to Historically Black Colleges and Universities* (New York: Amistad, An Imprint of HarperCollins Publishers), 29.

3. Norris, "St. Philip's College," 85.

4. Last letter to Miss Bowden from Bishop Johnston, March 24, 1923, San Antonio.

5. Milbrew Davis, *History of St. Philip's Episcopal Church: San Antonio, Texas 1895–1985* (Trader Publications, 1986).

6. Esdale Malloy, interview by Clarence W. Norris Jr., March 1973, transcript, St. Philip's Archives.

7. Letter from Dean J. L. Hawkins to Rev. Capers refusing to accept cut in pay, May 1933, OHC.

8. Malloy interview, 1973.

Chapter 5: Four Acres and a New Home

1. Eddie Harris, interview by Marie P. Thurston, April 2003, transcript, OHC.

2. Journal of Proceedings of the Fourteenth Annual Council, Diocese of West Texas, Grace Church, Cuero, May 1918, 45.

3. Milbrew Davis, *History of St. Philip's Episcopal Church: San Antonio, Texas 1895–1985* (Trader Publications, 1986), 95. Milbrew Davis, interview by Marie P. Thurston, May 2003, 8 Archives OHC.

4. Journal of Proceedings of the Twenty-Third Council of the Diocese of West Texas, January 1927, 35.

5. Letter from J. R. Reid to Bishop Capers making St. Philip's a junior college for negroes, May 1928.

6. Letter from Bishop Capers accepting approval of St. Philip's College for junior college, May 1928.

7. Report from Bishop Capers, Twenty-Seventh Annual Council, Diocese of West Texas, May 1931, 42.

8. Ibid.

9. Walter W. McAllister Sr., interview by Clarence W. Norris Jr., September, 1973, OHC.

Chapter 6: Struggling to Survive: the 1930s

1. Letter to Board of Trustees of the college and Dr. Patton, December 13, 1933, from Bishop Capers and Miss Bowden requesting that school be taken over and supported by the city. Archives, Diocese of West Texas.

2. This special committee, well-versed in the circumstances surrounding finances of the college, conferred with the Board of Trustees of St. Philip's Junior College and recommended that the school be continued only if Miss Bowden were relieved of managing the school. Archives, Diocese of West Texas.

3. Ibid.

4. This undated page three of letter from Dr. Patton to Bishop Capers is in response to Bishop Capers's letter of December 13, 1933, Archives, Diocese of West Texas.

5. Letter from Dr. Patton to Bishop Capers, undated but possibly in late December 1933 in response to letter from Capers to him dated December 13, 1933.

6. Ibid.

7. 12:46 a.m., Rev. Patton sent a telegram to the college, April 16, 1931. Telegram was sent by Rev. Patton informing Bishop Capers that the institute would no longer give funds to St. Philip's College.

8. Bishop Capers to Dr. Robert Patton. Letter dated December 13, 1933, San Antonio.

9. Report of ninth year from President Artemisia Bowden to Board of Trustees, St. Philip's Junior College and Vocational Institute, August 20, 1936 "to record outstanding points worthy of note and new developments which have taken place during the year 1935–1936."

10. This letter, dated May 16, 1931, was sent by a group of Negro citizens of San Antonio to the Trustee Board, St. Philip's Junior College. Letter and signatures are in the appendices. Archives, Diocese of West Texas.

11. S. C. Timpson & Sons to Rt. Rev. W. T. Capers, January 11, 1932 Archives, Diocese of West Texas.

12. H. M. Taylor, Taylor & Co. Engineers, Falfurrias, TX, to Bishop Capers, January 1932, Archives, Diocese of West Texas.

13. Porter A. Whaley, General Manager, Chamber of Commerce, to Bishop Capers, San Antonio, June 4, 1932, Archives, Diocese of West Texas.

14. E. H. Keator to T. D. Anderson, San Antonio National Bank, May 17, 1938, Archives, Diocese of West Texas.

15. The *Afro-American* was a national newspaper published weekly. It began publishing in 1892. The Sunday, March 19, 1934 issue announced the organization of the Board of Trustees.

Chapter 7: Oral History Interviews, 1930s

1. *St. Philip's Junior College and Industrial School Catalog*, 1929, vol. 29.

2. Rev. Claude Black, interview by Marie P. Thurston, November 2002, transcript, St. Philip's Archives, OHC.

3. Ibid.

4. Ibid.

5. Mrs. Vernice Warner, interview by Marie P Thurston, May 2008, transcript, St. Philip's Archives, OHC.

6. Ibid.

7. Tommy Crayton, interview by Marie P. Thurston, May 2003, transcript, St. Philip's Archives, OHC.

8. Mrs. Georgia Taylor, interview by Marie P. Thurston, 2003, transcript, St. Philip's Archives, OHC.

9. Mrs. Henrietta Stevenson, interview by Marie P. Thurston, December 2002, transcript, St. Philip's Archives, OHC.

10. Ibid.

11. Ibid.

12. Ibid.

13. Sylvester Mitchell, interview by Marie P. Thurston, November 2002, OHC.

14. Audre Adams, interview by Marie P. Thurston, December 2002, transcript, St. Philip's Archives, OHC. From a copy of the Registrar: "St. Philip's spelled with two ll's."

15. Ibid. *San Antonio Express-News*, July 20, 1980.

Chapter 8: An Awesome Responsibility: the 1940s

1. "This seems like a fearful burden to place upon you, but you voluntarily assumed it. It is because the Board of Trustees of St. Philip's Junior College has faith in you that your promise to raise ten thousand dollars in behalf of the current budget of the school was accepted and has become an accredited source to the school." *West Texas Journal*, January, 1941, 41.

2. Letter from Bishop Capers, presiding Bishop of West Texas, to Miss Artemisia Bowden, November 24, 1928.

3. Bowden voluntarily assumed the debt owed though it was not her personal debt. Letter from Edward Keator to the diocese explaining the circumstances.

4. Bishop Capers told Edward Keator at one time that Miss Bowden's brother had stopped keeping a record after passing a $1,500 total.

5. Keator's letter to the Board of Trustees protesting unfair treatment of Miss Bowden, salarywise. She failed to receive a full salary for many months.

6. Richard Perry Mallard Bowden (R. P. M.), interview

by Marie P. Thurston, March 2008, transcript, St. Philip's Archives, OHC

7. Stonewall Jackson Davis, interview by Dr. C. W. Norris Jr., September, 1973, transcript, St. Philip's Archives, OHC.

8. Clarence W. Norris Sr., *Up from Poverty* (American Printers, 1987), 75.

9. Ibid., 81.

Chapter 9: The 1940s, Continued

1. Letter from Bishop Capers to Rev. George A. Wieland, New York, September, 1942, informing him of S.A. school board decision agreeing to supervise St. Philip's Junior College and make it a part of their educational system.

2. Telegram from Edward H. Keator in San Antonio, sent to Bishop Capers in Colorado, August, 1942, requesting that he call a meeting announcing the Board of Education agreeing to take over the operation of St. Philip's Junior College. Archives, Diocese of West Texas.

3. Clarence W. Norris Jr., "St. Philip's College: A Case Study of a Historically Black Two-Year College," PhD dissertation, University of Southern California, 1975, 175.

4. Ibid.

5. Dr. Jerome Weynand, interview by Marie P. Thurston, December 2003, transcript, St. Philip's Archives, OHC.

6. Ibid.

7. St. Philip's Branch, San Antonio Junior College Bulletin, 1943, 1944. Stonewall Davis, interview by Clarence W. Norris Jr., September 10, 1973, transcript, St. Philip's Archives, OHC, by special consent of Norris family.

8. Minutes of the Trustee Board, San Antonio Union College District (SAUJC), August 1946, St. Philip's Archives, OHC.

9. Walter W. McAllister Sr., interview by Clarence W. Norris Jr., September 1973, transcript, St. Philip's College Archives, by special consent, OHC.

10. Ibid.

11. Dr. Ernest Stevenson, interview by Clarence W. Norris Jr., September 1973, transcript, St. Philip's Archives, OHC.

12. Norris, "St. Philip's College," 200–201.

Chapter 10: Students, Faculty, and Administrators from the 1940s

1. Rose McCann Hall, interview by Mark Barnes, 2003, transcript, St. Philip's Archives, OHC.

2. Serelia McCann Sanford, interview by Mark Barnes, 2003, transcript, St. Philip's Archives, OHC.

3. Rose McCann Hall, interview by Mark Barnes, 2003, transcript, St. Philip's Archives, OHC.

4. Hazel Calhoun Hays, telephone interview by Marie P. Thurston, 2009, St. Philip's Archives, OHC.

5. Clara Etta Williams, interview by Marie P. Thurston, June 2003, transcript, St. Philip's Archives OHC.

6. Madelyn Gardener, interview by Marie P. Thurston, 2011, transcript, St. Philip's College Archives, OHC.

7. Mattie Mathis, interview by Marie P. Thurston, May 2003, transcript, St. Philip's College Archives, OHC.

8. Joyce Thompson, interview by Marie P. Thurston, May, 2003, transcript, St. Philip's Archives, OHC.

9. Napolean Byrd, interview by Marie P. Thurston, May 2004, transcript, St. Philip's Archives, OHC

10. Sylvester Mitchell, interview by Marie P. Thurston, November, 2002, transcript, St. Philip's Archives, OHC.

11. Murray Slaughter, interview by Marie P. Thurston, 2003, transcript, St. Philip's Archives, OHC.

12. William Hudgins, interview by Marie P. Thurston, 2009, transcript, St. Philip's Archives, OHC.

13. Lois White, interview by Marie P. Thurston, August 2009, transcript, St. Philip's Archives, OHC.

14. Col. Roy Burley, interview by Marie P. Thurston, November 2002, transcript, St. Philip's Archives, OHC.

15. 1964 *Echo*, student yearbook.

16. Dr. Lanier Byrd, interview by Marie P. Thurston, May 2004, transcript, St. Philip's College Archives, OHC

17. Rev. Alzo Cole, interview by Marie P. Thurston, February 2002, transcript, St. Philip's Archives, OHC.

18. Bishop Gerald McAllister, interview by Marie P. Thurston, May 2003, transcript, St. Philip's College Archives, OHC.

19. Archives, St. Philip's College, Container List, box 1, folder 8. Programs of Turbon Student Center Dedication.

20. Bishop Gerald McAllister, interview by Marie P. Thurston, May 2003, transcript St. Philip's Archives, OHC.

21. Edith McAllister, interview by Marie P. Thurston, 2003, transcript, St. Philip's Archives, OHC.

Chapter 11: The Norris Years

1. Letter from Artemisia dated June 8, 1943, from Miss Bowden to Clarence W. Norris Sr., urging him to accept a position at St. Philip's College.

2. Ibid.

3. Clarence W. Norris Jr, "St. Philip's College: A Case Study of a Historically Black Two-Year College," PhD dissertation, University of Southern California, 1975, 256.

4. Clarence W. Norris Sr., dean of the college, interview

by Clarence W. Norris Jr., transcript, St. Philip's Archives, OHC, by permission of the Norris family.

5. Dr. Waylon P. Moody, interview by Clarence W. Norris Jr. Date unknown.

6. Minutes of Board of Trustees for San Antonio Union Junior College District in Bexar County, Texas, 7th day of April, A.D., 1948.

7. Clara Etta Williams, interview by Marie P. Thurston, June 2003, transcript, St. Philip's Archives, OHC.

8. Dr. Lanier Byrd, interview by Marie P. Thurston, May 2004, transcript, St. Philip's Archives, OHC.

9. *The Tiger*, vol. XXIII, no. 29, April 13, 1984.

10. May 20, 1952, Item 4, Minutes of a Regular Meeting of the Board of Trustees of the San Antonio Union Junior College District.

11. Dr. Theodore Williams, interview by Marie P. Thurston, 2003, transcript, St. Philip's Archives, OHC.

12. Dean William Hudgins, interview by Marie P. Thurston, 2003, transcript, St. Philip's Archives, OHC.

13. Dr. Levi Jackson, interviewed by Marie P. Thurston, May 2004, transcript, St. Philip's Archives, OHC.

14. Dorothy McClinton, interview by Marie P. Thurston, September 2003, transcript, St. Philip's Archives, OHC.

15. Virginia Tatum, interview by Marie P. Thurston, January 2004, transcript, St. Philip's Archives, OHC.

16. Trusse Norris, interview by Marie P. Thurston, September 2005, transcript, St. Philip's Archives, OHC.

17. Norris, "St. Philip's College," 1975, 206.

Chapter 12: The Surprise Election of G. J. Sutton

1. Minutes of a Called Meeting of the Board of Trustees for the San Antonio Union Junior College District Held on April 20, 1948.

2. Handbook of Texas Online, http://www.tshaonline.org/handbook/online/articles/SS/fsu11.html (accessed August 24, 2010).

3. Percy G. Sutton, interview by Marie P. Thurston, June 2003, New York City, transcript, OHC. Percy Sutton passed away on December 26, 2009.

4. Theodore R. Williams, interview by Marie P. Thurston, March 2003, transcript, OHC.

5. William A. Hudgins, interview by Marie P. Thurston, February 2003, transcript, OHC.

6. Johnetta Slaughter, interview by Marie P. Thurston, April 2004, transcript, OHC.

7. Jerome Weynand, interview by Marie P. Thurston, June 2003,transcript, OHC.

8. Rev. Claude Black, interview by Marie P. Thurston, November 2002, transcript, OHC.

9. Col. Roy Burley, interview by Marie P. Thurston, April 2004, transcript, OHC.

Chapter 13: Integrating the Schools: the 1950s

1. Minutes of a regular Meeting of the Board of Trustees of the San Antonio Union Junior College District held on May 20, 1952, Item no. 4, 13.

2. Jerome Weynand, interview by Marie P. Thurston, June 6, 2003, transcript, OHC.

3. Ibid.

4. Dean Hudgins, interview by Marie P. Thurston, February 2003, transcript, OHC.

5. Jerome Weynand, interview by Marie P. Thurston, June 2003, transcript, OHC.

6. Norris, "St. Philip's College," 1975, 218. Minutes of a called meeting of the Board of Trustees of the SAUJC District held December 20, 1954, reflected that a swimming pool was added later.

7. Dr. Lanier Byrd, interview by Marie P. Thurston, May 2004, transcript, OHC.

Chapter 14: Oral History Interviews, 1950s

1. Dr. Lanier Byrd, interview by Marie P. Thurston, May 2004, transcript, OHC.

2. For copy of Supreme Court decision, contact The National Center for Public Policy Research, 501 Capitol Court NE, Washington, DC, 20002.

3. Jeralyne Castleberry Williams, interview by Marie P. Thurston, May, 2003, transcript, OHC.

4. See note 1.

5. Eddie Harris, interview by Marie P. Thurston, April 2003, transcript, OHC.

6. Virginia Littlefield-Tatum, interview by Marie P. Thurston, January 2004, transcript, OHC.

7. Martha McNeil, interview by Marie P. Thurston, December 2002, transcript, OHC.

8. Alzo Cole, interview by Marie P. Thurston, December 2002, transcript, OHC.

9. Nettie Hinton, interview by Marie P. Thurston, April 2004, transcript, OHC.

10. Rev. Hamice James, interview by Marie P. Thurston, June 2003, transcript, OHC.

11. Gloria Bryant, interview by Marie P. Thurston, November 2002, transcript, OHC.

12. Ralph Wells, interview by Marie P. Thurston, June 2010, transcript, OHC.

13. Joyce Turner-Ferrier, interview by Marie P. Thurston, February 2010, transcript, OHC.

14. Theodore Williams, interview by Marie P. Thurston, transcript, OHC.

15. Dr. Georgene Bias, interview by Marie P. Thurston, September 2009, OHC.

Chapter 15: Learning to Adjust: Students and Faculty from the 1960s

1. Olga Samples Davis, interview by Marie P. Thurston, Wednesday, January 19, 2005, transcript, OHC.

2. Ibid.

3. Johnnetta Slaugter, interview by Marie P. Thurston, April 2004, transcript, OHC.

4. George Clark, interview by Marie P. Thurston, August 2009,transcript, OHC.

5. Ivory Lee, interview by Marie P. Thurston, September 2009, transcript, OHC.

6. John Coleman, interview by Marie P. Thurston, transcript, OHC.

7. Solomon Wells, interview by Marie P. Thurston, September 2009, transcript, OHC.

8. Dorothy McClinton, interview by Marie P. Thurston, September 2003, transcript, OHC.

9. Don Coleman, interview by Marie P. Thurston, April 2003, transcript, OHC.

10. Elwood Plummer, interview by Marie P. Thurston, May 2012, transcript, OHC.

11. Obituary, *Lynchburg News and Advance*, July 7, 2011, Lynchburg, Virginia.

12. Kenneth Pulliams, interview by Marie P. Thurston, September 2011, transcript, OHC.

13. Patricia Wright Williams, interview by Marie P. Thurston, June 2011, transcript, OHC.

Chapter 16: The Evening Division

1. Clarence Hill, interview by Marie P. Thurston, August 2003, transcript, OHC.

2. Browning McKinney Samples, interview by Marie P. Thurston, January 2005, transcript, OHC.

3. Ibid.

4. Dr. Levi Jackson interview by Marie P. Thurston, May 2004, transcript, OHC.

5. Lillian Burley, interview by Marie P. Thurston, April 2004, transcript, OHC.

6. Handbook of Texas Online, Jo Eckerman; "Artemisia Bowden: Dedicated Dreamer," *Texas Passages*, Winter 1987; Files, University of Texas Institute of Texan Cultures, and San Antonio and Archives, St. Philip's College.

Chapter 17: The Murphy Years: 1969–1984

1. *St. Philip's Update*, November 20, 1992, 10.

2. *Palo Alto Review Journal of Ideas*, fall/spring 2009–10, Ellen Shull, ed.

3. John Brown Murphy, interview by Marie P. Thurston, April 2003, transcript, OHC.

4. Mary Pierson Mackey, interview by Marie P. Thurston, February, 2004, transcript, OHC.

5. Betty Johnson, interview by Marie P. Thurston, August 31, 2009, transcript, OHC.

6. Terry Guajardo, interview by Marie P. Thurston, November 2004, transcript, OHC.

7. Charles Anthony Bowers, interview by Marie P. Thurston, transcript, OHC.

8. Gregory Hudspeth, interview by Marie P. Thurston, May 2004, transcript, OHC.

9. Ibid.

10. Mary Gilford, interview by Marie P. Thurston, January 2004, transcript, OHC.

11. Janie N. Gonzales, interview by Marie P. Thurston, January 2010, transcript, OHC.

12. Elizabeth Dolly Hudspeth, interview by Marie P. Thurston, January 2010, transcript, OHC.

13. Olga Samples Davis, interview by Marie P. Thurston, September 2009, transcript, OHC.

14. Dr. William Conan Davis, interview by Marie P. Thurston, September 2009, transcript, OHC.

15. Dr. Jeannette Passty, interview by Marie P. Thurston, October 11, 2011, transcript, OHC.

16. Terry Gay Puckett, interview by Marie P. Thurston, August 2009, transcript, OHC.

Chapter 18: A Procession of Presidents, Era of Contention: The 1980s

1. *The Tiger*, vol. XVI, no. 2, October 25, 1985.

2. Byron McClenney, interview by Marie P. Thurston, June 2003, transcript, OHC.

3. *The Tiger*, October 25, 1985.

4. Theodore R. Williams, interview by Marie P. Thurston, March 2003, transcript, OHC.

5. *Building for the Future: Bond Referendum Proposal.* Election information from the ACCD.

6. *San Antonio Light*, December 14, 1982.

Chapter 19: A Tumultuous, Progressive Time: The 1980s

1. Dr. Gloria Jackson, interview by Marie P. Thurston, January 2004, transcript, OHC.

2. CL Leonard, interview by Marie P. Thurston, November 2004, transcript, OHC.

3. Dr. Byron McClenney, interview by Marie P. Thurston, June 2003, transcript, OHC.

4. Dr. Douglas Harlan, interview by Marie P. Thurston, June 2003, transcript, OHC.

5. Gerardo Gonzalez, interview by Marie P. Thurston, November, 2009, transcript, OHC.

6. George Ozuna, interview by Marie P. Thurston, January, 2004, transcript, OHC.

Chapter 20: Poised for Change

1. Dr. Stephen Mitchell, interview by Marie P. Thurston, November 2002, transcript, OHC.

2. *San Antonio Express-News*, July 18, 1985, Metro Section, reprinted with permission of the Hearst Corporation.

3. Dr. Stephen Mitchell, interview, OHC.

4. Ibid.

5. Gaynell Gainer, interview by Marie P. Thurston, November 2010, transcript, OHC.

6. Dr. Julia Briggs, interview by Marie P. Thurston, May 2011, transcript, OHC.

7. Mary Kunz, interview by Marie P. Thurston, February 2010, transcript, OHC.

8. Bryon Skinner, eighth president, St. Philip's College, 1992–1993.

9. Jeanette Passty, *Palo Alto Review Journal of Ideas*, Ellen Shull, ed., Fall/Spring 2009–2010.

10. Rev. Hamice James, interview by Marie P. Thurston, June 2003, transcript, OHC.

Chapter 21: Keeping Watch: The 1990s

1. Dr. Elizabeth (Dolly) Hudspeth, interview by Marie P. Thurston, January 2005, transcript, OHC.

2. Dr. Lanier Byrd, interview by Marie P. Thurston, May 2004, transcript, OHC.

3. Rebecca Sanchez, interview by Marie P. Thurston, November 2004, transcript, OHC.

4. Dr. Karen Sides, interview by Marie P. Thurston, January 2005, transcript, OHC.

5. Dr. Sharon Crockett-Bell, interview by Marie P. Thurston, 2011, transcript, OHC.

6. Randall Dawson, interview by Marie P. Thurston, November 2004, transcript, OHC.

7. Gool Castleberry, interview by Marie P. Thurston, January 2012, transcript, OHC.

8. Rita E. Castro, interview by Marie P. Thurston, August 2009, transcript, OHC.

9. D. Hamilton, e-mail correspondence, November 21, 2011.

10. *San Antonio Express-News*, June 23, 1999, Section 1B. Printed with permission of the Hearst Corporation.

11. Ibid.

12. Ibid.

Chapter 22: A New Year, A New Place: The 2000s

1. Dr. Angie Runnels, interview by Marie P. Thurston, August 2005, transcript, OHC.

2. Pearlene Conyers, interview by Marie P. Thurston, April 2012, transcript, OHC.

3. Dr. Runnels, interview, August 2005, OHC.

4. Dr. Burton Crow, interview by Marie P. Thurston, December 2010, transcript, OHC.

5. See appendix for a list of artists, activists, authors, and others who presented for the President's Lecture Series through 2011.

6. Dr. Gregory Hudspeth, interview by Marie P Thurston, May 2004, transcript, OHC.

7. Tracy Shelton, interview by Marie P. Thurston, November 2005, transcript, OHC.

8. John Gomez, interview by Marie P. Thurston, January 2004, transcript, OHC.

9. DJan (Jan) Aggrey, interview by Marie P. Thurston, December 2003, transcript, OHC.

10. Diana Garza, interview by Marie P. Thurston, November 2004, transcript, OHC.

11. John Westerbeck, interview by Marie P. Thurston, December 2004, transcript, OHC.

12. Raymont Donyale Pann (Donny), interview by Marie P. Thurston, January 2005, transcript, OHC.

13. John Martin, interview by Marie P. Thurston, September 2011, transcript, OHC.

14. Dr. Patricia Candia, interview by Marie P. Thurston, October 2004, transcript, OHC.

Chapter 23: A Brand New Leader and a Brand New Day

1. Denver McClendon, interview by Marie P. Thurston, February 22, 2010, transcript, OHC.

2. Rev. Dr. Richard Thayer, Address to the Council of the Diocese.

3. *President's Newsletter*, vol. 3, issue 2, July 2010.

4. Texas Higher Education Coordinating Board.

5. American Culinary Federation.

6. http://www.militaryfriendlyschools.com/pr09.aspx

7. *Hispanic Outlook in Higher Education.*

8. Prepared by Texas Board of Nursing based on data provided by Pearson/VUE.

9. SPC Second Annual Scholarship Publication.

10. Texas Higher Education Coordinating Board.

11. 2009 Community College Survey of Student Engagement

12. Loston received this award from Psi Kappa Chapter of Phi Beta Kappa.

13. Dr. William David Bentley, interview by Marie P. Thurston, 2012, transcript, OHC.

14. Erick Akins, interview by Marie P. Thurston, February 9, 2011, transcript, OHC.

15. Alamo Colleges, St. Philip's College publication entitled *S. E. G. Student Engagement Grants: Your Generous Donations at Work.*

16. Dr. Christopher Pate, interview by Marie P. Thurston, February 2010, transcript, OHC.

17. Rosemary Spruill, interview by Marie P. Thurston, February 2010, transcript, OHC.

18. Dr. Bruce Leslie, chancellor, Alamo Community College District. Meeting of the ACCD Board of Trustees and the San Antonio community regarding moving the nursing school from St. Philip's to the medical school area.

19. Pablo Pena, instructor, S. W. Campus, auto and body, interview, Marie P. Thurston, January 28, 2005, transcript, OHC.

20. Ibid.

21. Dr. Adena Loston, president, St. Philip's College, interview by Marie P. Thurston, June 2010, transcript, OHC.

Chapter 24: Conclusion

1. The mission statement can be found in the opening statement in the general information section of the St. Philip's college catalog, it can be accessed on the Internet, and it can be found in a publication issued by the school called "Quick Facts."

2. Proposed by the 108th meeting of the Diocesan Council meeting during a convention in McAllen, Texas.

3. Denver McClendon, interview by Marie P. Thurston, February 22, 2010, transcript, OHC.

Index